Tennessee Williams and Company

His Essential Screen Actors

To
Reggie + Peter,
my dear dear
wonderful friends!.

Love,
John

Tennessee Williams and Company

His Essential Screen Actors

John DiLeo

HANSEN PUBLISHING GROUP

International Standard Book Number: 978-1-60182-423-3

Book design and typography by Jon Hansen

Cover Photograph: Tennessee Williams with Anna Magnani on the set of *The Fugitive Kind* in 1959.

All photographs courtesy of Photofest.

Hansen Publishing Group, LLC
302 Ryders Lane,
East Brunswick, NJ 08816

1-877-876-4716
http://hansenpublishing.com

Book web site
http://www.tennesseewilliamsandcompany.com/

Contents

Acknowledgments

Thank you to Gary Bagley, Carol and Ralph Bowman, Randy Buck, Marty Casella, Reggie Cheong-Leen, Marion Gillease, Abby Hansen, Audrey Lanham, Michael Milton, Tony Razzano, Dixie Rich, Eric Rockwell, Bill Schill, Craig Seligman, Becky Spencer, Peter Spielhagen, and the staff at the Pike County Library in Milford, PA.

Thanks, always, to my parents John and Vera, my sister Lenore, my brother Michael, as well as a special note of gratitude to my cousin Jim Azzara.

Jon and Jody Hansen, my dedicated publishers, have also become treasured friends.

After 27 years together, my partner, Earl McCarroll, and I got married in 2009. Thank you Massachusetts, thank you Mardy Wheeler. thank you Lee McClelland, and thank you Earl for every day of the last 28 years.

Preface

To commemorate March 26, 2011, the 100th anniversary of the birth of Mississippi-born playwright Tennessee Williams (1911-1983), I wanted to write a book about the movies based on his works. However, the standard format for such a project—a chronological film-by-film analysis—had already been done twice. As I thought about Williams' movies, I was reminded of how many performers appeared in more than one of the films, creating an unofficial stock company of Tennessee Williams screen actors, which includes some of the most gifted acting talents of the 1950s and 1960s. Several of these names—Marlon Brando, Karl Malden, Mildred Dunnock, Geraldine Page, and Madeleine Sherwood—should come as no surprise, since these men and women had performed (and originated) roles by Williams on the stage. Others, such as Anna Magnani and Vivien Leigh, both foreign-born, could hardly have been foreseeable as brilliant interpreters of such a distinctly American writer (though Leigh's Scarlett O'Hara had certainly proven her Deep-South credentials). Also included are the two most famous screen-acting couples of Williams' Hollywood heyday: Paul Newman and Joanne Woodward, and Elizabeth Taylor and Richard Burton. Each of the aforementioned appears in two Tennessee Williams movies, with Ms. Sherwood gracing three of the films, and Ms. Taylor the only person ever to star in three Williams pictures. Apologies to Rip Torn, who technically belongs here, having appeared in both *Baby Doll* and *Sweet Bird of Youth*. But Torn's role in *Baby Doll*, a one-scene bit as a dentist, hardly bears analysis, making his inclusion here a stretch.

This book is a critical look at these eleven screen actors and their roles, bonded by their sustained connection to one of the greatest dramatists of the twentieth century. Though I do not address every single work in the filmographies of my eleven subjects, I will be taking you through their whole careers, addressing the important highs and lows of their non-Williams films. But the emphasis remains on their professional association with Wil-

liams, specifically the success, and sometimes failure, of their interpretations of his characters for the screen, resulting in some of the more remarkable performances in movie history. Each of these roles, no matter its size, is given center stage. Six of Williams' feature films do not make the cut, each lacking a repeat player: *The Glass Menagerie* (1950), the first Williams film, which is assessed in my chapter on Joanne Woodward, the star of the 1987 remake; *Period of Adjustment* (1962), an exceedingly minor and depressingly conventional film of a lesser Williams play, though it is enlivened by its one golden asset, a prize comic turn from a young and fearless Jane Fonda (as a newlywed) in her first significant screen performance; *This Property Is Condemned* (1966), an underrated picture containing what is arguably Natalie Wood's finest performance, though it can barely be called a Williams picture, merely using his very short play (of the same title) as a springboard for three writers to craft an ostensibly original screenplay; *The Last of Mobile Hotshots* (1970), a very poor and distorted film of an unsuccessful play (*The Seven Descents of Myrtle*), adapted for the screen by two former Williams filmmakers, director Sidney Lumet (*The Fugitive Kind*) and screenwriter Gore Vidal (*Suddenly, Last Summer*), neither of whom could prevent the movie from becoming a garish cartoon (unaided by the script's strenuous butching-up of the play's effeminate mama's boy); *The Loss of a Teardrop Diamond* (2009), the latest addition to the Williams films, based on his unproduced original screenplay from the late 1950s, a good-intentioned but underwhelming movie, proving that Williams had considerable rewriting to do before his script was camera-ready; and, finally, the Italian *Senso* (1954), a visually striking but dramatically uninvolving historical epic from director Luchino Visconti, a numbing display of what grand opera might look like if it were devoid of singing. Alongside Paul Bowles, Williams received a dialogue credit for *Senso*, but in his autobiography, *Memoirs*, he admits to doing "little work" on the project. Also absent here are any of the television productions of works by Williams.

I write about some of the films in multiple chapters, depending on how many of my subjects appear in a given film. For example, *A Streetcar Named Desire* is dealt with three times, each from a different perspective, with the Marlon Brando chapter concentrating on the character of Stanley, the Vivien Leigh chapter focused on Blanche, and the Karl Malden chapter concerned exclusively with Mitch's scenes. (The big winner here is *Sweet Bird of Youth*, featuring four of Williams' repeat players.) Details about a film's origins (and those of the play on which it is based) are primarily addressed whenever one of these films makes its first appearance in the book.

In my previous books, I was careful not to reveal the endings of movies, unwilling to deprive others of the pleasures certain films had given me. This time, though, it is crucial to take each performer and role to its final moments. And as I am dealing with adaptations, it is vital to consider what was lost or gained in translation, which sometimes involves a revised ending.

Tennessee Williams and Company

His Essential Screen Actors

Marlon Brando

Nothing was ever the same on stage or screen after Marlon Brando played Stanley Kowalski in **A Streetcar Named Desire**.

Marlon Brando: Filmography

- *The Men (1950)*
- *A Streetcar Named Desire (1951)*
- *Viva Zapata! (1952)*
- *Julius Caesar (1953)*
- *The Wild One (1953)*
- *On the Waterfront (1954)*
- *Desirée (1954)*
- *Guys and Dolls (1955)*
- *The Teahouse of the August Moon (1956)*
- *Sayonara (1957)*
- *The Young Lions (1958)*
- *The Fugitive Kind (1960)*
- *One-Eyed Jacks (1961) (also director)*
- *Mutiny on the Bounty (1962)*
- *The Ugly American (1963)*
- *Bedtime Story (1964)*
- *Morituri (1965)*
- *The Chase (1966)*
- *The Appaloosa (1966)*
- *A Countess from Hong Kong (1967)*
- *Reflections in a Golden Eye (1967)*
- *Candy (1968)*
- *The Night of the Following Day (1969)*
- *Burn! (1970)*
- *The Nightcomers (1972)*
- *The Godfather (1972)*
- *Last Tango in Paris (1972)*
- *The Missouri Breaks (1976)*
- *Superman (1978)*
- *Apocalypse Now (1979)*
- *The Formula (1980)*
- *A Dry White Season (1989)*
- *The Freshman (1990)*
- *Christopher Columbus: The Discovery (1992)*
- *Don Juan De Marco (1995)*
- *The Island of Dr. Moreau (1996)*
- *The Brave (1997)*
- *Free Money (1998)*
- *The Score (2001)*

Marlon Brando (1924-2004)
Academy Award Wins

- **Best Actor** of 1954 for *On the Waterfront*
- **Best Actor** of 1972 for *The Godfather*

Academy Award Nominations

- **Best Actor** of 1951 for *A Streetcar Named Desire*
- **Best Actor** of 1952 for *Viva Zapata!*
- **Best Actor** of 1953 for *Julius Caesar*
- **Best Actor** of 1957 for *Sayonara*
- **Best Actor** of 1973 for *Last Tango in Paris*
- **Best Supporting Actor** of 1989 for *A Dry White Season*

Stanley Kowalski in *A Streetcar Named Desire* (1951)
Val Xavier in *The Fugitive Kind* (1960)

*M*ore than any other performer, Marlon Brando has the strongest and most enduring association with the work of Tennessee Williams. One could easily imagine that this is based on a string of projects, yet it actually involves only two Williams pieces: *A Streetcar Named Desire,* in the theatre and on film, and *The Fugitive Kind,* the film version of Williams' play *Orpheus Descending.* Since *The Fugitive Kind* was both a critical and commercial failure, it's safe to say that our intense association of these two men is based solely on the impact of Brando's performance as Stanley Kowalski in Williams' *Streetcar.* Their involvement was relatively brief, but the repercussions were not only groundbreaking but long-lasting, with the influence of Brando's performance keenly felt in every subsequent generation of film and theatre actors. Brando and Williams emerged as major creative forces of the post-war era. Their connection was a case of two artists needing each other for the fullest expression of his own talent. When the original Broadway production of *Streetcar* opened on December 3, 1947, Williams was already the American theatre's latest golden boy, thanks to the 1945 success of *The Glass Menagerie,* his exquisite memory play. (*Streetcar,* another domestic drama with an unhappy arc, was markedly different from *Menagerie* in its exploration of the more physical and erotic aspects of human experience.) Brando was far less well known than Williams in 1947, with a few secondary Broadway roles to his credit. Their union was an ideal joining of actor and playwright, with both men sharing and displaying natural inclinations to push the boundaries of what was considered acceptable adult fare (conspicuously in sexual terms) in American drama. Brando and Williams helped make each other possible: Brando provided Williams with a presence of explosive and unapologetic male sexuality, while Williams gave Brando the perfect vehicle to unleash his blazing and unpredictable talent. Without Brando's portrayal of Stanley Kowalski, would *Streetcar* have caused quite the same sensation that it did in 1947? And without Williams' creation of Stanley,

how long would Brando have had to wait before the right role catapulted him to his inevitable stardom? Together, they unalterably changed both American theatre and American film.

Marlon Brando was born in Omaha on April 3, 1924, the son of a bullying father and an alcoholic mother who had dreams of being an actress. Young Brando was a practical joker, a poor student, and a military-academy failure. A football injury to his knee led to 4-F status and exemption from World War II service. Following his two older sisters to New York in 1943, he studied acting under the tutelage of Stella Adler, a proponent of Konstantin Stanislavsky's acting methods and a member of the prestigious Group Theatre (1931-1941), which had turned out many celebrated Broadway productions of didactic plays by writers such as Clifford Odets and Sidney Kingsley, works that often expressed left-leaning sympathies with regard to social ills. The "lessons" in these plays have made many of them seem very dated today, while *Streetcar,* which refuses to deliver messages or instruct audiences, continues to fascinate. Brando quickly became Adler's star pupil and soon had his first taste of Broadway success in the heartwarming *I Remember Mama* (1944), playing the fifteen-year-old son of Scandinavian "Mama," which now sounds like a most unlikely situation in which to find even a very young and unformed Brando. The arrival of the "real" Brando, the actor of startling spontaneity (and the target of accusations of onstage mumbling) occurred in Maxwell Anderson's *Truckline Café* (1946), a play that lasted a mere thirteen performances on Broadway but provided Brando with considerable attention for his role as a World War II veteran who returns to a cheating wife whom he kills. It was co-produced by Elia Kazan and also featured Karl Malden in its ensemble cast, both of whom would become part of the *Streetcar* team a year later, respectively, as director and actor. Brando already had a reputation as a non-conformist, a rule breaker without a visible desire to climb the ladder of success or to market himself eagerly to produc-

Inside and Out

Fittingly, the Actors Studio emerged just two months before *Streetcar*'s opening, practically simultaneously with Brando's burst into stardom. Formed by acting teacher Robert Lewis, producer-director Cheryl Crawford, and Elia Kazan, the Actors Studio was a place for professional actors to experiment with their craft, searching to find ever deeper levels of truth in their work. The so-called Method became the Studio's calling card, a system of looking inward in the creation of a role. Sensitive to psychology, behavior, instinct, and one's own "sense memory" (which substituted personal experiences for characters' situations), the Method moved the American theatre away from elocution and manners and style, though the Method soon looked very much like an identifiable and mannered style of its own. The biggest danger in burrowing inward to investigate a character is the distinct possibility of turning acting into a self-indulgent and uncommunicative operation. For talents less inspired than Brando, the Method could offer very limited effects, resulting in performances that were boringly alike because they stuck so closely to an actor's own reality, insufficiently incorporating imagination and insight. The process could satisfy an actor's *feeling* of connection while never translating beyond his innards. The Method is an inside-out way of working, a way to unlock a character through emotional identification rather than the more traditional outside-in technique, which could reveal character through a special walk, or a funny hat, or a putty nose. It all comes down to whatever works, and actors could choose to incorporate the Method in one role and not in another, or even work inside-out and outside-in within the same role. It would be silly to adhere too fervently to any method in something as mysterious as the process of illuminating the human experience. Group Theatre member Lee Strasberg, who took over the Actors Studio in 1951, was the Method's staunchest guru, though many feel that the Method had by then gotten far from Stanislavsky's intentions. In 1934, Stella Adler studied with Stanislavsky in Paris and returned with the news that the Group had been misusing the master's technique, which actually stressed an actor's use of a play's "given circumstances" and his own imagination more than his personal experiences. (Stanislavsky had modified his teachings and was not rigid about them.) This caused a professional rift between Adler and Strasberg, who held fast to his version of the Method, the version taught at the Actors Studio, which then became, for better or worse, the dominant style in American acting.

ers. He was a poor auditioner, showing up for readings as a gloomy fellow who lacked proper theatre diction (or any other identifiable "actor" traits), but he possessed frighteningly exciting gifts.

After *Truckline Café*, Brando appeared opposite legendary theatre star Katharine Cornell in a Broadway production of George Bernard Shaw's comedy *Candida* in 1946, in the role of the young poet, Marchbanks, another decidedly un-Brando kind of role with regard to his later persona. He made one other pre-*Streetcar* Broadway appearance, in *A Flag is Born,* a short-lived 1946 play by Ben Hecht about the founding of the new state of Israel and starring Paul Muni, another acting legend. (Muni's commitment to total immersion in a character made him the Daniel Day-Lewis of his time.) Brando then toured briefly with Tallulah Bankhead in Jean Cocteau's play *The Eagle Has Two Heads* in 1947, but Bankhead, maddened by his erratic onstage manners and upstaging antics, had him replaced with the more malleable Helmut Dantine. For all Brando's associations with the innovative post-war theatre scene, his work with Cornell, Muni, and Bankhead shows that he got a considerable taste of the previous generation's more theatrical, less "realistic" brand of performing. It would be easy to imagine that he dismissed all three as phony and old-fashioned. However, in his autobiography, *Songs My Mother Taught Me,* Brando gives high marks to Muni, though he was not impressed with either Cornell or Bankhead. He must have learned a great deal from watching all three of them, even if much of what he learned fell into the "what not to do" category, but he also must have grasped something of the conviction and sheer weight of people who "owned" the stage and held audiences in their thrall. Brando was a great intuitive actor, but acting on the stage is also a technical process, a mix of inspiration and skill, and he was lucky to witness first-hand how stars could command the attention of hundreds of people every night.

The Talented Mr. Garfield

John Garfield, a Group Theatre actor in the 1930s, as well as a movie star of the late '30s and 1940s, was an obvious choice to play Stanley Kowalski. Famous for playing tough guys and other street-wise types, Garfield would have been excellent as Stanley. Not nearly as well remembered today as he should be, Garfield had a gift for naturalism, giving screen performances of simplicity and honesty that resonated as unembellished depictions of real life. The Group Theatre had championed the techniques devised by Stanislavsky at the Moscow Art Theatre (which began in 1897) in their quest for a more reality-based acting style, eventually to be labeled in America under the umbrella known as "Method acting." From his screen debut in *Four Daughters* (1938), a performance that garnered him a Best Supporting Actor Oscar nomination, Garfield was a new kind of Hollywood actor, combining cynicism with vulnerability, and he was most definitely the key forerunner to Brando. Garfield's most important legacy in American acting is as the transitional link between the Cagney-Robinson-Bogart trio of tough-guy actors to the Brando-Clift-Dean trio of rebel actors. No other actor fit as comfortably into both those worlds. Garfield carried the angst and introspection, as well as the intensity and sexuality that would have made him precisely right for the kinds of roles that Williams would create in the 1940s and 1950s. It would be easy to imagine Garfield in Brando roles, not only in *Streetcar* but also *The Men* (1950) and *On the Waterfront* (1954), or to visualize Brando in Garfield's roles in, say, the boxing picture *Body and Soul* (1947) or the underrated drama *The Breaking Point* (1950). You might say that without Garfield there could not have been Brando, and, by turning down Stanley (when the producer wouldn't meet his demands), Garfield was unknowingly passing the baton to Brando as the new generation's symbol of brooding, complicated males capable of both harsh impulses and unbearable sensitivities. Among the reasons cited for Garfield's opting out of *Streetcar* was his feeling that Stanley's role needed to be expanded because it was overshadowed by the character of Blanche DuBois (and, on the page, who could argue with him?). To make matters more interesting, Garfield had recently finished working with *Streetcar* director Elia Kazan on the eventually Oscar-winning drama *Gentleman's Agreement*. Brando was eleven years younger than Garfield, and his age (a mere twenty-three when *Streetcar* opened) worked to the play's advantage. Stanley's youth and immaturity go some distance in explaining his thoughtless cruelty, while a man in his thirties, behaving as Stanley does, would seem more calculatingly cruel. The final irony is that Garfield died of a heart attack at age thirty-nine in 1952, just months after Brando had electrified the movies in *Streetcar*'s film version.

Brando famously clinched the role of Stanley Kowalski when, at director Elia Kazan's urging, he went up to Provincetown to read for Williams, who was sufficiently bowled over. Despite the thrills one can imagine at seeing Brando perform Stanley in a theatre, there seems little doubt that he was built for film. The greatness of Brando has always been in the unpredictability of his choices, the depths that he could locate in unexpected gestures and line readings. It is a style whose foundation derives from the finding of the truth in any given moment, a way of working that's more easily suited to the screen because in film one is not called upon to repeat a performance eight times a week for months or even years. Stage acting could quickly become a bore for Brando's kind of talent, and it's no surprise that he never returned to Broadway once the movies beckoned. On-screen, he had only to do things brilliantly *once*, captured on celluloid. Brando played *Streetcar* on Broadway for eighteen months (understudies and replacements included Jack Palance, Ralph Meeker, and Anthony Quinn). During the run, he gained a reputation as a prankster, so frustrating for him was the process of doing the same play and the same lines every night. Not that he ever did things the same way twice, which made for a rather unsettling work situation for the rest of the cast.

Brando was the Method's poster boy, but wasn't he just doing what came naturally? Wasn't he employing the Method instinctively, with the capacity to look within and pull out the different aspects of himself that a specific role required? Wasn't Brando an acting phenomenon because nothing was in the way between himself and a given role? In the 1950s, the Method stamp was affixed to any actor who mumbled lines, got all sweaty, and had uncombed hair and torn clothing. Though Brando was Stella Adler's protégé rather than Lee Strasberg's, his opening night in *Streetcar* is probably the moment that most people would cite as the night the Method became the hottest trend in American theatre. It certainly was a style that fit snugly into the highly charged mix of sex and psychology exemplified by the plays and films written by Tennessee Williams.

Williams won the Pulitzer Prize for *Streetcar,* but the newly formed Tony Awards were freaked out enough by the play to opt instead for *Mister Roberts* as the big winner that season. Best Play for *Mister Roberts* over *A Streetcar Named Desire?* How's that for recognizing what's bold and brilliant in your own profession? Tony voters opted for something likable, reassuring, and funny (with a bit of tears thrown in at the end), instead of the play that challenged, exposed, and pulsated. Brando didn't win a Tony that year, though three actors were awarded Best Actor medallions (among them, Henry Fonda as Mr. Roberts). Ironically, Brando's acting sister, Jocelyn, was in *Mister Roberts. Streetcar*'s only Tony went to Jessica Tandy, who created the role of Blanche DuBois.

In their autobiographies, both Elia Kazan and Karl Malden speak of Brando's thrilling stage presence tipping the play toward Stanley rather than Blanche, but that the film, thanks to the director (Kazan again) deciding where your eye will look, restored the balance, making *Streetcar* Blanche's story as intended. Stanley's role is easily half the size of Blanche's, and he's gone from the movie for sizable stretches (though his presence hovers). Williams seems both to love and hate Stanley, savoring his humor and directness and bad-boy eroticism, while loathing his spitefulness and ignorance and violence. Something disquieting had been unleashed by Brando's Stanley, something uncontained, combining beauty and ugliness, comedy and cruelty, sex and sadism. Audiences rightfully were made uncomfortable (including those Tony voters). Stanley is simply too nuanced a character to be perceived and dismissed as an outright villain. In his autobiography, Brando claims he was the antithesis of Stanley in real life (though I imagine it was hard getting people to believe him) and that he felt he never played the part "successfully." An added attraction for him in the screen version was Vivien Leigh as his co-star, replacing Broadway's Jessica Tandy. In his book, Brando admits connecting with Leigh as he never did

with Tandy. Coincidentally, on the night that Tandy won her Oscar for *Driving Miss Daisy* (1989), over forty years after *Streetcar* premiered, Brando was a supporting-actor nominee for *A Dry White Season* (but, naturally, he was not in attendance).

Between the stage and screen *Streetcars,* Brando made his first movie, Fred Zinnemann's low-budget drama *The Men* (1950), not a male sequel to *The Women* (1939), but, rather, one of those post-war docudramas about returning WWII veterans, in this case paraplegics facing arduous assimilations back into "normal" American life. Zinnemann, a superb film director much honored in his time but now neglected, had recently guided Montgomery Clift to movie stardom (and an Oscar nomination) in *The Search* (1948) and was a logical choice to do the same for Brando. *The Men,* from the creative team that would later produce the superior *High Noon* (1952), is not one of Zinnemann's better films; it's worthy and well-intentioned but marred by a forced script with falsely rapid transitions. Brando makes a fine screen debut as the main paraplegic, conveying a painful adjustment to civilian life. It is a prime showcase for him because the role shows off both his volatility and vulnerability, elevating a decent movie beyond its obvious limitations. Ironically, the role confines this most physical of actors primarily to a bed and a wheelchair, but what stands out is how much the camera loves him. You can't, as they say, take your eyes off him. *The Men* delivered not only an exciting new actor but a born movie star.

Elia Kazan's film of *Streetcar* remains the greatest film adapted from a Williams play. (Isn't it nice that his finest play became his finest film?) It is an intensely concentrated and gripping piece of work. With Kazan re-imagining it for the movies, and Williams writing the screenplay, *Streetcar* was protected on its way to the screen, and, despite a few changes for the censors, it's a remarkably uncompromised translation. (Warner Brothers, which produced *Streetcar,* had botched the film version of *The Glass Menagerie* the year before, but this time wisely got out of the way and trusted the original creators.) Screen credit is given to Oscar Saul for "adaptation," a reference to an unused version he wrote, at Kazan's request, that dramatized scenes only talked about in the play. Kazan wisely realized that the material's power came from its rising tensions in confined spaces, tensions that shouldn't be relieved. The screenplay is essen-

Another Rebel in Town

Montgomery Clift was another New York-based theatre actor who would, with Brando, and then James Dean, influence the course of movie acting in the 1950s. Brando and Clift could be called rivals (both were beautiful, immensely talented, and complicated), though their screen personae were decidedly different, with Clift the more achingly sensitive and Brando the more volatile and overtly sexual. What they shared was that postwar feeling of something new, something more exposed and personal.

tially the play, yet the film is "cinematic" without being forcibly "opened up." The textures and contrasts in the black-and-white cinematography of Harry Stradling are stunning, alternately stark and dreamy and always adjusting to the shadings in Blanche's character and her own perceptions. The art direction by Richard Day is also first-rate, placing you inside a suffocatingly cramped living situation in all its slovenly detail, while also supplying a lively yet decaying feel for New Orleans' French Quarter just outside. And Alex North's jazzy score is a throbbing and plaintive accompaniment to all the yearnings and conflicts in the drama.

Streetcar depicts the final stages of a woman's destruction as she is increasingly forced to confront all that she has been trying helplessly to avoid. Some would call it a piece about brute forces destroying the weak and sensitive. It does pit two colossal characters against each other in a battle of wills: Blanche DuBois, a woman on the verge of a breakdown who is not going down without a ferocious fight; and Stanley Kowalski, the brother-in-law Blanche is unlucky enough to clash with when she barges into his life. It is about survival, or, more pointedly, survival of the fittest, and it also addresses the lies we tell ourselves, and others, in order to keep on going. With Brando recreating his towering Broadway performance, and Vivien Leigh's Blanche as the new element in a cast predominantly transplanted from New York, *Streetcar* became one of the American screen's most potent dramas, a timeless work because of its refusal to reduce any of its elements to easily digestible meanings. The characters are flawed, neither all good nor all bad, and the drama vacillates between fireworks and intimacy.

Brando's entrance into the film is not what you expect. Rather than a star's entrance, Brando first appears as part of the background. Stanley is glimpsed in the distance at a bowling alley, playing with his pals as his wife, Stella (Kim Hunter), points him out to Blanche, her visiting sister. Brawling with his buddies over the game, and very comfortable in his surroundings, Brando immediately sets up the character as an extroverted man with big emotions and little sense of public propriety. Stella remarks on Stanley's great looks and there's no mistaking it: Marlon Brando is a god-like specimen, a snarlingly handsome and muscled Adonis. Stanley is not just a big deal to his wife and friends. In World War II, he was "a master sergeant in the engineers corps" and decorated four times, a bona fide hero. Now he's an up-and-comer at the plant where he works, often traveling for the company. In his small chunk of the Quarter, Stanley has it all, and now there's a baby on the way to make things even sweeter.

The overriding sexual breakthrough of this movie is its use of a male as the object of lust. Of course, male stars had always been used for their virility and beauty, playing into audiences' fantasies of sexual availability, but never so explicitly as a film's main sex object. Kim Hunter is no competition, nor is Leigh as a woman past her prime. Brando's Stanley is the ultimate bad boy, a preening rooster, a gum-chewing wise guy, a blustering he-man. Stanley is a giver of sexual gratification, a man comfortable with his erotic appeal. In his first major scene, meeting his sister-in-law, he is not the brute he'll later be. With no reason yet to dislike Blanche, Brando introduces Stanley as a casually likable young man, and there's a moment when it almost seems as though they might get along, coasting on small talk and both exhibiting senses of humor. Revealing a sweaty T-shirt under his jacket, he announces that "Be comfortable" is his motto, stripping off the T-shirt after asking Blanche if she would mind. He then faces her, shirtless, before covering himself. Brando exudes the confidence of someone who knows he has a beautiful torso and beefy arms. To feel powerful he doesn't have to do anything but stand there. If Blanche has always used her attractiveness and charm to disarm men and win them over, Stanley appears to have done the same with women, but with more directness than charm. When she touches his arm at the sound of a screaming cat, Brando

Out of Her Class

The play and the film were landmarks in their depictions of lust, particularly in women. Stella is no vamp, but the writing makes it plain that she loves having sex with Stanley and cannot bear it when he's out of town. Previously, only a "bad girl" would have been able to imply such thoughts on the screen. (That wasn't the case in the early 1930s, before the Production Code was enforced, but it was the way things had been since 1934.) However, I can't say that Kim Hunter was the ideal actress to convey this to film audiences. Perhaps she was acceptable in 1951 because she was so unthreatening. Hunter was not an especially pretty girl, and not helped here by an unflattering hairdo. Putting her opposite a devastatingly attractive male says something about the characters. Perhaps Stanley got excited by the fact that this girl with a privileged background jumped off her pedestal to be with him. It was some kind of victory in the class war to have her making his meals and doing his laundry while she worshipped him. Maybe he's the type who likes to feed his ego by being in a relationship in which he is clearly the more attractive party. (Stanley wasn't reaching up, as poor-boy Montgomery Clift does with rich-girl Elizabeth Taylor in *A Place in the Sun;* Stanley pulled his privileged girl *down*.) In Williams' stage directions of the play, he describes Stella as "of a background obviously quite different from her husband's." She was raised at Belle Reve, an admittedly crumbling piece of the Old South, but nonetheless a grand Mississippi home with white columns. Secure as Brando's Stanley is in his world, he knows that he's "common." But doesn't Hunter seem every bit as common as Brando…even commoner? Where in Hunter's Stella is the girl who *chose* something baser than the old-fashioned gentility into which she was raised? She appears to have been born right into the dump she shares with Stanley, and I think it's a major weakness in Hunter's performance that we sense not a whiff of Stella's background in her current incarnation. There is no visible trace of Stella having made any adjustments to be with Stanley, no feeling that she was pulled down from anywhere. This diminishes the relationship, depriving it of colors and subtleties that would make their union something far less mundane than it appears. I believe in Stella as written by Williams, but not Stella as played by Kim Hunter, even though she created the role on Broadway. It's a boringly conscientious performance, proving that you can be honest and "real" and still be unconvincing. Coming off of *All About Eve,* Anne Baxter might have made a fine Stella, with her combination of sophistication and ordinariness.

takes a second to notice it, feeling her attraction to him and savoring the effortless victory.

Brando expanded the margins of behavioral realism on the American screen much the way Anna Magnani had done for Italian cinema. They didn't appear to be movie stars, just magnetic people caught by the camera and living somewhat more intensely than the average person. Another key element of Brando's impact is his line readings that don't *sound* like line readings. Sentences come out of him not just naturally, but without any sense of his having planned how he was going to phrase the words. Sometimes his Stanley, a man of verbal limitations, is downright monotone, but that doesn't mean that Brando is ever careless with Williams' dialogue or intentions. And he finds laughs waiting to be mined in lines that aren't necessarily comical. Stanley can be a very funny character because Brando never looks as though he is *trying* to get a laugh or even gets the joke. That's because Stanley believes everything he says. Brando is so completely this character that he cannot make a false move. He is so alive to the reality of any given moment that he can pick lint off a fellow actor while he's talking, or try to grab a stray feather floating by him. These are incidental moments, yet they speak to Brando's commitment to what is happening to Stanley *now,* regardless of how many times he played him on the stage. Brando reacted to what was happening at the time it was happening, which sounds easier than it is when there are a million things to think about in trying to make a scene work. His performance is one of total freedom, whether he's scratching himself, talking with his mouth full, eating with his hands, sticking a finger in his mouth to remove food from his teeth, slapping his wife on her buttocks, or anything else Stanley feels like doing.

Brando's Stanley is a man who just *is,* who comes up against a woman, Leigh's Blanche, who can't just *be.* Stanley is straightforward, while Blanche is all detours. Stanley tells Blanche, an English teacher, that he wasn't a good English student, but it doesn't bother him. He has done fine, *his* way, whether in the war or with women or at the plant. Among Stanley's virtues is his honesty, tied to his impatience with pretense and games, thus damaging the possibility of his being able to tolerate Blanche, who has a far more casual relationship with the truth. Stanley is a man of direct questions, and his power over Blanche comes from his ability to see right through her. As the story proceeds, Brando locates a core of insecurity in Stanley, his inability to be made a fool by anyone, or to be laughed at or bested. He simply can't take it. Perhaps someone got the better of him long ago and he vowed that it would never happen again. Maybe that's why he has such good radar in pinpointing phonies. The central conflict between Stanley and Blanche is that he has her number, almost on sight, and none of her "show" is going to have any sway with him. The more she acts "superior," the more he will brandish his contempt. The news that Belle Reve has been lost is the first serious fracture in the Stanley-Blanche relationship. It should be obvious even to Stanley that Blanche is incapable of plotting a financial swindle on anyone, what with her head being in the clouds, but he becomes incensed that, as Stella's husband, *he* has been swindled. No one gets the better of Stanley Kowalski!

In one of his funniest scenes, he explains to Stella what the Napoleonic Code is, "that what belongs to the wife belongs to the husband." He then launches into a speech regarding the goods overflowing from Blanche's trunks, a mass of cheap junk that he mistakenly interprets as valuables, including "a solid gold dress," a "genuine fur fox a half a mile long," a "treasure chest of a pirate." He tells Stella, "Here's your plantation," ridiculously, and she's wisely unconvinced. It is a hilarious attack, and yet the point is that, however remote the idea that Blanche swindled the Kowalskis, Stanley cannot let even the slightest possibility go by without confrontation. His ego will not allow it. Brando, whether comically or dramatically, stresses the pride in Stanley, his fear of being anyone's chump. Though playing opposite Leigh, Scarlett O'Hara herself, Brando has the more Scarlett-like role. Like Scarlett, Stanley can be rather funny, which makes him and Scarlett more likable than they have any right to be; he's gorgeous and knows it, wielding his beauty as Scarlett once did; and he's a winner at all costs, more consciously cruel

than Scarlett but just as self-absorbed. Brando was fifteen when *Gone With the Wind* came out. Could he have imagined that he would become Leigh's *other* great leading man of the movies?

Stanley will not take Blanche's bait with regard to her need for compliments, in one instance telling her flatly, "You looks okay." This leads to another comic speech about how women know whether or not they're good-looking without being told. On once being informed by a date that she was the glamorous type, he responded, "So what!" (His response shut her up but didn't end the relationship, he says, implying that he still took her to bed.) Stanley's patience with Blanche grows thin rather quickly. Her buzzing chatter prompts a loud outburst of, "How 'bout cutting the rebop?" and later a violent grab of her arm. But the most disruptive thing about her is her threat to his status quo. Stanley's world is stable before Blanche's arrival. He probably wouldn't mind her so much if she didn't cramp his style. At first it's minor things, like Stella fixing him a cold-plate dinner because she and Blanche are going out, but it starts to take its toll on the marriage, including the lack of privacy for their all-consuming sex life, with Blanche just a curtain away. Things become more serious with Blanche's direct pleas to Stella to leave him. Blanche's tragedy is her underestimation of Stanley, too easily disregarding him as a blue-collar mug. "Domestic violence" is a term that didn't exist back then, but it applies to the Kowalski household. Stanley is the kind of man who, after a night of drinking with the boys, is prone to taking a punch at his wife. Stella tolerates this because she knows how much he really loves her and because he's so sweet and apologetic the next day. And so the cycle continues without complaint, seemingly because the make-up sex is so good. No one seems to mind, until Blanche. Here again, she is a threat in pointing out things that have heretofore gone on as unremarkable, certainly at this address, where the brawling upstairs neighbors make the Kowalskis sound dull. If Blanche could keep her mouth shut, she would have less trouble with Stanley, but she can't, and, naturally, his disdain for her grows steadily.

In smoke-filled poker games, Brando is all business. Stanley's world is small but in it he's always a winner, in his mind anyway. If the game isn't going his way, and with all those beers flowing, he becomes a creep. Brando's sheer presence continually tells us that Stanley does not lose, whether in the army, the bowling alley, or at the poker table. So, when he does lose at something, he's a poor loser, as he is the night Blanche is playing the radio in the bedroom. In a childish reaction to losing at cards, he smashes the radio through the window, taking his frustration out on Blanche, whom he can blame for distracting his game. This is also the kind of hot-tempered moment that made Brando the most jolting new force in movies. He is not to be controlled. Stanley is soon punching Stella (his pregnant wife), until the poker players pull him off and put him under the shower, prompting a second outburst in which he attacks his pals. Once alone, and soaking wet, Brando begins the scene for which his Stanley is best remembered and most imitated. His T-shirt is so torn that it's backless. Brando reveals the post-violence childlike side of Stanley, which comes to the surface as if he were waking from a spell, aching with regret as he tries to figure out exactly what he has done in his latest blind rage. As Brando brings the realization of Stanley's assault on his wife to consciousness, the sobs overtake him. Not since Cagney had a macho man come to tears so easily and unashamedly, without fearing a loss of masculinity. Out in the courtyard, and knowing that Stella is in the upstairs apartment, he delivers the famous primal scream, "Hey, Stella!" four harrowing times. It is a cry of longing, a brat's cry for the toy he loves best, and most definitely a mating call. Pure need, pure feeling, unfettered by thought. Stella's reaction, considered to be too much for 1951 audiences, was part of the four minutes cut from the film, right before its release, to placate the Legion of Decency. These minutes (about a dozen scattered lines and visuals throughout) were restored in 1993; all of them had blessedly been saved. The restored footage enhances the film's faithfulness to Williams' original intentions and the overall adult nature of the film. The only weak restored moment is Kim Hunter's "lusty" descent down the curved wrought-iron staircase. Hunter is clearly uncomfortable, trying to suggest something, but don't ask me what. She doesn't look aroused. Does she smell something bad? It is a joyless stupor rather than an anticipation of sexual gratification. She schlumps her way down the stairs as Brando falls to his knees in sorrow and gratitude. Hunter finds her bearings once she connects with Brando, touching his hair and then smoothing her hands down his naked back. Had a

man's back ever before been made the focus of a heterosexual love scene? Perhaps what was so offensive and terrifying to censors was that the scene depicted a woman's aggressive desire and a man's passivity. They kiss and he carries her off to bed. He is sorry, naturally, fulfilling his usual role in their routine of anger, violence, forgiveness, and orgasm.

The next day Stanley overhears Blanche's pleas to Stella about running away with her. She has irretrievably crossed a line with her brother-in-law. When he makes his presence known, long after he has been listening, Brando plays the scene in a smiling, low-key fashion. Stanley knows that Stella will always choose him over her sister: when Kim Hunter leaps into his arms, Brando smiles at Leigh. As Stanley learns more about Blanche's secret past, Brando plays his scenes with Leigh with increasing impatience and open contempt. It is not so much that Blanche has a shady background; it is that she has tried to convince him otherwise. Blanche is the character we associate with vanity but that quality applies to Stanley as well. He has an inflated image of himself that fuels all aspects of his life. Neither Blanche nor Stanley is an easy personality, which is another reason for their conflict. In Brando's characterization, Stanley is free not to feel any sympathy for Blanche once he knows that she has been lying to him. Whatever happens to her will be what she has brought upon herself. To his way of thinking, he is no bad guy; he is shielding himself and others from a scheming liar and poser. What might have happened if Blanche had come to her big, strong brother-in-law and confessed her "sins" and begged for his protection? That might have been the way to wheedle Stanley, though it doesn't address the matter of what's to become of her. When he offhandedly asks her about a man named Shaw, knowing full well that she knew him, Brando displays a restrained vindictive pleasure in the panic he has generated. Stanley quietly revels in the knowledge that he has all the power in their relationship from this point on (not that there was much doubt prior).

Stanley tells Stella about the escapades he has uncovered in Blanche's recent past. In what could easily be one of Stanley's least likable scenes, Brando finds considerable gentleness in his handling of it. Though he does show some enjoyment at Stanley's victory in exposing the sexual exploits of a woman who has lorded her genteel superiority over him for five months, Brando is completely focused on Kim Hunter, sensitive to how Stella absorbs this shocking news. In deadpan, nearly monotone, reportage, Brando states the facts of Blanche's time at the Hotel Flamingo and her job-losing relationship with a seventeen-year-old male student. Brando's playing is subtle and straightforward, putting the focus on the facts and his listener and not on himself. It is a speech that could easily be turned into a big moment, but Brando realizes that he doesn't have to work hard to put it across. His keen awareness of Stella's feelings is an astute choice here, deepening Stanley's richness as a character with a reaction more complex than an obvious roar of vindication. From Stanley's point of view, he isn't being cruel to Blanche, who stormed into his life under false pretenses and then tried to fool his best friend, Mitch (Karl Malden), into marrying her. Though Brando's Stanley often radiates self-satisfied smugness when he scores points against Leigh's Blanche, this time he is simply the bearer and upholder of truth.

At Blanche's birthday dinner in the apartment, Stanley has turned a corner in his relationship with her. Why put up with nonsense from a fraud and a hypocrite? Brando expresses this with higher doses of blatant sarcasm and vulgar behavior. He sucks on chicken bones and licks his fingers, arousing the disgust of Stella, who reprimands him. Infuriated by her insult, Brando, in another classic moment, bangs his hand on the table and slides his plate off of it. The anger is more about the reason behind Stella's remark than the scolding itself. Would Stella have been offended by his table manners five months ago? It is Blanche's influence at work here, the threat to the way things were. Stella is suddenly (finally!) acting like she's from Belle Reve, all because of Blanche, whom Stanley knows is none of the things she pretends to be. It is hilarious when he quotes Huey Long, with regard to all men being kings, but the unfunny truth is laid bare: Stanley wants his old life back and sees no reason now for any delay. To stress the point, he crashes his coffee cup against the wall and facetiously asks Stella, "My place is all cleared up, now you want me to clear yours?" Brando manages to be both sharply funny and coolly terrifying, while still allowing us to see Stanley's need and frustration. He can no longer abide being called "Polack" by Blanche, especially now that he knows she is not better than anyone. He is a king, a hun-

dred-percent American, all puffed up and proud. By now Brando's attitude in his scenes with Leigh is pitiless. Stanley gives Blanche a birthday present, a one-way bus ticket home, reducing her to tears. He angrily reminds Stella, "I pulled you down off them columns and you loved it." Stanley tries to make Stella see how right he is, and how protective he is of their future. They were uncomplicatedly happy until Blanche brought confusion into their marriage. The scene ends with Stella going into labor.

When Stanley comes home from the hospital that evening (Stella's baby isn't due until morning), he finds Blanche dressed in a gown and tiara and talking to herself. Brando is so in command of the power in this showdown that he can amusedly allow Leigh's Blanche to overindulge her fantasy of a telegram containing an invitation to a Caribbean cruise. He's pretty high himself with the news of the impending birth and appears not to be in any way confrontational or even unkind, though his sarcasm never quite leaves him. In such relaxed moments, Brando permits us to see the easygoing young man Stanley is when unthreatened, a happy and immature guy who doesn't analyze things. He shakes his beer and lets it shoot high out of the bottle and all over himself, a flagrant sexual image connoting potency and abandon. He seems not to notice just how strange a scene he has stumbled into. But when she starts lying again, he cannot let it go by. He confronts her about her imaginary telegram and then heatedly reminds her that she has never fooled *him.* For all his ignorance and insensitivity, Stanley is about to become unambiguously cruel, primed for a final clash, with Stella nowhere in sight to stop him. After getting into his silk pajamas, he begins his smirking assault. In the bedroom, he traps Blanche like a caged animal but is faced with her weapon of a broken bottle. In a perverse and altogether believable touch, Brando exhibits grinning titillation at the prospect of this becoming "a little roughhouse." Sex and violence are two of Stanley's great talents and here he combines them to show Blanche unquestionably who is boss. Any sexual attraction between the characters is beside the point. The rape is about demolishing Blanche, placing her beyond repair.

In the final scene, life is almost back to normal, or will be as soon as Blanche makes her imminent departure to a mental institution. Stanley is having his card game with the boys. He mentions his time in

Salerno during the war and how he knew he was going to be lucky, a feeling he carries to this day with his wife and new baby. His meddling sister-in-law will soon be gone for good, and with no one the wiser about what happened between them. For all his bragging about his luck, and his sustained cockiness, now it is Stanley who is the liar, regarding that night with Blanche. From his standpoint, his victory came with the rape, so let's hurry and get back to life as it was. Brando allows for a suggestion of guilt in Stanley, as Blanche moves closer to her final exit. When he feels the need to go so far as to tell his buddies, "I never once touched her," Brando has the unsure composure of a man who is hiding something, which isn't something we're used to seeing in Stanley Kowalski.

But Stanley knows that they all played their parts in Blanche's demise, even if his role was the most decisive. He will learn to dismiss her from his thoughts. She was, after all, a dangerous troublemaker who tried to degrade him and bust up his marriage, right? When Blanche finally leaves, Stella says to Stanley, "Don't you ever touch me again." She then tells her baby that they're *never* going back into the apartment. These lines came about as a sop to the censors, affording Stanley some kind of punishment, but, of course, it has the opposite effect because you don't believe Stella for a second. This plays as Stella's way of assuaging her own guilt regarding Blanche, a fleeting moment of outrage that probably won't last the night. In the play, Stanley and Stella come back together immediately, with Stanley consoling her. Normalcy arrives without delay. But the movie's ending is more believable and psychologically more interesting. Stella *would* feel the need to make herself feel less guilty, so it is plausible that she would choose not to return to her happy life *instantly*. It is a feeble gesture but a credible response. By satisfying the watchdogs, the filmmakers came up with an ending that is more complex than the play's. Williams, however, was not pleased, telling author Gene D. Phillips (in *The Films of Tennessee Williams*) that *Streetcar* was "a brilliant film until the very end." The new ending also provided the perk of allowing Brando to reprise his cries for "Stella!" as Kim Hunter runs up the stairs away from him. She will be undoubtedly be back, making love to her husband, caring for their baby, and finding a way to compartmentalize what happened with Blanche, maybe even visiting her now and then (by herself,

Upsetting Upset

Streetcar lost the Best Picture Oscar to *An American in Paris,* the Gene Kelly MGM musical, a movie not without its charms but nowhere near *Streetcar's* caliber. Like *Dr. Strangelove* losing to *My Fair Lady* in 1964, or *Bonnie and Clyde* losing to *In the Heat of the Night* in 1967, or *Brokeback Mountain* losing to *Crash* in 2005, and many other instances, *Streetcar* was the film that scared Oscar voters, who reacted by hiding behind a Best Picture selection deemed classy and high-minded—it ended with a seventeen-minute ballet, for God's sake—when it was actually safe and undeserving. *Streetcar* lost in the director, screenplay, cinematography, costume design, and score categories to *A Place in the Sun,* the year's other big adult drama (from director George Stevens), with Montgomery Clift's perspiring anguish causing a stir nearly as great as Brando's. *Streetcar's* only win beyond the three in the acting categories was for art direction (and richly merited it was).

of course). Stanley, Stella, and Mitch can figure out what lies they need to tell themselves regarding Blanche. Stanley isn't punished, which is part of the point about how life works. Five years later, the 1956 film version of the Broadway smash *The Bad Seed* ruinously "punished" its title character, creating a ludicrous substitute finale, a complete cop-out. *Streetcar* is a great film partially because its drama and its characters refused to be modified for more palatable consumption.

A Streetcar Named Desire was a huge box-office success, proving again that sexual elements always help in getting audiences to see prestige pictures. It was nominated for twelve Academy Awards, including nominations for Brando and Leigh, Kim Hunter and Karl Malden in the supporting categories, plus those for picture, director, screenplay, cinematography (black and white), art direction (black and white), costume design (black and white), sound recording, and score. Isn't it interesting that though Leigh, Malden, and Hunter all won, Brando and the film did not? You can chalk this up to the countless instances of cowardice by the Academy, a group that usually favors a movie that was less threatening than the movie that should have won. Brando's Oscar loss is easier to accept than the film's since he lost to

Not Only Garfield and Clift

Though it's easy to think of Hollywood as a place that was pre-Brando and post-Brando in terms of both acting styles and on-screen male sexuality, Marlon Brando didn't spring from a vacuum. In addition to being influenced by John Garfield and sharing similarities with Montgomery Clift, Brando certainly owed a debt to James Cagney, another male who exploded on the screen (in the early 1930s) with terrifying unpredictability and spontaneity, appearing to live "in the moment" with exhilarating intensity. A more immediate predecessor was Gene Kelly, with his penchant for tight-fitting pants, as well as his blue-collar grace and ease, making him an earlier male star who obviously wanted to be noticed as an object of desire. There had also been actors who didn't seem to be acting, men like Spencer Tracy from whom dialogue flowed without any self-consciousness and who just seemed to *be* on-screen. But, taken all together, there hadn't been a star quite like Brando.

Humphrey Bogart in *The African Queen,* a marvelous performance from a legendary star who had never won before. It wasn't groundbreaking like Brando's work, but it surely was smart, funny, touching, and vastly entertaining, unlike anything Bogart had done before. The other nominees were Clift in *A Place in the Sun,* Fredric March in *Death of a Salesman,* and Arthur Kennedy in *Bright Victory.* Rebels Clift and Brando perhaps split the new-Hollywood vote, paving the way for Bogart. Though New York Film Critics' awards went to *Streetcar* as best film and Vivien Leigh as best actress, Arthur Kennedy, as *Bright Victory*'s blind war veteran (a role similar to Brando's in *The Men*) was the critics' best-actor choice. Brando didn't win a single major prize that year, yet his performance changed the face of his profession.

Brando was the titanic, untamed force of a film that had clearly unsettled the industry and the censors. He became the decade's most influential, most copied, and most inventive film actor. His impact could be seen quickly, in the work of newcomers Paul Newman and James Dean, then later, across the Atlantic, in a performance such as Richard Harris' in *This Sporting Life* (1963). The Brando effect could be easily discerned in Al Pacino and Robert De Niro in the 1970s and continues to thrive in Sean Penn,

Brando's current heir apparent. Proving that he was more than a T-shirt-ripping mumbler, the Brando of the 1950s embarked on a streak of challenging artistic successes rivaled by few actors in movie history. Within this wide range of roles, he had some misses, but they were overshadowed by the triumphs.

Viva Zapata! (1952) is another Kazan-directed picture and Brando was again nominated for an Oscar, this time playing Mexican revolutionary Emiliano Zapata, with Anthony Quinn (another former Stanley) at his side in a deservedly Oscar-winning turn as Zapata's brother. Though politically muddled and overly talky, it is a good, visually dynamic film, if not the occasion for one of Brando's best performances. With a mustache and heavy eyebrows, and looking great in a sombrero, Brando relies too heavily on brooding and moodiness. His portrayal of a selfless rebel hero is often quietly intense and interestingly *un*magnetic, but it is outshone by the varied colors of Quinn's more recognizable (and flawed) humanity. Then, in the biggest risk imaginable for this most modern of actors, Brando met Shakespeare in Joseph L. Mankiewicz's *Julius Caesar* (1953), which included master Shakespearean John Gielgud (as Cassius) in its ensemble. As Marc Antony, Brando acts with clarity, comfort, and a full voice. This test of diction and all-around legitimacy was a victory, notably in his key "Friends, Romans, countrymen…" speech, which he rightfully handled as the cunning manipulation of a crowd. Antony is not a large role (half the size of James Mason's fine Brutus), but Brando's shrewd and secure performance, assisted by the fact that he looked like a Roman statue, nabbed him a third consecutive Best Actor Oscar nomination. The overall film is more admirable than exciting, especially lackluster when compared to a vibrantly imagined Shakespeare film like Laurence Olivier's *Henry V* (1944). Moving as far from "the classics" as possible, Brando next starred as a motorcycling delinquent in *The Wild One* (1953), a decidedly lowbrow affair. Though not much of a movie, it was certainly an iconic moment in Brando's stardom, the rebel actor as an all-out rebel. Brando does more posing than acting, embodying an attitude (cool, insolent, inarticulate) and a look (leather jacket, sunglasses, jeans). His crew is about as scary as the gang members in *Grease* (1978), a film that utilized *The Wild One*'s bad boy-good girl plotting. Unworthy of his talent,

The Wild One is an immeasurable part of his legend.

Kazan's tough and powerful *On the Waterfront* (1954) is a film to rival *Streetcar,* and Brando, as Terry Malloy, a character far removed from Stanley Kowalski, is at his most extraordinary. Stanley and Terry may both be low-class and verbally deficient, but Terry is a young man of enormous sensitivity and low self-esteem. Able to feel guilt, he's the anti-Stanley. This outstanding film about dockworkers charts one mug's redemption from bum to local hero. Brando's acting is reverberatingly alive, filled with poignancy and pain on his way to becoming whole and connected, particularly in the tender love story he shares with Eva Marie Saint. Brando has humor and charm amid the sadness and insecurity, and his transition to courageous purpose, enhanced by love, is deeply moving and stunningly detailed. He finally becomes the "contender" he missed out on being in the boxing ring. The film's only flaw is its too-easy sort-of-happy ending (though it is emotionally satisfying). A perfect example of Brando's genius is the moment when Saint drops her glove and he picks it up, cleans it off, and then puts it on his own hand for a while (before she finally pulls it off). In his autobiography, *A Life,* Kazan states that Saint's dropping of the glove was a happy accident, with Brando improvising the rest, a grace note to their conversation and an exquisitely natural way for his character to detain this young woman, as well as an early (and subliminal) revelation of Terry's surprising softness, wearing a woman's glove without self-consciousness and easily retaining his masculinity. The glove business shows an actor so connected to what he is doing that he instinctively enriches his character by using whatever is available, instead of, say, picking up the glove merely to steal focus or behave self-indulgently, or even to keep the audience at a distance. This scene, like the entire performance, feels like life captured rather than enacted. Brando finally won the Best Actor Oscar, and, at thirty, was the youngest man to do so up to that time.

Opposite Jean Simmons in the title role, Brando played Napoleon in *Desirée* (1954), a big financial success but no more than a romance-novel version of history. As an ambitious young man with a sense of destiny, Brando, speaking beautifully in a British accent, submerges himself in the character, trying to bring some heft to a glossy costume picture. Though he is easily the best thing about *Desirée,* his role is practically a supporting one, with Napoleon's affairs

of state secondary to Desirée's affairs of the heart (and gown changes), resulting in a trivial movie. Such paper-thin material did not allow for the full-scale characterization of which Brando was capable, though he displays constant glimmers of what that performance might have been. In the mega-hit *Guys and Dolls* (1955), an adaptation of Broadway's 1950 musical-comedy classic, Brando was again directed by Joseph L. Mankiewicz and again paired with Jean Simmons (his only two-time female co-star). Singing the role of Sky Masterson was perhaps an even larger gamble for Brando than tackling Shakespeare. Though the film preserved Frank Loesser's great score, Michael Kidd's fabulous choreography, and Vivian Blaine's sublime Miss Adelaide, it is poorly paced and visually flat. As for Brando, his energy is of too low a wattage. His usual self-confidence is plainly lacking, maybe because Frank Sinatra, who should have been playing (and singing) Sky, is standing right next to him (miscast himself as Nathan Detroit). Though Simmons was also no musical star, she exhibits vitality and self-assurance, succeeding where Brando foundered. He may have bested her in *Desirée,* but she outclassed him in *Guys and Dolls.*

There would be additional offbeat casting, as the Okinawan interpreter Sakini in the box-office champ *The Teahouse of the August Moon* (1956), a leaden and static film version of the smash Broadway comedy about U.S. Occupation Forces in post-war Okinawa. Despite his convincing makeup and ease in speaking Japanese, Brando is borderline offensive as an Asian, giving a one-note performance of tediously smooth manipulations. He has his funny moments, as well as an agile physical grace, but he doesn't seem comfortably cast in this kind of manufactured commercial comedy. As in *Desirée,* Brando finds himself becoming subordinate to the main action, which is led by frazzled U.S. captain Glenn Ford, who strains for laughs and is all too representative of the film's overly cute and sexually coy tone. The movie's final line is Brando's "Sayonara," as if he were literally announcing his next project. Joshua Logan's *Sayonara* (1957) is another Japanese story but this time Brando plays a Caucasian, a Southern-accented American military major in love with a Japanese actress. *Sayonara* continued Brando's prowess as both a reliable audience draw and the most admired screen actor of the decade, garnering him Oscar nomination number five. A good and handsome prestige picture, *Sayonara,* like *Giant* (1956) and *South Pacific* (1958), deals with prejudice and social change within the confines of an expensive and profit-minded romantic movie. Brando's performance, as a tradition-bound fighter pilot (and good old boy) who discovers, through love, his individual identity and a new consciousness, was his finest and most nuanced since *On the Waterfront.*

What *hadn't* Brando played by now? He had proven his versatility, stretching far beyond the realm of Stanley Kowalski and wild-one Johnny. It was only a matter of time before he played a Nazi, but, of course, it wasn't going to be your standard Nazi. In *The Young Lions* (1958), Brando, shockingly blonded to full Aryan status, gives a performance noted more for its tortured conscience than its villainy. The film, bloated and flabbily directed by Edward Dmytryk, co-stars Montgomery Clift and Dean Martin as American servicemen; Brando never appears with either actor. (Clift essentially does for Martin what he did for Sinatra in 1953's *From Here to Eternity*, legitimizing him as a dramatic star.) The film would be better without Clift and Martin, focused solely on Brando, who, utilizing a strong German accent, gives the subtlest and most intriguing performance. The introspection he brings to his character, a naïve lieutenant who slowly realizes and finally confronts the horrific magnitude of the Third Reich, is the film's prime asset. (Brando would play another German, working for British intelligence, in 1965's *Morituri,* a seafaring WWII picture and another flawed film he pretty much holds together.) In the western *One-Eyed Jacks* (1961), Brando not only starred but directed, and, ironically, did a far superior job of directing than acting. One of the few exceptional westerns of its decade, *One-Eyed Jacks* is visually ravishing and mostly absorbing, a revenge-fueled drama and the rare western set by the ocean (in Monterey). Karl Malden scores as the bad guy, while Brando, perhaps too sidetracked by the enormity of his directorial tasks, gives one of his dullest performances, logy to the point of going slack.

Between the shooting and release of *One-Eyed Jacks,* Brando made his second film based on a Tennessee Williams play. *The Fugitive Kind* (1960) is an adaptation of *Orpheus Descending,* Williams' short-lived 1957 Broadway drama, with Brando assuming the role created by Cliff Robertson, though it had been originally conceived by Williams with Brando in mind. *The Fugitive Kind* was not a success com-

mercially or critically, and it marked the beginning of the end of Brando's days as a box-office star and the screen's foremost actor. The sixties would be as problematic for his career as the fifties had been enviable, with *The Fugitive Kind* the clear demarcation. It was ironic that one Williams film made Brando an Oscar-nominated movie star and another began his reversal of fortune. The irony continued because *The Fugitive Kind,* which finished Brando's reign as a dependably low-risk investment, made him the first actor to receive one million dollars for a single picture. But, while *Streetcar* is the best of the Williams films, *The Fugitive Kind* is the most underrated, especially considering that it came directly after *Cat on a Hot Tin Roof* (1958) and *Suddenly, Last Summer* (1959), two vastly inferior pictures that got major Oscar nominations and sizable audiences.

Directed by Sidney Lumet, *The Fugitive Kind* is one of the more affecting and visually evocative (in black and white) of the Williams pictures, and it features two great performances. Unfortunately, Brando's isn't one of them. Despite my considerable admiration for the film, I find Brando's performance to be one of his weakest. However, it must be said that his role is virtually unactable, murky and wispy and burdened with symbolism, much different from the two visceral female roles so thrillingly played by Anna Magnani and Joanne Woodward. Although Brando's Val Xavier is the catalyst for all the action, he is the least interesting of the main trio, frustratingly inert, even boring. Brando almost seems to give up, as if discovering along the way that his role isn't very good and that his two co-stars are wiping the floor with him. As with Montgomery Clift appearing with Elizabeth Taylor and Katharine Hepburn in *Suddenly, Last Summer,* Brando is used as a prop for two intense females, and, also like Clift, he doesn't connect with either actress. But even stuck in a repetitive and malformed role, shouldn't Brando have offered more than flickers of his celebrated inventiveness? He seems defeated, almost not to be acting at all (but not in the good way). He is unengaged, uninterested, and he lacks variety. (Even when he sings, briefly, it's not his own voice!) Though Stanley Kowalski, too, was secondary to a female, Val offered no potential as a scene-stealing threat to either female beside him.

Valentine Xavier (meaning "love savior," a case of Williams overstressing a point) is a New Orleans party boy and guitar player on the circuit since age fifteen. The film, vague on just how checkered Val's checkered past is, opens with him standing before a judge (a disembodied voice) and explaining his trashing of a joint and subsequent arrest. With Val's beloved snakeskin jacket over his shoulder, Brando approaches the bench and plays a five-and-a-half minute scene in one uninterrupted take. Val is ready to leave New Orleans and start over, away from the temptations of living wild, which appears to have included taking money for sex. (The role marked Brando's final appearance as a desirable stud.) While he is utterly spontaneous in his line readings and honest in his emotions, Brando is also rather lethargic (however tired Val informs us that he is). Impressive as the long take is, there is little pay-off, and Brando gets the picture off to a ponderous start, setting the pattern for his performance. Whenever he starts talking, he drifts into a lulling sameness, even when speaking lovely passages. No scene resonates more than any other, and Val increasingly functions as little more than the male desired by both females. The weight of the role is unnecessarily heavy, with Val, the play's "Orpheus," a music-making artist here to rescue his "Eurydice" (Magnani's Lady Torrance) from Hell, only to be undone by harsher forces. (Orpheus' harp is replaced by Val's guitar.) Everything about Val feels like a playwright's idea of a character, a literary fantasy, rather than a living-breathing man. Though Magnani represents Eurydice, and Woodward's Carol is ultimately a Cassandra, those roles and actresses transcend any burdensome origins by becoming fully human. Brando is thwarted by Val's arty, soulful, erotic purposes, and he cannot make the character *somebody*.

Accompanied by his guitar ("my life's companion"), Val has car trouble during a downpour and pulls over in a two-bit Mississippi town. Brando, at thirty-five, is playing a thirty-year-old, and though convincing as an artist, lover, humanitarian, as well as the proverbial outsider, he seems too physically and emotionally mature to be playing something of an eternal innocent (despite his hard living). Perhaps the only way for Val to seem real is if he's played by a beautiful young man able to exude a kind of purity untarnished by the character's experiences, making this more an issue of casting than acting ability. Further separating himself from the mundanely human, Val will tell Lady that his temperature is always

a couple of degrees higher than a normal person's. Brando is still a looker, not as head-turning as he was a decade prior but still credible as a commotion-causer. As in most of the Williams films, the sex object is male and his presence arouses lust, but Val is less animal than Stanley Kowalski, more spirit than body. (Val is more the Blanche of the piece, the vulnerable artistic type, rather than its Stanley, who is Lady's husband.) When Vee (Maureen Stapleton), the sheriff's wife, lets Val into her house, out of the rain, you wonder why. Brando doesn't look like the type of stranger you would open your door to when all alone during a storm, yet Val *should* be that kind of unthreatening figure. Instead, Brando seems mysterious enough to insinuate darkness and menace, neither of which is appropriate. Vee is an amateur painter, and she and Val will later talk about art making sense of existence. (Williams is always on the side of art and artists able to wring beauty from an ugly world.) After Val tells her of his time as an entertainer in New Orleans night spots, Vee decides to help him get a job at the Torrance Mercantile Store. Jabe Torrance (Victor Jory), the film's "Death" figure, is seriously ill and Lady, Jabe's wife, will need assistance.

Before meeting Lady, Val takes a ride with the local "bad girl," Carol Cutrere (Woodward), who remembers him from last New Year's Eve. As Val resists her attentions, Brando keeps his distance from Woodward, giving her no competition in their shared scenes, perhaps sensing that it would be futile to try. He remains thoughtful and observing but essentially impenetrable. Val doesn't want to return to the high-living madness in which Carol swirls, though it's hard to imagine Brando's Val as ever being any kind of fun at all. Wearing his snakeskin jacket and carrying his guitar, he finally meets Lady later that night, startling her from a phone call. Though she first resists him, the scene is about her finding her way to the decision to hire him, but it should also be about his powers of persuasion. As he did with Woodward, Brando lets Magnani dominate. Despite the lack of intensity and charisma emanating from him, Magnani has no trouble getting Lady where she needs to be by the end of the scene, ready to take a chance on him. Both characters are fed up with where their lives have brought them: Val wants a simpler life, away from hedonism; Lady is crushed by a loveless marriage, her father's death, and her incompatibility (as an Ital-

Though Brando is in the driver's seat, both Joanne Woodward (seated beside him) and Anna Magnani steal **The Fugitive Kind** *from him.*

ian) with this nowhere town. Val tells her that there are two kinds of people, those who buy and those who are bought. He then reveals a third kind, *his* kind, the kind who doesn't belong anywhere, like the species of bird without legs who cannot land, flying and floating till death. (Williams used this exact bird imagery in his 1950 novella *The Roman Spring of Mrs. Stone,* and it reappeared in the 1961

Ready When You Are, Mr. Lumet

Sidney Lumet directed one other Williams film, *The Last of the Mobile Hotshots* (1970), a dud adaptation of Williams' unsuccessful play *The Seven Descents of Myrtle* (1968). *The Fugitive Kind* was Lumet's fourth film in a big-screen career that began with *12 Angry Men* (1957), soared high with *Long Day's Journey into Night* (1962), and reached its zenith with *Dog Day Afternoon* (1975). Some would cite *Network* (1976) as his peak, but to me that is one of the more overrated and smugly self-congratulatory of all movies.

film version, uttered by Vivien Leigh, one year after *The Fugitive Kind*.) Brando's "bird" monologue, another unbroken take (which, according to Sidney Lumet in his book *Making Movies,* took thirty-four tries), is Val's most lyrical (if self-conscious) speech. The gentleness comes through, as does Val's poetic nature, but Brando's impact is no different than in the courtroom scene. He speaks the words without artifice yet they are unconnected to Val as a specific character. There are so few moments in this movie when you simply believe anything Brando says.

Both Val and Lady seem to know that a sexual liaison between them is inevitable, and Val certainly is aware of his seductive power over most women. In one scene with Woodward, Brando listens to her with his fingers casually placed down the front of his pants. But most of Brando's choices seem more vague than complex. His moments of sexual suggestiveness with Magnani belie both Val's spiritual essence and his determination to live differently. Again, there's a dangerous quality about him that doesn't seem in keeping with his free-spirited embodiment of elevating impulses and restorative powers. When Lady eventually asks him to move into the store, in a tiny main-floor room behind a curtain, Val figures that she wants him sexually. He later clasps her hand and tells her, "Nobody ever gets to know anybody" and that "We're all of us sentenced to solitary confinement." This seems truer of Brando than Val here, since the actor appears isolated in generic brooding. It would make more sense if Val instinctively understood Lady's need, expected her overtures, and was willing, without affront, to console her sexually. Later that evening, when he announces that he's quitting, angered at the prospect of (yet again?) doing "double duty,"

his reaction isn't believable. It is Magnani's stunning vulnerability that makes the scene work, despite his presence as the inauthentic device who keeps the plot moving. Once Val and Lady begin their passionate affair, it makes sense that Val, at this point in his wandering life, needs a relationship built on love rather than just sex, yet little of this comes through because the character, unlike Lady, isn't fully dimensional enough to bear such analysis.

Val becomes further entwined in Lady's life with her preparations for "Lady's Confectionery" at the back of the store, a re-creation of her father's wine garden, which was long ago destroyed by vigilantes when her father, who died in the ensuing fire, served to blacks. When the sheriff (R.G. Armstrong), a pal of Lady's husband, questions Val about being "wanted" and Val says that he isn't, the sheriff replies, in quintessential Williams, "Good-looking boy like you is always 'wanted.'" He then threatens Val with death unless he leaves town. Val's subsequent panic diminishes the character further; it is too late for Val to be so ordinary. Williams can't have it both ways, treating Val as both a heightened figure of love, art, and freedom *and* a man sensibly in fear for his life and looking to run. As Magnani and Woodward continually elevate the story with their fine-tuned modulations of turbulent emotions, Brando grows smaller, advancing little from the first scene to the last. When he tells Magnani, near the end, "I feel true love for you, Lady," and then offers to meet her elsewhere (after his escape from town), you realize just how hollow a conceit Val is, unimaginable as a person existing beyond the confines of Williams' text. Lady, consumed with the confectionery, and revenge on her evil husband, believes that Val is running off with Carol. Her calling him a liar rouses Brando for a moment, but not in any precise way. Whether he is slapping her or hugging her, there's never the kind of specificity expected from an actor of Brando's caliber. Vengeful Jabe, through fire and gunshots, brings it all to an end, not just the confectionery but the lives of Lady and Val, with nothing left behind but his snakeskin jacket. *The Fugitive Kind* becomes the first Williams film to kill off its lead characters, though once again, as in *Streetcar,* cruelty and violence are the victors.

Released by United Artists, *The Fugitive Kind* was the first box-office flop of a Williams film since *The Glass Menagerie* (1950), with five successes in between. Like Kazan's work on his two Williams films, *Streetcar* and *Baby Doll* (1956), Lumet directed *The Fugitive Kind* without gloss, building slowly but steadily, through expansive emotion and atmospheric visuals, to a shattering climax. The play is opened up quite naturally, including scenes at jail, a bar, a cemetery, etc. In *Making Movies,* Lumet says that *The Fugitive Kind* is about "the struggle to preserve what is sensitive and vulnerable both in ourselves and in the world," which might describe any number of Williams' works (including *Streetcar*) in which lost souls and nonconformists struggle (and fail) to live outside the norm. *Orpheus Descending* was actually a rewrite of *Battle of Angels,* Williams' 1940 play and his first to receive a major professional production. Despite the star power of Miriam Hopkins as Myra, the non-Italian "Lady" role, the play bombed in Boston. In *Battle of Angels,* Val is a writer rather than a musician, twenty-five instead of thirty, and even more of an object of lust, with one additional female chasing him. It is a precursor of *Picnic,* William Inge's 1953 play in which a drifter drives some small-town females to distraction. (Inge, like Williams, was a gay man writing about an irresistible male.) The 1940 Val is more of a Christ figure than an Orpheus, with the Vee character going so far as to paint him as Jesus. In both versions of the play, Val's death involves the off-stage use of a blowtorch. Though the phrase "the fugitive kind" is uttered in both plays, there was also an unrelated 1937 play by Williams titled *Fugitive Kind. Orpheus Descending* finally found success in London and New York in a 1980s production starring Vanessa Redgrave, inexplicably cast as Lady. (Having seen it, I can't tell you why it was so well-liked.) Neither *Battle of Angels* nor *Orpheus Descending* is among Williams' best plays, yet *The Fugitive Kind* surpasses most of the films based on his work, on par with *Baby Doll* and *The Night of the Iguana* (1964) as the three next-best Williams films after *Streetcar.* The *Fugitive Kind* screenplay, faithful to *Orpheus Descending,* is credited to Williams and Meade Roberts, with the finest writing going to the characters of Lady and Carol, two major Williams females. Particularly in its use of Val, the film has a fanciful, pretentious side, but Lady and Carol sustain its defiantly human core. The portrait of the Deep South is hellish and somewhat overblown, particularly in the scenery-chewing performance of Victor Jory as Magnani's monstrous husband. Like *Baby Doll, The Fugitive Kind* was hauntingly shot in black and white by Boris Kaufman, who gave the film a surreal beauty within its frightening Southern-set Hades. It wasn't, however, filmed in the South, but, rather, in Milton, New York, and inside a Bronx studio.

Brando next starred as Fletcher Christian, the old Clark Gable role, in *Mutiny on the Bounty* (1962), a long and lavish remake of the impressive 1935 Best Picture Oscar winner. Despite an endless shoot, a change in directors (from Carol Reed to Lewis Milestone), and the ultimate unfavorable comparison with the previous version, the remake is a gorgeous-looking, underappreciated epic with considerably more dramatic complexity and depth of character than the 1935 picture. Whereas Gable gave a straightforwardly strong and heroic performance, he was also miscast as an English gentleman, using no accent and in no way suggesting an upper-class fellow. Brando, in one of his more outrageous turns, plays Christian in a foppish manner, impeccably clad (first seen wearing a flaming red cape) and very much a high-born character. His performance is a daring subversion of Gable's famously lean and direct stamp on the role. Reversing the earlier film's dynamic, in which Charles Laughton's flamboyantly sadistic Captain Bligh is the over-the-top counterweight to Gable's understatement, Brando is the 1962 version's flashy attention-grabber while Trevor Howard's Bligh is a more human-sized villain. Brando's Christian is a heterosexual dandy with a dry humor, but he is much more than he seems, setting in motion a colossal character transition. If his Christian finally bears little resemblance to the fop he once was, it looks more like a fascinating transformation than the results of lazy acting. As this initially frivolous character finds meaning, Brando strips away all the exterior nonsense no longer of use to Christian. And, with a faultless English accent, he never mumbles. The older version may be better at basic storytelling and is more conventionally entertaining, but I prefer this strange and complicated remake. In 1963, Brando starred as *The Ugly American,* but his scrupulously intelligent performance as a naïve, idealistic U.S. ambassador wasn't enough to make this serious-minded Southeast Asian Cold War drama more than a labored and uninvolving misfire.

An all-star, sex-drenched drama of booze, racism, and murder, *The Chase* (1966) is a series of souped-up Southern shenanigans yearning to be a Tennessee Williams movie. Directed by Arthur Penn, a year before his *Bonnie and Clyde, The Chase* has Brando as a Texas sheriff, a good man in a lousy job. In reaction to all the overacting coming at him, Brando underplays, giving a resolutely contained performance but not an especially exciting one. Married to Angie Dickinson, he also shares screen time with Robert Duvall, his future *Godfather* co-star. *The Chase* flopped, as it should have, and Brando's decline in popularity continued with *The Appaloosa* (1966), sort of a western version of *The Bicycle Thief,* all about a man and his horse. Bare-boned, basic genre fare, it made a slow-moving contribution to the late-sixties demise of the western. No kind of stretch for Brando, he again pulls way back, this time in response to John Saxon's gleaming villain (who has alarmingly white teeth).

An especially low point for Brando was the shockingly poor ocean-liner comedy *A Countess from Hong Kong* (1967), the final film written and directed by Charlie Chaplin. On paper it sounded great, a romantic comedy starring Brando and Sophia Loren, helmed by the master himself. But it turned out not to have a laugh in it. Painfully old-fashioned and coyly carnal, it's a door-slamming farce in which Loren stows away in Brando's stateroom (where they discover that they have no chemistry, while supposedly falling in love). Miscast as Cary Grant, Brando is particularly disappointing, showing little humor and visibly disengaging as the hectic picture proceeds, positively stiffening in his refusal to have any fun. Loren fares far better, simply by allowing her lusciousness to shine and by being such a good sport on a sinking ship. John Huston's *Reflections in a Golden Eye* (1967) was a failure of a different kind, though it has something of a cult following today. Brando is a sexually closeted military officer and Elizabeth Taylor is his unsatisfied wife. Based on a Carson McCullers novel, the film (like *The Chase)* plays like faux Tennessee Williams, extravagantly Southern and extremely overheated. Brando doesn't help things by playing his role as someone too blatantly on the edge, rather than a seemingly well-adjusted fellow with agonizing secret desires. His repression seems as weird as his unintelligible Southern accent, with the character much too dour and anti-social, someone everyone would be talking about behind his back. More creepy than sympathetic, Brando's acting is self-indulgent, though he does have one great moment, fixing his hair in a mirror when he mistakenly thinks that his object of desire (Robert Forster) is coming to make love to him. But that kind of subtlety is rarely on view elsewhere in a picture mired in American movies' gay self-loathing of the 1960s, as homosexuals miserably found greater visibility.

You couldn't blame audiences for not wanting to sit through, and ultimately avoiding, the following trio: *The Night of the Following Day* (1969), a worthless thriller in which Brando gives a nondescript performance as a blond kidnapper; *Burn!* (1970), an ambitious but fumbling epic, with Brando, again blond, as an eighteenth-century Englishman meddling in colonialism; and *The Nightcomers* (1972), a sickening prequel to *The Turn of the Screw,* in which he gives a slovenly (though perfectly Irish-accented) performance as the sadistic Peter Quint. Of these projects, only *Burn!* seems to have aroused his energy and imagination fully, yet his British accent is distractingly insecure, even though he had done flawless English dialects in past roles. Each of these films, however, did its part in deepening Brando's slump.

His long-lasting critical and box-office doldrums ended resoundingly when he played Vito Corleone in the Francis Ford Coppola classic *The Godfather* (1972), for which he won and famously refused his second Best Actor Oscar. The film is one of America's great popular epic entertainments, a male-centric *Gone With the Wind* not only about the Mafia, but family, business, and America itself. A highly emotional and ritualistic film, it is exemplary in every department, perhaps most notably as an ensemble-acting piece. Here was proof of Brando's impact on the next generation of screen performer, watching him act with young men whose talent had been molded under the influence of *Streetcar* and *On the Waterfront*: Robert Duvall, James Caan, and especially Al Pacino, whose film *The Godfather* ultimately is. As family power is transferred from Brando's Vito to Pacino's Michael, it also feels like an acting legend is anointing his successor. Brando's portrayal is iconic (and much-parodied for its hoarse mumblings), but the role is too small for a lead Oscar. Though he vanishes for long stretches, he does start the film, establishing and grounding the story and its milieu, then hovers over it, revisiting it later as a sadder, weaker, and wiser man, before expiring in his tomato plants.

The performance is most effective as an unexpectedly poignant portrait of loving fatherhood. From the commercial high of *The Godfather,* Brando went the X-rated art-house route in Bernardo Bertolucci's controversial and much-lauded *Last Tango in Paris* (1972), receiving some of his best notices. About half the performance is in French, and much of it consists of sexual activity with Maria Schneider (an unappealing screen presence), though Bertolucci protects Brando by letting Schneider handle all the frontal nudity. Brando plays a suddenly widowed forty-five-year-old man (his wife has just committed suicide) who escapes into an anonymous and complication-free sexual odyssey with a twenty-year-old stranger, though he will ultimately feel the need for an emotionally intimate connection. The back story for Brando's character is a perplexing mess, and the transitions of both characters are mystifying. As for Brando's performance, it plays like individual scenes that don't accumulate into anything, a series of moods, improvisations, and bits that never add up to a whole character. To watch Brando in *Last Tango* is to watch a famous actor navigate a risky undertaking, rather than experience a full-scale, involving characterization. With much of its shock value long gone, *Last Tango* rests primarily on Bertolucci's hypnotic filmmaking technique. Released in America in 1973, this crashing bore netted Brando another Oscar nomination. But the one-two punch of *The Godfather* and *Last Tango* was only a brief respite from the erratic and increasingly bizarre trajectory of Brando's movie career.

Subsequent Brando screen roles were often cameos and/or take-the-money-and-run gigs. *The Missouri Breaks* (1976), which reunited him with director Arthur Penn (*The Chase*) and also added Jack Nicholson to Brando's list of next-generation co-stars, may contain the oddest Brando performance of them all. The film is a meandering folly, a dreary muddle of violence, slapstick, and romance tied to a threadbare plot: Brando is hired to capture horse rustler Nicholson. Brando offers self-amusement that doesn't translate to the audience, making this perhaps his most masturbatory performance, an incoherent bag of tricks that makes him seem simultaneously bored and a crackpot. After his undemanding bit as the title character's white-haired father in *Superman* (1978), Brando made *Apocalypse Now* (1979), again with Coppola. A staggering visual achievement, *Apocalypse Now* is a flawed but visionary war movie, touched by greatness, as convincing a journey into Hell as has ever been filmed. But Brando, showing up near the end, is at his most lugubrious and disrespectful, barely present and nearly destroying the movie. He is a dead weight (and by now quite heavy). *The Formula* (1980) teamed him with George C. Scott, a tempting joining of the two actors who refused Oscars, but the result is a jumbled thriller. As a big-oil businessman baddie, Brando is in his Sydney Greenstreet mode, portly and overbearing. He received a late-career Oscar nomination, his only one in the supporting category, for *A Dry White Season* (1989), a very bad and shallow film about the very worthy subject of apartheid. Brando, in his two scenes as a barrister, is the only good thing in it. Reminiscent of Charles Laughton in *Witness for the Prosecution* (1957), in terms of girth and age and deceptive sharpness, Brando rises to the occasion and gives the film some momentary gravity with his wily, disciplined performance. I assume his social conscience led him not to turn in one of his phone-it-in appearances.

In the last decade of his life—he died at age eighty in 2004—Brando made contact with yet another generation of actors shaped by his legacy, appearing in *Don Juan De Marco* (1995) with Johnny Depp and *The Score* (2001), his final film, with Edward Norton. (*The Score* also teamed him with Robert De Niro, the other actor who played Vito Corleone.) The roles weren't taxing, the films weren't special, but Brando still carried the aura of the man who altered the course of American screen acting, a craft that will always carry "pre-Brando" and "post-Brando" among its more significant classifications.

Vivien Leigh

The great Vivien Leigh as Blanche DuBois, Williams' greatest role, with Brando's Stanley hovering in **A Streetcar Named Desire**.

Vivien Leigh: Filmography

- *Things Are Looking Up (1934)*
- *The Village Squire (1935)*
- *Gentleman's Agreement (1935)*
- *Look Up and Laugh (1935)*
- *Fire over England (1937)*
- *Dark Journey (1937)*
- *Storm in a Teacup (1937)*
- *A Yank at Oxford (1938)*
- *St. Martins Lane (1938)*
- *21 Days (1939)*
- *Gone With the Wind (1939)*
- *Waterloo Bridge (1940)*
- *That Hamilton Woman (1941)*
- *Caesar and Cleopatra (1945)*
- *Anna Karenina (1948)*
- *A Streetcar Named Desire (1951)*
- *The Deep Blue Sea (1955)*
- *The Roman Spring of Mrs. Stone (1961)*
- *Ship of Fools (1965)*

Vivien Leigh (1913-1967)

Academy Award Wins

- **Best Actress** of 1939 for *Gone With the Wind*
- **Best Actress** of 1951 for *A Streetcar Named Desire*

Blanche DuBois in *A Streetcar Named Desire* (1951)
Karen Stone in *The Roman Spring of Mrs. Stone* (1961)

*V*ivien Leigh is the first of the performers in this book whose association with Tennessee Williams is a surprise. After all, what would Leigh, a British actress and Golden Age film star, be doing with a post-war American dramatist? Her stardom was rooted in pre-war Hollywood's dream factory and London's posh theatre scene; Williams became most famous for his ability to go beyond the recognized boundaries of what had been deemed good taste, exploring sexual themes in ways no one had dared to do in the more glamorous pre-war days. Besides, Williams' milieu was the American South, so what could a British actress be doing in Williams' environs? Ah, there we have the connection! Leigh may have been British, but no one could *ever* forget that she became an international star when she played Scarlett O'Hara in David O. Selznick's 1939 adaptation of Margaret Mitchell's best seller *Gone With the Wind.* Leigh had come out of nowhere, or so it had seemed to most Americans, to snag the most coveted female role in movie history. Bridging the gap between Golden Age Hollywood and post-war Hollywood, Leigh proved, with her awe-inspiring performance as Blanche DuBois in Williams' *A Streetcar Named Desire,* that she was more than capable of staying relevant, triumphing in a work by the most modern and provocative American playwright of the times. Leigh showed 1950s audiences that she could be part of the current scene, much the same way her husband, Laurence Olivier, would demonstrate when he starred in the stage and film versions of John Osborne's *The Entertainer* less than a decade later. Of the more glittering past, yes, but they were very much of the present as well.

Leigh was born Vivian Hartley on November 5, 1913, in India (to British parents) and educated all over Europe. She had already appeared in four forgotten English films in two tiny roles and two larger roles (in tiny pictures) when she made her mark on the London stage in the comedy *The Mask of Virtue* in 1935, which led directly to a film contract with producer Alexander Korda. Leigh got a break as a lady-in-waiting to Queen Elizabeth I

(Flora Robson) in the Korda-directed *Fire over England* (1937), also featuring a young and handsome Laurence Olivier. The film is one of those comic-book versions of history, dramatically thin and obviously a "rah-rah England" propaganda piece for the impending war. It is nowhere near as good as Bette Davis' "Elizabeth" picture, *The Private Lives of Elizabeth and Essex* (1939), but it is a testament to Leigh's unmistakable potential and her natural gift for acting before a camera. Olivier, however, though dashing, is stagy, hammy, and unable to connect with the lens, while Leigh shines radiantly as his love interest, a supporting role. Later that year, Leigh and Olivier starred on-screen in *21 Days,* a ragged melodrama whose only virtue is the sight of them in their youthful splendor, plus the pleasure of hearing her call him "Larry," just as she would have in real life. The movie was meager enough to be shelved in the U.K. until 1939 and was released in the U.S. in 1940 as *21 Days Together,* after Leigh and Olivier had both become Hollywood stars. They would appear jointly in the theatre for the next two decades, with Olivier by far the more acclaimed and Leigh always in his shadow. But, despite his many outstanding film performances, it was she who had the intuitive gift for the screen.

In 1937, Leigh also starred in *Dark Journey,* in which she plays a World War I spy (for the French) who passes messages in the evening gowns from her dress shop. Her romance with the monocled and middle-aged Conrad Veidt, spying for the Germans, seems improbable, and, as romantic intrigues go, it is pure tripe. *Storm in a Teacup,* her final 1937 release, is a slight but amusing light comedy, with a crackerjack Rex Harrison as her leading man. The stars don't quite mesh as a couple, but Leigh's role is not much more than decorative. She got a better comic opportunity in *A Yank at Oxford* (1938), her first American film (produced by MGM) though it was filmed in Britain. Maureen O'Sullivan is the love interest to Robert Taylor, the film's title-role star, with Leigh in the secondary part of a frisky flirt, a married woman with a much-older husband. The

Her *First* Role of a Lifetime

Despite the film's unfortunate and undeniable sympathies for the slave-owning Old South, *Gone With the Wind* remains one of Hollywood's supreme entertainments, a compulsively enjoyable historical fiction driven by Leigh's mesmerizing star turn. In one of the longest of film roles, Leigh delivers a sensational display of sheer magnetism and star quality, abetted by the ferocity of her concentration and the steeliness of her will. She is a one-woman charm offensive who can plausibly juggle a phalanx of suitors at an afternoon barbecue. Scarlett often behaves badly, selfishly, ruthlessly, but she is a beloved character for some potent reasons: she makes us laugh quite often, thereby disarming us; she is breathtakingly beautiful, so much so that it is hard to hold any grudges against her; and she has the enviable capacity to make things happen and get things done, fearlessly and cunningly breaking any convention in her way. Leigh's Scarlett is a dazzling schemer, a misguided child living an unexamined life, a woman able to adapt no matter how bleak the situation. You can love her without liking her. Leigh astonished audiences with her wit, sensuality, and indomitability. You can't "act" fascinating; you either are or you aren't. Leigh manages to fascinate for nearly four hours. Her relationship with Clark Gable's Rhett Butler feels positively ageless and consistently adult, both sexually and psychologically, with some of the Scarlett-Rhett showdowns looking like they were filmed yesterday. Carrying this masterly epic (a soap opera of the highest order), Leigh became an overnight sensation and the winner of the Best Actress Oscar. So, yes, Leigh knew a thing or two about the American South. And it now seems that she was just as destined to play Blanche DuBois. In both films, it is her character's story being told, with the male leads occupying far less screen time. Both films are *hers,* and both performances are definitive.

movie is formulaic, with the cocky Taylor, a star athlete, learning all about teamwork and good sportsmanship in terms as moralizing as those in an Andy Hardy picture. Hardly subtle herself, Leigh is animated, naughty, and bright. Before her first scene, Taylor tells his Oxford tutor, "I'm still reading *Gone With the Wind*, but I'm only halfway through." Two minutes later, Leigh enters the movie, with only one more movie between her and *GWTW*.

In *St. Martins Lane* (1938), known as *The Sidewalks of London* in the U.S., Leigh is more beguiling and spirited than polished, but her impact is tremendous. Opposite her is the remarkable Charles Laughton, who is in full masochism mode (warming up for the Hunchback of Notre Dame?) and not at his best, too broad and self-conscious. Leigh plays a character similar to Scarlett O'Hara in her self-absorption, gutsiness, and irresistibility. The role is a lovely street entertainer (a "busker") who becomes a London stage star. There's a tingling moment when she gets a phone call on the morning after a triumphant opening night, an offer from Hollywood! *Gone With the Wind* was not hers at this point, but the scene gives you a shiver. There she is, this exquisite English film actress, about to be swept away and taken to new heights, just as her excited character presumably will be. You can't help but feel that it's David O. Selznick who has made the call in *St. Martins Lane*, interrupting a mediocre movie to snag its stunning star before anyone else can.

Leigh had hoped to star opposite Olivier in Hollywood in William Wyler's *Wuthering Heights* (1939) but, lacking box-office value, Wyler instead offered her the role of Isabella, eventually played so memorably by Geraldine Fitzgerald. Leigh's refusal made her available when Scarlett O'Hara came along. Olivier would become a Hollywood star as Heathcliff in Wyler's film, and an Oscar nominee as well, though he, like Clark Gable as Rhett Butler, lost the award to Robert Donat *(Goodbye, Mr. Chips)*. After their joint success on *GWTW*, Selznick rightly wouldn't give Leigh the lead role she coveted in *Rebecca* (1940), opposite Olivier, even after she screen-tested. Selznick knew that she would have been unacceptable playing a mousy paid companion, especially after the world had come to know her as Scarlett. Leigh was actually the model image for *Rebecca*'s unseen (and dead) title character, an intimidatingly ravishing creature. Similar to the way he had entrusted Leigh with Scarlett, Selznick cast a relative newcomer, Joan Fontaine, in the role, catapulting another young actress to major stardom.

Instead, Leigh went over to MGM to star in their remake of *Waterloo Bridge* (1940) opposite Robert Taylor. (It had been a mere, but highly eventful, two years since Leigh had been a supporting player in Taylor's *Yank at Oxford* vehicle.) She gives an exceptionally touching performance as Myra Lester in *Waterloo Bridge*, a British ballerina who turns to prostitution after learning that her soldier boyfriend (Taylor) has been killed in World War I, only to discover that he lives after all. Any post-Scarlett role would have seemed an impossible encore, but *Waterloo Bridge* turned out surprisingly well, impeccably mounted and elegantly handled by director Mervyn LeRoy. Leigh's performance doesn't trade on her audience's identification with her as Scarlett. Myra is a far softer role, tender and melancholy, closer to Blanche DuBois than Scarlett in that both Myra and Blanche try to overcome their tarnished pasts. But, starting with Scarlett and Myra, Leigh's film roles usually addressed challenging sexual themes for contemporary audiences, especially for an era in which the censorious Production Code was in its heyday as the enforcer of morality and good taste. Leigh was becoming a key portrayer of female sexuality and its repercussions in several provocative roles that she would play on-screen in the next two decades.

Leigh and Olivier married in 1940. While still in Hollywood, they made the very English *That Hamilton Woman* (1941), another stodgy British historical epic in the *Fire over England* tradition, again directed by Alexander Korda. It is a stately and attractive snooze, and, again, obviously propagandistic (merely substitute "Hitler" for every mention of "Napoleon"). As with *Fire over England*, it is again stolen by Leigh. Emma Hamilton is conceived as a somewhat watered-down variation of Scarlett, and Leigh brings enormous reserves of winsome vitality to the part. Unlike Scarlett, Emma is a poor girl (with a past) who becomes the mistress and eventual wife of the British ambassador (Alan Mowbray) to Naples. Aside from Leigh's beauty and charisma, the film's chief asset is its rather mature depiction of infidelity, with Emma and Lord Nelson (Olivier), both married, carrying on a long-lasting and fairly open love affair. It is ironic that Leigh and Olivier don't have much in the way of on-screen chemistry. I blame Olivier, who, up to this point, gave impressive but rather contained screen performances, rarely making himself emotionally available to his leading ladies, whereas Leigh had had such palpable chemistry with Clark Gable in *Gone With the Wind* and an intimate rapport with Robert

Taylor in *Waterloo Bridge*. As Lord Nelson, Olivier gives a self-consumed performance, disappointingly heavy and stiff, lacking any appeal. (Maybe he was miffed that Leigh got top billing.) The film's most enduring pleasures are watching Leigh waft through ornate sets in extravagant gowns. The dullness isn't alleviated by the dreary framing story that shows the old Emma, now destitute, carted off to prison for shoplifting. Here is censorship at work again, just in case any young woman in the audience had decided to use Emma as a role model. The film also manages the neat trick of praising British imperialism while denouncing Napoleon.

Leigh and Olivier returned to England for the war years, depriving Hollywood of their talents for the duration. Still under contract to Selznick, Leigh sacrificed what could have been a glorious decade as a Hollywood star, at the peak of her beauty and youth and at the top of the list for any number of great roles, however far short they fell of Scarlett. Selznick would find a new object of fascination in Jennifer Jones, another dark-haired beauty (whom he later married). Leigh never did get to indulge her post-*GWTW* prowess, and I guess we should be thankful that she stayed in Hollywood long enough to give us *Waterloo Bridge*. Leigh continued to work in the theatre, notably in the British premiere of Thornton Wilder's *The Skin of Our Teeth* in 1945, recreating the role originated on Broadway by Tallulah Bankhead. There would be two more films from Leigh in the 1940s, both made in England. The 1945 screen version of George Bernard Shaw's *Caesar and Cleopatra* would be Leigh's first color film since *Gone With the Wind* and it looks nearly as expensive as its predecessor. But despite its colossal sets and raptur-

All in the Timing

There is no doubt that if *Gone With the Wind* had come down the pike in the mid 1940s, rather than the late 1930s, Selznick would have cast Jennifer Jones as Scarlett. She probably would have turned in a competent performance but it is hard to imagine her in Leigh's league. Besides, by then Gable would have been too old for Rhett, and Selznick might have opted for Gregory Peck, another of his hot young contract players. (To imagine the potential results, check out Selznick's *Duel in the Sun*, which did star Jones and Peck and became an instant camp classic.)

ous color, the whole enterprise is a very uncomfortable clash between film and theatre. Shaw's play was never intended as realism, which becomes obvious at the sight of such heightened material being played against all that massive and elaborate detail. Shaw didn't scale the play on those terms and the strain shows. Call it a misguided attempt by director Gabriel Pascal to turn a witty comic delicacy into an all-out screen epic. As was her habit by now, Leigh is the main reason to see the movie. As Cleopatra, another role for which she was born (with its decided similarities to Scarlett O'Hara), she makes an enchanting transition from frightened, superstitious child to commanding queen. With all her bewitching resources at her disposal, including her feline smile, Leigh's Cleopatra moves toward womanhood and power under the tutelage of Caesar (Claude Rains), finding confidence, seriousness, and wisdom, as well as shrewdness, petulance, and cruelty. And her eye-popping costumes provided Leigh with a fashion parade second only to her amazing array of Walter Plunkett-designed gowns for *Gone With the Wind*. The great Rains is not at his best, too monotonously dry and casual, even low energy, though he certainly doesn't have as interesting an arc to play as Leigh has. She and Flora Robson switched places: Leigh had once been lady-in-waiting to Robson's Elizabeth I (in *Fire over England),* but now it was Robson playing servant to Leigh's queen.

Greta Garbo had a major success when she starred in *Anna Karenina* (1935), a success not to be repeated when Leigh starred in a 1948 remake directed by Julien Duvivier. Leigh never fuses with the role, never makes Anna *hers.* Without a compelling connection to Anna, Leigh's performance, though effective in spurts, feels uninspired, as does the whole movie. Leigh lacked Garbo's poetically tragic demeanor, her overall "Russian-ness." Leigh's Anna veers too heavily on the side of foolishness and mental instability, which is less affecting than Garbo's aching sadness and closer to Emma Bovary than Anna Karenina. (*Madame Bovary* was filmed the following year, starring Mrs. Selznick, Jennifer Jones.) *Anna Karenina* marked Leigh's final screen appearance as a drop-dead beauty, again exquisitely clad (this time by Cecil Beaton). Despite Leigh's intelligence and warmth, the film was a non-starter. But Leigh's unraveling as Anna foreshadows her Blanche DuBois in *Streetcar,* though the results are

far less convincing or moving. Despite being a passionless movie, *Anna Karenina* marked the first time Leigh had an on-screen romantic involvement with a younger man, something she would deal with to varying degrees in all four of her remaining movies. Anna also occasioned Leigh's first on-screen descent into a form of madness, something repeated, also to varying degrees, in those same four movies.

In her real life, Leigh had begun having her own troubles with mental unsteadiness, which throughout the 1940s had increased, manifesting itself in manic depression and bouts of hysteria, further inflamed by a 1944 miscarriage and a 1945 diagnosis of tuberculosis. Vivien Leigh and Blanche DuBois were uncomfortably close by the time they met, and it is hard not to imagine that this is one of the reasons she connected with the role so deeply. In 1949, Olivier directed Leigh as Blanche in the London stage premiere of *Streetcar.* The production opened on October 11, and Leigh played Blanche for eight months, never missing a performance. Many of the London critics were appalled by the play's seamy content, but Leigh herself was widely praised. *Streetcar* became the property that led to Leigh's return to Hollywood after a decade away. She was no longer young by movie-industry standards (though only thirty-six during *Streetcar*'s filming) and no longer a surefire box-office attraction after such a sustained absence. Most American filmgoers hadn't seen a new Leigh movie since *That Hamilton Woman* because *Caesar and Cleopatra* and *Anna Karenina* were strictly art-house fare.

Having starred opposite Clark Gable, the King of pre-1950 Hollywood, and Marlon Brando, soon-to-be the King of post-1950 Hollywood, Leigh triumphed in both halves of Hollywood's first century. And she connected on-screen with both men equally well, on Gable's terms as a gigantic movie star and on Brando's terms as a great actor, not to say that Gable wasn't a fine screen actor or that Brando wasn't a genuine film star. Leigh made a sensational sparring partner for both men (and won two Oscars in the process, though both men lost their Oscar bids playing opposite her). Each, coincidentally, played Fletcher Christian in *Mutiny on the Bounty;* Gable in 1935 and Brando in 1962. It is worth noting that both Stanley Kowalski and Rhett Butler have Leigh's number from the start and are able to see right through her (and she doesn't like it in either movie). The only other actress seriously considered for the film version of *Streetcar* was Olivia de Havilland, also of *Gone With the Wind*. Who would have imagined that Scarlett O'Hara and Melanie Hamilton could have possibly been thought of in the same breath when casting *any* role? De Havilland was riding high at this point, having scored a big success as a mental-institution occupant in *The Snake Pit* (1948), plus winning two Oscars for *To Each His Own* (1946) and *The Heiress* (1949). But, not unlike John Garfield's negotiations to play Stanley back in New York, de Havilland's demands were more than what Warner Brothers was willing to offer, paving the way for the less expensive Leigh, whose price would naturally have been lower due to all that time back in England. But, still, imagine Melanie being more expensive than Scarlett! There are other con-

nections between *GWTW* and *Streetcar*; the former was produced by David O. Selznick, and the latter was produced on the stage by his ex-wife, Irene Mayer Selznick, the daughter of MGM boss Louis B. Mayer. So, the man who made Leigh a Hollywood star was once married to the woman who produced the play that led to Leigh's top-billed return to California. But the most delicious bit of overlap between the two films is the casting of Mickey Kuhn: in *Streetcar*, he's the young sailor who assists Blanche when she gets off the train in the opening scene; in *Gone With the Wind*, he's Ashley and Melanie's son, Beau, the child who has the crying scene when Melanie is dying. Vivien Leigh and Mickey Kuhn, together again, at last!

With her past association with the South via *GWTW* (which had to be good for marketing), and

Jessica Tandy, Screen Actress

When *Streetcar* was being brought to the screen, Elia Kazan, the play's original director and now the man who would helm the movie, brought along virtually the entire Broadway cast, with one major exception. Warner Brothers, the studio mounting the picture, decided that it wanted a film star in the role of Blanche, rather than Jessica Tandy, Blanche's first interpreter. Though Tandy is now beloved for her Oscar-winning performance in *Driving Miss Daisy* (1989), it is hard to disagree with the studio on this point. However good Tandy had been onstage, her track record in the movies was unimpressive. In her few pictures of the previous decade, the best being *The Seventh Cross* (1944) in which she appeared with husband Hume Cronyn, Tandy never really registered on camera. She was competent but exhibited little personality, and she wasn't especially photogenic or attractive. True, she was wasted in thankless roles in most of these movies, such as *Dragonwyck* (1946) and *Forever Amber* (1947), but even in juicier parts, opposite Gregory Peck in *The Valley of Decision* (1945) or Charles Boyer in *A Woman's Vengeance* (1947), she doesn't really take hold of the screen. Nothing she does stays with you, nor is she fun to watch. With her failed track record, why would she be offered the plum movie role of 1951, despite being the role's creator? Ironically, Tandy did appear on-screen that year, as the wife of Rommel (James Mason) in *The Desert*

Fox. It is a minor role, and, again, she makes little impression. When Vivien Leigh proved revelatory as Blanche on-screen, how could anyone have regretted the decision to bypass Tandy? You can see Tandy perform two of Blanche's monologues in the 1973 documentary *Tennessee Williams' South*, a cheap-looking Canadian television special. Though the circumstances are far from ideal, and Tandy, in her sixties, is twenty-five years past her stage performance, there isn't a glimmer of magic in her work. Speaking directly to the camera, she pushes for effects and emotion in an over-emphatic and actressy fashion. She lacks fragility, charm, and warmth, and barely uses any Southern accent. Tandy speaks Williams' lines much too slowly, without music or flow. It is not my intention to disparage Jessica Tandy, a distinguished actress who impressed me immensely the four times I saw her onstage in the 1980s, particularly in her Tony-winning performance in *Foxfire*. I just find it hard to imagine that an on-screen Blanche of hers could have rivaled Leigh's. Kazan and Karl Malden are both on record as preferring Tandy's stage Blanche to Leigh's on film, while Brando, in his autobiography, preferred Leigh, citing Tandy (as well as himself!) as miscast. So, the two most famous Blanches, Leigh and Tandy, were both British actresses with many classical roles to their credit, both of them custom-built for conflict with Marlon Brando, the young man who represented everything that was forward-looking in American acting.

the fact that she had starred in the play in London, it made sense to offer Leigh the role. Kazan was famous for getting to know his actors well enough personally so that he knew which buttons to push to get what he wanted from them professionally. He fanned Raymond Massey's real-life enmity for James Dean as a way to augment the force of their on-screen father-son clash in *East of Eden* (1955). He shrewdly used James Dunn, who had a history with the bottle, casting him as the alcoholic father in *A Tree Grows in Brooklyn* (1945), a role that won Dunn an Oscar. Leigh's mental troubles would not have been deemed a detriment for Kazan in accepting her as Blanche. Were the similarities between Leigh and Blanche (mental fragility, deteriorating beauty, rumors of sexual voracity) the reason why Leigh is so incredibly good in the film? She may have had a window into Blanche's predicaments, and even felt a kinship of understanding, but that doesn't explain her artistry in illuminating the character. Her performance is a phenomenal peeling away of a character's protective layers, an intrepid venturing into a character's multiple dark corners. Leigh's personal history was among the many factors (along with her talent, perseverance, and imagination) that enhanced her portrayal. Part of the appeal for her in accepting the film was the fact that Olivier had agreed to star in William Wyler's adaptation of Theodore Dreiser's *Sister Carrie,* now to be called simply *Carrie* (not to be confused with Sissy Spacek and buckets of blood). So, once again, Leigh would be following her husband to Hollywood so that he could star in a William Wyler movie, and again her success would overshadow his.

The film opens at the New Orleans train station at night. Leigh's Blanche emerges from the steam of a locomotive, an almost ghostly figure. Her featherweight costumes throughout (designed by Lucinda Ballard) highlight the ravaged poetry in Leigh's look, with garments that take on a diaphanous look that suggests a wounded butterfly. She looks carefully put together, in terms of clothes and makeup, but worn out from the journey and filled with unease. In a subliminally touching contrast, a happy wedding party flits by a moment before Leigh's wilted entrance. That kind of joy seems worlds away from the bruised figure who steps out of the mist. It is an unmistakably *Anna Karenina*-like opening, recalling thoughts of Leigh's previous film, as well as other train-station imagery from her pictures, nota-

In His Wife's Shadow (Again)

Though the woefully underrated *Carrie* (1952) turned out to be one of William Wyler's finest films, it was not well-received and failed commercially. This was especially unfortunate for Olivier, who, playing opposite the ubiquitous Jennifer Jones, gave what is arguably his greatest screen performance, a profoundly moving and multi-faceted piece of acting devoid of any of the staginess that had sometimes marred his film work. The triumph that would greet Leigh's Hollywood return should have been a triumph for both of them, but it was not to be.

bly the standout scene in *Waterloo Bridge* in which she, a prostitute looking for tricks, accidentally runs into the lover she believed was dead. (Train stations in Leigh's films do not foreshadow good things.) Audiences might not even have recognized Leigh on her entrance, since she looks nothing like the Scarlett O'Hara they had perhaps come to see. She is a blonde, no longer a budding youth, and, perhaps most distressingly, fragile. Blanche appears lost, literally and figuratively. She's looking for a streetcar named Desire, which transfers to another called Cemeteries, which will lead her to Elysian Fields. Got that? Desire leads to Death, which leads to Heaven. (Never again is Williams' touch this heavy.) Blanche is a woman aimlessly on the run with nowhere else to go. Elysian Fields, the address of her sister, Stella (Kim Hunter), and brother-in-law, Stanley Kowalski (Marlon Brando), is her last resort, the final stop, but from the look of things it seems she has landed back in the harsh reality from which she has escaped. In Leigh, you can feel how Blanche has somehow pulled all her nerves together to try to begin again, but that her underlying panic comes from a very real and terrifying sense that time is running out.

After tracking down Stella at a bowling alley, Blanche is reunited with her sister. There's little "opening up" in the movie, a wise decision made by Kazan to keep the tension taut and claustrophobic. In a story rife with Blanche's memories, mercifully none of them are visualized. The bowling-alley ambiance is loud and low-down, and Leigh sustains that unnerved feeling of being out of one's element.

Scarlett and Blanche, Red and White

And so, Leigh, who had already played American fiction's most famous Southern belle, would now do the same for American drama's most famous Southern belle. In her hands, these characters became American *film's* two most famous Southern belles, yet they could not have been any more different from each other. Aside from Scarlett being a brunette from Georgia, and Blanche a blonde from Mississippi, there are more substantive differences. Scarlett is a survivor; Blanche's survivor skills are crumbling. Both face desperate times, but Scarlett always bounces back, handling whatever crosses her path, whereas Blanche is increasingly weighed down and barely coping. Even at the end, when Scarlett learns that her dream of Ashley was pure fantasy, she seems immediately able to adjust and go after Rhett, whereas Blanche feels everything too deeply and can't make the successful transitions of which Scarlett is capable. Both women share a strong bond with their familial homes, Tara and Belle Reve, but Scarlett saves Tara from ruin, nearly single-handedly, while Blanche watched Belle Reve slip away. Blanche clearly notices Stanley Kowalski's sexual appeal, while Scarlett appears *never* to notice how good-looking Rhett Butler is. In *GWTW*, Rhett wants only to nurture and spoil Scarlett; in *Streetcar*, Stanley is going to destroy Blanche. Both women try to avoid self-reflection, but Scarlett succeeds, thinking about things "tomorrow," while Blanche can't seem to keep her demons at bay. One thing Scarlett and Blanche share is their desire to be loved *not* for who they are. Scarlett wants (or so she thinks) the love of a man (Ashley) who seems baffled and frightened by her, rather than the love of a man (Rhett) who sees her for exactly who she is; Blanche wants to be loved as the shimmering sorceress she presents to naïve Mitch, knowing that the real Blanche would be a much harder sell.

In this first major scene, a conversation between the sisters at a table in the bar, Leigh establishes Blanche as a woman of rapid-fire mood shifts, one minute breezy and humorous, then suddenly dark and silent. Blanche is able to segue effortlessly from the subject of her unchanged weight to Stella's abandonment of their ancestral home. Throughout the film, Leigh's quicksilver transitions are spellbinding and always make clear sense as to her state of mind. Blanche says and does whatever she feels she must in the name of self-preservation. One of the more heartbreaking aspects of Leigh's performance is how her Blanche, though clearly close to the edge, works so hard to project hopefulness and possibility. Without the hope in her desperation, the movie would carry the weight of a foregone conclusion, with the last scene hanging over the whole enterprise. There's enough fight and passion in Leigh's every jittery nerve ending to make us not give up on her.

Blanche's vanity, which includes her sensitivity about her age, is a defining character trait. All we know is that she's over thirty. In the play, Williams' stage directions identify Stella as around twenty-five, and Blanche as about five years older. Has anyone ever seen a professional production of *Streetcar* in which Blanche was played by a thirty-year-old actress? She is invariably cast older, especially today when thirty is considered much younger than it was back in the last mid-century. Leigh was thirty-six during the filming; Jessica Tandy was thirty-eight when the play opened. The casting of Leigh is ideal in that she is certainly lovely enough to be believable as a woman who would define herself by her looks, yet she also looks past her prime, more than her thirty-six years. There are moments when Leigh looks as beautiful as she did as Scarlett, and other times when she looks decidedly old and lined. Call it the magic of acting (as well as the magic of lighting and camerawork), a feat similarly achieved when Katharine Hepburn played Mary Tyrone in the 1962 film version of *Long Day's Journey into Night*. Both roles are former beauties, depleted by time and circumstance, who look back wistfully on their youth, a time before disappointments and realities turned their hope and promise to pain and defeat. Blanche and Mary are probably the two greatest female roles in the American theatre and it is fortunate that their translations to film resulted in two of the greatest of female screen performances.

Blanche's confidence was tied to her beauty, to the impression she made as an attractive being. But she can't count on this any longer. Blanche is self-deprecating about her looks, but that doesn't stop her from fishing for compliments. You could imagine her dissolving if someone told her that she looked old and haggard, even though she herself makes jokes about being "so total a ruin." There's a brilliant touch when the sisters are seated in the bowling-alley lounge. Leigh notices the light coming from a small lamp above her. Without a beat, she forces the shade downward, casting the glare off of her. It is an off-hand, instinctive moment that speaks volumes. Age is her stumbling block, the cause of her doubts in being able to go on and be of interest to men. Though sensitive regarding herself, she has no problem telling Stella that she's plump, not knowing that Stella is expecting a baby. Later, when Stanley lets it slip that Stella is pregnant, even though Stella told him not to say anything, Leigh has an inspired moment sitting before a mirror. As she takes in the news, you see her notice how old she looks, followed by the sad realization of her own childlessness. Her happiness for her sister is genuine, rising to the surface, but not until this flicker of darkness has passed. These nuances of feeling rise and fall in an instant. It is the kind of moment that only a great talent can pull off, a seemingly unconscious flow of impulses, an ambivalent expression of how a piece of news is absorbed.

It was a definite advantage, with material as rich as this, that all four leads, as well as most of the supporting cast, had played their roles on the stage. Blanche is meeting Stanley and Mitch for the first time, so Leigh didn't have to hurry to develop on-screen comfort levels with Brando and Karl Malden. The challenge would lie in Blanche's relationship with Stella, the one character with whom Blanche has a history. Though Leigh and Hunter are quite comfortable displaying a sisterly physical intimacy, with Leigh sometimes positively clinging to Hunter, you do not believe they are siblings, since absolutely nothing appears to connect them. The blame falls to Hunter, Broadway's Stella yet nonetheless miscast. Stella left Belle Reve behind and never looked back, but we are led to believe that the sisters were raised in a style of Southern aristocracy, however deluded and fading. Some semblance of their upbringing would have stayed with Stella and it should be visible, even if unconsciously displayed. However eagerly she chose to leave Belle Reve behind, Stella is a well-bred Mississippi girl who would not have lost all traces of a Southern accent simply by moving to New Orleans. There's no reason to expect strong

Southern accents from characters residing in a place as cosmopolitan as New Orleans, especially from characters whose birthplaces aren't identified, but Stella's history is clear. Hunter's performance would have made more sense if it were discernible that Stella is also a product of Blanche's world, though a much more practical and down-to-earth model. Stella should have a foot in both worlds, the background that made her, which she shunned, as well as the "common" world she chose and in which she revels. But there's only one Stella here, the slattern married to Stanley, and Hunter is unable to suggest the girl from Belle Reve, which makes Blanche seem even loonier by contrast. There's always the possibility that Belle Reve was never quite the Tara of Blanche's memories, but we do know that it has big white columns, which denotes some level of one-time grandeur. If Blanche married Mitch and had to adapt to a lowbrow New Orleans life, she would still be someone clearly from somewhere else. Hunter's performance, though earnest and engaged, is just all wrong (and must have been so on the stage as well).

In Leigh's portrait, Blanche is a high-energy person who uses whatever is at hand to keep herself going, whether it's a cold drink ("a lemon Coke with plenty of chipped ice"), a hot bath, a shampoo, a shot of liquor. She often dabs herself with a handkerchief to cool herself down. She's always bathing and cleansing, always trying to revive herself. These are her temporary means of warding off the fears and encroaching nerves that could, and will, devour her. Then there's the persistent chatter. Leigh had already mastered the verbal skills of Southern charmers when she played Scarlett, and so she masterfully speaks Williams' lines with astonishing fluidity, breezing through the words without ever sacrificing their meaning or emotional shadings. Leigh's deft handling of the dialogue enhances our perception of Blanche's intelligence. Only a sharp mind could come up with words as beautiful and vivid in everyday speech. She may operate on emotion, but she isn't stupid. If she had been less bright, she might have been able to get past things faster, refusing to dwell on them. Her well-honed knack with language matches her keen, though not infallible, intuition for sizing up a situation and then supplying what is required. A character like Blanche, one who talks incessantly, could grow tiresome in less skillful hands, but there's a wonderful musical-ity and variety in Leigh's Southern-accented inflections. Flowery phrases pours easily from her lips; she takes ownership of Blanche's flights of fancy and excels in the art of self-conscious Southern gaiety. The role never gets away from Leigh; she is credible as someone who really talks like that and who talks *that much*. Leigh also possesses a dancer's liquid grace, a lyrical theatricality that is an apt physical accompaniment to the syrup in her speech. Her body slinks and glides with corresponding remarks, and her arms and hands are gracefully keyed to her vocal fripperies. Leigh's voice is as light and melodic as a fluttering schoolgirl's when she is waxing poetic or pouring on the honeyed charm, but it is a much darker instrument that it was in *Gone With the Wind* twelve years earlier. In Blanche's scenes of unvarnished truth, bitterness, or rage, Leigh sounds shockingly raw and stripped of all delicacy. The hurt and angry Blanche arises when provoked. Girlish breathiness can suddenly give way to a powerfully low rumble that scrapes her vocal cords.

It isn't easy for Blanche to hide her taste for alcohol. In the bowling alley, she opts for a Scotch with the implication that it's because she needs something strong after such an exhausting journey. Her "one's my limit" lie is tough to sustain as the weeks drag on. Unsurprisingly, she uses alcohol to relax and distract herself, while it ironically takes its toll on her looks and behavior. She confesses to Stella that she's not very well, but she needn't have said anything. Leigh is something of a time bomb, a mercurial figure by turns pretty and captivating and then morose and shaky. Blanche has arrived under mysterious circumstances. Though a high-school English teacher, she has come to New Orleans before the end of the spring term. No one is suspicious about the details, but Leigh makes it plain, in her edgy defensiveness, that there's something murky in Blanche's story about her "leave of absence." Leigh also makes it easy to imagine the kind of English teacher Blanche is, the type who would really rather be teaching drama. You can picture her passionately reciting poetry to her students or organizing class presentations, behaving in ways that are alternately inspiring and embarrassing. But this Blanche was never the schoolmarm type. In Karl Malden's autobiography, *When Do I Start?* he says that Jessica Tandy was the only Blanche who showed audiences the schoolteacher side of Blanche, implying some degree of author-

ity and formality, as well as an ordinariness, none of which I long to see. If Blanche could have been a more conventional person, would she have ended up on the Kowalskis' doorstep? Leigh's characterization offers a full image of an unconventional teacher who stood out, an enthusiastic and attention-getting magic maker who tried her best to infuse students with her own love of the higher things in life.

Blanche is consumed with guilt, primarily for a major event that she will reveal later, but also for the loss of Belle Reve, the fact of which she must inform Stella. Blanche may now be a homeless poor relation, but she's quick to point out Stella's role in all of this, trying to pass some of the guilt onto her by bringing up the miseries that Stella missed, such as their family's "long parade to the graveyard." Blanche's line, "Funerals are pretty compared to deaths," acknowledges Stella's visits as well as her periods of detachment. Leigh brings to the surface the depths of pain and self-pity that Blanche usually keeps submerged. Though unlikely, perhaps Belle Reve might have been saved (and, consequently, Blanche herself) with Stella's help. It is this feeling—that Stella owes her—that allows Blanche to rationalize her moving in for an indefinite stay. As Leigh floats through the movie, she perfectly captures Blanche's self-absorption, transparent in the way she doesn't figure the repercussions of her actions on others, such as the burden she is as a guest who will not leave.

Blanche is a consummate liar, not yet a delusional one. She knows what she wants to reveal and what she prefers to fabricate (or at least sugarcoat). But in the moments when Blanche is forced into telling the truth (when found out), or when she volunteers the truth, it pours out of her. Blanche is a fantasist *because* she remembers everything, not because the truth has been blotted out. It is all there, simmering below, informing every waking moment. Little that she tells Stella at the beginning is true, about school, about her drinking. She speaks of not being able to be alone, but is that due to a fear of loneliness or more from an inability to trust her own behavior when a panic strikes? In her first serious encounter with Stanley, she learns that he is immune to her usual bag of tricks. His physical appeal is overwhelming, which Leigh makes a definite point of noticing, but how do you wheedle a man who will not be wheedled? She doesn't know it yet, but she has met her worst nightmare, a man impervious to feminine wiles, someone with no stomach for illusion. When he interrogates her on the loss of Belle Reve, she oozes with charm and ladylike deference, but to no avail. Blanche has no playbook with a man like Stanley. She fishes for a compliment with her dimpled smile and a coquettish pose, framing her chin with a fur. She gets nowhere, and the scene is properly embarrassing, whether she is squirting him with her atomizer or praising his "impressive judicial air." It is invariably poignant to watch Leigh behave as if her surroundings are grander than they are, as if Blanche's predicament isn't as dire as it is.

I love the stunned look on Leigh's face when caveman Brando starts lecturing her on Louisiana's Napoleonic Code, a look that says, "Where the hell did that come from?" He mentions having "ideas about you," which in this instance appears to be more about her untrustworthiness than her appeal, though she interprets it as flirting. "Such as what?" she replies, but he's not playing. She later notes to Stella that he's "not the type that goes for jasmine perfume," and she's right, and she's also lucid enough to realize that "maybe he's what we need to mix with our blood," acknowledging that the DuBois family is not all that good at the realities of living. If Blanche had approached Stanley in a different way, coming to him in need of his protection as her heroic and dependable brother-in-law, then maybe she would have had a chance with him. In the play, Blanche refers to Stanley as her "executioner," recognizing his harmful potential and raising the possibility that Blanche has come here to be put out of her misery. I'm sorry that line didn't make it into the film.

Blanche is unwise in her dealings with all three main characters: she doesn't curb her style around Stanley, though she knows she irritates him, especially in such cramped quarters (which she tries to improve without being asked to); she foments trouble by encouraging Stella to leave Stanley; she lies to Mitch. She can be a maddening pest. You can imagine her aging into *The Glass Menagerie*'s Amanda Wingfield, another faded belle lost in the past and determined, however misguidedly, to recapture a life built on youthful illusions. Blanche is too complicated to be seen as a flat-out victim, and it wouldn't be a great role if she could be dismissed so easily. Part of the greatness of the material is that Williams doesn't pigeonhole his characters or make them clearly classifiable. Ambivalence is inherent in

each of them. In his autobiography, Kazan is proud that he and Williams left things in a state of discomfort, refusing to dispense moral lessons or traffic in characters who could be labeled as all-good or all-bad. The play has lasted because it's an authentic depiction of the complexities of living, revealing the kinds of cross-purpose impulses in each of us. We sympathize with Blanche because we come to understand her (and what she has endured) and are able to feel her struggle for a happy ending. She is nearly as resilient as Scarlett O'Hara but resilient at going from one bad situation to the next, rather than, Scarlett-like, vanquishing her obstacles. When Blanche at last puts her "cards on the table" with Stanley, Leigh offers one of those startling moments when her voice grows hoarse yet rises from her gut. She tells him that she fibs and that "a woman's charm is fifty percent illusion." Blanche is usually "on," but canny enough, when it matters, to adjust her tactics to make the required impact. With Stanley, truth-telling is the way to go, though she can go only so far on that score. When she tells him that she has never cheated anyone, Leigh's voice finds its gravelly tone. Whenever she gets down to business, we hear ugly, stripped-bare sounds from her.

When Stanley demands to see Belle Reve's papers and grabs a stack of her letters, this prompts a violent response from Blanche. They are love letters, poems actually, written by Blanche's young husband. Regarding her husband, she tells Stanley, "I hurt him the way that you would like to hurt me, but you can't." (Oh, yes, he can.) The full story will come out later, but it's the first glimpse into the role that guilt plays in Blanche's downfall. Though she tells Stanley that she isn't young and vulnerable anymore, Leigh conveys Blanche's affecting mixture of strength and weakness, exposing the remaining shards of fight within her battered presence. An earlier mention by Stanley about her marriage led to the first of several times in the film in which she covers her ears and waits for a gunshot that only she can hear. "The boy died," is all she tells Stanley. But the boy's death, when Blanche was still a teenager, was the turning point in her life.

When she meets Mitch in an awkward encounter at the Kowalski bathroom door, she immediately senses something different in him, compared to everyone else she has met in New Orleans. You can see the wheels turning in Leigh's brain as Blanche fixates on Mitch as her possible savior. After he rejoins the poker game, Leigh has a quiet reverie in her slip in the "master bedroom," feeling sensuous (at the prospect of Mitch), then turning on the radio and dancing to a hot bongo number, a cunning way of arousing Mitch's imagination in the next room. Stanley bursts in to turn the radio off, and, again, Blanche has thoughtlessly provoked Stanley, interfering with his precious card game. But Malden's return to the bedroom results in a smile from Leigh (now in a robe) that is pure Scarlett O'Hara, the smile of an irresistible minx at the peak of her seductive powers. It is fascinating to watch Leigh with Malden here because, at last, we witness Blanche in her element, using her wiles successfully and making a man putty in her hands. The flirtatiousness and the coyness arise automatically. After all the combustion between her and Brando, the scenes with Malden are refreshingly soft and gentle. She tells him that her name, in French, means "white woods…like an orchard in spring," and then proceeds to lie that Stella is her *older* sister. Playing on his male ego, she daintily asks him to place a paper lantern over the room's naked light bulb, telling him that a naked bulb is something she cannot stand, along with "a rude remark or a vulgar action." She is really playing the great lady, but it's true that all three of those things represent unkind reality, rather than life as she would like it to be. Leigh displays the Blanche that the character aches to be again (if she ever was), the Blanche she is in danger of being too old to be. She tells him she's "very adaptable to circumstances," which first sounds like another bold lie since we haven't exactly seen evidence of this, but as the story continues it becomes clearer that Blanche has adapted far beyond anything she could have imagined, up to and including crashing in on her sister's married life and then trying to make Mitch her rescuer. If Blanche weren't adaptable, she would have been dead by now.

When Mitch turns on the light, with its newly affixed paper lantern, and Blanche switches on the radio, she exclaims, "We've made enchantment!" and then waltzes around the room. Leigh does give off a fanciful sense of wonder here, a moment that plays like vindication for all the Blanches everywhere. She has just turned the drabbest of rooms into a magical place simply with her gift for seeing the world as better than it is, merely by tweaking a few details.

It truly is a gift. Stanley smashes the radio through the window, thus, not for the last time, destroying Blanche's "enchantment." His ensuing loss of control, including an attack on his wife, is the kind of display that Blanche cannot process, especially her sister's acceptance of it. The next day it's Kim Hunter who has the morning-after scene, recalling Leigh's slyly naughty moment in bed in *Gone With the Wind,* the dawn after Clark Gable carried her up the grand staircase. Hunter can't compare with Leigh in suggesting carnal pleasures happily revisited. Both sisters are sexual beings, but Stella's appetite, though explicit, is unconvincing as forced by Hunter, whereas Blanche's longings, thanks to Leigh's openness, seem to be readily available. When Stella asks her about the titular streetcar (after Blanche brings it up), Blanche says, "It brought me here." Yes, desire brought her here, this final outpost in a life in which desire has not led to happiness. Her references to Stanley's "brutal desire" and his being "common" hold no sway with Stella, nor do references to their own upbringing, which, again, seem ridiculous in light of Hunter's blatant lack of breeding. Stanley is an animal to be reviled by Blanche, but he's also a temptation to human impulses, something Blanche has tried unsuccessfully to suppress. She clings to art, poetry, and music as ways to transcend nature. "Don't hang back with the brutes," she tells Stella.

When Stanley confronts her another day, dropping hints that he's uncovered her past, it's quite a blow. This is the moment Blanche has been dreading, when the past would catch up with her. Leigh plays Blanche's denials in great-lady fashion, but the character's pathetic panic sears through. Later, with Stella, she broaches the subject of possible gossip. She semi-confesses: "Soft people have got to court the favor of hard ones" and "You've got to shimmer and glow." Each time Blanche lets down a piece of her guard, Leigh's performance goes a layer deeper, confronting another chord of stinging reality. She asks Stella for a shot in her Coke. "I love to be waited on," she says, and it is a sad moment of yearning for a long-ago happy time when life was not an ongoing struggle. Didn't Blanche imagine herself being waited on throughout her whole life? In one of Leigh's most alarming moments, she screams when the Coke overflows in her glass, a response wildly out of proportion to the event yet an instinctual expression of her mounting dread. Gently blotting her skirt, she laughs and cries about the Coke not making a stain. This is a chilling, pitiable scene among many to follow. Leigh manages to convey both Blanche's terror and exhaustion, both of which are increased by the pressure she has imposed on herself to get Mitch to the altar. They've been dating, yet she has offered no more than a good-night kiss, determined to portray herself as a lady at all costs. She tells Stella, "I want to rest. I want to breathe quietly again. Yes, I want Mitch." The constant push-pull struggle of Blanche's hope and hopelessness is ingeniously sustained by Leigh. The actual Mitch is immaterial. She clearly doesn't care for him especially, though she realizes that he is a pleasant enough fellow. But he's the best thing likely to come along and she's got to snag him. It doesn't feel like cold calculation, though it certainly is, because the need behind it is so great and her prospects so dismal. It is easy to root in favor of Blanche's designs on Mitch because she would make him far happier than he is now.

Before Mitch arrives that evening, there is a scene that has become one of the play's most famous. Blanche is alone when the doorbell rings. It is a young man (Wright King) collecting for the Evening Star newspaper. He enters in the shadows, vague enough for Blanche to confuse him with the image of her young dead husband. Though the details of her marriage are still to be revealed, it's here that we can see how Blanche has gotten into so much trouble since then. Wracked with guilt over her husband's death, she has been making futile attempts to correct history ever since, reliving that relationship with many young men and trying to effect a different outcome, a happy ending. But nothing can alter what happened or the guilt she carries. Leigh shifts into seduction mode, fiddling with a scarf as a tantalizing prop. She detains the boy with questions, turning on the charm and the smile and her gift of gab. When she mistakenly guesses what kind of soda he just had, and he tells her that it was actually "cherry," Leigh repeats "cherry" with an abundance of warmth and delight that overflows with feeling, followed by the suggestive "You make my mouth water." Calling him "young man," and then repeating and savoring the word "young" several times, Leigh moves into a zone outside reality, a hazy and wistful alternative universe. She plants a gentle kiss upon his lips. It is one in a long line of Blanche's kisses meant for the husband she loved and lost. She tells the boy,

"It would be nice to keep you but I've got to be good and keep my hands off children." (That's one of the lines that was cut to appease the censors, but it was restored to the film in 1993.) The line denotes another of those strange moments for Blanche in which she's lost in a reverie of the past and yet shockingly alert to what is really happening. The boy and Mitch nearly run into each other outside.

She calls Mitch her "Rosenkavalier" and asks him to bow before he presents flowers to her. Blanche loves the protocol of ladies and gentlemen and their mannered courtship rites, a world gone with the wind. They go to a jazz club on a pier. (In the play, this scene happens at the Kowalski home, but it's more fitting for such a haunting scene to be played on a setting as softly romantic and dreamy as this.) Blanche seems to hold the power in the relationship, however perilously. Leigh continues to be rather prim in her physical contact with him, but continues to be generous with her amusing airs and her ability to make every situation feel heightened. She is all femininity. When he asks her to punch him in the belly so he can show off his hard tummy, Leigh, in a gloriously girlish moment, daintily pokes him briefly and then breathily cries, "Gracious!" When he lifts her to try to guess her weight, the over-the-threshold image is fraught with the agonizing suspense over whether or not they will *actually* get to such a place. (In his book, Malden recounts that on Broadway he lifted Tandy straight up, like a ballerina, which he preferred. It was Leigh who wanted the "threshold" lift from her London production. She won out, and she was right.) Blanche continues to speak of her "old-fashioned ideals" when he reaches for a kiss. It is a tightrope walk, seeing how withholding she can be without losing him. The clock is ticking a bit faster now that Stanley has heard those rumors about her. Being asked about her age by Mitch is an automatic setback, just by bringing that issue into the conversation, an issue of importance to his mother. Leigh furtively suggests that, while Blanche compassionately asks Mitch about his mother's health, she is secretly entertaining thoughts of the woman's impending demise, one more hurdle out of the way.

At last comes the monologue about Blanche's husband, the most altered piece of text in the transition from the stage to the screen. In the play, Blanche's husband, Allan Grey, is a homosexual. Stella tells Stanley about Allan: "This beautiful and talented young man was a degenerate." Blanche recounts to Mitch how she walked in on Allan with another man and then later confronted him about it on a dance floor, telling him that he disgusted her. Allan exited and moments later blew his head off. There was no way a speech like that could have made it into the film, but the success of Williams' own revision derives from the implication of Allan's gayness, with references to his "tenderness," "uncertainty," and the fact that he wrote poetry. Stereotypes, yes, but that's what was required to get the point across to those able to absorb it. For those familiar with the play, it's easy to substitute the original lines in your mind because it still appears that Leigh is talking about a gay husband. The inner truth hasn't been gutted; it's just that the lines are now more suggestive than explicit. It is not as though the basic truths have been tampered with, as they would be in later Williams adaptations such as *Cat on a Hot Tin Roof*. Naturally, the lines about walking in on Allan in a sexual situation are gone, but, perhaps because Leigh knew those lines so intimately from having said them onstage, they still seem to be present as her potent subtext. What hasn't been altered is the distance Blanche felt between herself and Allan, and the reason, in both versions, is something that she couldn't understand. For the most part, the monologue is faithfully transferred and one of the most beautiful passages Williams ever wrote. Blanche goes back to the age of sixteen, with her discovery of love and how it cast "a blinding light" on the world. Leigh luxuriates in the word "love," then turns quietly heart-wrenching as she stresses how she loved "unendurably." Before uttering the details of Allan's death, she tells Mitch simply, "I killed him." (Why did Blanche go back to her maiden name? Wouldn't it be preferable to be known as a widow than thought of as an "old maid"? Perhaps Blanche Grey sounded too bleak, not nearly as hopeful as "White Woods," especially for someone who doesn't want to see the greyness in anything.)

Blanche's deep love for the boy is richly evoked by Leigh, who appears to become a girl again, lost in the sensations of first love. Leigh is utterly believable as the kind of woman susceptible to falling in love with an artistic gay man. Blanche was a girl smitten with the arts—elevating forces in her corroding world—and here was Allan, a good-looking poet, a boy in whose company Blanche would have felt witty and cultured, perhaps more than a Missis-

"Grey" Area

Allan Grey, Blanche's husband, is the first of three off-screen gay male characters in the films of Tennessee Williams of the 1950s, all of them—the others being Skipper in *Cat on a Hot Tin Roof* and Sebastian (briefly glimpsed) in *Suddenly, Last Summer*—reaching a sad end. The messages were negative, but the visibility was important. In bringing the subject out into the open, Williams is the granddaddy to all the playwrights, primarily gay themselves, who would deal with the subject ever after.

sippi girl on a deteriorating plantation. Like Scarlett O'Hara's infatuation with Ashley Wilkes, Blanche's love for Allan reflected well on herself, furthering her own image of herself as a special girl with rarefied tastes. And, also like Ashley, there was obviously something elusive and unattainable about Allan. In another moment of stark clarity, Leigh cuts to the undistorted truth, the revolver in Allan's mouth and the words Blanche spoke that prompted it: "You're weak. I've lost respect for you. I despise you." It is not quite the play's "I saw…I know…you disgust me," but the essential meaning is unchanged, and we now know the incident from which Blanche has never recovered. She speaks of the "searchlight" being turned off. Love and life have never returned as brightly, and she lives with the fact that it was she herself who turned out that light. Guilt and regret are powerful barriers for someone trying to move on, especially if she feels she merits punishment. Allan was a young man who knew he was "different," yet he tried to make it work with this lovely and loving young woman. He soon realized it was a hopeless failure and took the only way out he could imagine. If Blanche, who adored him, despised him once she knew what he really was, then maybe he could no longer believe that any future happiness was possible. But he also lied to her and took advantage of her feelings, so he isn't exactly a gay martyr. Williams was a groundbreaker in bringing the topic of homosexuality to the stage and the screen, even if it was technically off-stage in *Streetcar*.

The monologue is staged on the walkway of a foggy pier, a dreamscape setting in which emotion and feeling trump the vague physical surroundings. After the speech, Mitch speaks of them both needing somebody, and they kiss. In what is overwhelmingly the most piercing moment in the film, Leigh exhales out of the kiss and says, haltingly and overcome with a kind of rapture, "Oh…sometimes… there's God…so quickly." It is a gorgeous line and it's delivered by Leigh with a profound mix of gratitude and relief. Mitch and Blanche are connected by their isolation, and, no matter how many times you've seen *Streetcar*, it's possible to get so caught up in this transporting scene that you can believe this is the time that Blanche and Mitch are going to find happiness. After her extraordinarily intimate rendering of Blanche's painful past, Leigh quietly exults in the overwhelming surge of feeling that maybe Blanche's anguish is really over and she has found her place of rest. Leigh looks at Malden as a life saver; the fact that the life-saving isn't one-sided doubles the moment's satisfaction.

At Blanche's birthday dinner in the apartment, Mitch is a no-show. Stanley has become more confrontational with Blanche, presenting her with a bus ticket home as a birthday present. As Leigh starts Blanche's unraveling, sped up by the apparent loss of Mitch, she continues to fight. There's a pointed moment when Leigh pushes Kim Hunter away, not willing to accept or bear Stella's consoling pity. Leigh's reaction makes it acutely clear that accepting such pity is an acceptance of defeat for Blanche, something for which she's not ready. When Mitch finally shows, much later, Blanche is alone, asleep, and drunk. The sound of his voice at the door prompts Leigh to look heavenward, as if God hasn't let Blanche down yet. Naturally, her first impulse is to check her face in the mirror. When he bursts in, she tries keeping things light, reverting to her usual chatty self and flitting around the room. Leigh cannily chose to keep Blanche in perpetual motion, as if she can't be hurt if she remains a moving target. The final humiliation is her being chased by Mitch as he turns on all the lights, insisting that the time has come to get a good look at her. Before he thrusts her under a bare bulb, Leigh delivers one of the play's most famous lines: "I don't want realism, I want magic." Blanche has been chasing magic her entire life, trying to make ugly things look pretty, trying to use social graces to make dull situations shine. She got close to magic, or so she thought, with Allan, and has clung to the idea of magic even as life became grimly real, which only made the need for magic all the greater. "I tell what ought to

be truth," she continues. But she has no one left in her audience. The degradation of Mitch's assault inspires her own brand of fury. Leigh, in a scene of blistering anger as Blanche rises to her own defense, tells him how she took her "victims" to the "Tarantula Arms." Without pretense, and with more brains and verbal dexterity than either Mitch or Stanley is capable, she speaks of her meetings with strangers, presumably young men (stand-ins for the Allan she destroyed), attempts at filling the void of an empty heart. Leigh's voice descends to its guttural recesses; Blanche is a hardened woman fighting for her life. She acknowledges that her youth is gone and that she's "played out," but also that it's not too late for them as a couple. They do still need each other. When Leigh tells him, "I never lied in my heart," it is spoken *from* the heart, and Blanche believes it, but isn't she lying to herself? She has been systematically trying to close the deal with Mitch. Alas, the happy ending is averted.

When the female vendor (Edna Thomas) arrives, selling flowers for the dead, it's a somewhat heavy-handed device, or would be if the sequence weren't visualized as a hallucination. Is the woman really there? No one else sees her. She becomes a barricade against Blanche's escape. Before Mitch leaves, Blanche does tell him more than he'd like to know. Leigh paints a haunting picture of Blanche's dark days, of the decaying Belle Reve as the family declined. "Death was as close as you are," she tells him, with death's opposite being desire. This offers another motivation for Blanche's promiscuity, a way to feel alive in a hopeless world. She chose life, spasms of excitement and danger and fantasy, even getting to be known by a group of soldiers stationed nearby. (Nothing in the play or the film goes so far as to say that Blanche was ever a prostitute.) Leigh giggles at the window, suddenly a young woman back at the mansion and not the pitiable creature in this dingy room. She is briefly the sexual being she became when she first blotted out an unhappy past and a grim-looking future. When Mitch grabs her, with desire rather than a plea for reconciliation, she thinks that perhaps all is healed. Her appeal to "Marry me, Mitch" is utterly bare (she has no more secrets), followed by his declaring her "not clean enough," though obviously still hoping to bed her. The rage that rises in Leigh, chasing him out with threats of screams and finally screams themselves, as passersby take notice, comes from Blanche's comprehension that her last chance has just gone by and her resilience gone with it.

Blanche used Southern charm and manners as her means of operating in a callous world, as well as a shield, but finally it's all she has left. You have to wonder how well she functioned immediately after Allan's death and before she began her string of sexual encounters. Was her Southern-belle routine already kind of moldy, a somewhat comical anachronism in mid-century America? Did she ever really have a Scarlett O'Hara time of glory as a manipulator of men? Were there gentleman callers lined up? The emotional baggage of her marriage, and her disbelief in ever finding true love again, were issues that not even Blanche's illusions could subside. I would imagine that Blanche's sexual experiences fell into two categories, both presumably assisted by alcohol: sex with adult strangers who provided temporary relief from loneliness and life's disappointments, as well as offering some much-needed attention and fleeting affection; and sex with very young men, substitutes for Allan, but "Allans" who desired her sexually, briefly allowing her to believe that Allan's tragedy never happened. Despite her breeding and high-minded ideals, sex surpassed charm and manners as her mode of connection, though it perhaps provided little satisfaction. I don't think that Leigh overdoes the sexual aspect of Blanche. I'd say that her performance, especially by 1951 standards, is frank and unafraid, fusing intuitively with Williams' text and subtexts. Feeling too old to be enticing anymore, Blanche tries to believe that her breeding is as valuable an asset as her looks had once been. It comes down to the simple, basic yearning to be cared for and not be hurt or disrespected. She chased culture and sophistication as portals to a world that would raise her up spiritually, as Allan once did, but didn't that arise from insecurity and feelings of inferiority? One of her most famous lines is, "Strange that I should be called a destitute woman when I have all these treasures locked in my heart." Who called her destitute? Someone back home, as they were running her out of town? Does she have any friends? Perhaps her hypocritical mix of snobbery and salaciousness made her someone to avoid. No one seems to appreciate those treasures locked in her heart, and it doesn't appear that anyone ever will.

Blanche is later seen in the apartment in what is essentially a mad scene, all dolled up and talking to herself. She is wearing one of those gowns from her trunk, plus her rhinestone tiara, as she makes small talk and giggles as if at a cocktail party. The mood is broken by Stanley's arrival. A harsh light is turned on, literally and figuratively, and it brings Blanche back to earth. It is a devastating transition as Leigh lets go of the fantasy, moving to a state of confusion and then to one of stark isolation. But Blanche rallies and launches into a spiel about a wire arriving with a yacht-cruise invitation from an old beau. Leigh plays the off-balance beautifully: Blanche knows that she's telling a fat lie, but she also achieves a victorious high from her own soothing words. When Stanley mentions her Miami millionaire, she tells him that the man, Shep Huntleigh, is from Dallas, with all the snooty pride of a woman who would be offended by the mixing up of those cities. After her debasing encounter with Mitch, and now all glamorized, she revels in her pipe dream, speaking of Shep Huntleigh as a man who wants the companionship of "a cultivated woman, a woman of breeding" rather than a bedmate. She suggests that sexual relationships are beneath intellectual and spiritual connections, implying either that she never took much pleasure in her past sexual activities, or simply that she deems it improper ever to admit how much she likes sex. This is partially fueled by her ongoing ache to be loved as she was by Allan, who didn't love her as a sex object but as a loftier companion, and it also has to do with her dimmed confidence in her physical appeal, shifting the focus to her personality. She revises the latest Mitch episode for Stanley's benefit, speaking of Mitch's imagined return with roses, begging her forgiveness (which she refused to give). And then Leigh forcefully utters the play's key line: "Deliberate cruelty is not forgivable." She adds that it is the one thing of which she's never been guilty, yet she doesn't really believe that. If deliberate cruelty is not forgivable, then that is why she has never forgiven her words to Allan before his suicide, words that made him feel sub-human. Leigh is astounding in her flexibility of emotion, appearing convincingly shaken mentally while also exhibiting searing flashes of unadorned clarity. She manages to be simultaneously sad, brave, ridiculous, and incandescent.

If Blanche entertained sexual fantasies about Stanley, and was jealous of her sister's good fortune in the bedroom, all that is gone as he moves in for the kill. Despite her many vulnerabilities, Blanche has survived thus far because she fights back. The fear Leigh evokes is harrowing, leading to the moment when Blanche makes a jagged weapon by breaking a glass bottle. Scared as Blanche is, Leigh embodies a last-stand capacity for violence that would allow Blanche to kill Stanley to save herself. But, in the struggle, her bottle crashes into a mirror and her battle is lost. In the final scene—it is unclear how much time has lapsed, though it's described in the play as "some weeks later"—Blanche believes that Shep Huntleigh is coming to get her, when it's actually a man and woman from a mental institution who will arrive to take her away. Leigh's second mad scene continues but in a gentle yet nervous vein as she touchingly focuses on the details of her outfit. While Blanche is in the bathroom, Stella tells her upstairs pal (Peg Hillias) that she couldn't believe Blanche's story about being raped by Stanley and still go on living with him. Blanche's demise is complete and each of the main characters has played a part. As Leigh makes her way to Blanche's final moments, she flickers back and forth between a dulled reality and her make-believe plans. When told that her expected man has arrived with a lady, Leigh turns the moment into something richly resonant, moving between twinges of jealousy at the appearance of a rival (and possibly a younger one) and concern about what the woman is wearing. Being dressed appropriately is as vitally important to her as the potential competition for a beau.

Leigh plays the shattered Blanche as a woman determined to hold on to her dignity in a situation fraught with confusion. The sight of the elderly gentleman (Richard Garrick) who has come to get her, clearly not the Prince Charming she was expecting, is an unhinging moment. Leigh offers him a polite, half-hearted smile before darting back to the bedroom. Here the actress opens up completely in a full-fledged panic attack, quivering as she tries to find an exit where there isn't one. But the final blow is the paper lantern that Stanley offers her, a blatant representation of her failed world of magic. It is unbearable to watch Leigh convulse and emit distressing primal sounds (snorts and grunts and groans), like a wounded animal. The matron (Ann Dere) brings her to the floor, and it's deeply disturbing to see this lovely, delicate woman so dehumanized. Blanche asks the old man to allow the matron

to free her, which he does. When he raises her to her feet, and then takes off his hat and offers his arm, it revives Blanche: "Whoever you are, I have always depended on the kindness… of strangers." One-night stands and other casual lovers had certainly provided Blanche with temporary relief, and strangers, in general, are unable to cause the kind of emotional damage inflicted by close relationships. Leigh exits the film trance-like, as a kind of peace washes over her, maybe with thoughts of the rest Blanche has been seeking. We are not meant to imagine a future for Blanche since she appears to be finished, but is there hope? This is not like wondering if Scarlett will win Rhett back at the end of *GWTW.* Maybe the best we can hope is that Blanche will find kindness at the institution, but, then again, how good a facility can it be? (There's no money for a really good place.) It is hard to imagine a comeback for her.

Blanche DuBois is Williams' supreme creation. Just about all of his major characters, including those that came before her, share certain qualities with Blanche, one or a few of her many facets, though none of them is as inexhaustibly complex as she is. It is no wonder that Vivien Leigh won almost every prize available for her magnificent and uncompromising interpretation of such a role. The commitment she brought to the part is staggering, and Kazan aided her greatly by shooting the film in sequence, aside from the location shots of the New Orleans opening, which were filmed last. Leigh got only two Oscar nominations in her career and she won both times, receiving an Oscar for *Streetcar* as a companion to the one she received for *Gone With the Wind.* At the 1951 Academy Awards, Leigh beat Jane Wyman—who had bombed the year before as Laura in the misbegotten film of Williams' *Glass Menagerie*—for *The Blue Veil,* Eleanor Parker for *Detective Story,* Shelley Winters for *A Place in the Sun,* and Katharine Hepburn for *The African Queen.* In any other year, Hepburn's glorious transformation in *The African Queen* would have been the victor, but Leigh's performance was unbeatable. Just about the only citation she didn't receive was the best-actress honor from the National Board of Review, who opted for Jan Sterling's stinging and sarcastic turn as a cold-blooded wife in *Ace in the Hole,* a terrific bad-girl performance but hardly a leading role. Sterling wasn't nominated for the supporting Oscar that year, though she deserved to win it. The undeserving victor was *Streetcar*'s Kim Hunter, riding the *Streetcar* wave. Actually, Sterling, with her real-life upper-crust background and her talent for playing down and dirty, might have been the screen's ideal Stella (even matching Leigh's blond hair).

It is mind-boggling to read Kazan's comments, in his autobiography, about Leigh's performance. Though he says he was "full of admiration" for her and her work ethic, and ultimately calls her "excellent" in the big scenes, he also cites her "small talent." It is hard to absorb those two words in light not only of her work as Blanche but in the rest of her screen career. Just about everyone, including Kazan, Malden, and Brando, agreed that the film of *Streetcar* surpassed the original stage production. Leigh and Brando were two people the camera loved, two people you could never tire of looking at, and they raised each other to dizzying heights in *A Streetcar Named Desire.*

When Leigh won her second Oscar, she was appearing on Broadway with Olivier in alternating productions of *Caesar and Cleopatra* and *Antony and Cleopatra.* She would devote most of the 1950s to her stage career alongside Olivier, notably in Stratford-upon-Avon productions of *Macbeth, Twelfth Night,* and *Titus Andronicus,* as well as the London premiere of *The Sleeping Prince,* Terence Rattigan's 1953 comedy, which Olivier, as director and star, later filmed as *The Prince and the Showgirl* (1957) with Leigh, deemed too old, replaced by none other than Marilyn Monroe. It was *The Deep Blue Sea,* also a Rattigan play, that would provide the vehicle for Leigh's first completed film since *Streetcar.* In 1953, she had begun work on *Elephant Walk,* a movie she eventually withdrew from due to a nervous breakdown. Despite the sad circumstances, her departure was hardly a bad career move. *Elephant Walk* would have been an inexplicable follow-up to *Streetcar,* no more than a colorful "B" picture, the kind of junky fun associated with Saturday matinees, a movie in which you wait patiently for an elephant rampage. (It's not the natives who are getting restless this time.) It is ridiculous to imagine Leigh in the role eventually assumed by Elizabeth Taylor, nearly twenty years Leigh's junior and much more appropriate as a naïve bride. Taylor's size and coloring matched Leigh's, thus allowing the finished film to use some of the long shots of Leigh in her Indian location footage. Though the plot is an unofficial re-

working of *Rebecca,* set on a tea plantation in Ceylon, what would the great Vivien Leigh, a two-time Oscar winner with Shakespearean credentials, have been doing in a silly jungle melodrama in which she would have been chased by pachyderms?

The Deep Blue Sea (1955) was certainly more suitable material, with Leigh in a role originated by Peggy Ashcroft in London and Margaret Sullavan on Broadway. Unfortunately, it's the kind of bloodless drama (so British it almost feels like a spoof) that young forward-looking English playwrights like John Osborne would soon be reacting *against.* From the *Anna Karenina* playbook, Leigh's character leaves her polite fifteen-year marriage to a judge (Emlyn Williams) for the virility of a brash test pilot (Kenneth More). The movie opens with her failed suicide attempt and then offers explanatory flashbacks. The effect is more artificial than probing and Anatole Litvak's direction is stagy, while Leigh's acting is disappointingly forced and mannered. Like Anna and Blanche (and Mrs. Stone to come), Leigh was again a well-bred woman who abandons propriety, but her heart just wasn't in it this time.

Beginning with *Streetcar,* Leigh played Americans in three of her final four films (she's British in *The Deep Blue Sea*). Her first American film since *Streetcar* was *The Roman Spring of Mrs. Stone* (1961), another Warner Brothers picture and her other film based on Tennessee Williams material. But *Roman Spring* was not adapted from a full-length Williams play, or even a one-act. Instead, it was based on his 1950 novella of the same name. Therefore, there had been no previous dramatic incarnation with which to compete, no previous cast to be measured beside. Perhaps this goes some way in explaining why Williams, in his autobiography, *Memoirs,* calls this film "a poem" and "my favorite of all the movies based on my work." That is an astonishing assessment because the movie lacks the intricate depths of *Streetcar* and never ignites emotionally in any comparable way. *Roman Spring* is at best a good film, and, fine as Leigh is, her work cannot rank as an achievement equal to her portrait of Blanche. But Karen Stone was an ideal role for Leigh as she neared fifty, and it seems more than fitting that there was a prime Williams role waiting for her as inevitably as Blanche had a decade before. What is remarkable about Leigh's performance is that it's her most subdued since *Waterloo Bridge,* only seldom allowing for the kind of lavishly emotional moments offered by her more recent screen roles.

In the pre-credits sequence, Karen Stone, a Broadway star, is appearing as Rosalind in *As You Like It* in Washington, D.C. Leigh is first glimpsed backstage in boy garb, then in her dressing room, primping for her entrance in an opulent wedding gown. As she succumbs to nerves and an overriding sense of inadequacy, she gets a strong talking-to from her dresser (Bessie Love, the long-ago star of the Oscar-winning Best Picture *The Broadway Melody* [1929]), yet nothing can assuage this tide of inferiority. Leigh begins the film in a state of defeat, an actress not up to the demands of Shakespeare, a star too middle-aged for the leading-lady roles that made her name. Here the role had to touch a chord with Leigh, who, like every other contemporary pushing fifty, was dealing with a paucity of good roles. But her affinity with Karen may have been keener with regard to shared doubts about their Shakespearean abilities: Leigh had never been considered Olivier's peer as a classical artist. A more coincidental similarity between Leigh and Karen is their newfound single status: Leigh and Olivier divorced in 1960; Karen will soon be a widow. If the realities of aging, professional insecurity, and sudden unattachment played their part in Leigh's identification with the role, her performance never feels self-indulgent or self-exploiting, remaining disciplined and understated, sticking to the character as written. Karen is never seen onstage, but it is later revealed that she was more a personality than an actress. (Shouldn't she have a stage name with more glamour than her ordinary married name?) Karen knows she isn't very good as Rosalind and decides not to bring the production to New York. She and her husband, Tom (John Phillips), a millionaire and an investor in her plays, set off for Europe, despite his heart trouble. Tom, twenty years older than Karen, suffers a fatal heart attack on the plane. Karen comes to Rome as a retired actress and a childless widow. The pre-credits sequence has ended.

Roman Spring was filmed in England and on location in Rome, but it is apparent that Leigh never set foot in Rome, since Karen (presumably Leigh's stand-in) is seen only in long shots of the city. Enormous credit goes to production designer Roger Furse who created sets of Roman exteriors that fit rather comfortably beside scenes shot in Rome itself. Leigh's Karen, like her Blanche, is a blonde; her only two screen blondes were her Williams characters.

Her coiffure is almost helmet-like in its immovable perfection. While Blanche's wardrobe was one of shabby elegance, Karen's is worthy of a queen, the height of smart, impeccably tailored Paris fashions (Balmain of Paris, to be exact). Leigh is costumed resplendently in couture dresses and evening gowns in varied colors and fabrics. She wears them like a true star, shimmering nonchalantly. Leigh embodies regal poise and refinement, creating a character of effortless sophistication and unerring taste, perfectly matching the character's dignified hold on her private emotions. Leigh hadn't played an actress on film since *St. Martins Lane* (1938), and, despite looking older than her forty-seven years, she is still remarkably beautiful. Her American accent is fine, despite an occasional overly pressed "r" on words like "darling" and "of course."

It is unfortunate that, after the credits, the movie restarts with unnecessary narration. This goes on, oddly, for several minutes, but then, odder still, is dropped abruptly, never to return. Karen is seen in her fashionable and spacious apartment in an ancient palazzo whose terrace overlooks the famed sun-drenched Spanish Steps. The narration introduces an important character, a homeless and handsome young man (Jeremy Spenser) in the plaza below, seeming to be "keeping watch" on Karen and waiting for her "signal." The narrator tells us more about Karen (her lack of self-knowledge) and her husband (his pampering of her), things that could easily be clarified in Leigh's acting and the dialogue, specifically the theme of "drifting" as her life loses purpose and meaning. The official plot begins with the arrival of the Contessa Magda Terribili-Gonzales (Lotte Lenya), an older-woman pimp, and Paolo di Leo (Warren Beatty), the Contessa's arrestingly handsome companion.

Warren Beatty, a Tony Award nominee for William Inge's *A Loss of Roses* (1959), had made only one other film, appearing opposite Natalie Wood in Elia Kazan's 1961 *Splendor in the Grass* (another Inge script). Though *Splendor* would make him the hot new serious-actor heartthrob in the Brando-Clift-Dean-Newman tradition, it had not yet been released when Beatty was making *Roman Spring*. His erotic appeal and New York acting style made him a natural for works by Williams, but in *Roman Spring* he plays an atypical Williams role, an Italian (not an Italian-American). Though not yet

Leigh's Karen Stone during her brief romantic resurgence, gazing into the eyes of Warren Beatty's studly Paolo di Leo in **The Roman Spring of Mrs. Stone**.

a star, Beatty is given a star's entrance. His face is teasingly shielded from the camera as he makes his way to Karen's apartment, revealed only at the moment they are introduced, permitting the viewer to get the same first impression of his good looks that she gets. As in most of the previous Williams films (*Streetcar, Rose Tattoo, Cat on a Hot Tin Roof, The Fugitive Kind, Summer and Smoke*), the sex object here is a male. Beatty is a beautiful young man, smoothly confident in his appearance whether nattily attired or sunbathing in black swim trunks. (He, unlike Leigh, clearly went to Rome.) The Contessa has brought Paolo here in the hope that Karen will be sufficiently enticed to invest in him as her way out of her aimless stupor. (The Contessa has a fifty-fifty arrangement with her "boys.") The surprise here is Leigh's cool reaction, showing little more than politeness in Beatty's presence, in no way desperate or needy. Her grace and reserve, as well as her lack of interest in him, are intriguing. He pursues her, and

she remains pleasant but remote. Twice in the film, Beatty unclenches one of her fists, a loosening of her unconscious tension, emotional as well as physical. Leigh slowly relaxes Karen's defensive arsenal, letting her guard down incrementally, which simultaneously makes her stronger (willing to live again) and weaker (allowing herself to be vulnerable).

Lotte Lenya, too, had appeared in only one previous film, as Jenny in the 1931 German film of *The Threepenny Opera*, a role she repeated onstage to acclaim in New York in the mid 1950s. The Contessa is a flamboyant role ideally suited to Lenya's theatrical grandeur and decadent persona. Unlike Karen, the Contessa is a survivor at all costs, sometimes pathetic but never pitiable as she does whatever humiliating task is required to keep the money rolling in. (No "drifting" for her.) Her bordello-red lair is a fabulous caricature of a place intended for wicked doings. She is a jaded Dolly Levi with an Austrian accent, a booking agent for a stable of young studs.

The Priest and the Prostitute

I must acknowledge Williams' use of my own rather rare last name for his main male character (created in the 1950 novella), an instance made even more unusual by Williams' almost simultaneous use of another variation of the name in the character of Father De Leo in his 1951 play *The Rose Tattoo*. While traveling through Italy in the late 1940s with his life partner, Frank Merlo, Williams must have seen the name somewhere and liked it, or perhaps he had some contact with a distant relation of mine. How interesting that he used the name for both a priest and a prostitute.

Everything about Lenya is tinged with a touch of the cheerfully Satanic: she has flaming red hair, red fingernails, red lipstick, even an orange cat (which she strokes like Blofeld, her boss in her next film). Her wrap is one of those dead animals biting its own tail. Publicly she is a personable madam, but privately more of a shrewd witch. Ruthlessly hardworking, she pounces on potential clients under the infectiously enthusiastic guise of bringing companionship to the lonely. She is also an iron-fisted watchdog over her boys, always ready to suspect a swindle. Fun to be with it if she's making money off you, she is trouble if you cross her. Lenya gives a richly entertaining and amusingly vulgar performance, the lurid and gaudy alternative to Leigh's muted Mrs. Stone.

The device of the looming, mysterious young man could become pretentious, a heavy symbol of inescapable death. Perhaps because he is a purely visual component, his presence is actually one of the film's strongest ingredients. As he periodically appears, frightening Karen despite his general passivity, he gives the film more dimension than it would have as a straight soap opera about a doomed affair between an older woman and a younger man. On some level, Karen knows that her death can be evaded only temporarily, and that it is somehow connected to the young man's persistent presence. Suicide is an option, since Karen is suddenly without all that once defined her and completely lacking the motivation to continue. The young man is her Angel of Death, though he is not a phantom; he is seen by others, including Paolo. (When Paolo asks her about him, she denies ever having seen him.) It adds an unexpected

poignancy that the young man doesn't seem to know why he is there, looking up at her terrace, drawn by some inexplicable force and waiting to perform a service for which he was meant. The option of death is there at her convenience, with the male stranger stalking more boldly as the film proceeds, showing up in other shadows and corners of Rome. Even her happiest times with Paolo do not prevent sightings of the lurking youth, who continues to make his availability known. This character works better in the film than in the book because in Williams' novella he is less mysterious and more aggressive (even once flashing his genitals), altogether too informal and realistically grungy. His relative passivity in the film makes for more powerful imagery, that of an attractive urchin in a state of perpetual waiting. If portrayed in a more everyday fashion, such as a down-and-out version of Paolo, he would be minimized as a force. Any back story would serve only to trivialize his potency. He never speaks (though he murmurs in the book), just waits and watches, knowing he must be ready. Like the lady selling flowers for the dead in *Streetcar*, the young man is an embodiment of death, on hand to fulfill a function he is strangely compelled to gratify. Even when questioning him, Leigh intuitively plays her rattled moments with him as if Karen subconsciously knows exactly who he is and what he signifies. They share a spiritual connection, an otherworldly feeling of some dark fate to be shared. Their pantomime gives the film moments of haunting visual poetry and its most original emotional resonances.

Karen Stone is a woman who wonders if her life will have a third act. Without the glittering career that focused her, or the wealthy and undemanding husband she leaned on, or the power she wielded by virtue of her youthful loveliness, she has the chance, however frightening, to reinvent herself in Rome. The role is mired in grief and hopelessness, a woman stuck in a numbing melancholy. The arrival of Paolo, though she first resists him, changes everything, but can it be anything more than a brief episode? Leigh plays Karen as a careful woman, a fascinating contrast to her reckless, emotionally expansive Blanche DuBois. Things don't end well for either character, but each approaches life in a completely different way. Karen, with every advantage of affluence and celebrity, seems almost always on the verge of giving up, while Blanche, with so little going for her, fights creatively and valiantly. Karen is prone to being

Gay and Happy

Roman Spring offers the first *alive* gay male in a Williams film, coming after the three dead homosexuals who constitute the back stories of *Streetcar, Cat on a Hot Tin Roof,* and *Suddenly, Last Summer.* True, the gay character here, the Baron Waldheim (Carl Jaffe), is a minor presence, which made it easier for him to survive the translation from novella to film, but it's also true that the strictures on gay screen content had loosened considerably by 1961, the year of *The Children's Hour.* The Baron is a client of the Contessa, and since she handles only young men it's clear what the baron wants. British screenwriter Gavin Lambert, who adapted Williams' book for the screen, gave the Contessa a tip-off to the audience when, right after she easily sets up one of her female clients, she tells the Baron, "For you, I need a little bit more time." This slyly implies that it will be harder for the Contessa to find a young man willing to sleep with men, even though it is doubtful that the baron's request would have been unusual in these circumstances. Wouldn't half, if not most, of the Contessa's clients be men, especially in less openly gay times? (In the novella, the baron was one of Paolo's previous "protectors.") In a later nightclub scene, the baron, who wears a monocle, is unmistakably paired off with a young man. Because the baron's presence is so secondary, he didn't have to come to a bad end in the manner of most gays-on-film in the 1960s. He is last seen actually enjoying the pleasure of his match-up. Even less connected to the plot is another gay moment, early on, during the narration about assignations on the Spanish Steps. The first duo to be seen is a younger man-older man hook-up, clearly not father and son. *Roman Spring* was a fairly gay enterprise, considering the contributions of Williams, Lambert, and the film's director, Panamian-born José Quintero. It is not surprising that there would be as much gay visibility as possible, however peripheral.

sensible and honest (if not exactly self-examining); Blanche opts for ever-deepening delusions. However, Karen, in believing that Paolo loves her and that she isn't merely paying for his attention, eventually does find herself living in a mirage. Age is a mutual enemy, with Karen having a very Blanche moment, a mirror scene, when a lamp's sudden light provokes a harsh reaction to her own image and a brisk move away. Both characters have easily identifiable executioners: Blanche has Stanley; Karen has the young man awaiting his cue. Both women are undone by a taste for young men, and both carry the pain of widowhood. Each finds a last-chance new man to bring potential happiness but neither can hold him. Though fortified in her tower, Karen turns out to be just as vulnerable as Blanche, but even in humiliation, and then death, Karen never loses a certain decorum, whereas Blanche is often teetering toward embarrassment. Karen has had "magic," a life of it eight times a week on stages, and is now looking for a reason to go on, something more than the latest fashions and swanky cocktail parties. She is not a pitiable figure, merely a lost soul trying to find out who she is *now*, fearful that she isn't really much of anybody.

There's one other character of importance, Meg Bishop (Coral Browne), Karen's old school chum and now an established political journalist. The Meg-Karen scenes serve a distinct purpose because Meg is the film's truth-teller, the one who says the things that Karen doesn't want to hear. Their encounters invariably end badly, with Meg going too far and Karen feeling wounded. In the novella, Meg is a lesbian, but I don't sense any sexual heat being emitted by Browne for Leigh, though Meg, perhaps cunningly, manages to put down all aspects of Karen's life aside from their friendship. Pooh-poohing Karen's denigration of her own talent (though not really disagreeing), Browne's Meg gets off one of Williams' best lines: "What's talent? Being able to get away with something, that's all." Meg tries to turn every conversation into a soul-barer, and she's not pleased to see Karen succumbing to the charms of a gigolo. She also refers to Karen's husband of twenty years as an "elderly invalid" with "filthy millions" and their marriage as Karen's way of avoiding love. Meg calls Karen an "escapist," perhaps closer to Blanche than first suspected, but more in the way that most people tend not to overanalyze choices they suspect may not be good for them. When Meg makes a reference to all the people who love Karen, Leigh has an illuminating moment, responding with "Who are these people who love me? I want names."

Jeremy Spenser, All Grown Up

In a coincidence as curious as *GWTW*'s little Beau Wilkes showing up later as *Streetcar*'s train-station sailor, Jeremy Spenser, *Roman Spring*'s nameless figure, had appeared as a child with Leigh in *Anna Karenina*, in a scene in Venice rather than Rome. As a little Italian boy, the son of Anna's servant, Spenser sits on Leigh's lap and is given a sweet by her. They speak Italian together, and the scene ends with a cuddle. All in all, a far cry from their disturbing encounter in Rome thirteen years later.

It is an admission of feeling unloved as herself, rather than as a star. The alertness of Leigh's reaction denotes Karen's underlying sensitivity, whether or not she is as unloved as she believes. If Karen was primarily the roles she played and "never ever myself," then Rome is a daunting opportunity for self-actualization without the armor—career, husband, youth—of her past. Coral Browne is just right as a well-meaning busybody and overall abrasive woman. After her delicious Vera Charles, the bitchy foil to a formidable Rosalind Russell in *Auntie Mame* (1958), Browne next appeared on-screen as Meg, another supposedly dear friend but nowhere near as good company as stage-star Vera. If the young man is Karen's Angel of Death, then Meg is her Voice of Doom. It is no fault of Browne's that we are never glad to see Meg, for the simple reason that she is certain to upset Karen.

Paolo, like Karen, plays hard to get, though he is impressed by her as "a very great lady." Leigh gradually breaks down Karen's defenses, with Paolo the only thing to have roused her since leaving America. Their dates bring him progressively closer to her bedroom. When he notices that even her smiles are sad, it's an accurate perception of Leigh's performance, in which sad smiles, from the moment Karen arrived in Rome, delicately express a lack of love and purpose, a fear of vulnerability, and a frustrating ennui. The basic May-December plot was franker and more affecting when Simone Signoret fell for Laurence Harvey in *Room at the Top* (1959), and had been more audaciously imagined when Gloria Swanson flipped over William Holden in *Sunset Boulevard* (1950). If *Roman Spring* feels comparatively undernourished and rushed, it is still an admirable piece of work

made with considerable care. Paolo is by necessity a vapid creature, a hustler looking for the best deal. Though he has pangs of feeling for Karen, the character is not explored fully because he isn't meant to be more than a petulant and grasping hunk, a greedy child incapable of the kind of self-analysis that might tell him why he does what he does (beyond his quest for luxury). It is Karen's story, and it doesn't matter who Paolo is beyond being the guy she thinks she loves. Beatty is certainly competent, endowed with obvious star potential, but, as far as being convincing as an Italian, he isn't as good—and I can't believe I'm going to say this—as George Hamilton in *Light in the Piazza* (1962), a far more believable "Italian" performance, surer in both accent and physicality. *Roman Spring* was the fourth Williams film with Italian ties, following the Italian-American characters in *The Rose Tattoo* (1955), *Baby Doll* (1956), and *The Fugitive Kind* (1960).

Leigh and Lenya share a scene at a cocktail-party buffet. The Contessa, mistrusting Paolo and wanting to show him who is boss, tries to sabotage his chances with Karen by revealing his next move. Leigh reacts in an unfazed manner, still in control, saying about him, "People who are very beautiful make their own laws," a simpler and more pointed observation than Williams' comparable line in the book. Karen admits to knowing the truth of her comment first-hand, and the line has an extra frisson of meaning because Leigh, too, would have known the advantages of remarkable beauty. Then, directly from the book, she says, "Americans aren't as romantic as their motion pictures," an ambiguous moment since it allows for the possibility that the American motion picture being watched may prove to be more romanticized than expected. Leigh remains cool and composed; Karen foolishly assumes her objectivity and detachment to be inviolable. When Paolo later launches into his cheap ploy, a story about a friend in need of cash (just as the Contessa predicted), it is a stinging moment that begins the key transitional sequence in Leigh's performance. Karen is being played like all the other rich ladies and she must make a choice. At first it looks as though she will simply accept Paolo for what he is and literally pay the price, going so far as to ask when his "friend" would need the money. But then her pride makes one last attempt to preserve her dignity, a move that will lead to her undoing because it is here that she blurs reality. She tells him, "When the time comes when nobody desires me for myself, I'd rather not be desired at all," and then leaves the terrace. It is a theatre star's dramatic exit, an absence that makes clear she is available to him in her bedroom. It is a risky gambit because he could walk out. But if he beds her without any financial promises, then she can imagine that she *isn't* like the others, having snagged him on her own. Or have her proud words really just been a defensive cover, a face-saving gesture despite their both knowing that she *is* agreeing to pay for all that's to come?

Choosing to stay or go prompts Paolo's most complicated moment, though he would naturally assume that after bedding her he would instantly be in a better position to get more from her. He is a good enough hustler to know that what this client needs is to feel special and wanted. In bed in her slip, she stares at her bedroom door expectantly. Beatty, all in black, makes a studly entrance into the boudoir, wordlessly closing the door and then the drapes. After they kiss, the screen fades to black. It feels like a victory for her, having gotten him without the promise of anything more, but sexual gratification will make her relinquish whatever power she thought she had. Neither character wants to see the situation as sordid, that they are preying on each other. But without the honesty of an up-front client-gigolo relationship, Karen has set herself up for a fall. She convinces herself that her sexual yearnings and her attraction to a younger man are validated by true love. Leigh's projection of vanity, a by-product of Karen's years of fame and accomplishment, allows for mistaking a high-class whore for boyfriend material. Karen is no innocent, and it is perhaps true that many years ago, when as beautiful as Paolo, she landed the much-older Mr. Stone by offering her allure in return for his fortune. Yet she loved her husband, so can't Paolo love her? Leigh lets go of Karen's tentative approach, her *drifting*, and liberates the character into the uncharted waters of unfettered feeling.

Instead of a Scarlett O'Hara morning-after giggle in bed, Karen's carnal bliss is expressed with a new hairstyle from Elizabeth Arden. When she then runs into a couple from back home, she is so disconnected from her past that it takes a while for these old friends to be recognizable as the dear chums they once were. The suddenness of Leigh's

realization informs just how deeply Karen is immersed in her reinvention. She tells the woman that she is dying and wishes her privacy to be respected. Leigh barely contains Karen's glee in delivering this outrageous ruse and clever trick, while positively glowing with health. Her confession of a terminal disease is ironically one of Leigh's happiest moments. For most of the film, even in romantic delirium, she carries undercurrents of innate pessimism, which explains those continuing appearances, as if summoned, by the young man. There is no montage of happy times between Karen and Paolo, though Paolo certainly implies that he cares for her, thus augmenting an impassioned situation for her from which it is too late to turn back. *Roman Spring* is suffused with a bleak outlook, however glamorous and expensive its suffering may be. The scene in which she takes Paolo to a tailor to be fitted for new suits is right out of *Sunset Boulevard*. Karen finds pleasure in being able to bring him pleasure; Paolo finds pleasure in the suits. Williams' novella predates his 1959 play *Sweet Bird of Youth*, in which another past-her-prime actress flees desperately from her career and seeks solace with an ambitious and great-looking boy toy (though the end result is markedly different).

When Lenya corners Leigh at a basement nightclub (in which a young Cleo Laine is the bandstand singer), she is in full black-widow attire, asking for $1000 because of hard times. (Karen offers her $500 instead.) The subtext behind the transaction is that the Contessa, who hasn't gotten one lira from the supposedly legitimate Karen-Paolo romance, deserves at the very least a finder's fee, no? It is gifts, rather than cash, that have been accumulating for Paolo. There's an excellent scene when he, giddy over the perfect fit of his new suit, runs home to the palazzo. Leigh, wearing a sumptuous pale-green gown, is looking at herself admiringly in a mirror. When Beatty bursts into the room, Leigh smiles with the anticipation of a compliment, only to be nearly knocked down as he rushes to preen before the mirror. Leigh's inspired response is unbridled laughter, not *at* him but at the characters' shared vanity. Karen immediately regrets the laugh, realizing how misinterpreted it was, but it can't be easily taken back, especially after he leaves the room hurt and embarrassed. This brief scene makes a startling transition from light to dark.

The Contessa telephones Paolo about a pretty red-headed American film star's interest in him, a ploy to attach Paolo to someone willing to pay for him. Starlet Barbara Bingham (Jill St. John) might even be able to get Paolo into the movies. (Bombshell St. John is twice heard wishing that she could go to New York and study the Method, which sounds like a satiric swipe at Marilyn Monroe.) As Paolo starts plotting his exit, he grows increasingly unpleasant, perhaps partially out of guilt over his impending treatment of Karen. He tells her the story of a woman like her who was found dead in her bed, murdered by a lover. After her joke about whether *he* is going to kill her, Leigh says, with casual and chilling humor, "Three or four years is all I need. After that a cut throat would be a convenience." (Leigh herself lived six more years.) Later, she asks, "Shall I never know if you love me unless you hurt me?" referring to his satisfying (to her) explanation for his hurtful remarks earlier in their relationship. Now he flirts openly with younger women, perhaps trying to drive her away or at least give her the opportunity to end it herself. The pain in Leigh's performance comes in her realization that she *is* like the others, that Karen *has* lost her dignity. And yet *Roman Spring* doesn't play like masochism because Karen isn't given time to wallow; her humiliation is brusque and swift. The spiteful Contessa, certain there's nothing left to be gotten out of Karen, joins in the degradation, bringing the movie star to Karen's home. There's a masterfully bitchy moment when Leigh, trying to hold on to Karen's grace, asks Miss Bingham about her latest picture and then glides by her as the young star begins to answer. Neither Karen nor Leigh had spent a lifetime in the theatre for nothing.

As home movies are shown of Karen and Paolo, ostensibly the reason for this uncomfortable gathering, the scene evokes a similar one in *Rebecca* (1940) in which happy home-movies play as counterpoint to the serious situation unfolding. Leigh girds herself for the final confrontation with Beatty, prompted by his furtive moments with St. John on the terrace. At last comes the unguarded anger in Leigh, with Karen knowing she has lost Paolo to a higher bidder. She says she will not deal in such "ugly traffic," but she has already. His exit prompts her to throw out her remaining guests as the home movies continue in playful contrast. Lenya's "Wunderbar!" is followed by her slow, slithering exit, slamming the

door behind her. If Karen's story had truly ended with the finish of her career and marriage, then her Roman episode was a kind of limbo, an in-between existence, a last gasp before the final resignation. Leigh collapses in tears, a release of everything that has been building inside of Karen since her arrival in Rome, from her initial dearth of feeling to her current anguish of feeling too much. Like Blanche and Stanley's "date with each other from the beginning" (Stanley's line in the play, cut for the movie), Karen and the mysterious young man reach their destined moment. She puts her keys in a white handkerchief and flings the small bundle to him while he paces below, as if already sensing that the time has finally arrived. Leigh plays this date with death calmly, resolutely, as if Karen is freed by a proactive choice to drift no more. She sits and begins to light a cigarette as the door opens. The young figure isn't scary, looking rather frightened himself. Moving slowly, he walks directly into the camera as the screen is enveloped by the black shadow of his coat. Karen's death is thankfully not treated as a punishment for sexual sins, but, rather, as a choice against an intolerable open-ended "drift." Her murder-assisted suicide connects her to Sebastian in *Suddenly, Last Summer*, another Williams character who instigates his own dark and violent fate.

Considering this was director José Quintero's first and only feature film, he did a laudable job, despite a few scenes that end much too abruptly. *Roman Spring* is a colorful, elegant-looking movie, a bit leisurely paced though its dreamy, unrushed feeling is also one of its assets. Quintero had directed the celebrated Off-Broadway production of Williams' *Summer and Smoke* in 1952, starring Geraldine Page, and went on to become the foremost interpreter of the works of Eugene O'Neill, including the original production of *Long Day's Journey into Night* in 1956. Quintero later directed the Broadway premieres of two lesser Williams plays, *The Seven Descents of Myrtle* (1968) and *Clothes for a Summer Hotel* (1980). In his autobiography, *If You Don't Dance They Beat You,* Quintero writes about the marvelous friendship he forged with Leigh during *Roman Spring*'s making. Her trust in him, despite his initial nerves at making his first film, is evident in her performance.

Leigh went on to win the Tony Award for Best Actress in a Musical for *Tovarich* (1963), a singing-and-dancing departure for her in which she

I Demand a Recount

Lotte Lenya's performance resulted in the film's sole Oscar nomination, but she lost, amid much misguided fawning over *West Side Story,* to Rita Moreno for her imitation of Chita Rivera. Lenya went on to screen immortality as Rosa Klebb, the great lesbian villain with the poison-knifed shoe in *From Russia with Love* (1963).

performed a show-stopping Charleston. But there would be only one more film role, a final sad middle-aged American beauty looking for love, in Stanley Kramer's heavy-handed and flat-footed *Ship of Fools* (1965), a *Grand Hotel*-style drama set in 1933 (though it looks utterly like 1965). Situated on an ocean liner going from Mexico to Germany, this self-important commentary on pre-war Germany is almost saved by three of its stars: Oskar Werner, who, as the ship's doctor, has the greatest screen heart attack of all time; Simone Signoret, as a brave mistress and drug addict being sent to an island prison; and top-billed Leigh as a rich and jaded divorcee. Leigh's role is a sketch of what had by then become a stock character for her, combining bits of her three previous films. Despite insuf-

ficient screen time, she is sharp and droll and vivid, doing a mean Charleston (perfected in *Tovarich,* I guess) and improbably walloping the hulking and boozy Lee Marvin with just her high heel. She has the requisite scene of confronting her aging face in a mirror, drunkenly applying too much makeup. (It's the reverse of Jan Sterling's famed makeup-removal scene in *The High and the Mighty* [1954].) Despite a raft of Oscar nominations, *Ship of Fools* is a bad prestige film, never sinking lower than when the incomparably abominable José Ferrer, as a Nazi-party member, hijacks the screen.

Though she became a major star as an indomitably strong character, Leigh spent the remainder of her film career primarily playing characters facing humiliation, madness, and suicide. Scarlett O'Hara was increasingly less visible in Leigh's subsequent, more fragile screen performances, in which she often looks aged beyond her years. Her bipolar status was an ongoing problem for the last two decades of her life. She died at fifty-three in 1967 due to a recurrence of her tuberculosis. Because Miss Scarlett could always take care of herself, you are more likely to be haunted by Blanche DuBois and Karen Stone, Leigh's two bruised Williams characters sorely in need of basic human kindness and understanding.

Karl Malden

*Mitch listens as Blanche opens up about her past in **A Streetcar Named Desire**.*

Karl Malden: Filmography

- *They Knew What They Wanted (1940)*
- *Winged Victory (1944)*
- *13 Rue Madeleine (1946)*
- *Kiss of Death (1947)*
- *Boomerang! (1947)*
- *The Gunfighter (1950)*
- *Where the Sidewalk Ends (1950)*
- *Halls of Montezuma (1950)*
- *A Streetcar Named Desire (1951)*
- *The Sellout (1952)*
- *Diplomatic Courier (1952)*
- *Operation Secret (1952)*
- *Ruby Gentry (1952)*
- *I Confess (1953)*
- *Take the High Ground! (1953)*
- *Phantom of the Rue Morgue (1954)*
- *On the Waterfront (1954)*
- *Baby Doll (1956)*
- *Fear Strikes Out (1957)*
- *Bombers B-52 (1957)*
- *Time Limit (1957) (director)*
- *The Hanging Tree (1959)*
- *Pollyanna (1960)*
- *The Great Impostor (1961)*
- *Parrish (1961)*
- *One-Eyed Jacks (1961)*
- *All Fall Down (1962)*
- *Birdman of Alcatraz (1962)*
- *Gypsy (1962)*
- *How the West Was Won (1963)*
- *Come Fly With Me (1963)*
- *Dead Ringer (1964)*
- *Cheyenne Autumn (1964)*
- *The Cincinnati Kid (1965)*
- *Nevada Smith (1966)*
- *Murderers' Row (1966)*
- *Hotel (1967)*
- *The Adventures of Bullwhip Griffin (1967)*
- *Billion Dollar Brain (1967)*
- *Blue (1968)*
- *Hot Millions (1968)*
- *Patton (1970)*
- *The Cat o' Nine Tails (1971)*
- *Wild Rovers (1971)*
- *Summertime Killer (1972)*
- *Beyond the Poseidon Adventure (1979)*
- *Meteor (1979)*
- *Twilight Time (1982)*
- *The Sting II (1983)*
- *Billy Galvin (1986)*
- *Nuts (1987)*

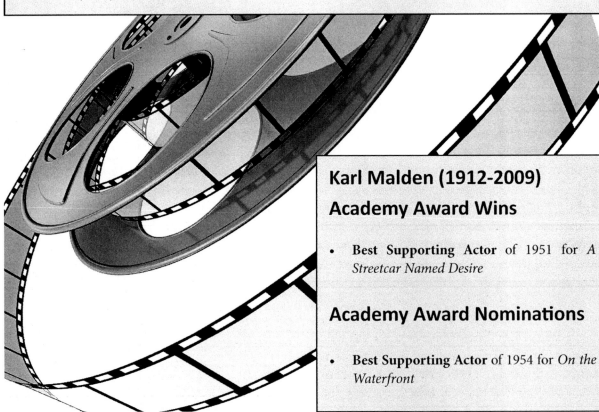

Karl Malden (1912-2009)
Academy Award Wins

- **Best Supporting Actor** of 1951 for *A Streetcar Named Desire*

Academy Award Nominations

- **Best Supporting Actor** of 1954 for *On the Waterfront*

Harold Mitchell in *A Streetcar Named Desire* (1951)
Archie Lee Meighan in *Baby Doll* (1956)

*I*t is easy to forget that Karl Malden was a product of the same theatrical forces and trends that produced John Garfield, Marlon Brando, and other performers identified with the Group Theatre and the Actors Studio. Since Malden was an ordinary-looking fellow, he was not the type to wear an eroticized ripped T-shirt onstage or appear in a torrid love scene. He was a character man, an all-purpose fellow, the kind of actor who never seemed like an actor or who would even be mistaken for one. And he never seemed a tortured soul, almost a prerequisite for a Method-style actor. Though he was part of both the Group Theatre and the Actors Studio, he never considered himself a Method actor (according to his autobiography), just someone who sensibly used the Method when he thought it would help. Malden appeared to have more in common with the reliably no-fuss supporting players working in Hollywood—regular guys like himself who would invariably be cast as cops, priests, detectives, businessmen, and doctors—than he did with angst-ridden theatre actors influenced by the teachings of Konstantin Stanislavsky or Lee Strasberg. Malden was always believable as an average person, which made him a very useful actor.

He was born Mladen Sekulovich in Chicago in 1912 to a Czech mother and a Serbian father. Twelve years older than Brando, and a year older than Garfield, Malden had a theatrical pedigree that went back to the Group Theatre's triumphant 1937 Broadway production of Clifford Odets' *Golden Boy,* in which he had a small role as a fight manager. Elia Kazan was also a member of the *Golden Boy* cast, meaning that Malden's connection with Kazan predated Brando's by about a decade. Malden followed *Golden Boy* with another supporting role, this time as an Irish cop, in the Group Theatre's 1939 production of Irwin Shaw's drama *The Gentle People,* which, again, featured Kazan. Later that year, Malden appeared in Maxwell Anderson's *Key Largo,* which starred Paul Muni. Malden continued to work on the New York stage until his participation in World War II, in which he served in the Air Force. After the war, Malden, as a drunken sailor,

appeared with Brando on Broadway in *Truckline Café* (1946), co-produced by Kazan. Though it flopped, it brought together three of *A Streetcar Named Desire*'s major players just one year before they made theatre history. Malden's professional regard for Brando was always enormous; he calls him a "genius" in his autobiography.

Malden had already found time to test the waters of film acting. He appeared in a minor role in *They Knew What They Wanted* (1940) and, while in the service, was seen in both the stage (1943) and screen (1944) versions of *Winged Victory.* After the war, he was back before the cameras in two pictures directed by Henry Hathaway, the war movie *13 Rue Madeleine* (1946), starring James Cagney, and *Kiss of Death* (1947), the film noir that catapulted Richard Widmark to stardom and gave Malden one of his many law-enforcement roles. *Boomerang!* (1947) was Malden's first film directed by Kazan, who had recently staked claim to that enviable position of being equally in-demand as a director both in Hollywood and on Broadway. A fairly solid and compact movie, *Boomerang!* is the kind of "realistic" docudrama, like *Call Northside 777* (1948) and *The Na-*

Early Elia

The success of Kazan's 1945 directorial film debut, an evocative and unforced adaptation of the novel *A Tree Grows in Brooklyn,* made him one of the more promising of post-war screen directors. Kazan hadn't yet mastered the visual aspects of filmmaking, but his skill with actors was readily apparent. In *A Tree Grows in Brooklyn,* he got several superb performances from a cast who didn't share his Group Theatre background: song-and-dance man James Dunn, who gave a charismatic and emotionally bare portrait of a pipe-dreaming alcoholic (and won a supporting Oscar); wisecracking Joan Blondell, who, as Aunt Sissy, revealed new depths beneath her flashy and likable persona; and little Peggy Ann Garner, in one of the more accomplished child performances in movie history.

ked City (1948), that was all the rage right after the war. Malden, part of a large ensemble cast, plays a detective, in what now seems a dated and simplistic account of the real-life murder of a minister and the hunt for his killer. Kazan's direction is efficient yet uninspired, though he was clearly starting to show more interest in the technical aspects of moviemaking. You don't much notice Malden, but then you aren't really supposed to. He was paying his dues.

Malden spent 1947 appearing on Broadway as the son of the main character's business partner in Arthur Miller's *All My Sons,* which ended its run a month before the opening of *Streetcar* in December. After a year in *All My Sons,* Malden spent two years as Mitch in *Streetcar.* The success of these back-to-back prestige hits brought him back to the movies with improved opportunities. He was cast as the new police lieutenant in Otto Preminger's fine, if implausible, film noir *Where the Sidewalk Ends* (1950) and then as a friendly saloonkeeper in the masterful Henry King western *The Gunfighter* (1950), starring a never-better Gregory Peck. The films had improved, even if the roles were still essentially unnoticeable. When Kazan was ready to bring *Streetcar* to the screen, Malden came along with the bulk of the original cast.

Mitch (actually Harold Mitchell) is a mama's boy whose off-screen relationship with his mother seems sad and even a little creepy. He is a grown man whose life revolves around his sickly mother. Mitch behaves as his mother would like him to behave, catering to her and apparently sacrificing his own future for her. (He may remind you of Russ Tamblyn's maternally browbeaten character in 1957's *Peyton Place.*) Mitch is a man in stasis, unable to move forward, and you may wonder if his mother is as sick as she makes him think she is. His best pal and war buddy, Stanley (Marlon Brando), is everything Mitch isn't: handsome and sexy, free and easy, the center of attention. Malden makes you believe that it's a constant thrill for Mitch to be in Stanley's light, as if some of it might rub off on him. He is all the better for being in Stanley's company, which at least brings some excitement into his life. Stanley's confidence emphasizes Mitch's awkwardness, but it's worth it for Mitch to be part of Stanley's social circle. The quietest of the gang, Mitch doesn't appear to fit in, especially when wearing a jacket and tie to Stanley's poker games. But he is proud to be included. Mitch and Stanley

work at the same plant, with Mitch "on the precision bench in the spare parts department." Imagine how dazzling Blanche (Vivien Leigh), Stanley's genteel sister-in-law, would seem to a man like Mitch, mired in drudgery. Malden is first seen bowling with his buddies, not more than an extra in a scene that plays as background for the first scene between Blanche and her sister Stella (Kim Hunter).

Mitch and Blanche meet as he comes out of the Kowalskis' bathroom. (Had there ever been a movie with as much bathroom activity as this one?) At the sight of Leigh's Blanche, Malden wipes his hands nervously on a towel. It is an alternately touching and funny visual of a large man trying to appear comfortable in a less than ideal situation. Heightening the humor, Malden walks away with the towel, then realizes what he has done and quickly hands the towel to Kim Hunter's Stella before vanishing as swiftly as possible. He's both unerringly polite and boyishly embarrassing. His interest in Blanche is soon ignited by the "hot" music coming from the radio behind the curtain, while he hopelessly tries to pay attention to his all-male poker game. In another instantly endearing bit of business, he administers some breath powder before re-entering the boudoir on his supposed revisit to the bathroom. His shyness and insecurity are increased in her poised presence. Talk of the inscription on his cigarette case opens him up a little, as he reveals the story behind it, all about the girl (now dead) who gave it to him. Perhaps it was a girl he loved and never got over, similar to Blanche's attachment to her dead husband, but it's nonetheless clear that these characters connect in their shared loneliness and dead-end lives. Malden, through his enthusiasm and increasing pleasure, makes plain what a unique experience it is for Mitch to be paid attention by a woman of such class and refinement. He's thrilled to be of manly assistance to her when he places a paper lantern over a bare light bulb. After the sustained tension associated with Brando's Stanley, it's a welcome respite to be in the presence of Malden's sweetness and innocence.

Stanley screams for Mitch, but a return to the poker game would break this beautiful spell, a fall to earth for which Mitch isn't ready. He guesses that Blanche taught art or music because to him she's not like ordinary folks. Malden winningly combines uneasiness with giddiness, wholly out of his element with this elegant woman but swept away by the way she makes him feel, as if he belongs in her company. After he switches on the lantern-covered light and Leigh goes into her entrancing dance, Malden, too, becomes "enchanted." He applauds her dancing and then lurches to the music himself, trying to match her movements and almost, but not quite, partnering her. He's hopelessly clumsy but quite engaging, laughing happily. When Stanley turns the scene into a riot, Mitch's twice-uttered response is, "Poker should not be played in a house with women!" Mitch is a gentleman among the brutes, but gentlemen, like fragile ladies, are vulnerable to being hurt by those less gentlemanly.

Mitch is tickled by Blanche. She makes him feel romantic and gallant, like when she has him bow to her before he presents her with flowers. When egged on by her to behave in such ways, his delight always trumps his embarrassment, which is a masterstroke of Malden's performance. It is as if Mitch, like Malden himself, has stepped into a Hollywood movie and found himself playing opposite a stunning actress. He's so respectful with her, so timid, that he allows her to control the relationship on her terms, not knowing that he's really holding all the cards. If Stella is the high-class girl who liked being brought down a few pegs when she married Stanley, then Mitch is the regular Joe who loves feeling elevated by his contact with a regal woman. (Both Stella and Mitch become caught between Stanley and Blanche: for Stella, it's husband versus sister; for Mitch, it's best friend versus girlfriend.) The sense of wonder that Blanche brings to Mitch's life is the core of Malden's performance, and the reason he is so affecting when he later loses his innocence. Unlike Stanley, Mitch enjoys a little magic, even craves it. He can play along when Blanche begins a make-believe situation, such as their being in a café on the Left Bank of Paris. She really gets him talking, too. Malden opens up in a way that suggests Mitch has been bursting to tell someone about himself, but no one until now has shown any interest. His Mitch is kind and vulnerable, decidedly unworldly, and "ashamed of the way I perspire." But he holds forth proudly about how much time he spends at the gym. He even asks her to punch him in the belly to see how hard his stomach is. When her reaction is properly impressed, it makes him feel like a million bucks. He decides he can guess her weight by lift-

ing her and does so, again being made to feel manly in her feminine presence. But he's also dangerously close to needing a cold shower.

Mitch doesn't care how old Blanche is but his mother does. (You can imagine dear old Mother plotting ways to break them up.) Malden, in his autobiography, talks about his subtext being that Mitch hated his mother for holding him back and controlling his life. Though the lines say otherwise, it makes sense that Mitch is not quite as selfless as he seems. He usually keeps his feelings bottled, yet he has dreams of escape and freedom and romance, dreams that at the moment seem to be matching up quite nicely with Blanche's. At the end of Leigh's sorrowful monologue about the death of Blanche's husband (Allan), Malden approaches her from behind and ever so gently touches her shoulders. He tells her, "You need somebody and I need somebody too." They kiss. At this point, Malden's Mitch *is* Prince Charming, a man sensitive enough to feel her pain and want to take care of her and have her take care of him. The thwarted happy ending is nearly as devastating for Mitch as it is for Blanche. You might guess that as he goes through life, he will carry the memory of Blanche in much the same way that she has carried Allan's memory all these years. The joy is short-lived because Stanley tells Mitch what he's learned about Blanche's sexual exploits, leading to Malden's first scene of uncontrolled anger. Not only has Mitch's world collapsed in on him, keeping him stuck with his mother, but he's also had his illusions shattered and been made to feel like a fool.

After deliberately missing Blanche's birthday party, Mitch bursts through the door hours later and confronts her. Malden continues to release the anger that he first unleashed at the plant, when Mitch heard the stories about her past. His is a scalding combination of infuriation and hurt; her lies have also destroyed his own dream of the future, a dream that was so close to fulfillment. In his impulse to hurt her, he starts turning on all the lights so he can get a good look at her. He throws to the ground the paper lantern he had once so valiantly affixed for her and then grabs her face, holding it under the bare bulb. Blanche's anguished reckoning with reality is also Mitch's. And her humiliation, too, is his. He pushes her into a chair in disgust. If he were strong enough to accept her words about the two of them still needing each other, despite what he's learned about her, then there still might have been a happy ending. But Mitch is too conventional a guy to absorb her past. How could he ever face his friends? Yet wouldn't he still love to protect this beguiling creature? At the end of the scene, he tells her that she's not clean enough to marry but that he's more than willing to make love to her. He still desires her but no longer wants her as his wife. Tennessee Williams acknowledges that all of us, even gentle Mitch, are capable of "deliberate cruelty," not exclusively the Stanleys of the world.

While I understand why Williams would want Mitch in the final scene—so that Mitch could witness his shameful part in Blanche's downfall—I find it implausible that Mitch would actually be there. How could he look on as Blanche is being carted away? Once she is subdued by the matron, Mitch explodes at Stanley, but, of course, what dominates Malden's performance is Mitch's guilt in being a key player in Blanche's destruction, worsened by the knowledge that she probably could have made him happier than he is ever going to be. It is vital that we see Mitch's fury at Stanley and watch him absorb his own guilt in what has transpired, collapsing in tears, but I can't imagine that he would be able to face Blanche again and certainly not on the day she is being dragged out the door. Sensitive soul that he is, Mitch will not be able to shake off the memory of Blanche, or find anyone quite so captivatingly unlike himself in his romantic future. *Streetcar* is filled with guilt that doesn't dissipate, as Blanche knows all too well. Mitch presumably returns to the grind of a life in which his biggest thrill is being attached to Stanley Kowalski. But hasn't the Blanche episode forever tarnished Mitch's perception of Stanley? Mitch is left without any illusions. He will probably always carry the memory of the night when he switched on the light with the paper lantern and ineptly danced with a bewitching beauty who briefly brought some magic into his life. Malden makes *Streetcar* a tragedy for Mitch as well as Blanche, leaving him consumed with regret and bereft of magic.

In the five years between his two Tennessee Williams pictures, Malden made eight films, most of them forgettable, yet he did manage to work with two legendary directors (both in less than peak form). The dreadful *Ruby Gentry* (1952) was a reunion for director King Vidor and star Jennifer Jones in an attempt to out-trash their *Duel in the*

Mitch Bests Nero

Seamlessly adapting a stage performance to the screen, Karl Malden won the Academy Award for Best Supporting Actor for *Streetcar,* beating Kevin McCarthy in *Death of a Salesman* (a play nowhere near as lucky as *Streetcar* in its path from stage to screen), Gig Young in *Come Fill the Cup,* and Peter Ustinov and Leo Genn, both of *Quo Vadis.* (Ustinov's sensationally entertaining Nero was Malden's main competition.)

Sun (1946) with regard to love-hate romances and heavy breathing. Malden, as the richest man in town, marries wrong-side-of-the-tracks but pointy-brassiered Jones after she is jilted by lover Charlton Heston (of the side-of-beef acting style). Call it lust in a North Carolina swamp, with Malden unable to make much of his role before being killed in a boating accident (but at least he's not terrible like his co-stars). *I Confess* (1953), one of Alfred Hitchcock's least persuasive innocent-man thrillers, has Malden playing one of his standard pre-*Streetcar* detective types, here convinced (wrongly) that lifeless priest Montgomery Clift is a murderer. Malden had to wait for his reunion with Kazan and Brando on the bruisingly powerful *On the Waterfront* (1954) to re-energize his movie career and garner him a second supporting-actor Oscar nomination. Among all those longshoremen and mobsters, Malden has the potentially thankless and dull role of the concerned priest, yet he plays it with backbone and unsentimentality, making Father Barry more admirable than annoying. Before heading south to star in *Baby Doll* (1956), Malden spent much of 1955 on Broadway in the hit thriller *The Desperate Hours* opposite newcomer Paul Newman.

Tennessee Williams' screenplay for *Baby Doll* was a considerably altered and expanded adaptation of two of his short plays from the mid 1940s: *27 Wagons Full of Cotton* and *The Unsatisfactory Supper.* Kazan returned to direct his second Williams film after their colossal success with *Streetcar.* In the years between, Kazan continued to reign as a top American film director, with films such as *Viva Zapata!* (1952) and *East of Eden* (1955), as well as the superb, multi-Oscar-winning *On the Waterfront. Baby Doll* offered Malden an actual leading role and top billing, though the film is more of a three-hander than a

A most "unsatisfactory supper" for Baby Doll (Carroll Baker), Archie Lee (Malden), and Silva (Eli Wallach) in **Baby Doll**.

star vehicle. His co-stars, Carroll Baker and Eli Wallach (in his screen debut) were fellow Actors Studio members. Kazan and company traveled to Benoit, Mississippi, for a Deep South authenticity that no studio could replicate. *Baby Doll* is a fine piece of work, one of the better Williams films, yet it is most famous for being condemned by Cardinal Spellman, who forbade Catholics to see it even though he hadn't seen it himself. As usual, a Williams film was the source of battles over content, censorship, and morality. Williams and Kazan were continuing to bring challenging sexual themes to the mainstream audience, unapologetically treating human sexuality as an undeniable and fundamental force. Such boundary-pushing unsurprisingly led to controversy and publicity. "Sex" had been helpful in making the two previous Williams pictures, *Streetcar* and *Rose Tattoo,* very popular. Without the sexual draw of his films, Williams would have been relegated to the

more academic and highbrow (and less commercial) status afforded writers like Arthur Miller. Some label *Baby Doll* a flat-out comedy, but I wouldn't, though it is indeed funny. It is also decidedly dark, consumed with jealousy, spite, and revenge. Oh, and lots of lust, too. In Williams' letter to Kazan, printed in *Notebooks* (edited by Margaret Bradham Thornton), he calls his original conception of *Baby Doll* "a grotesque folk comedy of the modern South, with some serious over-tones," and that's exactly what he got, which I mean as a high compliment. *Baby Doll* has the spirit of a low-budget art film, though a particularly playful and unpretentious one. Unlike *Streetcar* and *Rose Tattoo,* it's not a film with one or several *great* lead performances, but it is solidly played and lovingly crafted by Kazan and his team. For Malden, the role of Archie Lee Meighan was a plum, a man who makes the transition from sexual fool to wielder of violence and cruelty, someone in the grip of desperate and demeaning crises. Like *Streetcar*, *Baby Doll* deals with an interloper disrupting one man's hold on his power and self-image.

Malden is first seen outdoors in pajamas, shouting repair orders to a man on the roof of Archie Lee's crumbling mansion. He bought the house for his new bride, Baby Doll (Carroll Baker), with the promise of returning it to its glory days, something that now seems impossible because of the slump in business at his cotton gin. If that weren't enough to keep a man up at night, there's his pre-nuptial agreement. He accepted his eighteen-year-old bride's terms, consenting not to consummate their union until her twentieth birthday, now just two days away. Archie Lee has kept his promise, but he's a man on edge, both sexually frustrated and financially strapped. The film gets off to a kinky start when he finds his wife's door locked and goes into the adjoining room to spy on her through a peephole. Carroll Baker is first glimpsed in the most famous image from the film, that of a young and lovely blonde asleep in a crib (with the front slat down) and a thumb in her mouth. This was the visual that blazed across a Times Square billboard, covering an entire Broadway block, when the picture opened during the 1956 Christmas season. It is still a provocative image, especially from the point of view of a horny middle-aged man salivating over his young bride's virginity. This is the first of many instances in which Malden gets to play a mixture of titillation and humiliation, each feeling fueling the other in a not unpleasant way for Archie Lee (because he knows the end of his wait is near). Baby Doll awakens and catches him using a knife to make the peephole larger. In an audacious reaction, Malden smiles at being caught, making Archie Lee's naughty-boy arousal surpass his embarrassment. Later, interrupting her bath, he again intrudes and is swatted away. Malden plays these moments with the kick of knowing that each time Archie Lee is snubbed he is also getting closer to the time when she can no longer reject him.

Tensions are running high between husband and wife as consummation day approaches. Though Archie Lee is a man facing ruin, Malden is rightly focused on the impending sex act, the orgasmic distraction from the mess of his professional life. The actor's anticipatory excitement speaks to the character's agonizing time of pent-up desire. But Baby Doll has all the power because Archie Lee hasn't de-

livered on *all* his promises. Though he hasn't laid a hand on her, he also hasn't given her the home she was expecting. Not only is the mansion in a fragile condition, but trucks will soon be arriving to repossess most of the furniture. Baby Doll has wiggle room out of her bargain: no furniture, no sex. Malden aptly plays Archie Lee as a buffoon at first, an older man helplessly in the thrall of his trophy wife, though completely disrespected by her. Baby Doll is a teasing and sarcastic kitten, and she's not looking forward to bedding Archie Lee. She mocks his double chin and baldness but he keeps coming back for more. His emasculation is compounded by his business losses. Sexual need is the impetus for Archie Lee to behave reprehensibly in an attempt to save his business and thereby claim his wife. Malden makes Archie Lee a bellower, screaming her name, trying hopelessly to gain a feeling of authority in their marriage. They squabble constantly yet Archie Lee never wins. Without sex, they're just an angry parent and a bratty child. A doctor visit provides little help for what ails him, nor does the knowledge that the whole town is aware of his sexless situation. With his talent for playing ordinary men, not exactly the fellow who gets the girl, Malden is believable as a man stripped of his dignity and debasing himself for a prize that may never be his. Baby Doll is later told, "Your husband sweats more than any man I know." Malden understands that Archie Lee is a man in search of release.

Wickedly amusing as Malden is in the earliest scenes, I don't think he's as funny as he could be, or as appropriately comical as another actor might have been in the role. Malden is best in the film's final section, its most dramatic passage, as well as in the quieter moments. He certainly isn't as comfortable as Archie Lee as he was playing *Streetcar*'s Mitch, which is a more completely inhabited performance. His casting as Archie Lee is fitting and his performance is sturdy, but he's rarely surprising after those daring opening scenes. You might not even remember who plays Archie Lee if you haven't seen the movie in a long time. Perhaps Rod Steiger or Edmond O'Brien would have put more of an individual stamp on the role, though both would also have been more prone to overacting the part. Malden gets the values out of every scene, does well with the Southern accent, and never crosses over into redneck caricature, but sometimes his performance seems more functional than distinctive.

Once most of the furniture is taken away, the film is primarily set inside a bare and decaying mansion, a haunting and surreal setting, a massive tomb. It is a backdrop for stark and unusually beautiful black-and-white imagery. Living in a vacant house that is literally and symbolically falling apart around him, with a wife who is not really a wife, Archie Lee resides in a waking nightmare. For all the harmless bluster in Malden's performance, he makes a startling shift when Archie Lee turns arsonist. His victim is Silva Vacarro (Eli Wallach), the man whose cotton gin has destroyed Archie Lee's business. At Silva's party, celebrating his one-year anniversary as manager of the Syndicate Plantation (a year in which Silva has put many local men out of business), Archie Lee uses a can of kerosene to burn down Silva's new gin. Silva is an outsider, a Sicilian, someone who doesn't belong here. Archie Lee has shades of Stanley Kowalski, protecting the status quo while being threatened by an outsider's force, doing whatever he must to reclaim his position and self-worth. Malden reveals the darkness and recklessness beneath a seemingly innocuous good old boy. Entrenched in his community and its traditions, Archie Lee has no guilt about damaging the property of someone who, to his thinking, never should have been here in the first place. But old-world Sicilian justice and revenge are formidable adversaries for new-world Southern justice and revenge, not really all that different once pitted against each other, a Sicilian shark versus a Southern scoundrel. Following *The Rose Tattoo,* this was the second consecutive Williams film to have a major Sicilian-American character.

Silva rightly guesses the guilty party because Archie Lee was the only cotton-gin owner noticeably absent from the party (though anyone could have hired someone to do the deed). Keeping his enemy close, Silva brings all his cotton to be ginned at Archie Lee's place, the better to find out what really happened. To Archie Lee, the arson plan was a great success, giving him back his dignity. He exults in his financial upturn, which will mean the return of the furniture, and, therefore, the imminent attainment of Baby Doll. Malden brandishes Archie Lee's newfound confidence and sense of control. He is a smirking manipulator (until someone gets the better of him). Referring to Silva's name, he asks, "Like a silver lining?" Well, yes, Silva is a silver lin-

ing for Archie Lee, temporarily. Malden has many lines about the Good Neighbor policy and "tit for tat," an especially indelicate phrase once Baby Doll becomes the main objective in the men's war. Malden lays on the sociability, making Archie Lee feel slick and shrewd, not knowing that Silva isn't believing any of it. Archie Lee is forever being bested by somebody, whether he knows it or not. Ready to get back to overseeing the work at his gin, he makes the mistake of asking Baby Doll to entertain Silva. "So, you're a wop," is her opener.

This leads to the most famous sequence in the picture, a twenty-minute seduction as Silva tries to secure a confession from Baby Doll about Archie Lee starting the fire. This section is a triumph of subtly persuasive writing and imaginatively fluid direction, a consistent building of tension as the scene moves from the mansion grounds to the inside of a dilapidated car to a swing to the house's porch. It seems clear that Baby Doll knows the truth about the fire, but also that she isn't quite sharp enough to conceal what she knows. Malden disappears from the film for a long stretch, forgotten, as Eli Wallach puts an arm around Baker's shoulder, picks cotton lint off her chest, strokes her throat, breathes on her, and tickles her arm with his riding crop. Baby Doll is vulnerable because she isn't used to being touched or experiencing physical pleasure of this kind, and, apparently, the Sicilian is a master of seduction. Wallach gives a good performance (again as a Sicilian, as he was on Broadway in *The Rose Tattoo*), but his casting seems a stretch. Silva needn't be beautiful (Wallach's shortness and ordinary looks are not the problem), but the set-up would make more sense if he carried a palpable sexual charge. Baby Doll's ignorance and innocence are important factors here, but Silva still ought to be plausible as an erotic force. The underrated and sexy Italian-American actor Richard Conte, not a pretty boy, would have made a more stimulating Silva. With Wallach, you feel as though you are getting a fine New York actor, not a true Sicilian operator. Silva is conceived somewhere in the vague place between immigrant and first-generation American. He speaks of being a foreigner, yet Wallach opted for an accent that is Southern rather than Italian. The total effectiveness of the scene is enhanced by its length, as she grows weaker and succumbs to arousal, unaccustomed to being the manipulated rather than the manipulator. Archie Lee is back to being a fool, oblivious to what's going on, still feeling his oats at how crafty he has been.

Unfortunately for Malden, he is also not in the other "best" scene in the movie, the hide-and-seek mating dance between Baker and Wallach inside the shell of a mansion. Playing off the notion that the house is haunted by its former owner, Silva sneaks inside to frighten an unsuspecting Baby Doll with a swinging chandelier and a mysteriously swaying string-supported light bulb, plus a chair suddenly atop a table. Properly baffled, she then goes upstairs to change her dress, spending the rest of the scene in a white slip. When Silva follows, the scene becomes a farce, in and out of rooms as he tries to elude discovery. He "rides" the rocking horse in the nursery (and whips it with his riding crop), a blatant sexual image in keeping with his conquering mood. Covered in a blanket, she chases him with a boat paddle; he startles her with a bugle and a deer head. The sequence abounds with visual pleasures, and the overall effect is that of a particularly mischievous and vigorous bout of laugh-filled foreplay. Baby Doll has always behaved as a child and this is one more childish episode, though it ends with her sprawled on the floor with his foot on her belly, both of them in hysterics. She bites him on the calf. Baby Doll's libido is as constrained as Archie Lee's, only she didn't know it. Silva is the only one not sexually stymied, merely using sex as a tool. He gets her signed confession and is ready to go, but she offers him a nap in her crib.

The self-assured air that carried Malden through the middle of the picture is deflated when Archie Lee returns home. The film remains ambiguous about whether or not Silva deflowered Baby Doll. You believe Silva when he later tells Archie Lee that nothing happened, yet why is Baby Doll noticeably more mature now, as if something major has happened to her? What we see on Archie Lee's return, though he himself remains downstairs, tells us that nothing occurred between them: their positions appear unchanged from the last time we saw them. Silva remains fully clothed and blanket-covered in the crib, and Baby Doll is still in her slip, sitting on the floor beside him. In the "making of" featurette on the DVD, Baker and Wallach offer their opinions, with Baker certain that Baby Doll lost her virginity to Silva, and Wallach saying that she didn't.

These opposing views are transparent in their performances, adding further to the pleasurable ambiguity. Either way, *something* has happened to Baby Doll through her contact with Silva, plus her fed-up attitude toward Archie Lee. She is clearly more womanly, feeling "cool and rested" for the first time. When Archie Lee insults her intelligence, she caps her defense of her smarts with a proudly firm "And I'm a magazine reader!" It's one of Williams' best lines for Baker and she delivers it with the punch of knowing that it's a beaut. (Baby Doll's signature line is "My daddy would turn over in his grave," and she's probably right whenever she says it.) But Archie Lee continues to count the hours till her birthday.

Archie Lee employed arson to destroy this man's power but has inadvertently made Baby Doll the focus of his rival's revenge. The Sicilian appears to be the winner. There he is at the top of the stairs in Archie Lee's home. When Baby Doll then speaks of Silva's plan to give all his business to Archie Lee, leaving Silva free to be entertained by Baby Doll, it sets up a wonderfully perverse moral question for Archie Lee. Is he willing to pimp Baby Doll to keep his business booming? Doesn't that defeat the purpose? And can he have a showdown with Silva and risk losing Silva's business, which would ultimately mean losing Baby Doll? She knows exactly what she's telling Archie Lee, wanting to see him squirm. When Wallach slides down the banister, Malden reacts in a stunned manner to the familiarity and intimacy that has been advanced in his absence. You can see Malden's mind ticking quickly as Archie Lee tries to piece together what has happened, turning once again into the desperate and threatened man he was yesterday.

In the pathetically typical reaction of bullies backed into corners, Archie Lee turns on the weakest person available, Baby Doll's ineffectual Aunt Rose Comfort (Mildred Dunnock). But even she fights back admirably when pushed. Archie Lee will have to resort to old-fashioned vengeance by calling on reinforcements, plotting more violence since he can't win on his wits. A stewing and fuming Malden doesn't shy away from the fact that Archie Lee is mean and cowardly, a small man residing in a large body. Baby Doll and Silva flirt openly: she is emboldened by her feelings for him and their secret kisses (and is now wearing a grown-up black dress rather than one of her usual white frocks); Silva is secure in the knowledge that her signed affidavit is in his pocket. Malden's funny response to his mounting aggravation is a caveman holler of "Food!" two times to deaf Aunt Rose in the kitchen. Archie Lee isn't dumb; he's just not as sharp as those around him. He expected to coast on the Southern privilege of being a white man in business, part of the elite, and to remain unchallenged by foreigners, virgins, or live-in relatives. Egging him on, Baby Doll and Silva start sharing a messy meal of bread dipped in soupy greens, eating sloppily and laughing, further enflaming Archie Lee's wrath. Malden at last unleashes Archie Lee's alcohol-fueled rage, eventually grabbing her angrily and holding her face to tell her, "I got position," which is all he has left. And how long will that last once the truth comes out about the fire? His talk of having friends is a threat, his final advantage. Malden is superior at exposing the vulnerabilities of a man trapped, trying to hold on to what remains of his fading self-esteem. But losing out on his wife's virginity (as he believes) exceeds all else. Archie Lee is a loser, always has been and always will be. Malden chillingly whispers to Baker, "You think I'm gonna put up with this?" and then gleefully tells Wallach, "I'm gonna wipe that grin off your greasy wop face for good."

The final sequence of *Baby Doll* has Malden outdoors, shotgun in tow, chasing after Wallach. Malden is finally a man unhinged. *Baby Doll* is to some extent Archie Lee's mid-life crisis, the old story of a grown man's downfall caused by a nymphet, self-destructing in his attempt to possess her. The bristling triangle has led Archie Lee and Baby Doll to see things as they really are, rather than as the sideshow that they've been play-acting. Defeated (and out of bullets), he roars for "Baby Doll!" (This never quite competes with Brando's pleas for "Stella!" though the impulse is similar.) Moaning her name repeatedly and weeping openly, he is reduced to banging the back of his head on a tree, at last realizing that he has been a fool. The cops, called by Baby Doll, take his gun and handcuff him, but he's still consumed with whether or not Silva will remain on the premises. Silva goes off happily with Baby Doll's signature, showing only half-hearted interest in seeing her again. The movie ends with church bells tolling midnight, signifying Baby Doll's birthday. Archie Lee goes with the police, presumably to return home the next day after he has slept off the liquor. Baby Doll's memorable final line, to her aunt, is "We

Thank You, Mr. Kanin

Baby Doll is something of a deep-fried version of Garson Kanin's *Born Yesterday*, with its sexy and dim blonde, her crooked blowhard mate, and the stranger who disrupts everything by forever changing the blonde's outlook. And Silva's line to Baby Doll, "There isn't much of you but what there is is choice," is awfully close to Spencer Tracy's assessment of Katharine Hepburn in *Pat and Mike* (1952), also written by Kanin (and Ruth Gordon).

got nothing to do but wait for tomorrow and see if we're remembered or forgotten." She is hoping for Silva's return, but if he doesn't come for her it's unlikely that she will stay with Archie Lee. She's not the girl she was two days ago, but Archie Lee will never be anyone but who he has always been.

From his short play *27 Wagons Full of Cotton*, Williams took the plot points of the cotton-gin arson and the subsequent seduction scene. However, the play's Baby Doll character (Flora) is a large woman, and she and her husband (Jake, a man of sixty) have a taste for rough lovemaking. Jake tells Flora explicitly to lie about where he was when he started the fire. She sleeps with Silva, and it appears that her sexual betrayal will continue. Maureen Stapleton played Flora when *27 Wagons* opened on Broadway in 1955 as part of *All in One*, an eclectic evening of three short works (a drama, an opera, and a dance piece) by various artists. *The Unsatisfactory Supper*, the other one-act Williams play from which he fashioned *Baby Doll*, deals with the Aunt Rose Comfort subplot. In neither play is Baby Doll young, beautiful, or virginal, so there's nothing about a consummation agreement or repossessed furniture. Williams rightly received an Oscar nomination for Best Adapted Screenplay, even though his script is billed as an "original screenplay" in the film's opening credits.

Baby Doll isn't emotionally powerful, nor are its characters especially multi-faceted, but it's refreshingly offbeat (to this day), a neat little sexual mood piece deserving of the tag "ahead of its time." Though produced by Warner Brothers, *Baby Doll* has the feel of an independent film rather than a studio product. It may not be up to the quality of *A Streetcar Named Desire,* but it's nonetheless a major Williams film and a second high-caliber collaboration between him and Kazan. Though they would work together in the theatre again, it is regrettable that they never joined forces for another film. Most of the later Williams screen adaptations would have benefited enormously from Kazan's impassioned quest to mine material more deeply and inventively than most directors. Kazan gave *Baby Doll* a loose feeling, as if it were just happening unrehearsed, notably in the daringly elongated seduction and the magical hide-and-seek game. It is a movie that breathes, taking in the languor of its locations and emitting a pervasive mood of Southern decay, all gorgeously shot in striking contrasts of black and white, sometimes at imaginative angles, by Boris Kaufman (Oscar winner for Kazan's *On the Waterfront*). Along with Williams, Kaufman got an Oscar nomination for *Baby Doll,* as did Carroll Baker (Best Actress) and Mildred Dunnock (Best Supporting Actress).

Carroll Baker had just come off a supporting role in *Giant* (1956) and was taking her place as one of the more promising young actresses of the mid 1950s. Resourceful and well cast as Baker is as Baby Doll, moving nicely from petulance to arousal to maturity, it strikes me as a performance that could have been duplicated or even surpassed by other pretty and talented ingénues of the period, such as Lee Remick, who was just a year away from making her film debut in Kazan's *A Face in the Crowd.* It seems strange that Baker was Oscar-nominated in a year that overlooked Marilyn Monroe's sublime performance in *Bus Stop.* If you had to pick just one sex-bomb blonde to nominate that year, wouldn't you have to go with Marilyn? Eli Wallach's entry into the picture adds a low-key slyness that is welcome, especially after all the time spent with the battling Meighans. (Wallach had recently appeared on Broadway in Williams' *Camino Real* in 1953.) Perhaps the film's box-office muscle would have been stronger if the comely Baker had a better choice than either Wallach or Malden, two middle-aged character men. Who calls that a love triangle? And it is always a mixed blessing to use non-actors in small roles, in this case the citizens of Benoit. "Real people" provide verisimilitude, yet their obvious amateurishness usually cancels out the benefits of using them, which is occasionally true here. The black characters are used mainly as observers to the main action's wild goings-on.

Malden went on to play Carroll Baker's father in the all-star *How the West Was Won* (1963), a popular epic western that is punishingly long and a generic yawn. He and Baker also appeared together briefly in the western *Cheyenne Autumn* (1964), arguably the best of John Ford's films of the 1960s and the rare Ford film to qualify as underrated. Despite its beauty and somber force, *Cheyenne Autumn* is admittedly misshapen, often losing its focus, as well as being the occasion for an overacted Malden performance, a badly German-accented captain. Amid a predominantly restrained ensemble of actors, in a film more attuned to its theme (the mistreatment of the Cheyenne by the U.S.) than its plot or characters, Malden manages to stand out in the wrong way. Among his other post-*Baby Doll* films, a highlight is *Fear Strikes Out* (1957), a good biopic of baseball player Jimmy Piersall (Anthony Perkins), focused on his rise, mental breakdown, and recovery. As Piersall's ferociously ambitious and emotionally cruel father (a match for any stage mother), Malden gave what is perhaps his finest performance, certainly his most gripping. That same year he directed a tight little drama, *Time Limit,* with a cast led by Richard Widmark. This military mystery, adapted from a Broadway play, was manageable material for a first-time director, and, though he never directed another feature, Malden did an admirable job with both the script and his cast. In Disney's appealing *Pollyanna* (1960), a high point among the studio's live-action pictures, he is a fire-and-brimstone reverend who fervently delivers a memorably unanticipated sermon titled "Death Comes Unexpectedly." Malden reunited with Marlon Brando in *One-Eyed Jacks* (1961), the only film ever directed by Brando, a compelling and great-looking revenge-driven western (though overlong and much too leisurely paced). While Brando's own performance is surprisingly passive, Malden excels as the bandit turned villainous sheriff.

In the soapy tobacco-industry saga *Parrish* (1961), Malden is a ruthless millionaire businessman who implausibly romances Claudette Colbert (in her final feature film), yet he is no fun, lacking the panache to pull off a larger-than-life villain, a quality he displayed with no problem in *One-Eyed Jacks.* He then appeared in two John Frankenheimer prestige pictures in 1962, *All Fall Down* and *Birdman of Alcatraz,* with the latter, in which he plays

Hey, Don't I Know You?

Nuts offers the accidental pleasure of reuniting three key Tennessee Williams actors. In the courtroom, there's *Baby Doll*'s Malden and Eli Wallach (as a psychiatrist) sitting near each other, with Wallach and Maureen Stapleton, the original stars of *The Rose Tattoo,* also just a few seats from each other, marking their only film appearance together. Playing his wife, Stapleton interacts with Malden, but neither of them engages with Wallach. The courtroom seating area appears reserved only for Williams players, and you half-expect Jessica Tandy or Burl Ives to drop by.

a prison warden, the far better of the two (though it does lose some footing whenever its star, a very fine Burt Lancaster, gets too far from his birds). *All Fall Down* sinks under the weight of its hollow, heavy-handed histrionics, with Malden as Angela Lansbury's alcoholic husband, a performance that frequently resorts to empty yelling. He even made a musical, playing the thankless doormat role of Herbie, opposite Rosalind Russell and Natalie Wood, in *Gypsy* (1962), no more than a decent adaptation of the Broadway hit. (Once again, he yells a lot.) Malden got his shot at a camp classic when he co-starred with Bette Davis in her second "twins" drama, *Dead Ringer* (1964), playing a dull nice guy, the police-sergeant boyfriend of the "good" and frumpy Davis (the one who operates a cocktail-lounge dive). In a three-year period, Malden had on-screen romances with Claudette Colbert, Rosalind Russell, and Bette Davis, each a Golden Age legend. Not bad for a character actor without the handsome good looks to which those ladies had formerly been accustomed.

The Cincinnati Kid (1965) put Malden back in *Baby Doll* territory as another fool with a much-younger knockout wife (Ann-Margret) whom he cannot trust. This Steve McQueen vehicle tried to do for poker what *The Hustler* had done for pool, but, though entertaining, is nowhere near as good as its predecessor. Malden, as McQueen's best pal, gives a standard, uneventful performance, one he seemingly gave countless times. A very low point came with *Murderers' Row* (1966), one of those abysmal James Bond spoofs starring Dean Martin as Matt Helm, with Malden's performance the most unimaginative rendering of any character ever bent

on world domination. His final film of note was *Patton* (1970), the Oscar-winning biopic dominated by George C. Scott's all-ablaze performance. Who even remembers that Malden appears as Omar Bradley? The picture's chief problem is that there aren't really *any* characters other than Patton in a mighty long movie. There's no one, including Malden, for Scott to act *with*. Though billed above the title (after Scott), Malden is as colorless as the rest of the nonentities milling about WWII. *Patton* works only on one-man-show terms, but, unfortunately, that's not what it is. Malden made his final feature-film appearance in the Barbra Streisand vehicle *Nuts* (1987), based on a Broadway play (with more than a passing similarity to Tennessee Williams' *Suddenly, Last Summer* in its dealings with a woman's sanity, secrets, and persecution). Malden plays Streisand's stepfather, who had sexually abused her as a child and teen (and paid her for it), leading to her career as a high-class call girl. The drama feels rigged from the start, playing like a glorified television movie, as Streisand tries to prove her mental competency in court. Malden gives no more than a competent performance, a reminder of just how many times he was used as a dependable old pro who wouldn't steal focus from the leading players, an actor more inclined to be good rather than great.

Malden starred with Michael Douglas for five seasons on the television series *The Streets of San Francisco* (1972-77), returning to the kind of detective role with which his film career had first gained traction. He died at age ninety-seven in 2009 and will be remembered best for his top collaborations with Brando, Kazan, and Williams: *A Streetcar Named Desire,* with all three men; *On the Waterfront,* with Brando and Kazan; and *Baby Doll,* with Kazan and Williams. Both *Streetcar* and *Baby Doll* leave us with lingering images of Malden alone and brokenhearted, feeling all the worse for knowing that he got that way by his own making.

Anna Magnani

*Anna Magnani versus Jo Van Fleet (with Florence Sundstrom in between) in **The Rose Tattoo**.*

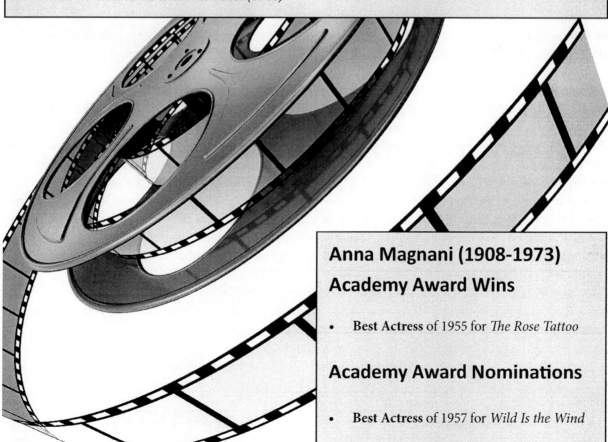

Anna Magnani: Filmography

- *Scampolo* (1928)
- *The Blind Girl of Sorrento* (1934)
- *Full Speed* (1934)
- *Cavalry* (1936)
- *Thirty Seconds of Love* (1936)
- *Princess Tarakanova* (1938)
- *A Light at the Window* (1940)
- *The Fugitive* (1941)
- *Teresa Venerdì* (1941)
- *Alone at Last* (1942)
- *Good Luck is Heaven-sent* (1942)
- *The Adventure of Annabella* (1943)
- *Life Is Beautiful* (1943)
- *Campo de' Fiori* (1943)
- *The Last Cab* (1943)
- *The Flower Before Your Eyes* (1944)
- *Crazy Quartet* (1945)
- *Open City* (1945)
- *Down with Misery* (1946)
- *A Man Returns* (1946)
- *The Bandit* (1946)
- *All Rome Trembled Beneath His Feet* (1946)
- *Peddlin' in Society* (1946)
- *The Stranger from San Marino* (1946)
- *The Honorable Angelina* (1947)
- *Assunta Spina* (1948)
- *L'Amore* (*The Human Voice* and *The Miracle*) (1948)
- *Many Dreams Along the Way* (1948)
- *Volcano* (1950)
- *Bellissima* (1951)
- *Anita Garibaldi* (1952)
- *The Golden Coach* (1952)
- *We the Women* (1953)
- *The Rose Tattoo* (1955)
- *Sister Letizia* (1956)
- *Wild Is the Wind* (1957)
- *…And the Wild Wild Women* (1958)
- *The Fugitive Kind* (1960)
- *The Passionate Thief* (1960)
- *Mamma Roma* (1962)
- *Josefa's Loot* (1964)
- *Made in Italy* (1965)
- *The Secret of Santa Vittoria* (1969)
- *Fellini's Roma* (1972)

Anna Magnani (1908-1973)
Academy Award Wins

- **Best Actress** of 1955 for *The Rose Tattoo*

Academy Award Nominations

- **Best Actress** of 1957 for *Wild Is the Wind*

Serafina Delle Rose in *The Rose Tattoo* (1955)
Lady Torrance in *The Fugitive Kind* (1960)

If you thought that Britain's Vivien Leigh was an unexpected Tennessee Williams colleague, then how about Italian powerhouse Anna Magnani? She didn't even speak English when Williams emerged as a noted American playwright. Separated by an ocean, Williams and Magnani both had their career turning points in 1945: Williams as the author of the Broadway hit *The Glass Menagerie;* Magnani in Roberto Rossellini's film *Open City,* a worldwide success that launched the Italian cinema's neo-realist movement. But how could Williams' poetic brand of realism ever fuse with Magnani's war-torn neo-realism? Following the stage success of *A Streetcar Named Desire* in 1947, Williams fell in love with Frank Merlo, an Italian-American with roots in Sicily. On vacation in Italy with Merlo, Williams became enamored with Sicily and then Rome, where he first encountered Magnani. All three became great friends. Williams' heady mix of love for Merlo, Magnani, and all things Italian led to *The Rose Tattoo,* his subsequent play. An astonishing departure after his shattering domestic tragedies, *The Rose Tattoo* is the work of someone too happy to write anything but a playful and life-affirming look at love, sex, and second chances. Williams' treatment of Italians is affectionate and uncondescending (there's not a single spaghetti scene). In *Memoirs,* Williams calls it "my love-play to the world," and says that it was "permeated with the happy young love for Frankie." He dedicated the play "To Frank in Return for Sicily." It would appear that the play poured out of him in one enthusiastic burst of appreciation and pleasure. Ironically, *The Rose Tattoo* is the only Williams work to win the Tony Award for Best Play. (Is this because it was the most conventional and least threatening of his hits?) Williams wrote the play's central role, Serafina Delle Rose, with Magnani in mind, but the actress wasn't confident enough to undertake a role in English on the American stage. *The Rose Tattoo* opened successfully on Broadway in 1951, but would have to wait until its 1955 screen version to be seen as it was intended, with Magnani, in her Hollywood debut, proving that she was worth the wait.

Though it was long considered fact that Magnani was born in Alexandria, Egypt, she was actually born (on March 7, 1908) in Rome, the city with which she would forever be associated. (Magnani was Rome's First Daughter; later, Sophia Loren would be the same for Naples.) The exotic Egyptian myth added a bit of luster to Magnani's unglamorous beginnings, born to an unmarried mother and raised by her maternal grandmother in a poor section of Rome. Because of her difficult childhood, as well as her extraordinary capacity for playing peasant-stock characters, it would be easy to assume that Magnani was simply one of those "real" people found by filmmakers and used to play herself. However, by the time Magnani achieved world fame as the embodiment of Italian cinema, she had pretty much done it all as a performer. In her early years, she sang in dives and music halls, learning how to keep an audience in her thrall and becoming an accomplished entertainer. She made one silent film but didn't begin her serious film career until 1934. Magnani was also one of Italy's leading stage actresses, including appearances in productions of such American plays as *Anna Christie* and *The Petrified Forest.*

When *Open City* came her way, she was best known to Italian moviegoers as a comedic actress. After its release, she would be regarded as one of the world's most thrilling dramatic stars. Filmed immediately after the final days of the German Occupation, *Open City* still carries the charge of being a drama captured rather than staged. There's no mistaking the film's authenticity and immediacy as a window into the Italian Resistance during the Occupation's waning days, and it stands as a testament and tribute to Italian courage. However, *Open City* is one of the more wildly uneven of international classics, in quality, tone, and style. For every arresting street scene, there's a bad (sometimes laughable) Gestapo scene, complete with clichéd Nazi officers and a glam lesbian agent. An essentially pedestrian drama is interrupted on occasion by startling and powerful sequences. What hasn't aged a day is Magnani. She is the most persuasive member of the film's ensemble cast. As a widow (with a young son) who is also the pregnant fiancée of an Underground member, Magnani is outstanding, an estimable force but also tender, loving, and fearful. The scene in which she is gunned down in the street, the film's most visceral and moving passage, belongs in any montage of the greatest moments in Italian film. As her lover is carried away in a truck with fellow prisoners, Magnani fights off Nazi guards to chase after him, repeatedly shouting for "Francesco!" as she runs along the street with one outstretched arm. She is stoppable only by bullets, and to see this volcanic woman stilled is devastating. How can all that life vanish in an instant? *Open City* is a landmark picture, but it never recovers from her loss (which comes about halfway through the film), descending into a variant of a low-budget, Hollywood-type melodrama.

In the decade between *Open City* and *The Rose Tattoo,* Magnani was the undisputed queen of Italian movies, though none of her films got the attention in the U.S. that had greeted *Open City* in 1946. There were headlines, though. In 1949, Roberto Rossellini famously dumped Magnani for Ingrid Bergman, which led to the scandal of Bergman's unwed pregnancy, effectively crushing the Swedish star's thriving Hollywood career for nearly a decade. *The Miracle* (1948), another Magnani film directed by Rossellini, caused censorship troubles when it was released in the U.S. in 1950, a battle that went all the way to the Supreme Court. The film became more famous for being condemned by religious groups and for its victorious court battle than for its considerable artistry. *The Miracle* is the story of a lonely and simple-minded peasant (Magnani) who interprets her rape by a wanderer as an Immaculate Conception by Saint Joseph. (Federico Fellini, who also wrote the story, plays the wanderer.) Merely forty minutes long, it was paired with *The Human Voice,* another Magnani-Rossellini short film, and released in Italy as *L'Amore.* When it arrived in America, it was attached to two short French films, becoming part of a trio known as *Ways of Love.* Whatever you call it, *The Miracle* contains one of Magnani's more glorious performances. She is especially astounding in the scene in which, soon after learning of her pregnancy, she enters a church overflowing with joy and gratitude at being so blessed, moving from statue to statue to altar, where she eventually collapses in rapture. (The film, however,

needed a better final third and a real ending.)

After Rossellini made Bergman his leading lady of choice, Magnani worked with Luchino Visconti on *Bellissima* (1951), a fine stage-mother drama (an Italian *Gypsy*), and then collaborated with Jean Renoir on *The Golden Coach* (1952). Renoir's masterwork was Magnani's first film in English. A stirring tribute to those most alive on a stage, *The Golden Coach* is one of the essential films about actors, the theatre, and vagabond lives. Set in South America in the eighteenth century, this magical and breathtakingly colorful film stars Magnani as an Italian touring company's leading actress. She is dazzlingly magnetic as she romantically dangles a soldier, a bullfighter, and a viceroy. Magnani may never have been a traditional beauty, with her strong Roman nose and those dark shadows under her eyes, but one never doubts her ability to command amorous attentions. Despite the discomfiting efforts of an international cast hopelessly trying to meld, *The Golden Coach* is an invaluable pairing of a great actress and a great director. Magnani overwhelmingly convinces the viewer that no off-stage romance could ever compete with the love her character receives from her art. Having now appeared triumphantly in an English-language film, Magnani was at last ready to play Serafina in *The Rose Tattoo.*

Maureen Stapleton made her name on Broadway when she created the role of Serafina, winning a Tony Award in the process (in the featured category, ridiculously). Stapleton was a terrific actress, but it's hard to imagine her as Williams' Sicilian-born seamstress. How "Italian" could Maureen Stapleton really be, and, even if she was *that* good, how could she compete with Magnani, the real deal? Stapleton had to "act" everything that Magnani brought to the role naturally. Call Stapleton a good sport, helping to make the play a hit and keeping the role warm for the author's original inspiration. But Magnani was still a big risk. American audiences had thus far not embraced Italian actresses—Isa Miranda, Alida Valli, Valentina Cortesa—in their attempts at Hollywood stardom. (Gina Lollobrigida and Sophia Loren were soon to change all that, almost concurrently with Magnani's *Rose Tattoo* success.) Since Magnani was virtually unknown to mainstream American moviegoers, *The Rose Tattoo* had to be brought to the screen carefully. Paramount wisely used their hit production of *Come Back, Little Sheba*

(1952) as a model. In *Sheba's* case, a Broadway play was brought to the screen with its original leading lady, Shirley Booth, a middle-aged theatre star—who happened to be plump and unattractive—making her screen debut. How did they make it work? Producer Hal Wallis used the play's original director, Daniel Mann, to guide Booth's transition from stage to screen, and hired master cinematographer James Wong Howe to ease Mann's own debut as a filmmaker. But what about bolstering this prestige project's box-office prospects? Though decidedly too young for the role of Booth's alcoholic husband, Burt Lancaster came onboard for commercial security. The film was well-received, won Booth an Oscar for her touching (both sad and lovable) performance, and it made a profit. Three years later, Wallis re-assembled Mann (who had also directed *The Rose Tattoo* on Broadway), Howe, and Lancaster to do for Magnani what they had done for Booth, which was to make it viable for the best actress to play the part regardless of her doubtful popular appeal and atypical movie-star looks. And it worked again.

Aside from the artists involved, the similarities between the films of *Come Back, Little Sheba* and *The Rose Tattoo* are substantial. Both black-and-white films star middle-aged women with hair frequently uncombed (rare for films of this time) and with costumes dominated by robes and house-dresses. (Paramount's resident costume designer, queenly Edith Head, designed both ladies' dowdy wardrobes.) Both films have young-love subplots, in contrast to the older ladies' romantic woes and disappointments. The two movies also share a Broadway-style maturity (on the subjects of sex and lust) and were adapted from works by gay playwrights (William Inge wrote *Sheba*). Both conclude with the women choosing to let go of the past and ready to make a real stab at a better future. Like Booth, Magnani nabbed the Best Actress Oscar and every other major prize that year.

Perhaps the most striking similarity between the films is the miscasting of Lancaster, though in utterly different ways. In *Sheba,* he's clearly not *really* a middle-aged man beaten down by disappointment, despite the powdered gray applied to his temples. In *Rose Tattoo,* he tries too hard to convince us he's a Sicilian-American goofball. In *Sheba,* he's repressed and controlled and respectable (until he falls off the wagon), whereas in *Rose Tattoo* he's the life of the

party. In a nutshell: in *Sheba,* he tries to be more mature than he is; in *Rose Tattoo,* he tries to be more *immature.* Neither extreme is a good fit. (On Broadway, Sidney Blackmer co-starred with Booth in *Sheba,* and Eli Wallach teamed with Stapleton in *Rose Tattoo;* both men won Tony Awards for their performances.) Though Lancaster isn't credible in either role, you can't help but be impressed by his gumption and commitment in tackling both roles. (Though top-billed in *Sheba,* he's billed below Magnani in *Rose Tattoo,* which makes sense because his part is hardly a leading role.) Though Fredric March would have suited the role in *Sheba,* and Anthony Quinn was the obvious choice for *Rose Tattoo,* I can't help but feel glad that Lancaster dared to throw himself into these parts and was so willing not to get in the way of his celebrated co-stars. His casting made it feasible for these actresses to play their roles and clutch their Oscars. Between the films, Lancaster starred in a little something called *From Here to Eternity* (1953), thus elevating himself to superstar status and making him an ever hotter prospect for Magnani than he had been for Booth.

Come Back, Little Sheba and *The Rose Tattoo* are both rather slight movies, especially considering the praise once heaped upon them. They are vehicles for actresses, and Booth and Magnani never disappoint. Daniel Mann was a more confident filmmaker three years after *Sheba,* and, again with James Wong Howe's immeasurable assistance, *The Rose Tattoo* became a much more visual experience than the kitchen-sink *Sheba.* (Mann's only film in between, 1954's *About Mrs. Leslie,* starring newly crowned Oscar winner Shirley Booth, is a turkey.) Serio-comic and most enjoyable, *The Rose Tattoo* is decidedly uncharacteristic Williams fare, despite being set on the Gulf Coast near New Orleans. The locations were filmed on Key West, where Williams and Merlo had a house. It was the first Williams screen adaptation since the phenomenal success of *A Streetcar Named Desire* (1951) and its change-of-pace nature could hardly have been what moviegoers expected. Like *Streetcar, The Rose Tattoo* boasted a screenplay by Williams, and like the former film it proved to be a hit with both critics and audiences. And Serafina gave Magnani the showcase in which to show all of America her magnificent talent.

Magnani is first seen at a grocery store, nicely dressed and buying Grade-A eggs for her Grade-A husband. Serafina is a woman defined by her man, Rosario (Larry Chance), a truck driver who hauls bananas. Magnani plays the scene with a superior air aimed at the grocer and the other shoppers, stemming from Serafina's belief that she has the husband of husbands. But doesn't that type of arrogant display usually come from insecurity? As the story unfolds, it becomes clearer that Serafina's view of her marriage is indeed "rose-colored," and that, on some level, she has always known that the truth is far less rosy. But right now she shines with the news that she is pregnant. In the play, Rosario never appears, but in the film he is seen in shadowed circumstances. Serafina returns home to find him in bed. In this one opportunity, Magnani conveys Serafina's passion for this man (who is half-asleep and bare-chested) as she inhales the rose oil in his hair and puts her cheek on his shoulder and tells him her news. He grabs her hand and promises that tonight's mysterious ride will be his last "night run." Visible on his chest is his rose tattoo. Magnani looks as though she could happily devour him. She kisses his back and rubs her hands across it in a gesture reminiscent of Kim Hunter's toward Marlon Brando in *Streetcar*, and, again, a male has been made the sex object of an on-screen marriage. Rosario's naked back is seen again as he peeks from the bedroom door to watch Serafina's encounter with a customer, Estelle (Virginia Grey), who wants a shirt made of rose-colored silk for her lover of one year, a man who is "wild like a gypsy." That man, unbeknownst to Serafina, is Rosario.

A smuggler, Rosario dies that evening when his truck crashes and burns in an armed pursuit by the police. In the play, Serafina knows that he smuggles for the mob. The movie is vaguer on the details, and it makes sense that Serafina would suppress any knowledge that Rosario is an outright smuggler, preferring instead to speak of his "night runs." When her priest and some female neighbors arrive with the bad news, it's the set-up for the film's most wrenching scene. Sitting at her sewing machine in a black slip, she hears their voices. Magnani clutches her throat in fear and moves toward them as they enter her house. As the priest approaches, her other hand moves to her heart and she says, "Don't speak," repeating this phrase as she moves backward. She clutches a curtain, puts a hand in her hair, and continues to whisper "Don't speak" as she crumples to the floor in tears. She continues to choke out the same phrase as they lift her. Each "Don't speak" grows more intense as her body grows weaker. What Magnani so beautifully articulates is Serafina's desperate attempt to delay reality: for as long as her visitors do not say what they have come to say, then it is not true. Serafina can stall the truth if she never hears their words. Magnani is especially poignant for bringing such physical expressiveness to internal agony. Her hands and arms, her entire body, give the scene expansive and resonant manifestations of loss. Serafina suffers a miscarriage.

The story jumps to three years later, with Rosa (Marisa Pavan), the fifteen-year-old daughter of Se-

From *Eternity* to Here

Before Marlon Brando was cast in *A Streetcar Named Desire* in 1947, Burt Lancaster, already a movie star, had been one of the few actors given serious consideration for the role of Stanley Kowalski. With *The Rose Tattoo*, Lancaster finally got his shot at a Williams role. He later starred in *The Rainmaker* (1956), another well-liked stage-to-screen adaptation (produced, like *Sheba* and *Rose Tattoo*, by Hal Wallis for Paramount), but this time, finally, Lancaster wasn't miscast, ideal in the smooth-talking flimflamming title role, a warm-up for his Oscar-winning performance in *Elmer Gantry* (1960). Directed by Joseph Anthony (like Daniel Mann another theatre director), *The Rainmaker* is a stagier film than either *Sheba* or *Rose*

Tattoo. Again, Lancaster's role is subservient to the female lead (Katharine Hepburn), but this time it's his film, with Hepburn the one who seems miscast (too old, too fancy, too "special" for her "old maid" role). Lancaster went on to appear in two other screen adaptations of plays in the 1950s, again lending his box-office stature to risky projects, again helping other actors win Oscars. He was seen in the overrated *Separate Tables* (1958), a low-grade *Grand Hotel*, in which he was again miscast but helped David Niven and Wendy Hiller collect Oscars. Then came *The Devil's Disciple* (1959), from George Bernard Shaw's play, in which Lancaster and Kirk Douglas (*both* miscast) were outclassed by Laurence Olivier, who was perfection as a British general in the Revolutionary War.

rafina and Rosario, about to graduate high school. (Her name, Rosa Delle Rose, means Rose of the Roses.) Following Serafina's decision to defy the Catholic Church by having Rosario cremated (because "I had to have something"), she has become depressive, reclusive, self-pitying, and an all-around mess. *The Rose Tattoo* is about grief, about holding on to illusions and memories and letting the present, and therefore the future, go by. Rosario has become a saint to Serafina. Their Rosa is sweet and pretty and well-mannered, and the contrast between mother and daughter is a source of embarrassment for the teenager. Serafina has tried to keep Rosa a child. This speaks to Serafina's deep-down awareness that Rosario *was* a wild thing, who endowed his daughter with the potential for trouble. Her overprotection also comes from her own appetite for sex (with Rosario), leading to fears that young Rosa may have inherited her mother's libido. Rosa meets blond Jack Hunter (Ben Cooper), the kind of boy-next-door sailor you would more likely meet in an MGM musical, far from being the randy threat of parents' nightmares. As Serafina eventually finds her way out of unresolved grief and into possible romance, the film distinguishes between her amatory complications and the simplicity of first love experienced by Rosa and Jack. When Rosa returns from a school dance at 1:15 a.m., on the night she first meets Jack, she finds Serafina wide awake. In the first example of Serafina using her Catholicism for quick results, she asks Rosa to kneel before the statue of the Holy Mother and swear that she spent the night studying (as promised). Magnani is commandingly funny whenever Serafina wields her religion to make a point or score a point, without any sense of irony at the humor inherent in such short-cut and easy-access methods to the Divine.

The mother-daughter relationship is central to *The Rose Tattoo,* and Magnani and Pavan (born in Sardinia) work excellently together, undoubtedly aided by their shared Italian heritage. Pavan has a light accent, unnecessary for a character born in the United States, but her casting is nonetheless appropriate because of her credible blood ties to Magnani and their informal physicality with each other. It is easy to accept them as a loving and squabbling mother and daughter. Paramount could have tried to get Natalie Wood for the role, and she would have looked right, but Pavan brings further Italian flavor

to a film that needs it, especially once Burt Lancaster arrives. When Magnani wallops Pavan across the face at her mention of daddy's smuggling, the scene isn't just about disrespecting or defiling the memory of Rosario. For Magnani, the moment is about Serafina's whole identity. If Rosario is diminished, then what does that make of the woman who dedicated herself to him? Her response to his death has been to devote herself even further to him, blocking out all else (except her watchful eye on Rosa). Magnani spends this section of the picture with tousled hair, shuffling around in a bathrobe. The women in the neighborhood, primarily fellow Italians, are afraid of her, and who wouldn't be? She's liable to go off at any moment. When a teacher (Dorrit Kelton, from the Broadway cast) stops by, Serafina launches into a verbal attack on the school's morals, specifically those dances at which young girls can meet sailors. When the scene moves out of the house, Magnani is wickedly funny as she blasts, "How *high* is this high school?" A humiliated Rosa calls Serafina "disgusting," and it cuts so deeply that all the fire goes out of Magnani as she painfully absorbs the blow. As she did with the "Don't speak" phrase earlier, Magnani keeps repeating the word "disgusting," each time feeling it more sharply. Throughout the film, the highs and lows of the mother-daughter bond are played frankly, with enormous love, as well as an anger that can accelerate quickly whenever tapped. Volatile Serafina and Rose are miles apart from the daintier Amanda and Laura of *The Glass Menagerie*, Williams' previous mother-daughter duo.

The "disgusting" scene leads directly to the comic sequence of Serafina, ready to turn things around, deciding to attend Rosa's graduation. With a hilarious lack of vanity, Magnani attempts to get into a girdle, which gets only as far as her thighs. She then tries to fasten a corset around her middle, another lost cause. By now in a dress, she's interrupted by the arrival of a client, Bessie (Jo Van Fleet), and Bessie's pal Flora (Florence Sundstrom, who, oddly enough, played Bessie on Broadway). Bessie wants the blouse Serafina was to have made for her, but it's not ready yet. Bessie and Flora are fun-loving gals on their way to a convention in New Orleans. Though eager to get to the graduation, Serafina agrees to finish the blouse. The women offend Serafina with their "dirty talk," allowing Magnani one of her amusing displays of great-lady respectability, despite her modest surroundings and barely assembled self. Calling them "man-crazy things," Magnani fully indulges Serafina's pride and self-delusion about her marriage, telling them she is "satisfied to remember because I had the best." But she's up against a formidable foe. Van Fleet is the rare actress able to hold her own against Magnani, physically (as they start pushing each other around), verbally (as they shout at each other), and talent-wise (as the scene ends in a draw). Bessie, enhanced by Van Fleet's gleeful spite, tells Serafina about Rosario's affair with Estelle, the Mardi Gras Club's blackjack dealer. Despite Magnani's screams of "Liar!" and her dazed composure, mixing fury with numbness, it's as though Serafina has been waiting for this moment for years, the moment when the truth is thrust before her. But, as in the "Don't speak" moment, it would not be true until someone said it out loud. Serafina never knew the details, but she knew *something*. It may have looked to outsiders that her depression was about losing her husband, but the flashes of insecurity and defensiveness in Magnani's performance connote a firmly suppressed heartache over a marriage that wasn't what she thought it was. If she can't continue to sustain the myth of her marriage, then what? Who is Serafina without that exceptional love? If Rosario was a deceiver, then has Serafina's whole life been a lie?

Why would Rosa bring Jack home to meet her mother tonight? The last time Rosa and Serafina saw each other was when Rosa called her "disgusting," and who knows what she will find? It's even worse than imagined. Alone in the dark at her sewing table, Magnani looks lost, too shattered and distant to be even vaguely friendly. If Serafina didn't believe the "lie," would she have taken it this hard? She might have been furious at those women for spreading gossip, but her devastated reaction implies that they merely confirmed dreaded suspicions. But the scene grows wonderfully comic when Magnani places her roused attention on cross-examining sailor Jack Hunter: "What are you hunting, Jack?" First she corrects his pronunciation of their name ("Delle Rose" has *two* syllables on "Rose"). Then she addresses Sicilian customs regarding the courting of young women, who are not to be left alone with boys to whom they are not engaged. When he confesses that he's a virgin, she laughs in disbelief. She's so obsessed with her daughter's innocence that she's unmoved by

the news that he's a Catholic: "You don't look Catholic to me." (Which means he's not *Italian*.) As the scene continues, there's an added element of almost farcical comedy as Magnani tries to keep Pavan exiled on the front porch, even blocking her peeks in the window until the interrogation ends. Magnani pointedly wants to know, "Why do they make them Navy pants so tight?" But the capper comes when she asks him to kneel before the statue of the Blessed Virgin and swear that he will respect Rosa's innocence, which he does willingly. Sighing with satisfaction, Magnani relaxes into Serafina's genuine relief that her tactics have produced the desired results. Having steamrolled over this sweet-faced boy, Magnani allows him to kiss her hand.

The centerpiece of the movie is the scene at the church bazaar, with Magnani the unconnected and preoccupied element in a sequence filled with pleasure seekers and merrymakers. Magnani is consumed with one thing and nothing can stop her: Serafina must find her priest. Here comes the other surprising variation of my own last name in a Williams film. Predating Warren Beatty's Paolo di Leo in *The Roman Spring of Mrs. Stone* by six years is *The Rose Tattoo*'s Father De Leo (Sandro Giglio). It is here, at fifty-one minutes into the film, that Burt Lancaster arrives as Alvaro Mangiacavallo. The film's

Triple Threat

In her first year in pictures, Jo Van Fleet had a sensational 1955 in three disparate roles, proving handily that she was a chameleon of a character actress, able to play seemingly anything. In *The Rose Tattoo*, she's a horrid playgirl—nasty, pushy, and vulgar—with a flagrant Southern accent. In Elia Kazan's *East Of Eden*, she's superb as James Dean's runaway mother, a hardened, low-voiced woman working as a madam, tightly concealing her pain and vulnerability. In *I'll Cry Tomorrow*, also directed by Daniel Mann, she is amazing as Susan Hayward's stage mother (though only four years older than Hayward), alternately loathsome and sympathetic, sly and theatrical, and speaking with nasal New York inflections. It is no surprise that Van Fleet won a much-deserved Best Supporting Actress Oscar that year, singled out for *East of Eden*. (Van Fleet beat Pavan, nominated for *Rose Tattoo*.)

stars are introduced at a bingo table, but Magnani hardly notices; Serafina's focus is clearly elsewhere. Revived by the sight of her priest, she then becomes nervous and fearful about her mission. Despite her misgivings, the priest brings her inside the church, the place where she was married. This prompts her memories of how she came to America for her arranged marriage, not knowing one word of English. She recalls being awed by her first sight of beautiful Rosario. Whether remembering that her first English word was "love," or so overcome with emotion that "I can't breathe in this building," Magnani is tremendously touching. The priest lectures her on her unkempt appearance, troubling behavior, and her self-indulgent grief. In her defense, she proudly responds, "I gave my husband much glory." She, the peasant girl who married above her class (Rosario was some kind of baron), cannot fathom that a man could betray such "glory." Magnani turns private pain to public anger as she confronts the laughter of eavesdroppers. Her anger at Rosario is foisted on all those around her, an easier response than facing the flaws in a so-called flawless marriage. The more she shouts that she doesn't believe the lie, the more Magnani heartbreakingly convinces that Serafina believes it all too well. There's one last hope, and it's the reason she has come here.

Serafina then asks Father De Leo if Rosario ever spoke, in the confessional, about another woman. She pleads with the priest to break a vow, knowing full well that what she asks is outrageous. Magnani is phenomenal here, so compelled that nothing else matters, employing whatever it takes to get her answer: asking gently, begging pathetically, crying openly, and finally grabbing hold of him furiously and refusing to let go. It is Lancaster who pulls her off him. Though the priest quickly (and wisely) escapes behind the church door, Serafina isn't finished. Magnani pounds the door until she slides to the ground in defeat. As Lancaster assists her exit, the final indignity is the cluster of women staring at her, inducing horror and shame on Magnani's face, which she covers in disgrace. The beauty of Magnani's handling of the scene is that it's all played as impulse, regardless of any embarrassment or inappropriate behavior. Magnani's Serafina *has* to do what she does because she needs this information, however wrong it is to ask, however large a commotion it will create. It is a last-ditch effort to save all that she held dear.

Magnani's surge of feeling and need, all the way to the outburst of physical contact and the humiliating conclusion, is unflinchingly vivid and exposed. Williams gave Serafina an added layer of complexity when he made her an unwaveringly religious person with a hypocritically bargaining relationship with her God. Serafina can follow the church's laws with which she is comfortable, but she does as she pleases if in conflict with those laws, first by cremating Rosario, and now by asking a priest to break his vow by satisfying her curiosity. Serafina is adept at using her Catholicism to get people to swear before statues, but she has definite limitations whenever life challenges her religious beliefs. Serafina has a recognizably compromising approach to religion, using what's needed and disregarding what's too difficult. She *had* to have Rosario's ashes, and she *had* to know what Father De Leo knew about Rosario's secret life. In the play, the Father De Leo scene happens at Serafina's house, in response to her phone call, but it has more propulsive conviction in the movie, with Serafina in actual pursuit of him.

In the truck scene, as Lancaster drives her home, Magnani finds her way back to reality, as if the previous scene had occurred in a state of possession. The first time Magnani really notices Lancaster is when he removes his shirt so that she can repair the rip she caused in the church scuffle. Magnani has a double-take reaction to Lancaster's sleeveless T-shirt, and for the remainder of the scene she keeps looking at his torso, or trying *not* to look at it, which is even funnier. She becomes amusingly troubled, dazed, and aroused by his distracting flesh. The resemblance between Mangiacavallo's body and Rosario's is uncanny, and Mangiacavallo is also a Sicilian trucker who hauls bananas. But she notes a major difference: "My husband's body with the head...of a clown." Mangiacavallo, whose name means "eat a horse," is a sweet lug and the grandson of a "village idiot." Lancaster acts with admirable gusto, attempting inflections with an Italian-American flavor and using his acrobatic background to make Mangiacavallo a cheerfully manic presence. His boisterous laugh feels forced, but Lancaster appears to be having a grand time. But how can a miscast actor, one who is so obviously "acting" (make that *overacting*), stand up to someone as authentic as Magnani? It is not a fair fight, and yet her grounding solidity and his unquenchable enthusiasm meet halfway. Their contrasts as actors luckily fit with their contrasts as characters. Serafina can be delighted by him, though she can swiftly find his humor annoying (with good reason). But she is able to open up with him, telling him about the rose tattoo on Rosario's chest and how she would smash his urn if she believed those ugly rumors. Mangiacavallo has three dependents (grandmother, father, and sister) and is looking for a mate whom he can offer "love and affection." Though Serafina isn't interested, Magnani brings flirtatiousness to the scene, as well as glimmers of a woman being awakened after years of dormancy. Shades of Blanche and Mitch from *Streetcar,* as two stalled people come together with the possible outcome of joint happiness. Serafina, like Blanche, is a widow obsessed with the memory of a young and beautiful husband. Both women are stuck in states of illusion, but whereas Blanche will be destroyed by the dismantling of illusions, Serafina will be freed by the truth, able to accept it and go on. This is, after all, a romantic comedy at heart.

Their date at Serafina's house later that evening is a comic dance between an amorous (and tipsy) bachelor and a nervous and uptight widow. Magnani is all fixed up, in a black dress, with her hair pinned, and the scene becomes a series of steps forward and back, as she moves alternately between enjoyment and discomfort. He can be such a child, as

One Clap Says It All

Speaking of Magnani's wondrous physicality, I must mention her signature gesture: the one clap. Not applause, just a one-time slapping together of her two hands. It is a move that can have countless meanings when Magnani chooses to utilize it, such as "Oh my God," "That's that," "Isn't that wonderful?" "This is too much," "Can you believe it?" "Where can it be?" "Go figure," "Impossible!" and on and on. I guess this comes under "talking with your hands," but it's a special delight when such "talking" instantly transmits a specific thought or feeling. And since Magnani's English can sometimes be a challenge for the listener, these gestures are priceless, even though I suspect that Magnani's Serafina is the kind of generously emotional performance that can be understood without knowledge of either English *or* Italian.

difficult to control as her daughter. When he shows her the rose tattoo he had put on his chest that afternoon, it kills the party. Magnani plunges Serafina back into her grief. After she tells him about the infidelity rumor, and discovers that he knows the woman in question, Magnani makes a marvelous transition, a pro-active decision to tackle the issue head-on and confront her nemesis at the Mardi Gras Club. She puts her hands through her hair and laughs, then shouts "Okay!" and slaps her thigh. She shouts "Okay!" again for fortification, then grabs her pocketbook and tells him, "Take me there!" Primed for a showdown, she opts for no longer hiding or brooding in fear. Magnani enters the club at her most unstoppable, locating Virginia Grey's Estelle and making intimidating taunts of "Liar!" The woman's brazen confession leads to Magnani bashing her across the face with her pocketbook. An even bigger moment comes when Grey opens her shirt to Magnani to reveal her own rose-tattooed chest. Magnani's face registers shock and anguish, but she rallies her rage to belt Grey with a second bash to her face. Did poor Virginia Grey know who she would be up against when cast in this role? Grey had been a dutiful and likable member of the MGM stock company in the late 1930s and early 1940s. With acidic asides, she had stolen Joan Crawford's telephone scene in *The Women* (1939), but had she been prepared to get belted around by the Italian dynamo? Lucky for her, the club patrons separate the two women (in effect, saving Grey's life). In the play, this showdown happens over the phone!

When Lancaster runs into the house after a loud crash, Magnani is on the floor in tears surrounded by the smashed urn and its content of ashes. Serafina must find a way to live with the knowledge that all the love she gave Rosario wasn't enough to satisfy him. She moves away from grief and on to revenge, focused on bedding Mangiacavallo. She asks him to make a noisy show of leaving, only to sneak back later. They boom their voices in overblown goodnight wishes. Magnani now concentrates Serafina's strength and determination in a new direction. But Mangiacavallo returns drunk and passes out. In the play, they do sleep together, but, up against Hollywood morality, the screen Serafina is protected from herself. Sex or no sex, you have to wonder if Mangiacavallo is a viable romantic option for Serafina. He may be a good egg, but he's such a fool that it is easy to hope for someone better to come along. Perhaps he is a good transition between her widowhood and a later, more sensible mate. But at least this boozing bozo appears unlikely ever to be the kind of smooth deceiver that Rosario was.

When he wakes the next morning on the floor of her sewing room, he discovers Rosa asleep on the couch, terrifying the girl and arousing Serafina's wrath after Rosa seeks her protection. Magnani emerges from her room with both arms swinging, a comic tempest who won't quit. Large Lancaster, suddenly seeming puny in her presence, shields himself with one of her mannequins. She throws him out, hilariously slapping all the way, and then hurls a coffee pot at him out the window. Rosa angrily assumes that her mother slept with this stranger. In her denials and mortification, Magnani gets to the line, "I closed my eyes and dreamed he was your father," which would make more sense if they *had* slept together as they do in the play. This scorching mother-daughter confrontation eventually finds its way to understanding. When Serafina gives her consent for Rosa to marry Jack, Magnani and Pavan, despite all their fireworks, again display their unmistakably rooted and heartfelt attachment. "Go with the boy," Magnani tells her. There's a lovely moment when Magnani is startled and then pleased by a second kiss on her hand from Ben Cooper's Jack, followed by a beautiful image of the young lovers running off into the distance.

But back to Serafina and Mangiacavallo and the movie's second happy ending. Bare-chested Lancaster, back in acrobat mode, is playing bird high atop a parked sailboat, eventually making his way to her, assisted by the interested neighborhood ladies. Serafina, no longer secretive, acknowledges a new openness with her community and looks ahead to a future unencumbered by the baggage of the past. As she switches on her electric piano to blare "The Sheik of Araby," a song that has annoyed her throughout the movie, it is a call to laugh and play and *live*. When Lancaster steps inside and she closes the door behind him, Magnani says, hand on breast, "Now we can go on with our conversation," followed by big laughs and a hug. Mangiacavallo is a new kind of romantic partner for a new Serafina. The play concludes with Serafina happily believing that she has been impregnated by Mangiacavallo, obviously not an option for the unconsummated screen couple.

And Howe!

James Wong Howe's career began in the silent era; the final film he photographed was *Funny Lady* (1975). In addition to *The Rose Tattoo,* he was the cinematographer on another of the year's Best Picture Oscar nominees, *Picnic,* which he shot in gorgeous Technicolor. Howe's other credits include *The Thin Man* (1934), *Kings Row* (1942), *Yankee Doodle Dandy* (1942), *Sweet Smell of Success* (1957), and *Hud* (1963), for which he received his second Oscar.

More than anything else, *The Rose Tattoo* is Williams' valentine to Magnani. (You can glimpse Williams as an extra at the Mardi Gras Club bar when Magnani storms through.) To say this is his best comedy picture may not sound like much of a compliment since only one other Williams film, the trifling *Period of Adjustment* (1962), can be categorized as purely comic. (Unlike the sinfully funny and altogether superior *Baby Doll, The Rose Tattoo* and *Period of Adjustment* are the only two comedies of his that *end* as comedies.) Marisa Pavan and Ben Cooper handle the first-love subplot nicely, with its refreshing (for the time) mix of a girl's sexual curiosity and a boy's timidity (augmented by his fear of God after making his vow). Pavan went on to play Catherine de Medici quite well in *Diane* (1956), while Cooper is best remembered as Turkey in Nicholas Ray's hyper-intense western *Johnny Guitar* (1954). Future 1950s film star Don Murray had played Jack on Broadway.

Embraced even more enthusiastically by the Academy Awards than *Come Back, Little Sheba, The Rose Tattoo* received a hefty eight Oscar nominations, for picture, actress, supporting actress, black-and-white cinematography, black-and-white art direction, black-and-white costume design, film editing, and score. It won not only in the Best Actress category, but also for art direction and cinematography. This marked the first Oscar for veteran cameraman James Wong Howe, who brought rich nocturnal textures to *Rose Tattoo*'s frequently darkened settings, as well as tangible feelings for a sweltering climate, a gritty neighborhood, and a ramshackle house (which was right next door to Williams' own house, on Key West). It was no surprise that Lancaster wasn't nominated, but I would have expected a screenplay

Marty...Really?

The big winner at the 1955 Oscars was *Marty,* which was coincidentally produced by the Hecht-Lancaster company (yes, *that* Lancaster). *Marty* was a rather dubious winner, a film whose thinness and lack of inspiration were interpreted as a new stride in realism. (*Open City* it ain't.) Easy to watch but extremely minor, *Marty* is merely low-gloss goo. So much for Oscar: *The Night of the Hunter,* far and away the year's best American film, didn't receive a single nomination. One other footnote regarding Oscar night: Sal Mineo, nominated in the supporting-actor category for his teen performance in *Rebel without a Cause,* had been in the original Broadway cast of *The Rose Tattoo,* playing one of the neighborhood children.

nomination for Williams and Hal Kanter (though Kanter was credited only with "adaptation"). Author Margaret Bradham Thornton, in *Notebooks,* reports that Williams' collaboration with Kanter was so "unpleasant and unproductive" that Williams refused to share the screenplay credit with him.

Magnani's chief competition in the Oscar race was Susan Hayward in *I'll Cry Tomorrow,* the biopic of alcoholic songstress Lillian Roth. Hayward was never better, gutsy and uncompromising and fiercely committed, but can anyone compete with Magnani? (Again, not a fair fight.) Imagine how Daniel Mann felt, having directed both of the year's most acclaimed female performances. I wonder who he and Jo Van Fleet, who appeared opposite both actresses, were rooting for on Oscar night. Magnani was in Italy that evening, and Pavan accepted the award on her behalf. Back-to-back Williams adaptations had resulted in Best Actress Oscar wins (the previous Oscar was Vivien Leigh's for *Streetcar*), just as the roles had won Tonys for their original interpreters. Mann would never become a major film director, but he surely was good with actors.

After the box-office success of *The Rose Tattoo,* and her Oscar win, it was inevitable that Magnani would make a subsequent Hollywood picture, and perhaps just as inevitable that Anthony Quinn would be her leading man, especially since he had missed out on playing Mangiacavallo. Quinn and Magnani had recently switched places, both to ac-

claim: she, the Italian star, had worked in America in *Rose Tattoo,* and he, the American star, had worked in Italy in Federico Fellini's *La Strada.* With his new Italian seal of approval, he was prepared to be an ideal Italian-*seeming* Magnani co-star. Their vehicle was *Wild Is the Wind* (1957), directed by elegant George Cukor, who was out of his comfort zone helming a torrid (and implausible) love triangle set on a sheep farm. Quinn is a big ham here, giving an overbearing performance as an overbearing Italian-American farmer. Newly married to Quinn, Magnani is another "arranged" bride from Italy, the sister of Quinn's deceased first wife. She is the film's chief asset, and her honesty shows up Quinn's phoniness. (Maybe his casting as Mangiacavallo wouldn't have been such a dream after all. He may have been just as overblown as Lancaster and not as nice to look at.) The film mirrors *They Knew What They Wanted* when Magnani begins an affair with young Anthony Franciosa, who is like a son to Quinn. Magnani is clearly closer to Quinn's age than Franciosa's, but the blatant twenty-year age difference goes unmentioned. Unlike *The Rose Tattoo,* it all feels so strenuously "Italian." Magnani provides some compelling drama as her character tries to assimilate while suffering the indignities of being confused with her sister, but there's too much florid writing, too many "big" scenes, and it's all rather tiring. Magnani and Quinn both got Oscar nominations, though.

When Williams rewrote his 1940 play *Battle of Angels* and it resurfaced as *Orpheus Descending* in 1957, the main character had evolved from a fair Southern lady to a Palermo-born woman transplanted to a dreary Mississippi town. Williams' continued fascination and admiration for Magnani, presumably even greater since her *Rose Tattoo* triumph, is the obvious inspiration for the character's conversion, but, again, Magnani did not play the role, Lady Torrance, on Broadway, once more holding out for the film version. Pinch-hitting onstage again was ever-reliable Maureen Stapleton, though this time the play was not a hit. When the screen version, directed by Sidney Lumet and adapted by Williams and Meade Roberts, was filmed in 1959, Stapleton was cast in the supporting role of the sheriff's wife, standing on the sidelines while Magnani swooped in, despite her ongoing difficulty with English. In *A Look at Tennessee Williams* (by Mike Steen), a book of interviews with the playwright's friends and colleagues, Staple-

In **The Fugitive Kind**, Magnani's Lady confronts David Cutrere (John Baragrey), the man who hurt her deeply so many years ago.

ton is quoted specifically on losing both Serafina and Lady to Magnani: "I would have hired Anna, too!" Not only a good sport, Stapleton was savvy enough not to let the business side of things affect her self-esteem. Though the *Orpheus* film, retitled *The Fugi-* *tive Kind*, would be deemed a failure in its day, it is superior to the *Rose Tattoo* film and contains a Magnani performance every bit as great as her Serafina. The sixth of the Williams films, *The Fugitive Kind* unfairly became the first not to result in a nomination for the Best Actress Oscar since *The Glass Menagerie* (1950), the initial Williams picture.

Lady is married lovelessly to Jabe Torrance (Victor Jory) and they own and operate a dry-goods store above which they reside. Jabe has just been released from the hospital but is dying nonetheless. (*Cat on a Hot Tin Roof* begins similarly, with the return home of the fatally ill Big Daddy.) When Magnani enters, emerging from a car and following Victor Jory to the store's entrance, her slow, deliberate body language suggests someone in no hurry to get back to the life waiting for her inside. She takes a weighted pause before entering. Mostly wearing black throughout the film, Magnani's Lady is in perpetual mourning for several people: her beloved father; the baby she miscarried; the still-living lover who spurned her; plus the ailing husband she cannot wait to *start* mourning. A gathering of neighbors wish Jabe well, but Lady remains apart, making no pretense of wifely concern. As a woman locked in a marriage of mutual antagonism, Magnani is hard, unsmiling, and hopeless. (Jabe notices her changes to the store in his absence and orders things restored to his liking.) This is the most miserable marriage in a Williams film, with hatred expressed openly and loudly. Jory, best remembered as Jonas Wilkerson, the creepy overseer in *Gone With the Wind,* here plays another vile Southerner, and he gives a large performance, slimy and sweaty and easily incurring an audience's antipathy.

Everything is about to change with the arrival of Val Xavier (Marlon Brando), the handsome drifter (and musician) looking for work. Val enters the store while Lady is on the phone in desperate need of sleeping pills, saying to herself, "I wish I was dead." Startling her, Val responds, "No you don't, ma'am." (Williams has his Orpheus arriving to lead this Eurydice out of her hell and back to life. Much later, Lady will tell him that she knew *someone* would be coming to rescue her.) The physical appeal of Val, enhanced by his snakeskin jacket, is not lost on her, but Lady is a woman skeptical of everything, too bruised by life to suspect anything but the worst in people. With her imposing self-possession, Magnani is firmly on guard, making Lady's eventual transition to passion and vulnerability even more earthshaking. Though Magnani and Brando, two of the era's greatest actors, don't have obvious chemistry, this is partially because the roles were

not conceived with equal conviction or plausibility. Though Brando coasts along unsurely, Magnani is in no way adversely affected by him. She plays Lady's inner and outer selves so powerfully that nothing seems able to get in her way. (Lancaster's miscasting in *The Rose Tattoo* was no problem for her and neither is Brando's hazy rendition of a hazy character.) Regarding Val's pitiful letter of recommendation, she says, "What people say about you don't mean much," which speaks to Lady's generally low opinion of humanity and her recognition of Val as an outsider like herself. (*Orpheus Descending* offers more information about Lady's Italian background, including her coming over from Palermo, which goes unmentioned in the film.) Lady and Val are both weary; they are ready for something new. Val's quest is deliberate, while Lady's is unexpectedly sparked by his fated arrival. Until now, the bitterness seething in Magnani was Lady's primary way of knowing that she was still alive.

Lady reveals to Val her dream of opening "Lady's Confectionery" in the back room of the store, something of her own, unrelated to Jabe. The confectionery will be modeled on the wine garden of her father, which was burned down, along with her family's house and orchard, one long-ago summer. As Magnani brings smiles and a more relaxed air into her performance, such as when Lady suggests to Val that maybe he can play his guitar and sing for the confectionery's patrons, the character is discovering the hope she hasn't had in a long time. After just a few minutes in this attractive young man's presence, Magnani has begun to expose Lady's burgeoning inclinations toward warmth and intimacy. Though she makes a firm point of telling him that he doesn't interest her sexually, Magnani plays this as a case of protesting too much. But her subtext is less about sex than power, making it known that she isn't someone easily taken advantage of. No man will ever again abuse her. Once Val begins clerking for her, the store increases business because of an influx of female customers. But Lady's above-the-store life is still a nightmare, a fact as unavoidable as Jabe's cane-banging calls for attention. The fluctuating tensions in Magnani's performance denote how Val's rejuvenating presence has made Lady's life with Jabe both more and less bearable, as her escalating happiness with Val serves to heighten the intolerability of her marriage.

After rowdy party-girl Carol Cutrere (Joanne Woodward) causes a commotion at the gas station, her brother David (John Baragrey) is on his way to retrieve her at Lady's store. This news begins the puncturing of Magnani's containment because David is the man Lady once loved, the rich boy who threw her over. She hasn't seen him since then and says that she won't allow him in the store. Magnani's proud exterior shields a character more scared and unsure than she allows people to see. Her hate and bitterness arise, but so does the fact that Lady still loves this man, or, rather, the man he used to be. David is a minor role, like the husband in *The Rose Tattoo,* which creates a casting conundrum. You can't have major actors in tiny roles, but you also must cast men believably worthy of Magnani-sized ardor. In both films, you never quite believe that these arbitrary actors could have aroused such love and devotion from anyone as vital as Magnani. Though you cannot imagine that *this* David was Lady's great love, actor John Baragrey is perfectly adequate in fulfilling his dramatic function as little more than the prop on the receiving end of one of Magnani's greatest scenes.

When David arrives, Lady calls down from the second floor, telling him never to come back (rather than just letting him leave without seeing her). "I hold hard feelings," Magnani says quietly, mixing great dignity with Lady's compulsion not to lose this opportunity for a showdown. She comes down the stairs to the landing, keeping herself formally a few steps above him. She speaks about the store's success and the forthcoming confectionery, a tribute to her father's wine garden, a site associated with Lady and David's young love. It is obvious that David was as destroyed by their split as she was, and, like her, still hasn't healed. But that's not enough of a victory. Magnani builds steadily, with Lady's composure harder to sustain as memories flood back into immediacy. Unable to let him go, she moves directly toward him and deliberately hurts him by revealing the pregnancy he never knew about: "I carried your child in my body the summer you quit me." (He rejected her and married a society girl. Lady married Jabe out of hopelessness.) Magnani's release, full and throbbing, is like that of an at-last performance of a scene rehearsed in one's head countless times. "I lost your child," she continues, as tears start to overtake her. (In *Orpheus Descending,* she aborted

the baby.) Lady wanted death herself "but death don't come when you want it," a particularly poignant utterance considering that death will come to Lady when she *least* wants it. When he moves to kiss her, Magnani unleashes what's left of Lady's long-clenched feelings, screaming for him to get out and halting this agonizing three minutes with a final "I just wanted to tell you my life." It is a scarring scene in which Magnani wrestles with the unresolvable nature of Lady's love-hate feelings for David, while taking some mirthless pleasure in wounding him for his destruction of their happiness. It is a scene she had to play, inexorable and cleansing but also instantly regrettable. After he exits, she tearfully laments throwing away pride for momentary satisfaction, then climbs back up the stairs. Magnani began in control, succumbed to fevered emotion, then exits sadly depleted, with Lady no happier or more gratified for having had her long-awaited confrontation. Like Serafina's altercation with her husband's lover in *The Rose Tattoo,* this scene is painful but cathartic, allowing Lady to move ahead with her life, whether she realizes it or not.

Lady and Val drive to the ruin of the old, overgrown wine garden, the place where Lady was a happy girl. Here Magnani has a short monologue about Lady's father and the vigilantes who set fire to his property after learning that he sold some liquor to blacks. Everything was lost in the blaze, including her father, and no one lifted a finger to help. When Magnani fumes, "I'm full of hate," it is expressed as though Lady hasn't had a moment of peace since that day, which was soon followed by David's dumping her. But Val has changed everything. When she invites him to move into the store and sleep in a small room behind a curtain, it is the beginning of a seduction. When Val later takes offense at being thought of as a stud service, Magnani surprisingly does not meet Brando's anger, choosing, instead, to be vulnerable, more needy than angered. There is lust in her, yes, but more than that, there is a longing to feel closer to him. She is plainly open to love, so grateful for his coming into her life. But when he insults her, she slaps him and he throws her onto the tiny room's cot, making her cry. It is a distressing sight to see the formidable Magnani suddenly looking so fragile and exposed, in just her black slip, with her hand over her face. As in all their scenes together, Brando does what's required without surmounting an essential emptiness, while Magnani keeps peeling away layers of Lady's protective covers. When he kisses her, she registers ecstasy, more the ecstasy of human contact and tender affection than sexual satisfaction.

The confectionery will be the monument to their new love and Lady's post-Jabe, post-David awakening. The set for the confectionery is magical and lightweight, all jingling wind chimes and flower decorations. Magnani's Lady is a woman reborn, and her energized commitment to this new life is ironically strengthened by a disturbing revelation. Jabe blurts out that he was among the vigilantes responsible for her father's death. Magnani grabs at Victor Jory as if she could kill him right then (though shouldn't Lady have suspected his guilt long before now?). She is more determined than ever to see the confectionery open, right under Jabe's nose. Magnani blots out all else; Lady works furiously for the scheduled opening that evening, ready to pick up where her father left off. As Lady intends to reverse a lifetime of defeats, Magnani plays this final section of the film with relentless drive. Even when Val's life is threatened and he wants to leave town, Lady will not listen to anything that might interfere with her impending triumph, which must be shared with Val. To the inhabitant of the bedroom upstairs, Magnani bellows, "Death must die before we can go."

This leads to one of the finest sequences in all the Williams films. After being fired by Lady, Jabe's snippy nurse (excellent Virgilia Chew) expects to shock and intimidate her by saying that she knew Lady was pregnant from the moment she laid eyes on her, adding that she also knew Jabe was not the baby's father. This is a brilliantly written moment, as one character, hoping to be bitchy, inadvertently offers joyous news. The scene appeared to be shaping up as a juicy face-off for two stirred-up actresses, but suddenly it shifts. Softly thanking the nurse for "telling me what I hoped for is true," Magnani puts Lady into an altered state. This transformation, informed by Lady's childlessness, is immense enough even to still her rage at Jabe. (As in *The Rose Tattoo,* a later-life pregnancy is a blessing, and, as in *Cat on a Hot Tin Roof,* talk of a pregnancy is the dramatic climax.) Inside the tinsel-strung confectionery with Brando, Magnani delivers, in one unbroken take, the great fig-tree monologue. (The text, though revised, goes all the way back to *Battle of Angels.*) As she holds him tenderly, Magnani, laughing and crying in the telling,

recounts Lady's childhood memory of the little long-barren fig tree that suddenly produced a fig. In her girlish excitement, she had run for the box of Christmas ornaments and hung the tree with tinsel, bells, birds, etc. It is extraordinarily moving to hear Magnani then tell Brando to "unpack the box of Christmas ornaments" and "put them on me, glass bells, glass birds, and icicles," as she pulls tinsel down onto her head and repeats "Put them on me" while running across the room and blissfully grabbing at more tinsel. The writing is beautiful, the setting enchanted, and the actress is an exhilarating mix of pure elation and profound gratitude. Further enhancing the celebration and its miraculous spirit, Magnani switches on the room's vast number of twinkling lights. But just as she speaks of her life beginning again, Lady is defeated once and for all. After Jabe starts a fire that quickly consumes the confectionery and eventually Val, he shoots Lady dead on the stairs. Her moment of victory, however brief, was full and satisfying, even though Lady is ultimately another Williams character (like Blanche DuBois) who cannot escape the world's cruel, destructive forces.

In *The Rose Tattoo,* Magnani had ventured a similar path to Lady's, away from rigidity (and a holding on to the past) and toward a chance-taking freedom. However, Serafina ends up ready to reap the benefits of her hard-earned life lessons. Magnani doesn't get to be funny in *The Fugitive Kind;* neither does she ever do her signature one-clap gesture, proving it was not something she did no matter the role. One last word about the valiant Maureen Stapleton. *The Fugitive Kind* was just her second movie, and she gives a gentle and thoughtful performance as the amateur painter married to the sheriff. Her sudden blindness is retained from *Orpheus Descending* but inexplicably gone are the lines about it being tied to her religious visions, making her blindness in the film both confusing and bizarre. Overall, the screenplay is true to the play, which, in turn, is closer to *Battle of Angels* than you might imagine. In 1961, one year after *The Fugitive Kind,* there would be another Williams film, *The Roman Spring of Mrs. Stone,* in which an older woman is vivified by her love for a younger man she first resists. Mrs. Stone and Lady awaken from numbing emotional stupors, yet things end badly for both of them.

Magnani had just one more major role in an important film before she died of cancer at age sixty-five in 1973. Pier-Paolo Pasolini's *Mamma Roma* (1962), not seen in the U.S. until three decades later, is a bleak portrait of contemporary Italy, with its Roman wasteland of cement housing projects and shards of ancient ruins. The film is rescued from complete despair by an electrifying Magnani as a prostitute trying to get out of the racket and lead a legitimate life for herself and her teenage son. Inventively filmed and unsentimentally conceived, *Mamma Roma* is a blistering look at Italy through one woman's struggle. As in many of her films, Magnani functions as a vibrant life force in a doomed situation. The film has two phenomenal sequences, both nighttime walks by Magnani, both uninterrupted five-minute takes. The first is her literal exit from prostitution, humorous and triumphant, and the second marks her sad return to the streets. Both scenes, monologues for Magnani, present her with revolving companions (other whores, a cop, two gay men, an athlete, etc.) as people drift in and out of the frame, listening to

her for a while, before being replaced by others. Her connection with Pasolini, another gay artist, feels similar to the bond she forged with Williams—intuitive and primal and expansive—encompassing life's highest highs and lowest lows.

There was one more American film, *The Secret of Santa Vittoria* (1969), a feeble WWII comedy from director Stanley Kramer, a reunion for Magnani with Anthony Quinn. *Santa Vittoria* is really an Anthony Quinn movie (he was still riding high from 1964's *Zorba the Greek*), with Magnani wasted, perhaps thankfully. Her final big-screen appearance, fittingly, was a cameo as herself in *Fellini's Roma* (1972), a final appreciation of her as Mamma Roma, the queen of Italian cinema. But we can thank Tennessee Williams for also making Magnani part of the American cinema with two of his prime roles, one comic and one dramatic. Whether laughing or crying (or doing both at once), Magnani seemed always to be covered in tinsel.

Paul Newman

*Paul Newman's Brick inhales Maggie's nightgown in one of many moments that exemplify what's so wrong with the movie version of **Cat on a Hot Tin Roof**.*

Paul Newman: Filmography

- *The Silver Chalice (1954)*
- *The Rack (1956)*
- *Somebody up There Likes Me (1956)*
- *The Helen Morgan Story (1957)*
- *Until They Sail (1957)*
- *The Left Handed Gun (1958)*
- *The Long, Hot Summer (1958)*
- *Cat on a Hot Tin Roof (1958)*
- *Rally 'Round the Flag, Boys! (1958)*
- *The Young Philadelphians (1959)*
- *From the Terrace (1960)*
- *Exodus (1960)*
- *The Hustler (1961)*
- *Paris Blues (1961)*
- *Sweet Bird of Youth (1962)*
- *Hemingway's Adventures of a Young Man (1962)*
- *Hud (1963)*
- *A New Kind of Love (1963)*
- *The Prize (1964)*
- *What a Way to Go! (1964)*
- *The Outrage (1964)*
- *Lady L (1965)*
- *Harper (1966)*
- *Torn Curtain (1966)*
- *Hombre (1967)*
- *Cool Hand Luke (1967)*
- *Rachel, Rachel (1968) (director)*
- *The Secret War of Harry Frigg (1968)*
- *Winning (1969)*
- *Butch Cassidy and the Sundance Kid (1969)*
- *WUSA (1970)*
- *Sometimes a Great Notion (1971) (also director)*
- *The Effect of Gamma Rays on Man-in-the-Moon Marigolds (1972) (director)*
- *Pocket Money (1972)*
- *The Life and Times of Judge Roy Bean (1972)*
- *The MacKintoch Man (1973)*
- *The Sting (1973)*
- *The Towering Inferno (1974)*
- *The Drowning Pool (1975)*
- *Silent Movie (1976)*
- *Buffalo Bill and the Indians, or Sitting Bull's History Lesson (1976)*
- *Slap Shot (1977)*
- *Quintet (1979)*
- *When Time Ran Out (1980)*
- *Fort Apache the Bronx (1981)*
- *Absence of Malice (1981)*
- *The Verdict (1982)*
- *Harry and Son (1984) (also director)*
- *The Color of Money (1986)*
- *The Glass Menagerie (1987) (director)*
- *Fat Man and Little Boy (1989)*
- *Blaze (1989)*
- *Mr. and Mrs. Bridge (1990)*
- *The Hudsucker Proxy (1994)*
- *Nobody's Fool (1994)*
- *Twilight (1998)*
- *Message in a Bottle (1999)*
- *Where the Money Is (2000)*
- *Road to Perdition (2002)*
- *Cars (2006) (voice only)*

Paul Newman (1925-2008)
Academy Award Wins

- **1986 Honorary Oscar**
- **Best Actor** of 1986 for *The Color of Money*
- **1994 Jean Hersholt Humanitarian Award**

Academy Award Nominations

- **Best Actor** of 1958 for *Cat on a Hot Tin Roof*
- **Best Actor** of 1961 for *The Hustler*
- **Best Actor** of 1963 for *Hud*
- **Best Actor** of 1967 for *Cool Hand Luke*
- **Best Picture** (as producer) of 1968 for *Rachel, Rachel*
- **Best Actor** of 1981 for *Absence of Malice*
- **Best Actor** of 1982 for *The Verdict*
- **Best Actor** of 1994 for *Nobody's Fool*
- **Best Supporting Actor** of 2002 for *Road to Perdition*

Brick Pollitt in *Cat on a Hot Tin Roof* (1958)
Chance Wayne in *Sweet Bird of Youth* (1962)

Alongside Marlon Brando is Paul Newman, the other male star closely identified with the work of Tennessee Williams, though neither of Newman's screen portrayals of Williams characters comes anywhere close to the high quality of Brando's performance in *Streetcar*. Newman would hone his acting skills significantly through the years, reaching his peak in his fifties and sixties, but initially he lacked the daring and originality of a major talent. Even so, in his first half-decade in movies his performances garnered respect for their reliable intelligence and serious-minded craftsmanship. But try picturing Newman and Brando in each other's roles for a moment. It is easy to imagine Newman as Stanley Kowalski in *Streetcar*, or in a non-Williams Brando role like Terry Malloy in *On the Waterfront*, but it also seems certain that neither film would have been as accomplished or complex with Newman in those roles. Then picture Brando in Newman's two Williams parts, Brick Pollitt in *Cat on a Hot Tin Roof* and Chance Wayne in *Sweet Bird of Youth*, and it isn't difficult to envision Brando baring aspects of both roles beyond what Williams wrote, adding the kind of unexpected touches that deepen a character and augment the meanings in the dialogue, thereby raising intriguing questions while supplying stimulating answers. Although Newman was merely ten months younger than Brando, he became a film star a half-decade later and always looked to be the noticeably younger man. (Newman would age incredibly well, while Brando seemed determined to destroy his beauty.) Both men were remarkable specimens in their prime, which merits mention because physical attractiveness was essential to all four of their Williams screen roles. Though Brando may have played Newman's two roles with more intricacy, Newman was the ideal physical type for Brick and Chance at the time the films were made, whereas Brando was already not quite the looker he had been a few years before. (By the time Newman starred in *Sweet Bird*, in 1962, Brando's years of playing studs were over.) Newman is unequivocally solid in his portrayals of Brick and Chance, but he rarely delivers more than what is on the pages of the scripts, offering clarity rather than illumination. This may not be constructive criticism but it is accurate: the main defect in these performances is that Newman isn't Brando, but, in fairness, even Brando could be accused, more than occasionally, of not living up to himself.

Born on January 26, 1925, in the fashionable Shaker Heights section of Cleveland, Newman was the son of a Catholic mother and a Jewish father, both of Eastern European extraction. After a youth inclined more toward athletics than dramatics, he enlisted in the Navy in 1943 and served in the Pacific. After the war, he more or less fell into acting, working in regional theatre before attending the Yale School of Drama in 1951. But he left Yale for New York in the summer of 1952, finding work in "live" television, the great training ground for actors of his generation. He also became a member of the Actors Studio (the *other* great training ground for any self-respecting New York actor of the day). Within a year, he landed a featured role in a Broadway smash, William Inge's *Picnic* (1953), playing the role assumed by Cliff Robertson in the 1955 film version, while also understudying Ralph Meeker in the lead. Hollywood took notice of Newman as quickly as Broadway had. Warner Brothers starred him, with "introducing" billing, in *The Silver Chalice* (1954), the studio's answer to Twentieth Century-Fox's Bible-themed mega-hit *The Robe* (1953). It was an inauspicious beginning for a legendary screen career, nearly annihilating his Hollywood future. *The Silver Chalice* has long been treated as a joke, notably by Newman himself, who certainly had the last laugh by becoming a superstar. Yes, *The Silver Chalice* is bad, but is it really any worse than a so-called *good* Bible-themed movie of its era (like, say, *The Robe* itself)? Crummy as it is, it has two stunning assets: a striking production design, filled with nonrealistic and imaginatively geometric sets; and Jack Palance as Simon the Magician. Palance, the John Malkovich (or Christopher Walken) of his day, offers a magnetically strange and flashy portrait of a megalomaniac who cynically plans to outdo Jesus' "tricks," and then comes to believe he is God. Unfortunately, Newman, who never appears with the subversive Palance, is stuck in the dull, virtuous part of the plot. No one can say that the critics were unfair to him. He is stiff and unsure, trying to be "real" but coming across as boring and stilted. (Apparently, it's problematic to bring the Actors Studio to the first century A.D.) Newman plays a great Greek artisan hired to craft the silver chalice that will house Jesus' cup from the Last Supper, but the best that can be said of his acting is that he has the lean, hairless torso of a classical statue. He is caught between two women, the anachronistically glamorous temptress Virginia Mayo, invariably gowned as if about to present an Oscar, and the incessantly pious Pier Angeli. You can't become a star behaving as passively as Newman did here, especially with that Palance fellow nearby.

After a successful return to Broadway as the bad guy in the 1955 thriller *The Desperate Hours,* co-starring Karl Malden and directed by Robert Montgomery, Newman soon found the Hollywood stardom that had eluded him. (When *The Desperate Hours* was filmed, also in 1955, Newman's role went to Humphrey Bogart.) His second film, *The Rack* (1956), is a respectable courtroom drama unsurprisingly (because of its visual limitations) based on a teleplay (by Rod Serling). Newman returns from a North Korean P.O.W. camp and is charged with collaboration. With its serious subject matter and thin psychology, *The Rack* feels both weighty and simplistic. It is also the first of Newman's father-son dramas, opposite Walter Pidgeon, paving the way for the familial showdowns of *Cat on a Hot Tin Roof* and *Hud.* Newman fared far better than he had in *The Silver Chalice,* but no one saw *The Rack.* It was the next one, another film with father-son rumblings, that made him a movie star. Designed as a vehicle for James Dean, *Somebody up There Likes Me* (1956), the biopic about boxer Rocky Graziano, came to Newman following Dean's untimely death. Graziano is a robust character who encouraged Newman out of his shell and into an extroverted and charismatic performance. The movie is conventional, tilted toward its feel-good aspects, but it's well made by Robert Wise, absorbing and beautifully shot in black and white. Though Newman is obviously "acting" rather than "being" Graziano, his confidence level is conspicuously higher than what it had been when he was paired alongside a chalice. Again, no signs of audacity or insight in his acting, but he does superbly in the ring (which gives further screen time

to his young-god torso). Newman was again teamed with Pier Angeli (as Mrs. Graziano), but this time, breaking their jinx, they were comfortably matched.

In the substandard musical biopic *The Helen Morgan Story* (1957), starring Ann Blyth, Newman has a Cagney-type role, a fast-talking bootlegger, but the hackneyed script was insurmountable, resulting in his two-dimensional acting. Opposite the lacquered and impenetrable Blyth, in what must be the most uninteresting performance of an alcoholic in movie history, Newman at least injects the picture with what little zip it has. *Until They Sail* (1957), his second film for Robert Wise, was a step up, a classy and reasonably adult WWII soap, a home-front drama set in New Zealand and focused more on sex than war, but, specifically, sex in wartime. Again subservient to a female star (Jean Simmons), Newman is a cynical U.S. major who finds love in Simmons' arms. In an undemanding role, Newman is nicely relaxed on-screen, free from the pressure of carrying a not quite good-enough movie. If 1957 seemed to stall his momentum, it was 1958 that solidified his stardom. First up was *The Left Handed Gun,* based on Gore Vidal's teleplay about Billy the Kid, which had starred Newman on the small screen in 1955. Arthur Penn's intermittently effective feature-film version is noted more for its violence than its storytelling, which is emotionally and dramatically uninvolving. The conception of Billy is that of a 1950s-style rebel youth, making the role more suited to a James Dean type than a thirtyish Newman. It would be his two other, more commercially minded (and financially profitable) 1958 films that really put him over. Martin Ritt's Mississippi-set potboiler *The Long, Hot Summer* was the first of Newman's ten big-screen appearances with Joanne Woodward, whom he married soon after the film wrapped. Based on several William Faulkner stories, *The Long, Hot Summer* is overheated and skindeep, but Newman brandishes the cocky sexuality of a full-fledged movie star. He plays a drifter, a good guy cloaked in a bad-boy pose, a misunderstood hunk who eventually thaws Woodward, a wealthy and strong-willed schoolteacher. (Orson Welles, over the top as Woodward's father, appears to be auditioning for *Cat on a Hot Tin Roof*'s Big Daddy.) It is hard to praise a drama that wastes Lee Remick and Angela Lansbury while flaunting Anthony Franciosa, with further damage inflicted by its romantic-comedy fade-out. But it surely is a pleasure to see Newman take such command. The performance won him the Best Actor prize at the Cannes Film Festival.

After *The Long, Hot Summer,* which feels like imitation Tennessee Williams, Newman got his shot at the real thing, the screen version of Williams' 1955 Pulitzer Prize-winning play, which Williams cites in *Memoirs* as his favorite among his plays. (Fine as it is, can it truly rate with the astounding beauty and lingering depths of *The Glass Menagerie* or *A Streetcar Named Desire*?) Like *The Long, Hot Summer,* the film of *Cat* is another steamy Mississippi-set drama, but it was an even bigger box-office winner and more of a critics' darling. With Elizabeth Taylor as his co-star, it was one of those match-ups in which the two best-looking movie stars of the moment are irresistibly united. Mr. Blue Eyes and Ms. Violet Eyes together at last! I wish I could report that the movie was worthy of the acclaim it received, but it is actually one of the more bowdlerized and exasperating of the Williams films. Perhaps the play would have fared better as a movie if the production had been delayed, just a few years, until the material wouldn't have had to be so gutted and tamed for the censors. MGM's first-class mounting, which made *Cat* the first Williams film to be photographed in color, was a definite prestige project. It had the bonus commercial advantage of being about beautiful people and their sexual problems. After all the lust aimed at Carroll Baker in *Baby Doll, Cat* restored the male as the object of desire in a Williams film, the place he had occupied in *Streetcar* and *Rose Tattoo.* But not since the debacle of the 1950 film version of *The Glass Menagerie* had a Williams piece been so distorted, so muddled in its meanings and simplified beyond recognition. Audiences must have been confounded as to what in heck was going on, but they were sufficiently pleased by the gorgeous stars, the glamorous treatment, and the blatantly erotic situations. Who cared if it was incoherent?

Newman has all the components of an ideal Brick: devastatingly attractive; scaldingly humorous; forceful when it counts; smart enough to get all the crackle out of Williams' words; and sure of his Southern accent. It is not his fault that the screenplay, as it veers further and further from the play, reduces Brick to a more standardized and less dramatically honest character. *Streetcar,* too, had made modifications on its path to the movies, but its integrity had been protected by Williams and direc-

tor Elia Kazan. When *Cat* came to Hollywood, it was transformed (and not in the good way) when Richard Brooks (who also directed) and James Poe handled the adaptation. (*Every* good line comes from the play.) In Pat McGilligan's book of interviews, *Backstory 2,* Brooks explains that Poe had written a complete screenplay for director George Cukor, a gay man who eventually withdrew because "it wasn't possible to deal honestly with the homosexuality" (Cukor's words to Gavin Lambert in the book *On Cukor*). The final *Cat* screenplay melds Poe's script with Brooks' alterations, which are most evident in his virtually brand-new third act. Without Williams or Kazan (who directed *Cat* on Broadway) at the helm, there was less of a responsibility to safeguard the material's original intentions and values. However, it must be said that *Cat* posed more of a challenge for Hollywood than *Streetcar* had (even though it was filmed seven years later), primarily because homosexuality, still a Production Code taboo, was more integral to *Cat*'s plot than it had been to *Streetcar*'s. There is nothing inherently wrong with the adaptation's approach; the problem is that none of the new scenes or dialogue is on par with Williams, with all the reworked motivations and revelations coming off as lame and empty. The play is used as a jumping-off mark for a movie that wends its way toward inoffensive blather, discarding anything genuinely provocative from Williams' text while trying to retain its bold and steamy aura. The first half of the film works moderately well because of its essential faithfulness to Williams, but then the disintegration begins and quickly accelerates. It is ironic that Brooks made an early mark as the author of *The Brick Foxhole,* a 1945 military novel about the murder of a gay man. When it became the film *Crossfire* (1947), adapted by another writer, the homosexual had become a straight Jew, replacing homophobia with anti-Semitism.

Cat's screen version opens on the night before the play begins, with a prologue showing how Brick broke his ankle. Newman is seen at a high-school field, downing a liquor bottle, hearing imagined cheers, and then attempting to run the hurdles and falling on his fourth jump. This is entirely unnecessary, since Brick is one of those Williams creations who evokes an iconic image: the comely young man in pajamas, with a crutch under one arm and a drink in his opposing hand. His "crutch" is essential to who he is, and it seems blasphemous ever to see Brick without it. The crutch and the cast on his ankle represent his handicap, his inability to live comfortably. Newman is next seen sprawled on a couch, with Brick back where he belongs dramatically, restored to his pajamas, his crutch, and his drink. The setting is the mansion of Brick's parents, Big Daddy (Burl Ives) and Big Mama (Judith Anderson). Worth ten million dollars, Big Daddy owns 28,000 acres of fertile land. Brick is the prodigal son, the favorite, whereas his older brother, Gooper (Jack Carson), who has played by the rules, is unappreciated. Brick is here from New Orleans with his wife of three years, Maggie (Elizabeth Taylor), for the double occasion of Big Daddy's return from a clinic, where he has been undergoing tests, and his sixty-fifth birthday. For the first section of the play and the film, Brick merely listens as Maggie does most of the talking, yet it is Brick who holds all the power in their relationship because he's the one with nothing to lose, having already given up. There's something wrong with their childless marriage, but it isn't yet apparent what that trouble might be. Maggie is consumed with protecting Brick's part of Big Daddy's fortune from Gooper's grasp, even though Brick shows no interest (in this or anything else). What does become clear is that Brick will not sleep with Maggie, despite her pleas. Here the film sets up an enticing hook: why in the world doesn't Paul Newman want to sleep with Elizabeth Taylor? (This is as mystifying a question as it would be in Hitchcock's *Marnie* [1964], when people wondered why Tippi Hedren wouldn't have sex with hubby Sean Connery.) And why is Brick still *with* Maggie if he detests her? *Cat on a Hot Tin Roof* is about getting Brick to talk, though Newman says very different things than Ben Gazzara's Brick said in the original stage production.

The biggest flaw in Newman's performance is that it feels too impeccably worked out. Every line reading sounds well-rehearsed, leaving little room for a spontaneous reaction or a fleeting nuance. Newman gets every intended value from Williams' lines, as well as the screenwriters', but nothing he does suggests an individual interpretation of the role. You can feel him reaching, in the big emotional moments, for a depth he can't deliver, as though he were imitating another actor rather than investing himself more intuitively (in the Actors Studio manner). He fares better in humorous moments. When he tries to hit Taylor with his crutch, failing and falling, he is discovered on the floor by one of his nieces who wants to know what's happened. Newman, with a wicked glint, tells her, "I tried to kill your Aunt Maggie." Then, on why he was jumping hurdles, he tells her, with smooth eloquence, "People like to do what they used to do, after they've stopped being able to do it." Williams has him call her "little girl," a clever way to tell us that Brick has no idea what the names of his nieces and nephews are. Newman also gets the comic dryness out of the moment when Big Daddy asks him why, as a committed alcoholic, he doesn't just kill himself: "Cause I like to drink." His sting is less comic but sharp and cool when Maggie tells him how fertile she is and he wonders how she can conceive "by a man who cannot stand you." Aside from such flickering examples of Newman's sly wit, the performance essentially operates in two keys, repressed emotion and flat-out anger, with a deficiency in riveting transitions and simmering ambiguities.

Brick (an obviously ironic name for someone who refuses to become erect) will not fight for anything, not his wife, not Big Daddy's money, not the sports-announcing job he recently quit. He was once a professional football player, but, at thirty, he's past his glory days. As Taylor rambles on, Newman has several moments in which to reject her blatantly: refusing to look when she asks if her nylon seams are straight; using his crutch to block her from getting too close; rising when she moves to kiss him; wiping her kiss off his mouth; not even drinking from a glass that has touched her lips. She catches him looking at her in the mirror, deducing that his look contains suppressed lust. The movie makes the same deduction, the first sign that something is awry. Is Brick *forcibly* denying himself the pleasure of Maggie's body as a way to punish them both? Is he avoiding contact because he *can't* resist her? (In the bathroom, Newman inhales her nightgown, caresses it, and then tosses it to the floor.) He speaks to her about "the conditions" (no sex) on which he has agreed to continue living with her. The conflict in their marriage goes back to Skipper, Brick's best friend and teammate. Any mention of Skipper riles him, even though that name is never far from his thoughts. In the play, Skipper is gay; he confessed his feelings to Brick (who hung up on him) and soon died from drugs and alcohol.

Though Big Daddy is told that the clinic tests have all come back negative, Brick is told the truth by the family doctor: Big Daddy is dying of cancer. When Big Daddy joins his son for a talk, Brick, at his father's urging, begins to talk about why he drinks. It is for the "click" he gets, the moment when he feels he has found temporary peace, an escape from reality. Brick is an alcoholic, but he was conceived by Williams as a poetic drunk, the kind who never seems to *be* drunk, who never sloshes words or laughs too much or goes into rages. Brick's alcoholism seems false, a theatrical and romanticized means of detachment. He drinks without losing lucidity and he's never embarrassing. Newman plays the alcoholism as written, with crisp self-pity and neatly organized bitterness, but wouldn't it be more appropriate to see Brick having more of a struggle, fighting the effects of the booze, or giving in to them, as he battles his wife and his father? But Brick, his drink firmly clasped in his hand, is never at a loss for just the right words. The reasons for his drinking begin to emerge: "disgust," "mendacity," "lies and liars." When Big Daddy mentions Skipper, thunder literally (and laughably) crashes. Newman's defensiveness—his references to "the gutter," his use of words like "shameful" and "filthy"—is a direct response to implications of gayness. But the homosexuality that remains in the movie is in the context of something to be accused of *falsely* (as in *Tea and Sympathy*) and as a horrible misinterpretation of hero worship or ideal friendship. Here gayness has the potential to put an unwarranted blight on Brick's clean masculinity. In the movie, Skipper died—in a far flashier death than his descent into self-destruction in the play—when he leapt from an eleventh-floor hotel-room window. Brick says, "Skipper is the only thing that I got left to believe in," which makes increasingly less sense as the screenplay desperately blurs and rewrites Williams into the mainstream.

"It was too rare to be normal," Brick says in the play, holding his bond with Skipper on a pedestal. Even if his subtext remains mysterious to an audience, any actor playing Brick has to decide just how gay, bisexual, or straight Brick is, unless you're in the 1958 movie in which it's a moot point. Brick can be played straight, ignorant of homosexuality and thoroughly blindsided by Skipper's feelings, which would cause him to re-examine the nature of their closeness. A heterosexual Brick would still

be wracked with guilt and depression over his key role in a friend's death. But latent homosexuality is obviously a stronger and more complex dramatic choice, and it is firmly supported in the text. Then there's the question of whether or not the "friendship" was sexual. Since Skipper's phone-call confession is such a huge event, it can be assumed that the relationship was not sexual. But a case could still be made that physical intimacy had occurred, the kind that was permissible as long as it was never spoken about or in any way acknowledged. Brick cannot forgive Maggie because she forced the issue with Skipper, directly challenging his feelings for Brick. Trying to prove himself straight, Skipper fumbled his attempt at having sex with Maggie. Then came his admission to Brick of his true feelings. Where Skipper erred was in expressing these feelings out loud, making them *real* and no longer avoidable, thus forcing Brick to address his own sexuality, something he preferred to keep compartmentalized. There would be obvious terror for him, a he-man football player having to face the prospect of being in love with his best friend. Knowing what the world, including himself, thinks of such men, Brick was ill-equipped to handle this. And Skipper's willingness (however agonized) to broach the subject made it impossible for the friendship to continue. The only response Brick could muster was to hang up on Skipper. Maggie connived to show both men the truth and they responded by turning to alcohol. All illusions of "hero worship" were shattered. To play Brick straight is to miss his ferocious, overemphatic defensiveness regarding his sexuality. His self-loathing blazes through the play's big scene with Big Daddy, as Brick rattles off a litany of gay slurs. What's most astounding is Big Daddy's tolerant and modern attitude on the issue, far more accepting and compassionate than Brick's. Big Daddy worked for a gay male couple, eventually inheriting their property and turning it into his empire. As Brick grapples with the meaning of his attachment to Skipper, and Big Daddy learns he has terminal cancer, the play is about facing substantial and demanding truths. The movie is too sanitized to compete. How can you make a movie about facing truth when one of the main characters is let off the hook?

In the play, Maggie doesn't appear in the father-son heart-to-heart, but the movie allows her to defend herself in the revised version of events. Not only is Skipper no longer gay, but he was more than willing to sleep with his best friend's wife. In the play, Skipper's tearful phone call was a disclosure of gay love, but in the movie it is his rather fuzzy and unconvincing expression of dependency on Brick's emotional and professional support. In both versions, Skipper needed Brick, but in the movie the need hardly reaches suicidal proportions. When Newman says the new line, "How does one drowning man help another drowning man?" what is he talking about? Why, at that point, was Newman's Brick drowning? Why did *this* Brick hang up, and why did *this* Skipper have to die? After the hang-up, Brick refused to answer his repeatedly ringing phone. (The "click" stops the ever-ringing phone in his head.) The screen Brick resents Maggie because he believes Skipper's lie about his sleeping with her. I guess you could say that Skipper lied to make Brick leave Maggie, the interloper. In short order, the movie has made Skipper merely weak, Maggie innocent of infidelity, and Brick unambiguously straight. Purified over the course of their rather bland and implausible admissions, Brick and Maggie are refashioned into more typically sympathetic movie characters, rendered less challenging for the 1958 audience. What is retained from the play is Brick's sense of guilt. In this respect, Brick is a male Blanche DuBois. Both characters plummet because of enduring remorse for their participation in the death of a beloved person, someone who took his life after their cruel rejection at a vulnerable moment, and, at least in the plays, for the exact same reason. Unable to forgive themselves, Brick and Blanche cannot seem to function in ordinary life.

Cat on a Hot Tin Roof is a play with two third acts, one that Williams originally intended and another that opened on Broadway after rewrites suggested by Kazan, who was correct in encouraging Williams to include in Act III a character as dominant and flamboyant as Big Daddy. But Kazan was wrong to propose that Brick needed to make discernible emotional progress, a way to make the play easier to digest. (Kazan writes in his autobiography how angry he was at Williams for writing—in the play's published edition, which features both third acts—that Kazan's influence compromised his play. Kazan states that Williams could have refused his ideas but didn't.) The movie applies the basic form of the Broadway third act, with much of Williams' rewritten dialogue, yet

it feels more like the handiwork of the screenwriters. The movie takes it much further, though, meaning that it makes it much worse. After Brick inadvertently reveals to his father the truth about the cancer and then realizes how deeply he has hurt him, Brick is, thereafter, and quite miraculously, a man reborn. (This is symbolically augmented by Brick's accidental breaking of his crutch.) And you don't believe it for a second. Newman, out of pajamas and into a shirt and trousers, is no longer interested in drinking. But with his instant cure comes smug superiority. (I liked Newman better when he was brooding and sarcastic.) He follows Big Daddy down to the cellar, a space cluttered with a museum-warehouse's worth of acquisitions accumulated from Big Daddy and Big Mama's European spree. Brick arrives to apologize in what quickly descends into the worst scene in the movie, a total invention and an utterly banal way to treat Williams' initially fascinating characters. The gist of it is that Big Daddy can't express love; he can only offer material things. Brick's closeness to Skipper is reduced to a Daddy-didn't-love-me-enough diagnosis. (Boys need Skippers when they have distant Daddys? Why not throw in the fact that Big Mama was too clinging?) All Brick wanted was Big Daddy's love, not his money. Newman gets a gratuitous breakdown, shouting "I don't want things!" as he trashes the joint, a moment sympathetically witnessed by Taylor's Maggie, discreetly hidden on the stairs. Newman, finally sober, *now* gets to act all-out drunk! It's a big, empty tirade climaxed with tears and delivered by Newman with a generic intensity. "All I wanted was a father not a boss," he says, as you cringe at what's being done to Williams. The platitudes keep on coming: "You own us but you don't love us."

But the scene still has lower to go, with a new monologue for Burl Ives about Big Daddy's hobo father, a painfully sentimentalized account of the happy bum Big Daddy adored. Brick allows Big Daddy to acknowledge his own father's love. *Cat on a Hot Tin Roof* has just become a male-bonding heartwarmer, with Brick suddenly so wise and preachy, the model son who a few hours earlier was a drop-out drunk. His unearned authority is rather unpleasant and it undermines him as a multi-faceted character. Peace has settled between father and son in just two conversations over the course of one day. Overtaken by literal-minded slop, this no longer feels like a Williams movie. When Maggie tells

Before Big Daddy

Cat on a Hot Tin Roof first began life as *Three Players of a Summer Game*, a 1952 Williams short story about Brick Pollitt, an alcoholic and former college athlete, and his wife, Margaret, a Mardi Gras queen and debutante. This Brick begins an affair with his doctor's widow, gaining back some of his self-respect. The "game" is croquet and the third "player" is the widow's daughter. Here we learn the origin of Brick's name, a nickname referring to his "flame-colored" face (not his onetime virility). A handsome redhead, Brick ends up with the conquering Margaret, returning to his drunken and emasculated state. *Three Players* is barely an outline for *Cat*, a starting-off point, an early formulation of its lead characters and their unhappiness, ultimately bearing little resemblance to the play it inspired. After all, there's no Big Daddy and no Skipper.

Big Daddy the lie that she is pregnant, Brick plays along (as he does in the Broadway Act III, and as he doesn't in the original version), standing up for his wife none too believably against his brother and sister-in-law. Brick is suddenly amused by his wife—and here Williams is again abandoned altogether—eventually calling for her to join him upstairs and then lowering the lights in their bedroom. With Brick's virility restored and Maggie softly feminized, all is right with the world. "We're through with lies and liars in this house," he tells her, and then asks her to lock the door. Newman and Taylor at last have a real kiss. The film ends with the memorable image of Newman tossing his pillow to join hers on their brass bed. Gone is the great final line from the non-Broadway ending, when Brick, submissively about to bed Maggie, responds to her declaration of love with "Wouldn't it be funny if that was true?"

The direction of Richard Brooks is so compromised by his writing that it's hard even to grant him credit for making such a good-looking movie, photographed by William Daniels (the favorite cameraman of Greta Garbo). Despite the attractive visuals, Brooks allows things to get fairly stagy and talky, especially once his script starts to deteriorate. The first Brick-Big Daddy confrontation is an attempt to open things up, moving from bedroom to stairs to living room to outside in the rain, which works well enough until Newman and Ives are ridiculously forced to act in a downpour. Brooks wisely didn't resort to dramatizing flashbacks of Skipper, an especially good decision considering what the film does to Skipper's story. (Brooks' major film before *Cat* was the taut and exciting 1955 schoolroom drama *Blackboard Jungle*, a far riskier and propulsive, though also dated, movie.) It is immensely disappointing that the massive Burl Ives, repeating his celebrated stage performance and billed above the title after Taylor and Newman, gives such a mechanical performance, never doing anything unpredictable or truly affecting. (Ives was a mere forty-eight when filming began!) He appears to be preserving his Broadway performance rather than re-inventing it for the movies, coming across as a powerful but distant force. Ives won the Oscar that year as Best Supporting Actor for *The Big Country*, a performance that contains all the magnetism and churning depths absent from his screen Big Daddy. As Big Mama, Judith Anderson gives an outsized performance, acting up a storm and never quite adjusting to the movie around her. (To see Anderson at her finest, check out her brilliant work in the 1950 Anthony Mann western *The Furies*.) I wish the original Big Mama, Mildred Dunnock, had gotten the chance to repeat her stage performance for the screen. The movie even softens Brick's relationship with Gooper, allowing them a truce at the end. Jack Carson, the 1940s Warner Brothers contract player, seems an odd, out-of-place choice for Gooper (only one year younger than Ives), but he does score in his emotional scene with Big Mama.

The film received six Oscar nominations, for picture, actor, actress, director, screenplay, and color cinematography. It won no statuettes, nor should it have, losing in its four non-acting categories to Vincente Minnelli's *Gigi*, a chic musical but unintentionally creepy (in its borderline pedophilia). *Gigi* was yet another example of the Academy opting for a safe (and seemingly highbrow) choice. The voters ran scared from the best of the five nominees, the race-relations drama *The Defiant Ones*, as well as *Vertigo* and *Touch of Evil*, the year's two non-nominated masterworks. Newman lost to David Niven in *Separate Tables*, an effective change of pace for the light-comic actor, shockingly cast as a sexually deviant military major (a movie-theatre masher). Niven gave an achingly clenched performance, poignantly masking his character's terror. He was the freshest element in, like *Cat,* an overrated and superficial adaptation of an adult Broadway hit. Newman and Niven later appeared together in the comic calamity *Lady L* (1965).

Newman finished 1958 in another pairing with Woodward, the woebegone suburban "comedy" *Rally 'Round the Flag, Boys!* which had him again alongside *Cat* brother Jack Carson, meanwhile juggling wife Woodward and temptress Joan Collins. Though he pushes for laughs, Newman does display some loose giddiness, at least in his drunken cha-cha with Collins. (*Rally 'Round* was the beginning of the Newmans' string of unfortunate collaborations.) Solidifying his matinee-idol status, Newman was kept occupied in glitzy soaps whose artificiality, matched to his inability to rise above hollow material, was no help in his progress as an actor or as any kind of challenge to Brando. *The Young Philadelphians* (1959) gave him one of his wonder-boy roles, a poor fellow who rises in the world of law, falling prey to the evils of mean old success! Newman is self-assured, if uninspired, as a corporate tax lawyer redeemed by his sudden emergence as a brilliant trial lawyer. Though the film is shallow to its core, it is surely better than the rancid *From the Terrace* (1960), in which Newman is a rich fellow, again dealing with Daddy troubles and again maneuvering ambition and ugly success, this time on Wall Street. His acting lacks the requisite drive, further dampened by his insipid romance with sweet and boring Ina Balin. Again opting for redemption, he chucks the rat race and his marriage to a cheating society-girl (Woodward). *From the Terrace* was a blazing box-office hit, but *Paris Blues,* his next with Woodward, wasn't, thus ending their brief time as a popular screen team. *Paris Blues* is all tired clichés revamped against the hip background of Parisian jazz clubs. Aiming for a French New Wave look, director Martin Ritt focused on the black-and-white visuals, all but abandoning the tepid dramatics involving Paris-based Newman, a trombonist yearning to be a serious composer, and his affair with a vacationing Woodward. Though socially, sexually, and racially liberal for its time, *Paris Blues* is a flimsy mood piece, all milieu and no verve. The sight of Newman and "saxophonist" Sidney Poitier jamming with Louis Armstrong is bizarre and monumentally unconvincing.

Newman also accepted more serious fare during this period, perhaps knowing that career longevity could not be sustained on the likes (however profitable) of *From the Terrace. Exodus* (1960) was a biggie, an Otto Preminger-helmed epic about the formation of the state of Israel, with Newman playing a Palestinian Jew of Russian descent (though he's completely American in every way). The film has its moments, yet it's remarkably uninvolving and is endlessly long. When Eva Marie Saint, as Newman's gentile love interest, asks, regarding the Middle East problem, "How is it ever going to end?" you're sure she's talking about the movie. Newman gives one of his worst performances, shockingly disengaged and uninteresting and matched by Saint's lifelessness. Their romance should personalize our investment in the historical elements but serves merely to drag things out further. However earnest and well-intentioned, the movie never rises to its subject. But the next one put Newman at the top of his profession, fulfilling the promise shown in his best work from the fifties.

The Hustler (1961), easily the best film he had yet made (and probably the best film he *ever* made), is a literate and psychologically probing drama set in the grubby world of pool halls. Robert Rossen directed with a conspicuous anti-Hollywood grit and maturity (though he couldn't resist a conventional ending). As "Fast Eddie" Felson, a born loser with the pool-shooting talent to become a winner, Newman excellently delivers the cocky bravado, the sexy charm, and the self-destructive tendencies, a believable combination of brains and stupidity. What he doesn't have is the imaginative instincts of a great actor, what a Brando or Cagney or Olivier could unleash at their very best. Good as Newman is here, it would still be years before he could deliver performances of uncommon depths and illuminating surprises, finally fulfilling the supposed mission of the Method with ostensibly "personal" acting. Newman often appears blocked in his early films, not yet free enough to be great, unable to give of himself fully. In *The Hustler,* he is somewhat shown up by the superb work around him, from George C. Scott's electrifying portrait of cool malevolence, and Piper Laurie's aching, unadorned work as Newman's sad girlfriend. (Laurie and Newman had previously shared one brief scene together in *Until They Sail.*) *The Hustler* is about mind games, in and out of the poolroom, and it gets muddled only at the end, self-

consciously reaching for profundity while also providing a too "satisfying" finish. Newman, in what had become almost a formula, grows up, ditches it all, and is cleansed. He deserved his Oscar nomination and was favored to win the gold-plated prize, but Maximilian Schell (*Judgment at Nuremburg*) was the victor for a far less intricate, though showy, role. Newman would, in fact, get an Oscar for playing Eddie, but he had to wait a mere twenty-five years.

Despite the steady stream of film work, Newman had opted to spend the bulk of 1959 starring on Broadway in Tennessee Williams' new play *Sweet Bird of Youth,* which opened just after Newman received his Oscar nomination for *Cat on a Hot Tin Roof,* making him very much *the* Williams actor of the moment. It was only a matter of time before *Sweet Bird* made it to the screen, and there was no need to look for a big movie star to play Chance Wayne because one of the biggest of movie stars just happened to be the actor who created the role. Not messing with success, the film version, like the celluloid *Cat,* would be an MGM production directed by Richard Brooks, who would also write the screenplay (by himself, without another writer receiving co-credit, which had been the case with *Cat.*) Also like *Cat, Sweet Bird* made the transition from an Elia Kazan-directed stage production to a Brooks-directed film. Between his Williams pictures, Brooks won an Oscar for his screenplay of *Elmer Gantry* (1960), a film he also directed, another adult drama and far superior to either of his Williams adaptations. Though *Sweet Bird* did not undergo the extent of censor-conscious (and distorting) rewrites suffered by *Cat,* it was still negatively modified by Brooks. (If Kazan had directed the films of *Cat* and *Sweet Bird,* he never would have condoned such tramplings over Williams' original material, which is one of the reasons why his films of *Streetcar* and *Baby Doll* remain so fine.) *Cat* is certainly a better play than *Sweet Bird,* and even in shards it is the more memorable film. *Sweet Bird* may be truer to Williams, but to a less-good Williams.

Brooks followed his model for success—the critical and financial feats of *Cat*—by giving *Sweet Bird* the same softening treatment, treating it as a customarily bombastic Southern melodrama of familial and political corruption, and also by sentimentalizing its romantic leads into star-crossed lovers. Brooks was clearly shaping the material for commercial success but was also making much of it forgettable and ordinary, sanding away the play's roughest edges and pulling back from challenging his audiences. *Sweet Bird* is still an often good, enjoyable movie, and it's never boring, but it's not as visually entrancing as *Cat,* despite its flashy editing techniques and multiple flashbacks. (Brooks made *Cat* without incorporating a single flashback, in a plot which had afforded him many an opportunity, while his *Sweet Bird* adaptation utilizes a significant number of flashed-back scenes.) With four major cast members from the Broadway production (Newman, Geraldine Page, Rip Torn, and Madeleine Sherwood), *Sweet Bird* has more heavyweight original-cast members on hand than any Williams film since *Streetcar.*

Chance would appear to be an ideal Newman role, a virile and ambitious operator out to climb to the top. About a decade ago, he was a poor, good-looking star athlete (a diver) who fell for rich-girl Heavenly Finley (Shirley Knight). Her father, Tom "Boss" Finley (Ed Begley), is a former governor and still the most powerful politician in the state (unnamed, but on the Gulf Coast). Boss Finley wanted Chance out of the way, and so he disingenuously encouraged the young man to leave St. Cloud and seek his fortune in New York. Chance found minor success in show business, including a cover of *Life* magazine as one of three chorus boys in a Broadway show (identified as *Oklahoma!* in the play but nameless in the movie). Though he continued to believe in his potential for stardom, Chance scored bigger as a sexual companion to wealthy ladies. As a beach boy in Palm Beach, he recently latched on to Alexandra Del Lago (Geraldine Page), an apparently washed-up movie queen who, compromised by booze and drugs, signed him to a personal contract. With the strung-out Alexandra in tow, Chance returns to St. Cloud and into the Regal Palms Hotel, expecting to reunite with Heavenly and whisk her away with him to Hollywood. He doesn't know that he impregnated Heavenly on his previous visit home and that she had an abortion. The plot is two-pronged, focused on both Alexandra and the Finley family, with Chance at the center of each scenario. Like *The Fugitive Kind,* *Sweet Bird* is concentrated on a male character but utterly dominated by female forces. Geraldine Page's Alexandra has about half the screen time allotted to Newman's Chance, but the person you remember is Page, just as in *The Fugitive Kind* it's Anna Magnani and Joanne Woodward who overshadow Marlon Brando. Chance is one more male sex object in a Williams film and, coming after Warren Beatty in *The Roman Spring of Mrs. Stone,* the second leading Williams role of a high-class male prostitute.

During the opening credits, Chance is seen driving Alexandra's white Cadillac convertible; she is passed out in the backseat. A sign reads "You Are Now Leaving Florida" as they ride west along the coast. The film's title sprawls across the screen, right to left, in the *Gone With the Wind* manner, soon followed by some unnecessary action involving Chance driving recklessly in the rain, mere filler before the "play" begins. On arrival at the hotel, Newman displays the strut of a man primed to show everyone what a big shot he has become. He orders a suite for himself and his movie star, knowing that word will spread quickly. Newman, in golden-boy mode, is a Southern-accented charmer who savors his good looks, and he's riding particularly high because it finally looks as though everything has come his way. His first real scene, in the suite, is with Dr. George Scudder (Philip Abbott), a nondescript fellow and the local hospital's chief of staff. The news of Chance's mother's death results in the first instance in which Newman's performance delivers the outer indications of emotion without anything underneath. He sits, holds his upper arms, wrinkles his eyes, and puts his chin on his chest, suggesting grief but devoid of honest, individual expression. Scudder warns Chance to leave town, the first of several people to do so, followed by the stunner that Scudder is to marry Heavenly. Though Newman's anger, here and elsewhere, often feels nonspecific and repetitive, he does come through with some intimate feeling regarding Heavenly. Chance later tells Alexandra that the biggest difference between people is "those that have had pleasure in love and those that haven't," a line from the play though it sounds more like the romanticizing Brooks.

Alexandra treats Chance like a servant, which he temporarily is, but Newman plays him with the spark of someone who thinks he is actually holding the position of power. Chance is a fairly naïve young man, never quite sharp enough to be the equal of the monsters he will encounter throughout this Easter weekend. (The play takes place entirely on Easter Sunday.) Chance, in the movie more than the play, seems surprisingly innocent despite his past,

and his and Heavenly's unwavering love is treated as something eternally pure, no matter what, all of which seems intended to provide balance with the film's more sordid elements. Chance is presented as a love-struck man trying hard to be a shameless conniver, though conniving doesn't come as naturally to him as it does to most of the characters around him. The Hollywoodized notion here is that Chance, however sleazy his actions have been, has done everything in the name of love, as a means to a happy romantic ending. He is not a very deep fellow, but in the play his struggles and hungers feel more complicated and compulsive, and his desperation more harried and vivid. Newman cannot make believable the fact that time is already Chance's enemy, with his heyday as a gigolo nearing its termination date. He says in the play that he is twenty-nine, but his exact age is omitted from the screenplay. In Williams' stage directions, he describes Chance as having a "ravaged young face" that is "still exceptionally good-looking" and a body that "shows no decline." Newman, in his mid-thirties, is at the peak of his handsomeness and appeal, with decades to go (as time would prove) of movie-star attractiveness. Nowhere near the first hint of waning beauty, Newman is simply too devastating to be Chance Wayne. Any Hollywood studio would sign this guy about five seconds after looking at him. But Chance is *not* going to be discovered, and he shouldn't be twinkling with Newman's obvious star quality. When Page, out of her stoned haze, finally gets a good look at him, watch Newman preen, enjoying his undimmed power over those who can appreciate the male figure. Such impact is too much coming from a delusional loser like Chance Wayne. The only way Newman could have compensated for his physical perfection would have been to heighten his level of desperation, with Chance truly believing, despite evidence to the contrary, that time is running out and that Alexandra might actually be his last chance to cash in on his charms. But there's no genuine anguish in Newman, even when Chance is scared or reduced to pleading. And there's never anything frayed about him, physically or emotionally. Newman is smooth and slick, and his Chance would be more interesting if he were able to penetrate the character's vulnerability, with Chance not as polished as, well, Paul Newman. His acting is too guarded to arouse much sympathy and is therefore

Geraldine Page's Alexandra can't help but notice the physical attributes of Paul Newman's Chance in **Sweet Bird of Youth**.

never affecting. It is a very tricky thing to cast a major role in which the actor must convince viewers that he doesn't really have the makings of a star, when, of course, he must be talented and charismatic enough to carry the movie. Tab Hunter, who had the kind of juvenile beauty whose boyishness could remain untarnished for only so long, would probably have made a more credible Chance, even though he was a far lesser actor than Newman. A thirtyish Tab Hunter would clearly not be the kind of "dish" he had been at twenty. Hunter, in his autobiography, *Tab Hunter Confidential,* reveals that he got an offer to replace Newman in the role on Broadway, but, to his lasting regret, he declined.

In his scenes with Page, Newman is appropriately eclipsed by her thrilling theatricality, and he is confident enough to stay out of her way, knowing he has all those scenes without her in which to regain his ground as the film's center. On his own in the hotel bar, he draws attention to himself by making it no secret that he's placing a phone call

to columnist Louella Parsons. Sporting sunglasses indoors, he stands before the bartender (whose job he once held), again hoping to suggest the return of a conquering hero. A flashback shows him with Heavenly at a country-club dance, then at a victorious diving contest—his slow-motion dive is a nice directorial touch, a stretching out of one of Chance's true shining moments—and finally in conversation with Boss Finley. Chance, content to remain in St. Cloud and marry Heavenly, was swayed by Boss Finley into following the go-getting hordes destined for New York, staked with a train ticket and a hundred dollars. Newman is convincingly guileless as a boy of around twenty, but this scene (not in the play) stresses the point that Chance's dreams were not his own. By placing the blame on Boss Finley for all that transpired, the movie makes Chance a misguided dupe in his pursuit of stardom and its consequential degradations. Unseen is Chance's transition into a man whose quest for success became all-consuming. A stint in the Korean War panicked him because it sacrificed some of his precious youth. (Nerves led to a medical discharge followed by a failed attempt to score in Hollywood.) But the kind of drive fueling Chance in his cunning dealings with Alexandra is either in someone or it isn't. It cannot be imposed upon anyone. He could not have sustained a dream for this long if it had never really been his, as it is in the play, in which he says, "I wanted, expected, intended to get, something better." The timid point of the film's flashback is that Chance's ambitions were *thrust* upon him, diminishing the character and minimizing his responsibility for his own actions. He is not necessarily more likable for being portrayed as a victim of manipulation.

Chance is focused on what he can get out of Alexandra, even resorting to tape-recording their conversation about her illegal drug use, meant to serve as blackmail insurance in case she decides not to honor their contract. Newman seems like a schoolboy doing a naughty prank, which fits the film's conception of Chance as a perennial innocent, but it belies the fact that he has been servicing and presumably exploiting rich women for a decade. True, he will always be something of a child when dealing with an Alexandra or a Boss Finley, but the film maintains the questionable assertion that, no matter how seamy his actions, Chance is ennobled by his purifying attachment to Heavenly. Why should he be so ashamed when he finally beds Alexandra? It is far from the first time he has used sex to get what he wants, and it is supposedly something for which he has a real talent, so why act so troubled about it now? Is it because he's in his hometown, so close to the one he loves? This moment of shame, present in the play as well, appears motivated merely by the fact that *we* are watching it, as opposed to Chance's many off-screen, and therefore unwitnessed, sexual escapades. The next morning a shirtless Newman is seen doing sit-ups, as if his stomach could get any flatter. Page's morning-after satisfaction assures Newman's fans that he is as good in bed as they had hoped. What is pleasing and rather unexpected is the developing rapport between Chance and Alexandra, despite the nature of their relationship as mutual users. Especially in their lighter moments, Newman and Page, who had played opposite each other on the stage, share a legitimate bond. Chance and Alexandra occupy different worlds but are made

of similar stuff and understand each other's clawing, high-reaching aspirations, even though hers are far more plausible than his.

At church for the Easter service, Boss Finley confronts Chance with the news of Heavenly's pregnancy (but not the abortion). This stirs up another flashback, a scene completely invented by Brooks, with Chance hopping off a freight train and sharing a rendezvous with Heavenly at an abandoned lighthouse, the location of their consummation. (There are no scenes in the play between Chance and Heavenly.) When he tells her about his inability to break into the movies, all I can think of is that I'm staring not at Chance but at Paul Newman and not buying any of this. Shirley Knight, with barely a trace of a Southern accent (the only Finley family member without a thick one), tells him that "my papa sold you that phony dream," again absolving Chance of any unsavory behavior. After lots of blather, and the lovemaking, Chance refuses her request to accompany him to his job in Palm Beach (where he will meet Alexandra, a scene described but not visualized). The lighthouse sequence is among those scenes that make *Sweet Bird* feel depressingly like a soap opera of two crazy kids in love simply trying to beat the outside forces against them. The characters are just as much in love in the play but appear much more bruised by their pasts. Newman's acting matches the banalities of Brooks' dialogue, lacking any distinctive fervor, while Knight, in what could have been the Joanne Woodward role, is extremely bland. (Get us back to Alexandra's bedroom!) He begs, "Don't ask me to give up my dream," but, again, was it ever really his? The film continues to remind us that no matter what Chance has done, or thinks he must do, he is basically good and true and our sympathies for him should remain unwavering. This isn't because the film is nonjudgmental, but, rather, because it is so afraid of alienating its audience. Making its way toward the happy ending not in the play, the movie opts for a less turbulent Chance and a safe, shielded Newman performance.

During Alexandra's phone call with columnist Walter Winchell, the film's finest scene, Newman is on the sidelines of Page's ingeniously funny and ardent self-absorption. Just as Chance keeps annoying Alexandra with his pleas to be mentioned to Winchell, so, too, does Newman seem a nuisance, interrupting our complete attention on Page.

Chance seems an idiot here, ridiculously oblivious to the bald fact that Alexandra is receiving life-altering news about the unforeseen triumph of her comeback, her own Easter resurrection. You would have to be a block away to miss what was happening, and Chance (in the play as well) should be savvy enough to know that now isn't the right time to be asking for a favor. After the call, and her full elevation to her former prowess, Alexandra delivers a bracing splash of reality upon him, identifying him as a mere distraction and, far worse, as someone who has gone past his youth. As Chance begs for her help, Newman's despair is unpersuasive, that of an actor going through the mapped-out pattern of a "big moment" but removed from the emotions in his words. Chance's pride won't allow him to accept employment as her chauffeur or butler, and he even refuses her offer to provide him with safe passage out of town. Like Carol Cutrere's climactic car-ride offer to Val Xavier in *The Fugitive Kind,* sparked by another premonition of doom, the gesture is rejected, but *Sweet Bird* turns imminent horror into romantic redemption. Following the Paul Newman formula, in which he does the right thing at the end of his pictures, *Sweet Bird* disparages the hunt for big bad success and promotes true love above all else. Chance is thereby decontaminated of his slutty opportunism, leaving Alexandra and Boss Finley to continue fighting their nasty battles to stay on top.

Chance runs to the front of the Finley mansion, screaming Heavenly's name (shades of "Stella!") when two cars pull up and four men emerge, including Heavenly's violent brother, Tom Junior (Rip Torn). As he is beaten, Chance continues to call her name before being dragged by his legs to one of the cars. Tom Junior, holding his daddy's cane, tells Chance he's about to "take away loverboy's meal ticket." In the play, Tom Junior and his crew enter the hotel suite to castrate Chance, a threat hanging over him throughout the play in response to the fact that what Chance gave Heavenly was not his seed but his venereal disease, which led not to an abortion but a hysterectomy ("spayed like a dawg"), thus making the Finleys' hatred of Chance more understandable. His castration is the price for Heavenly's own maiming. It is clear just how much of an impact the Williams pictures were having on Hollywood's grown-up future when a topic as controversial as abortion became the compromise, more palatable on-screen

than a hysterectomy brought on by V.D., which was simply too much even for a Williams picture. In the play, Chance permanently infected Heavenly; in the movie, he gave her their love child. The abortion was her father's doing, not Chance's. Brooks' line about Chance's "meal ticket" is a sly nod to the play because Chance's genitals could conceivably be labeled Chance's meal ticket. The film's Tom Junior bashes Chance's face with his cane, destroying the "meal ticket" of his beauty, though there's certainly the possibility that his face can heal into some semblance of what it had been. Audiences could endure Newman getting beaten to a pulp, but presumedly couldn't face the prospect of him as sexually diseased and then neutered. Consider the demises of some of Williams' male characters, from the cannibalization of Sebastian in *Suddenly, Last Summer* to the blowtorch death of Xavier in *Orpheus Descending* to Chance's castration, and, for all his lustful attentions on males, Williams certainly had a disturbing imagination when it came to violence against them.

Bloodied and swollen, the screen's Chance is reunited with Heavenly, with the added bonus of political trouble for Boss Finley, ignited at a rally when heckling about Heavenly's abortion raised questions about his family values. After sharing some tears and laughter, the lovers drive off for good, into the bliss denied them for a decade. The good have been rewarded, Boss Finley seems headed for punishment, and all has been tied up improbably and much too neatly. Chance has been cured of chasing the unreachable and can now find domestic normality with his dream girl, with the additional benefit of their undamaged ability to have other children. Not quite the Hollywood ending of Chance's fantasies but very movie-ish nonetheless. The play ends moments before his castration, without Heavenly there to rescue or soothe him; he will probably be left for dead. In his book *Tennessee Williams and Film,* author Maurice Yacowar, who dislikes the film of *Sweet Bird,* cites an interview in which Williams expressed his leanings for the movie over the play.

Sweet Bird of Youth netted three Oscar nominations for its performances, but Newman's was rightly not among them. Page, of course, was a contender, as was Shirley Knight, whose Heavenly was adequately sweet and sad but hardly meriting award consideration. As Boss Finley, *Sweet Bird*'s Big Daddy, Ed Begley won the Best Supporting Actor Os-

The Finley Men, Father and Son

Caricatured though he is in the film's garish vision of the mean old South, Boss Finley is still an all-too recognizable figure of political hypocrisy, preaching God, patriotism, and the commie threat, all the while serving nothing but his own self-interest. In the play, Williams stresses the character's seething racism and offers no promise of his political undoing. Rip Torn, who had gotten a Tony nomination for playing Tom Junior on Broadway, gives a more intriguing performance than Ed Begley's, sickeningly threatening and almost proudly stupid, hating his father while craving the man's approval. Torn combines good looks, sexual danger, and the frustrating inability to do anything right, anything that would make him more than daddy's henchman. (Torn got to play Boss Finley in a 1989 television production.) This father-son relationship has parallels to *Cat on a Hot Tin Roof,* with Gooper another son unable to please his father, and Big Daddy another father who cannot imagine such a son assuming his place.

car, the first winner for a Williams role since Anna Magnani won for *The Rose Tattoo* (1955). Unfortunately, Begley's performance is the most cliché-ridden element in the movie, a stout, suspender-snapping villain with a perpetual smile, just another ruthless Huey Long variation in a gumbo of florid scenes (several invented for the movie) that look like outtakes from *All the King's Men* (1949). Begley was a fine actor, of both stage *(All My Sons, Inherit the Wind)* and screen *(Stars in My Crown, 12 Angry Men),* but his Oscar was undeserved, a response to the exhibitionism of Boss Finley's loud personality and colossal vanity, both of which were conceived without subtlety or ingenuity.

Sweet Bird may not have been a Newman success on the order of *The Hustler,* but *Hud* (1963) certainly was. Fine commercial adult fare, *Hud* is a layered contemporary western that operates effectively on several planes: as father-son drama; as a boy's struggle between two very different role models (his grandfather and his uncle); and as a metaphor for a dying West. Though the movie doesn't offer much in terms of depth or nuance, it surely is compelling, spurred by excellent dialogue, interesting relationships, and first-rate acting. *Hud* was another Newman collaboration with director Martin Ritt, their best of six films, with Newman, as in *The Hustler,* in full anti-hero mode in what might be labeled an anti-western. Hud is another sexual bad boy, the womanizing black sheep of his family. Newman's performance is charismatic and knowing, but, yet again, limited by his characteristic holding back. His Hud isn't much different from his Eddie Felson or Chance Wayne, striding along on cocky charm and all-around savvy without exposing all that much beneath his seductive surface. Newman

was getting *On the Waterfront*-type opportunities, but he simply didn't have the resources to go beyond giving well-crafted sketches of roles with potential for greater complexity. As in *The Hustler,* he is outclassed in *Hud* by his co-stars, Patricia Neal and Melvyn Douglas. In a supporting role that won her a Best Actress Oscar, Neal endows her loose and likably sassy housekeeper with a beautifully lived-in feeling, an effortless authenticity. Melvyn Douglas, as Newman's principled father, won a supporting Oscar for bringing a Lear-like gravity and power to his role, as well as a painfully worn-out ache at his core. (Brandon de Wilde is the young man torn between grandfather Douglas and uncle Newman.) *Hud* broke the Newman formula by having him *not* learn a lesson at the end, leaving him unredeemed in a refreshingly downbeat ending. Newman received his third Oscar nomination but lost to his *Paris Blues* co-star Sidney Poitier *(Lilies of the Field).*

Though Newman had achieved top-tier stardom in dramas, he continued to strike out in comedies, making lackluster impressions in fizzling attempts. Consider *A New Kind of Love* (1963) and *Lady L* (1965), for example, and tally the piddling laughs generated by Newman and his co-stars. As mirthless and frenetic as they are dismal, these Newman comedies sink like stones of a very expensive but imitation variety. An exception is *The Prize* (1964), an enjoyably light Cold War thriller, a low-grade Hitchcock wannabe that borrows liberally from *North by Northwest,* with writer Ernest Lehman plagiarizing *himself.* Set around the Nobel ceremony, *The Prize* allows Newman a chance to give a reasonable facsimile of a Cary Grant performance, without ever quite matching Grant's wit or grace. Directed again by Mark Robson *(From the Terrace),* Newman carries the movie with his leading-man sparkle and infectiously high spirits. A dramatic risk presented itself on another project with Martin Ritt, *The Outrage* (1964), a western version of Akira Kurosawa's world-renowned *Rashomon* (1950). For Newman it was an attempt to disappear into a character part, a Mexican bandit complete with thick accent and raspy growl, plus a mustache and a fake nose. It was a Brando kind of dare, and, though it could hardly be called a triumph, Newman survived without humiliation, coming off better than co-stars Laurence Harvey and Claire Bloom. *Hud*'s Oscar-winning cinematographer, James Wong Howe, is the real star, but even his sublime black and white (and Ritt's faithfulness to Kurosawa's plot) could not generate involvement in this heavy-handed nonentity of a film.

After the success of *The Hustler* and *Hud*, Newman continued with "H" roles as his lucky charm. *Harper* (1966) is an update of the film-noir days of private detectives and an example of how a superstar can carry flimsy material on his confident shoulders. *Harper* is simply about Paul Newman, movie star extraordinaire, a pretext for him to be wryly amusing and super cool. Though he is clearly having a good time, that's no excuse for the movie's overlong running time and TV-mystery plotting, which keeps twisting long after anyone cares. Newman twinkles alongside Lauren Bacall, Janet Leigh, and Shelley Winters, yet these A-list ladies seem to be appearing in separate movies in different styles. *Harper* was another "H" hit, and Newman did a 1975 sequel, *The Drowning Pool,* another unoriginal and convoluted caper lifted by his undimmed star power. His next "H" movie, the somewhat slow and talky *Hombre* (1967), broke the string of successes, even though it was an honorable try, a good *Stagecoach*-style western with a modern social conscience and none of the slickness that had made *Harper* so popular. *Hombre* was the sixth and final Newman-Ritt picture, a far better western outing than *The Outrage,* with Newman in another risky role, an Apache-raised white man. He is properly stoic but not much else, out-acted once again, in this instance by Fredric March's villain and Diane Cilento's fallen woman. *Hombre* was also superior to another Newman hit, *Torn Curtain* (1966), a bona fide Alfred Hitchcock thriller, though disappointingly half-baked and dim-witted. Newman plays opposite Julie Andrews (on hand to build up her non-singing credentials), with neither star

proving to be a good fit with the Master of Suspense. Usually brimming with smarts, Newman has never seemed as dumb and vague as he does here as a nuclear scientist. The Cold War intrigue is contrived, and Hitchcock is nearly bereft of inspiration, leaving Newman to founder in one of his limpest and most vapid performances.

Stuart Rosenberg's *Cool Hand Luke* (1967) solidified Newman's status as the movies' premier dramatic male star of the decade, with Jack Lemmon his comedic counterpart. The film nabbed Newman his fourth Oscar nomination, but he lost the award to Rod Steiger *(In the Heat of the Night)*. *Cool Hand Luke* became a fondly recalled touchstone of an era, a pop classic, but don't ask me why. As chain-gang movies go, it cannot be spoken in the same breath with the great *I Am a Fugitive from a Chain Gang* (1932). Despite its detours into frat-house comedy—Newman bets he can eat fifty hard-boiled eggs in an hour—and its strangely martyring approach to the title character, *Cool Hand Luke* is essentially one of those stories about a man who will not be broken. But Newman's Luke is presented as an iconic figure rather than an actual human being. He's a macho fantasy of male heroism, a vacant creation embodied by a blue-eyed god, a nobody upon whom the film's strenuous and worshipful mythologizing is pinned. Despite some good escape scenes, the movie becomes increasingly full of itself, even though Luke represents nothing much and his martyrdom is pointless. The film is so smitten with its star that it concludes with a desperately upbeat finale, a photo montage of his assorted smiles, further deifying Luke, a beautiful cipher. The fuzzily imagined *Cool Hand Luke* was another chance for Newman to rely solely on personal magnetism, stranded without a character to play. I am as immune to this movie as I am to Newman's next smash, his decade-capping blockbuster, the movie that secured his stardom into the 1970s.

George Roy Hill's *Butch Cassidy and the Sundance Kid* (1969) is a wildly overrated comic western in which motiveless outlaws smirk their way into legend. As in *Cool Hand Luke,* the movie treats its central characters not as specific individuals but as the movie stars playing them, signifying that we are expected to forgive them no matter what they do. After all, they're so damned good-looking, right? Unlike *Bonnie and Clyde* (1967), which has the Depression as its context, *Butch Cassidy* offers a duo whose criminality defies reason: they don't seem to want anything; they aren't reacting to anything in their pasts; and they have no special grievances or passions. Newman's Butch and Robert Redford's Sundance exist merely to delight audiences with their dazzling chemistry, which is what they did, making *Butch Cassidy* a colossal success, a slick and cynically engineered product written by William Goldman. Newman is lively, perhaps too antic, more boyishly energetic than the younger, more composed (and funnier) Redford. Memorable lines and moments abound, but they do not disguise the overriding emptiness. There is spectacular, Oscar-winning cinematography by Conrad Hall, and an unusual and varied Burt Bacharach score, but little else to praise. The picture descends especially low when the boys are joined by Katharine Ross (dreadful as Redford's love interest) in their relocation to Bolivia and subsequent pilfering of a dirt-poor country, gleaming all the way. (Is the disposable Katharine Ross in the film only to distract us from suspecting any homoerotic tensions between the men?) The famous freeze-frame ending seems more about shielding viewers from seeing movie stars die bloody deaths than it is about Butch and Sundance. Despite their soulless shortcomings, *Cool Hand Luke* and *Butch Cassidy* provided a seamless transition for Newman into the New Hollywood. Instead of looking like an outmoded studio-system product with an accelerating expiration date (the way Rock Hudson did by 1969), Newman was primed to be part of the screen's new permissiveness. In fact, it was films like *The Hustler* and *Hud* (and their title characters) that paved the way for this burgeoning and uncharted era in American movies.

However, there was nothing forward-looking about *The Sting* (1973), the reunion vehicle for Newman, Redford, and director Hill, a winner of seven Oscars including Best Picture (*Butch Cassidy* had merely been a nominee). The stars were again cast as lovable and glamorous rascals, and the movie was every bit as overrated as *Butch Cassidy,* lots of wrapping with nothing inside, though it was a very different kind of movie. Replacing their cowboy duds for snazzy 1930s suits, this pair apparently looked great in any period. How strange that there's not a single gorgeous female on view, ensuring that these pretty boys have no competition from either sex. *The Sting* tries to be an old-style comedy in the Da-

mon Runyon tradition, but Hill's direction lacks the breezy style and rat-tat-tat pacing required (paging Frank Capra), resulting in a slight and mildly amusing movie, not even the visual treat that *Butch Cassidy* had been. Redford received an Oscar nomination but Newman didn't, mostly because Newman had the much smaller role. And yet it is Newman who steals the show, giving his most polished comic performance. Redford is too old and too preppy to be playing a young grifter (a part suitable for the early Cagney), while Newman, as the old-pro con man, gives the film its wittiest flourishes. His poker scene is the film's centerpiece, with Newman a particular pleasure in his pretense as a boozy, no-class jerk. Audiences (and the Academy) loved being conned by this irresistible twosome, and there is certainly cleverness in the construction of the titular scheme, but *The Sting* is a throwaway. It gets points for being a battle of smarts, and at least has a motive propelling its big con, but it shows that two personality stars can shine in a movie that has no personality of its own.

The 1970s saw Newman working with major directors not at their best. *The Life and Times of Judge Roy Bean* (1972) is one of John Huston's worst movies, a perverse bore and grotesque cartoon that cannot find a sustainable tone. A bearded and mustachioed Newman stars as the famed hanging judge, and he's gutsy and game, but Bean is another cipher, a violent "hoot" utterly undeveloped. The film's point and intentions are baffling, and Newman can't compete with Walter Brennan's great, Oscar-winning Bean from *The Westerner* (1940), a performance as fascinating as Newman's is perplexing. Unfortunately, Huston and Newman were at it again for *The MacKintosh Man* (1973), another bad movie (though *Judge Roy Bean* is more flagrantly awful). With a Cold War plot full of holes, *MacKintosh Man* is sloppy and dumbfounding rather than intricate and mysterious. Newman coasts, looking as miscast and uncomfortable as he had in the Cold War terrain of *Torn Curtain,* trapped inside a cardboard character and an incoherent drama. Newman's association with Robert Altman fared somewhat better, beginning with *Buffalo Bill and the Indians* (1976), a revisionist history lesson in the *Judge Roy Bean* mold but not a comparable disaster. The subject is worthy—the chasm between truth/reality and myth/legend, and the conscious reshaping of one into the other—and there are good bits throughout, but the film keeps making this same point over and over, lacking any narrative push and growing slower and flabbier until it becomes a shapeless drag. It is an admirable and great-looking Altman misstep, made with integrity and vision if not focus. Newman's attractive Buffalo Bill—with beard, mustache, and long wig, plus those fringed and colorful costumes—is more easygoing than flamboyant, though he does have bouts of entertaining bluster. But even he couldn't draw audiences for this rambling movie. Much worse was the Altman-Newman *Quintet* (1979), an agonizingly ponderous work set in a futuristic ice age. The title refers to a game played to the death, yet the film is as lifeless a thriller as can be imagined, a bewildering blank. Between the cold and the script, Newman stumbles through numbly.

Slap Shot (1977) was Newman's third and final film with George Roy Hill, sans Redford, an enjoyable (if repetitive) sports comedy set in the consistently raucous and testosterone-charged world of minor-league hockey. Newman is in top form, enviably relaxed and shrewd and altogether plausible as an aging player and coach on a losing New England team. Things change once they start playing more violently, gaining confidence and winning steadily as they turn hockey into a bloodsport on par with Roman Coliseum fare. One of the films in the decade's series of in-your-face sports movies *(The Longest Yard, Semi-Tough, North Dallas Forty), Slap Shot* is often muddled, and it sputters at the climax, losing its way whenever it veers too far from Newman. Wearing horrifying '70s fashions and easily flinging the "F" word, the past-fifty Newman proved that he was still in sync with the contemporary filmmaking scene. In Daniel Petrie's *Fort Apache The Bronx* (1981), a violent cop picture, Newman continued to display newfound ease on-screen, far removed from the tightness of his star-making performances. The film is long and exhausting, though decidedly action-packed, and Newman makes a strong impression as an honest cop. Good as he is, though, he doesn't exactly blend into the milieu, too sensational a presence for his blue-collar role. And his moral crisis—whether or not to rat on a murderous cop—feels very movie-ish, a return to Newman's days of doing the right thing just before the credits roll. If the film is disappointingly familiar and mediocre, it certainly upped the ante on police brutality in the movies.

The 1980s were a renaissance for Newman's stature as an esteemed screen actor. Having honed a limited talent for three decades, he had developed into a master craftsman, an actor of economy, simplicity, and unforced depths. Newman had truly learned by doing. No longer pushing for emotion or big effects, he trusted himself as never before, becoming the rare longtime star who got significantly better and less self-conscious with age, freer and more open, unlike, say, Jack Lemmon, a contemporary who became a mass of tried-and-true tics, tricks, and habits. *Absence of Malice* (1981), which brought Newman his first Oscar nomination in fourteen years, is a decent Miami-set newspaper drama that raises interesting points without being especially absorbing or having much impact. Despite the film's brains and ambition, it has a TV-movie texture thanks to Sydney Pollack's merely efficient direction and an overall lack of surprises. Newman, however, as an honest liquor wholesaler (and son of a bootlegger), is impeccably smooth, easily outdoing co-star Sally Field (as a reporter). But it was with another Sidney—Lumet—that Newman hit a peak, playing the alcoholic, ambulance-chasing lawyer in *The Verdict* (1982), a very fine courtroom drama, satisfying and well-paced and handsomely crafted by Lumet. Scripted by David Mamet, *The Verdict* is basically good pulp, featuring a femme fatale, a surprise star witness, corporate evil, and Newman's do-gooding crusader, an underdog desperately seeking redemption through a medical malpractice suit. Its cliché components were freshly spruced, creating a spiffy adult entertainment and a compelling character study. Newman was finally a skillful enough actor to encompass a multi-faceted role, which brings more weight to the melodrama of the court case. Newman is terrific, and has rarely (if ever) been better, charting his character's revitalizing and sometimes reckless struggle to regain his idealism and fight his insecurities. As in his other best movies, there's always some seasoned pro lurking to steal his thunder, in this case a brilliant James Mason as his adversary. Exceptional as Newman is, he is no Mason, who subtly imbues a stock character (the slimy lawyer) with mesmerizing strokes of implacable cool and smugly controlled arrogance. (Mason had previously played Newman's nemesis in *The MacKintosh*

Man under far less felicitous circumstances.) Both men received Oscar nominations but each went unrewarded, with Newman losing to Gandhi!

Newman returned to the role of "Fast Eddie" Felson in *The Color of Money* (1986), Martin Scorsese's sequel to *The Hustler.* Tom Cruise, a Newman heir in the brash-young-man department, plays a green but cocky and talented pool shooter taken under Eddie's wing. Though exceedingly well made, this sequel is nowhere near as good or pungent as the original film, but Newman is a much better actor this time around. The role of Eddie may not be as good as it was back in 1961, but Newman's performance is considerably more accomplished, a lesson in less-is-more character shadings. He doesn't gleam as brightly as he once did, yet you still can't take your eyes off him. Just as Newman wasn't quite able to hold his own alongside George C. Scott in *The Hustler,* now it's Cruise who is in the position of being the heartthrob movie star obviously not of the same acting caliber as his consummate co-star. Fast Eddie is now a liquor salesman (in the same business as Newman's *Absence of Malice* character), but, through mentoring hot-shot Cruise on the ways of the game, he revives his old self, eventually hitting the tables on his own. It is the *Verdict* formula of a "finished" fellow who isn't quite done after all. By the end, Eddie needs to prove to himself that he is a great player and not just an ace hustler, an arc that reflects the distance between *The Hustler* and *The Color of Money,* with Newman the actor having progressed from promising newcomer to elder statesman. With supreme self-confidence and concentrated emotion, Newman never makes an unnecessary move, by now a master in the art of thinking in front of a camera. Those blue eyes could say it all. Past sixty now, he won his Best Actor Oscar on his seventh nomination, his second for playing Eddie, and it was no shabby consolation prize. He won it one year *after* receiving an honorary Oscar, which *was* a consolation prize. (In 1994, the Academy bestowed upon him their Jean Hersholt Humanitarian Award.)

In his sixties and seventies, Newman accepted unexpected roles instead of resting safely on his laurels. *Blaze* (1989) took him far out of his comfort zone, casting him as real-life Louisiana governor Earl K. Long (Huey's brother), a Boss Finley-sized role. The film depicted Long's 1959 relationship with stripper Blaze Starr (Lolita Davidovich), as well as his po-

litical troubles stemming from his being a pro-civil rights progressive. The movie, written and directed by Ron Shelton, is a good try but the results are middling. By now an expert internal actor, Newman wasn't nearly as adroit in expansive parts (like Buffalo Bill), lacking Earl K. Long's star-spangled vitality, expansive gift of gab, and eccentric abandon. Newman's attempt is commendable, but his gusto has no oomph. The role cried out for Robert Duvall.

Because Newman was such a famous liberal, it was always fun to watch him tackle characters who would not have shared his ideals. *Fat Man and Little Boy* (1989) is a confused movie, lacking drive and too prone to speechifying, but it features Newman as the hard-nosed general passionately overseeing the construction of the atomic bomb. His succinct performance as a gruff non-intellectual gives the movie what little grounding it has. In *Mr. and Mrs. Bridge* (1990), a Merchant-Ivory production and Newman's final co-starring feature with Woodward, he was effectively cast against type as a stiff conservative, both a successful lawyer and a priggish husband-father. The film, however, is a maddening misfire, a period piece (set in the 1930s and '40s) heading nowhere. Woodward got an Oscar nomination, but I prefer Newman's offbeat work, more of a stretch than his wife's predictable performance. Later, he was the evil corporate shark in the Coen Brothers' bloodless whimsy *The Hudsucker Proxy* (1994), another "H" film (one with "Hud" in the title, no less) but one in which Newman's contribution was in support of star Tim Robbins. The film is a late-1950s reworking of *Mr. Deeds Goes to Town* (1936) with fantasy elements, set in a mythical New York. Like *Miller's Crossing* (1990), it's one of those pointless Coen films that leaves you doubting their affection for whichever old-movie genre they are reviving and strangling. Newman gives a sly portrait of greedy villainy, and only he and the spirited Robbins (unlike the stupefyingly bad Jennifer Jason Leigh) are able to surmount the stunt nature of this often hideous and mystifying project.

There was one more major leading role in the Newman filmography, in a movie that snagged him his first and only New York Film Critics' Best Actor citation (plus an eighth Oscar nomination). Robert Benton's *Nobody's Fool* (1994) is a nice little movie anchored by Newman's dexterity. Just about everything else in this slice of small-town life, from the

"Chance" Meetings

Nobody's Fool has two incidental Tennessee Williams connections. Not only does Newman share a brief scene with Angelica Torn, daughter of Geraldine Page and Rip Torn, but there he is, the original Chance Wayne, renting a room from Jessica Tandy, the original Blanche DuBois.

casting to its sentimentality, is uneven and a strain on plausibility. Even Newman isn't quite "regular" enough to be an ordinary Joe, a sixty-year-old Irish-American construction worker with a bum knee, a divorced father renting a room from an elderly landlady (Jessica Tandy). There's something too unmistakably "superstar" about Newman (as there had been in *Sweet Bird of Youth*) to allow for his complete credibility in a role more suited to Brian Dennehy, or, if you insist on a big name, then Gene Hackman or James Garner. If you can get past this, as most people did in 1994, then you can savor Newman's discerning underplaying of the deeper feelings and regrets of a man who has made a mess of his personal life. Newman, at nearly seventy, also does wonders with his many wisecracks, ultimately making *Nobody's Fool* seem better than it is. Newman and Benton reteamed on *Twilight* (1998), putting Newman back into *Harper* territory, acting with the aforementioned Hackman and Garner, and Susan Sarandon, but it was no more than an okay noir update, nowhere near as fine as *The Late Show* (1977), Benton's previous excursion into contemporary film noir. *Twilight* accomplished little beyond showing that Newman, now *past* seventy, was still able to carry a movie and bed his leading lady.

Newman is crusty comic relief as Kevin Costner's father in the otherwise slurpy *Message in a Bottle* (1999), and, in his final big-screen appearance, he plays an organized-crime boss in Sam Mendes' *Road to Perdition* (2002), for which he received his ninth Oscar nomination and his first in the supporting category. (*Road to Perdition* is not a lost Hope-Crosby picture.) Though a bit too arty for its own good, the film works as both a 1931-set action-filled gangster yarn and an intimate family drama. Based on a graphic novel, it stars Tom Hanks as Newman's hit man and unofficial adopted son. Playing Irish again, Newman does a sturdy job as a powerful man torn

between two sons: Hanks, for whom he feels genuine respect and affection; and a pre-Bond Daniel Craig, his biological son and a crazed and all-around rotten weakling. Hanks follows Newman's acting example—superb containment—tempering the film's visual extravagance while Craig and assassin Jude Law go straight over the top. It is appropriate that Newman would be seen on the screen for the last time in a father-son saga, a sub-genre of drama that had contributed significantly to his stardom, from *Somebody up There Likes Me* to *Cat on a Hot Tin Roof* to *Hud*. *Road to Perdition* made a classy capper to Newman's nearly fifty years on the screen.

He returned to Broadway in 2002 as the Stage Manager in a revival of *Our Town*, getting his one and only Tony nomination. (In 1955, he had appeared as George opposite Eva Marie Saint's Emily in a musicalized television production of the play, with Frank Sinatra as the Stage Manager, warbling "Love and Marriage.") Newman also provided the voice for one of the characters in the Oscar-nominated animated feature *Cars* (2006). When he died of lung cancer at age eighty-three in 2008, still married to Woodward after fifty years, he left behind not only a personal career of legendary proportions but a legacy of astonishing and ongoing hu-

Newman's Own

Newman also had his share of acclaim as a film director, including winning the New York Film Critics' award for *Rachel, Rachel* (1968), a starring vehicle for Woodward. As the film's producer, he received its Best Picture Oscar nomination. He went on to direct four other features: *Sometimes a Great Notion* (1971), in which he also starred; *The Effect of Gamma Rays on Man-in-the-Moon Marigolds* (1972), another Woodward showcase; *Harry and Son* (1984), for which he also co-wrote the screenplay, starring himself and with a supporting role for Woodward; and *The Glass Menagerie* (1987), a return to his association with Williams *and* a valentine to Woodward, giving her a plum screen role in her fifties. Aside from the expected sensitivity that is usually present when actors direct actors, Newman was a serviceable director at his best (*Rachel, Rachel*) and a hazy, meandering one at his worst (*Harry and Son*, despite the "H" in the title).

manitarian achievements, notably his Hole in the Wall Gang Camp for young cancer patients and the charitable proceeds from his Newman's Own food products. It may have taken him a few decades to become the actor he strived to be, but at least he got there, and he might never have done so had he not played the Williams roles that helped catapult and establish him. Without *Cat*'s Brick making him the hottest new leading man of late-fifties Hollywood, and without *Sweet Bird*'s Chance confirming his legitimacy as a theatre star, perhaps he wouldn't have gotten all the way to *The Hustler* and *Hud* and mega-stardom, meaning that his career might not have lasted long enough for him to do *The Verdict, The Color of Money,* or *Nobody's Fool,* when he was past needing the luck of an "H" in his titles.

Elizabeth Taylor

In **Cat on a Hot Tin Roof**, *there's no doubt about it: "Maggie the Cat is alive!"*

Elizabeth Taylor: Filmography

- *There's One Born Every Minute (1942)*
- *Lassie Come Home (1943)*
- *Jane Eyre (1944)*
- *The White Cliffs of Dover (1944)*
- *National Velvet (1944)*
- *Courage of Lassie (1946)*
- *Cynthia (1947)*
- *Life with Father (1947)*
- *A Date with Judy (1948)*
- *Julia Misbehaves (1948)*
- *Little Women (1949)*
- *Conspirator (1950)*
- *The Big Hangover (1950)*
- *Father of the Bride (1950)*
- *Father's Little Dividend (1951)*
- *A Place in the Sun (1951)*
- *Callaway Went Thataway (1951)*
- *Love Is Better Than Ever (1952)*
- *Ivanhoe (1952)*
- *The Girl Who Had Everything (1953)*
- *Rhapsody (1954)*
- *Elephant Walk (1954)*
- *Beau Brummell (1954)*
- *The Last Time I Saw Paris (1954)*
- *Giant (1956)*
- *Raintree County (1957)*
- *Cat on a Hot Tin Roof (1958)*
- *Suddenly, Last Summer (1959)*
- *Scent of Mystery (1960)*
- *Butterfield 8 (1960)*
- *Cleopatra (1963)*
- *The V.I.P.s (1963)*
- *The Sandpiper (1965)*
- *Who's Afraid of Virginia Woolf? (1966)*
- *The Taming of the Shrew (1967)*
- *Doctor Faustus (1967)*
- *Reflections in a Golden Eye (1967)*
- *The Comedians (1967)*
- *Boom (1968)*
- *Secret Ceremony (1968)*
- *The Only Game in Town (1970)*
- *Under Milk Wood (1971)*
- *X Y & Zee (1972)*
- *Hammersmith Is Out (1972)*
- *Night Watch (1973)*
- *Ash Wednesday (1973)*
- *That's Entertainment! (1974)*
- *The Driver's Seat (1976)*
- *The Blue Bird (1976)*
- *A Little Night Music (1977)*
- *Winter Kills (1979)*
- *The Mirror Crack'd (1980)*
- *Young Toscanini (1988)*
- *The Flintstones (1994)*

Elizabeth Taylor (1932-)

Academy Award Wins

- **Best Actress** of 1960 for *Butterfield 8*
- **Best Actress** of 1966 for *Who's Afraid of Virginia Woolf?*
- **1993 Jean Hersholt Humanitarian Award**

Academy Award Nominations

- **Best Actress** of 1957 for *Raintree County*
- **Best Actress** of 1958 for *Cat on a Hot Tin Roof*
- **Best Actress** of 1959 for *Suddenly, Last Summer*

Maggie the Cat in *Cat on a Hot Tin Roof* (1958)
Catherine Holly in *Suddenly, Last Summer* (1959)
Flora Goforth in *Boom* (1968)

Vivien Leigh and Anna Magnani were unanticipated Williams collaborators because they were foreign-born and therefore unlikely to become key interpreters of an American playwright. But since both women were great actresses, and because Williams wrote extraordinary female roles, their eventual associations now seem almost inevitable. Elizabeth Taylor, who topped both Leigh and Magnani by starring in three Williams films, was an unexpected Williams player for a different reason (though she, too, was foreign-born). Who would have guessed that an all-out movie star, one lacking stage experience and not even taken particularly seriously as a film actress, would eventually be thrice-paired with the work of Broadway's most illustrious mid-century dramatist? Their trio of films do not rank among the best of either artist, yet Taylor and Williams turned out to be very good for each other in career terms, at least for their first two efforts, *Cat on a Hot Tin Roof* and *Suddenly, Last Summer*. Taylor gained considerable prestige and acclaim (including two Oscar nominations), and Williams enjoyed tremendous commercial success, resulting in an acceleration of Williams-based films, with seven released in the 1960s.

Taylor was born in London on February 27, 1932, to American parents (her father was an art dealer). The family returned to the States when Taylor was seven, and her ambitious mother, a former small-time actress, was determined to get young Elizabeth into pictures. And with that glorious grown-up face framed by raven hair, it can't have been hard. After appearing in a "B" comedy, *There's One Born Every Minute* (1942), Taylor got a break when she was cast as an English girl in *Lassie Come Home* (1943), which is sort of *The Odyssey* with a canine Ulysses. This irresistible dog-driven picture was Taylor's first for MGM, the studio that would be her home for nearly the next two decades. Alongside Lassie and the unaffected Roddy McDowall (the picture's other star), Taylor attracted notice not only for her beauty but also for her presence, which seemed preternaturally wise and mature. On loan to Fox, she played

a small but memorable role as the sickly friend of the title character in *Jane Eyre* (1944), a moody and handsome but dramatically hollow adaptation of Charlotte Brontë's novel. The movie features not only Taylor but an excellent Peggy Ann Garner and a terrible Margaret O'Brien. (Natalie Wood is the only major female child actress of the 1940s *not* in it.) In her few scenes in the abusive orphanage, Taylor displays an ethereal goodness and an undeniable gift for connecting with the camera.

After playing the small role of an English farm girl smitten with Roddy McDowall in director Clarence Brown's war-themed family drama *The White Cliffs of Dover* (1944), Taylor was cast in the leading role of Brown's next film, *National Velvet* (1944). Not only did it make her a young star, but it remains one of the finest of family films, with Taylor memorably disguising herself as a boy to win the Grand National horse race. It is quite possible, though it may sound facetious, that Taylor never topped her radiant performance as Velvet, a girl exquisitely possessed by her love for a horse. Set in 1920s England, this colorful and moving film is anchored by Taylor's unforced and intuitive acting; her commitment is astonishing in someone twelve years old. (How could she have been overlooked for a special juvenile Oscar?)

As Taylor continued her tenure as an MGM contract player, no role comparable to Velvet came her way for the rest of the decade. Her next picture, *Courage of Lassie* (1946), was an unworthy follow-up, with the dog given the heavier emoting and Taylor relegated to a watered-down retread of her Velvet. *Cynthia* (1947) proved to be a bum vehicle for the blossoming teenage Taylor, who never experienced an awkward in-between phase, the ruination of many young careers. She was better served in *A Date with Judy* (1948), a Jane Powell vehicle with the sweet-sixteen Taylor cast as a snooty rich girl who warms up when paired with dreamboat Robert Stack, forming a couple too beautiful to be believed. Fresh and perky Powell (another valuable

MGM teenager) sings her heart out, but how can she compete with Taylor's womanly charms? In *Little Women* (1949), the least of the three main screen versions of the Louisa May Alcott classic, Taylor, as the blond and selfish Amy, is the only "little woman" whose performance tops the actress (Joan Bennett) who played her role in the beloved 1933 version. The 1949 movie is too immaculately pretty, looking like an MGM musical, but Taylor is its bright spot, vain and charming and wittily comic.

Taylor made a graceful transition to adult roles in *Conspirator* (1950), even though the film is a second-rate Cold War spy melodrama, a flop whose point is that marriage and espionage don't mix. Her on-screen (and secretly Commie) husband is MGM's other Taylor, Robert, two decades older than luscious Elizabeth. She and Joan Bennett, co-incidentally both former Amys of *Little Women*, were cast as daughter and mother (very convincingly, genetically and dramatically) in *Father of the Bride* (1950), the film that successfully launched the full-grown Taylor. This enjoyable, savvy domestic comedy is Spencer Tracy's show, but it is further enhanced by Taylor's glowing simplicity, as is *Father's Little Dividend,* the harmless, one-year-later sequel.

The arrival of the young-lady Taylor was solidified when she was loaned to Paramount for *A Place in the Sun* (1951), appearing opposite Montgomery Clift, her first encounter with the new "serious actor" breed of leading men. Directed by George Stevens, *A Place in the Sun* is hypnotically photographed in black and white and indeed compelling, but it's also flawed and not altogether satisfying. Poor-boy Clift starts moving up the corporate ladder and becomes romantically linked to debutante Taylor, only to learn that his drab girlfriend, Shelley Winters, is pregnant, leading to Winters' accidental drowning and Clift being sent to the electric chair. Clift appears too naïve and victimized, never quite the "operator" the story requires, while Winters plays her role much too pathetically, overdoing the dowdiness when all she needs to be is ordinary. (Stevens' direction works too hard at keeping Clift sympathetic, forgiving his actions at every step, while turning against Winters, trying to make us want her dead as much as Clift does.) Taylor's performance, in the least showy role, is the most fully realized, managing simultaneously to project complete innocence and innate maturity. It is a lovely,

unspoiled performance, enriched by the smoldering chemistry she shares with Clift.

Ivanhoe (1952), reteaming her with Robert Taylor, was less demanding fare, but it was another big hit, and, along with *Father of the Bride* and *A Place in the Sun,* another Best Picture Oscar nominee. Though it has rapturous color, *Ivanhoe* is no *Adventures of Robin Hood* (1938), and it marked the beginning of a perilous period in Taylor's career when she was pigeonholed as no more than a pretty young thing, as if *A Place in the Sun* had never happened. For the next four years, Hollywood offered her little that would challenge her potential or develop her abilities, including *The Girl Who Had Everything* (1953), a cheap quickie whose only real asset is its tempting title. In 1954, MGM consigned her to the amorous kitsch of *Rhapsody,* in which she is torn between two musical geniuses (while classical music soars!), and then came a Stewart Granger costume picture, *Beau Brummell,* in which the central relationship is not even the romance between Granger and Taylor, but, rather, the friendship between Granger and Peter Ustinov (splendid as King George IV). Taylor's dresses and hair styles were most becoming in these movies, but what had become of the promising actress?

The film that rescued Taylor from her window-dressing limbo was *Giant* (1956), a fine epic about capitalism, prejudice, and liberalism, but mostly about marriage and raising children. Again guided by George Stevens, the director who more than any other had a knack for tapping her talent, Taylor was better than she had been since *National Velvet* and never again would she be anything less than a major star. As the Maryland-bred bride of Texas cattle rancher Rock Hudson, she exhibits a strength and intelligence heretofore unseen in her work, even when eventually under age makeup. It is a flawless performance, far richer and more interesting than those of her co-stars, Hudson and James Dean, both of whom got Oscar nominations while Taylor was unfathomably ignored. The *Giant* role shows the Taylor I like best: honest and no-nonsense, fierce and fearless, and intensely likable. Plus she has strong chemistry with both Hudson and Dean. Unsurprisingly, Taylor made *Giant* on loan (to Warner Brothers), but MGM finally took notice of her strides. They built for her a *Gone With the Wind* of her own, complete with a Civil War-era setting and a Southern-belle leading

Princess Maggie?

MGM had purchased the film rights to *Cat* as a property for Grace Kelly, before she upped and married a prince. Though the thought of Kelly as Maggie the Cat now seems puzzling, remember that the role was created on Broadway by Barbara Bel Geddes, a well-bred blonde in the Kelly mold (though not a great beauty). In her Hitchcock thrillers, Kelly had proven her sexiness; her challenge would have been to convince audiences that she was an underprivileged girl who married into wealth.

role. Hardly *GWTW*, *Raintree County* (1957) has a plot unworthy of its nearly three-hour treatment. Though Taylor was again cast opposite Montgomery Clift, their chemistry seems considerably dimmed after six years between films. Clift suffered a severe car accident during *Raintree's* filming, disfiguring his breathtaking face, but this doesn't sufficiently explain his impoverished performance throughout. Miscast and too old, he's a drag. Taylor is the rich, unstable beauty from New Orleans who ventures north ("Raintree" is in Indiana) and marries Clift after making him believe he has impregnated her (at least Shelley Winters was *really* pregnant). Suffering from a childhood trauma (and a shaky, overblown Southern accent), Taylor plays her role with obvious strain as the character tries to hold on to her fragile sanity. Of course, Taylor looks stunning in her gowns by Walter Plunkett (Scarlett O'Hara's designer), but she shows little Southern-belle flair, coming off best in quieter moments. Her shrill voice, almost always an issue in her acting (yet not in *Giant*), is excruciating in her "big" scenes. Superficial as it is, *Raintree County* was another hit, and it brought Taylor her first Oscar nomination, with the award going to Joanne Woodward in *The Three Faces of Eve*, another story of a woman's mental troubles stemming from childhood trauma. By Oscar night, Taylor was already at work on *Cat on a Hot Tin Roof*, playing opposite Paul Newman, Woodward's new husband.

Richard Brooks, *Cat's* director (and co-adapter), had worked with Taylor on *The Last Time I Saw Paris* (1954), an unfortunate reworking of F. Scott Fitzgerald's story "Babylon Revisited," turning it into a real snooze of a soap opera. Taylor, as a pleasure-seeking bohemian, gives *The Last Time*

I Saw Paris its only allure and vitality, even though her role is secondary to Van Johnson's as her failed-novelist husband. *Cat* was a significant improvement: Brooks' direction shows considerably more enthusiasm, and Taylor is no longer trapped into being a pawn in a melodrama. But very early into the *Cat* shoot, Taylor suffered a tragedy, the death of her husband, Mike Todd, in a plane crash. By all reports, work became her therapy, and she threw herself into the role of Maggie the Cat, thoroughly impressing her colleagues both professionally and personally. (Todd was husband number three, following Nicky Hilton and Michael Wilding.)

Taylor literally drives into the movie, emerging from her car in a white blouse, beige skirt, and a bright red belt. Freed from the moldy histrionics and antebellum excesses of *Raintree County*, Taylor is indeed comfortable in Maggie the Cat's skin. Her Southern accent is far more controlled and acceptable than it had been in *Raintree*, and her voice, always her chief limitation—mostly because it hadn't really changed since *National Velvet*—also seems to be more manageable than unwieldy (though she does have her strident moments). Simply put, Taylor has as Maggie what she had in *Giant* and lacked in *Raintree*: confidence. Her first scene is a run-in with a niece, a daughter of brother-in-law Gooper (Jack Carson) and his wife, Mae (Madeleine Sherwood), one of a brood Maggie fiendishly refers to as "no-neck monsters." When the bratty child hurls ice cream at Taylor's ankles, she responds by scooping up the mess and smearing it across the girl's face. It is an apt introduction to Maggie, a Southern gal with nerve, grit, and a wicked streak. Another key asset of Taylor's work is her enjoyment of her looks and their sensual power. She uses her physical appeal to keep her millionaire father-in-law, Big Daddy Pollitt (Burl Ives), charmed and in her corner. The affection Taylor displays for Ives' Big Daddy feels sincere and relaxed. But Maggie can no longer get any attention from her husband, Brick (Paul Newman), who appears to detest her. Her first scene with Brick, in which she changes her ice cream-stained stockings, is a striptease for an uninterested audience. The properly baffling question here is why this goddess is unable to arouse her mate. She calls him "a back-aching Puritan," but there's obviously more going on than that.

Brick broke his ankle the night before, trying to relive his glory days on the high-school athletic field. He was drinking, as he has been steadily since the death of Skipper, his best friend. Since Brick has dropped out of life, including quitting his job as a sports announcer, it has fallen to Maggie to be their defender in family matters. They are here in Mississippi, at the family mansion, to be present for the results of Big Daddy's medical tests and also for the celebration of his sixty-fifth birthday. Big Daddy is dying of cancer, and Gooper and Mae are moving in to grab what they can. Maggie has taken it upon herself to fight for Brick's share (and her own). This offers an actress a nice bit of ambiguity: Maggie is in love with her husband enough to want to protect him, especially when he won't protect himself, but she is also selfish enough to want to secure money and material goods for her own future. Plus, she happens to loathe Mae and Gooper. Taylor is astute enough to provide a combination of all three motivations, in varying degrees, throughout. Unfortunately, the movie significantly softens the original material, with Maggie losing her initial edges and becoming more homogenized and "palatable" (and less fun) as the picture proceeds. It is to Taylor's credit that she retains a good bit of fight even as Maggie is increasingly portrayed as a faithful and dutiful wife and less and less a "cat."

There's one thing Maggie is powerless to do on her own, something of vital importance to her (and Brick's) standing in the Pollitt family. She has yet to produce a child, while her sister-in-law is due with number six! This is a source of extreme frustration for Maggie, particularly since she is so willing to oblige. It also provides some bitchy humor, with Taylor's malicious smiles and gleefully delivered zingers aimed at Madeleine Sherwood's Mae. Taylor meshes neatly with Williams' sense of humor, wringing his funny lines for all their flavorful juice, referring to Mae as "that monster of fertility" and flashing open disdain for those "no-neck monsters" (who are constant reminders of Maggie's failure as a daughter-in-law). Mae may not have Maggie's physical assets or personal appeal, but she is a baby-making machine and it drives Maggie to distraction.

Even if Maggie has an eye on Big Daddy's fortune, there's no doubt that her feeling for Brick is genuine. Taylor exposes Maggie's neediness and strength in equal parts. Even when nervous and frustrated and in pain, Taylor keeps Maggie forging ahead, sustained by her belief in her ability to change things. She often expresses her love for Brick openly, knowing that she will probably be rejected, which allows Taylor moments of frank vulnerability, when Maggie's emotional yearning outweighs her palpable sexual desire. But for what is Maggie being punished? "Haven't I served my term?" she asks, followed by her feeling like a "cat on a hot tin roof." The obvious metaphor—a cat in heat, so desperate for sexual release that she is going mad without it—applies here and goes a long way in explaining the film's popularity. After telling her to jump off the roof and take a lover, Brick asks to know what a victory would be for a cat on a hot tin roof. Taylor smiles slightly, assuming eventual triumph when she says, "Just staying on it I guess, long as she can." It is Maggie who has staying power, focus, and determination, qualities that shine through in Taylor. She may not come close to being great or inspired in the role, performing more commendably than brilliantly, but it's also true that the screen Maggie isn't as multi-dimensional a role as the stage Maggie. Still, Taylor never feels inauthentic, which is why she retains her likability and justifies her casting. Though she had been raised as a Hollywood princess, Taylor can appear remarkably "regular," someone you might affectionately call "a real broad." There's nothing remote or superior about her, and her down-to-earth charms resonate rather well in a part like Maggie, a role that could easily have been pushed into overkill on both its sexual and "Southern" terms.

The play's first act is a virtual monologue for Maggie, but the movie breaks things up, getting Taylor famously into her white slip—an iconic movie image of the 1950s—for her second scene with Brick. She is dressing for Big Daddy's birthday party, which Brick refuses to attend. Though Maggie accepts that they "occupy the same cage," she never gives up on Brick, sensing that she's wearing him down. (Here the movie is tipping its hand toward the revised ending to come.) By now Taylor is in that sumptuous white dress (by Helen Rose) that wafts so elegantly whenever she moves, her costume for the remainder of the movie. Brick's mother, Big Mama (Judith Anderson), soon corners her: "You're childless and my son drinks." That says it all regarding the way the marriage is seen by the family, but the screenplay pulverizes the play's explanations of how that state of affairs came about. The movie is terribly uncomfortable with every mention of Brick's best friend, the unseen (and now dead) Skipper, the play's unambiguous homosexual.

Taylor is credible as a woman raised without money, a deprived pretty girl who married "up" but cannot forget what financial humiliation and insecurity feel like. When she speaks of her wedding dress being "a hand-me-down from a snotty rich cousin I hated," Taylor offers a vivid picture of the kinds of humbling embarrassments that Maggie had to absorb gracefully. Though rich-boy Brick crumbles in difficult times, poor-girl Maggie dusts herself off and goes on. Taylor carries the red-hot spark of a girl who climbed out of her surroundings but preserved her hard-knocks sensibility, a quality not necessarily found in the great homes. And so we root for her. "Maggie the Cat is alive!" she shrieks at Brick, and no one could doubt her. If Taylor lacked Scarlett O'Hara-style finesse in *Raintree County*, she finds some of it as Maggie, mostly by chasing Brick as resolutely as Scarlett chased Ashley, two seemingly unattainable prizes.

But then it all goes screwy, leaving the play behind because homosexuality was still too controversial a subject for the mass audience, with no more than a hint of it allowed. The back story in the film resembles that of the play, with Maggie having planned to seduce Skipper (in the play, to prove he's gay; in the movie, to prove he's no good). The screenplay then goes its own way, with Maggie recounting how she was unable to go through with bedding the willing Skipper, out of fear that her plan would backfire. Maggie is reduced to someone misunderstood, an unfairly blamed victim. In both play and film, Maggie is threatened by Skipper's bond with Brick, feeling like an unwelcome intruder, but in the film she wants exoneration from a sin she didn't commit. Taylor handles this monologue—the film's revised account of Maggie's experience with Skipper—very well, again balancing tenacity and sensitivity, even though the writing isn't believable. In both versions, Maggie pressed the issue with Skipper, which led to his undoing, and that is why Brick can't forgive her. Since the screen Brick has never believed her explanation of what happened, she says, of Skipper, "I didn't get rid of him at all." But the stakes are so much lower in the movie, and the triangle so much vaguer. If Skipper was really just Brick's best friend, though personally too needy and professionally too dependent, then the plot doesn't rise to the level of

potent drama. Yes, Maggie would have felt jealous and left out, but without the sexual component is this really worth anyone's time? Taylor's straightforward delivery saves the scene, even though she's given a new and melodramatic end to Skipper's story, a lame line about his improbable utterance to her in the ambulance after his eleven-story jump: "Why did Brick hang up on me, why?" Anyone watching this movie will have the same question.

While Brick bonds with Big Daddy in the basement, Maggie fights Brick's battles with Gooper and Mae. Taylor shows compassion for Judith Anderson's Big Mama, which is an accomplishment; it's hard to get that close to someone *acting* that hard. The gutsy pleasures of Taylor's Maggie dissipate whenever she appears tormented by Gooper and Mae's attacks. But things pick up when Taylor lunges at Madeleine Sherwood's Mae (though they are prevented from coming to blows by Jack Carson's Gooper). Maggie stuns them all with her lie to Big Daddy that she is pregnant. She has a victory when her lie is defended by the new and improved Brick, who is sober and cleansed and magically transformed after one day of father-son forgiveness and truth-telling. When he calls her to their bedroom, Taylor is all aglow, shouting "Yes, sir!" and then racing to him obediently. She thanks him for backing her up, allowing him to take command. Consummation is moments away. In both versions of the play's final act, Maggie is the one still in charge, but a happy Hollywood ending could mean only that the husband has become "the man" again and that "the woman" has found joyful subservience.

Taylor received her second consecutive Best Actress Oscar nomination for *Cat*, losing the award to Susan Hayward's unbeatable journey to the gas chamber in the raw and grungy real-life drama *I Want to Live!* In a showier and more provocative role than the screen's diluted Maggie the Cat, Hayward proved tough and headstrong but also rather limited, lacking the variety, range, and vocal chops to astound as a woman headed for death row. (I prefer Hayward in *The Lusty Men* and *I'll Cry Tomorrow*.) Shirley MacLaine (*Some Came Running*) was the most deserving pick among the nominees, while non-nominee Shirley Booth (*The Matchmaker*) was also exceedingly Oscar-worthy.

Taylor's next film was her second Williams vehicle, an adaptation of his one-act play *Suddenly Last Sum-*

mer, a title without the name recognition (or catchiness) of *Cat on a Hot Tin Roof.* The play premiered Off-Broadway in 1958 as the second half of an evening called *Garden District;* the curtain-raiser was Williams' *Something Unspoken. Suddenly Last Summer* is a bizarre and self-conscious work more suited to the adventurous milieu of Off-Broadway than the commercial theatre, which is not to imply that the play was too good for Broadway, but, rather, a piece in which Williams appears to have been testing the limits of just how far he could go. Is he putting us on with *Suddenly Last Summer*? Was he daring audiences to take seriously this elaborate stunt of a play? Though its themes are remarkably similar to those in his previous hits, its plot is florid and fantastic. Up to this point, the Williams films were essentially realistic domestic dramas (or comedy-dramas), but *Suddenly, Last Summer* (which gained a comma for the screen) bears scant resemblance to what may be called "real life," even though it deals with familial relationships. The film would challenge moviegoers' suspension of disbelief as no previous Williams picture had. And if the public had been left wondering what exactly had happened in *Cat,* then what did they make of the black-and-white grandeur of *Suddenly, Last Summer,* with its stew of homosexuality, cannibalism, and the dominating threat of a lobotomy? (Williams' sister, Rose, had undergone a prefrontal lobotomy in 1943.) On a stage, this material can luxuriate in its theatricality and symbolism, but it becomes problematic in the more naturalistic realm of a Hollywood movie. A major problem with the film is how it turned Williams' dark fable into a ridiculously literal and heavy-handed drama, which inadvertently serves to make the material seem even screwier. Onstage and on film, *Suddenly, Last Summer* is minor Williams, but, to his credit, only he could have come up with something quite like it. And no one could ever accuse it of being boring.

Cat cashed in on the image of Taylor in her white slip, but *Suddenly, Last Summer* went a bit further, becoming the movie in which a wet Taylor could be ogled in a one-piece white bathing suit (with a cutout between her breasts). The bathing suit sold tickets, making the movie another hefty box-office hit, however unlikely the commercial appeal of its content. Despite the bathing suit, and all the praise her performance received, Taylor is not at her best; in fact, she's terrible. Gone is the actress' comfort in her

own skin, the component that made her Maggie the Cat so grounded. As the victimized Catherine Holly of *Suddenly, Last Summer,* Taylor gives an emotionally unconnected performance in which she screeches her lines in a hapless and effortful attempt to merge with the character. As was the case in *Raintree County,* she is most effective in quiet and simple moments, scenes in which she isn't pressured to deliver results. Her innate practicality as an actress makes her resist the role's extravagances: the uncontained emotion, the heightened language, the outlandish circumstances. And she doesn't possess the range to excel beyond her comfort zone. Some of the blame falls to Williams because Catherine lacks complexity; she is little more than a guiltless pawn with enemies on all sides. Though top-billed, Taylor does not appear until thirty-five minutes into the movie.

Suddenly, Last Summer is set in 1937 yet nothing about it says anything but 1959, not a dress nor a hairstyle, nothing more than a single automobile. I presume the point of identifying the year is a way to explain the story's medical background, specifically that this is the time when lobotomies were becoming a new surgical option. Mrs. Violet Venable (Katharine Hepburn), the richest woman in New Orleans, is interested in securing a lobotomy for Catherine, her niece by marriage, at the Lions View State Asylum. With the institution in dire straits, Mrs. Venable makes a generous offer (bribe): a million dollars for a new psycho-surgery building in exchange for Catherine's operation. The film opens at the asylum, with a cheesy *Snake Pit*-like prowl through the women's ward as every cliché screen-loony finds her way into the frame. This is director Joseph L. Mankiewicz's lame attempt at getting the movie off to a lurid, chilling start, and it might have worked if it weren't so laughably familiar. Dr. Cukrowicz (Montgomery Clift), a Chicago surgeon now employed at Lions View, arrives to perform his specialty, the lobotomy. (Cukrowicz later identifies himself as being Polish. Is this good-guy Pole the playwright's compensation for bad-guy Stanley Kowalski?) Cukrowicz, which means "sugar" in Polish, is the film's largest role. Clift is in nearly every scene, while Taylor and Hepburn have long breaks and never appear together without him. Yet Cukrowicz is a service role, merely a feed to the film's flamboyant females. Clift gives Taylor and Hepburn their cues, pays them due attention, and stays out of their way. He suggests a piece of dry

Pardon Me While I Steal This Movie

For Katharine Hepburn, the character of Violet Venable was a turning point. She had spent the 1950s in her spinster phase, winning Oscar nominations for playing lonely middle-aged women who find love and/or romance in *The African Queen* (1951), *Summertime* (1955), and *The Rainmaker* (1956). With Violet, Hepburn was embarking on her "mother" persona of the next decade, which would result in Oscar nominations not only for playing this character but also for the mothers she portrayed in *Long*

Day's Journey into Night (1962), *Guess Who's Coming to Dinner* (1967), and *The Lion in Winter* (1968). (She won for those last two.) Hepburn's triumph in *Suddenly, Last Summer* is similar to Vivien Leigh's as Blanche in *Streetcar,* another case of a 1930s movie star proving that she could be a stimulating addition to a more permissive screen era, able to ally herself with a groundbreaking writer and probe darker facets of her talent. Hepburn's performance is especially exhilarating because Violet is the only character in the movie explored with any nuance.

cleaning on a hanger, but he manages to make it to the end of the movie intact.

Suddenly, Last Summer is the third Williams film, after *A Streetcar Named Desire* and *Cat on a Hot Tin Roof,* whose plot hinges on a safely dead homosexual. The *Streetcar* film glossed over the play's details about gay Allan Grey (Blanche's husband), making the point obliquely. *Cat*'s film totally revamped Williams' play because the explicitly gay content (the character Skipper) got too close to the male lead (Brick), who on film became necessarily straight. *Suddenly, Last Summer* was able to go further than the previous films, while remaining faithful to its source, because its gay character, Sebastian (Violet's son), has no sexual connection to any other character in the story (unlike Skipper's link to Brick) and therefore could not "taint" any Hollywood actor through on-screen association. (Ironically, gay Montgomery Clift has to look suitably clueless regarding the mystery surrounding Sebastian.) I suppose someone could have dreamed up a way to make Sebastian straight, perhaps making drug addiction his secret, but this wasn't really necessary. The details of Sebastian's story are so baffling and outrageous that what audiences got was a metaphoric and macabre tale rather than a serious exploration of gay life. As with Allan and Skipper, Williams' portrait of Sebastian is depressing and hopeless. Sebastian died, reportedly from a heart attack, while traveling with his cousin Catherine in Europe last summer. Traumatized by his death, Catherine told stories about the surrounding events, stories that greatly offended her aunt. Catherine has been at St. Mary's (a home for the insane) ever since. She is unable to speak the truth, much of which she has suppressed.

The bulk of the pre-Taylor section of the film is

Hepburn's superb scene in her garden, the movie's best and most memorable sequence. Her disembodied (yet inimitable) voice signals her grand entrance, descending to the ground floor of her mansion in her one-woman elevator, seated like a queen. Hepburn uses no Southern accent, playing the widowed dowager as too superior for anything as common as a regional accent, even finding a later opportunity to mock the Southern accents of Catherine's relatives. Hepburn's usual rarefied speech is acceptable, though you wonder if laziness is the reason she isn't more "Southern." Past fifty, Hepburn looks lovely and elegant, all in white, radiating an enveloping charm, the better for Violet to wheedle the malleable Dr. Cukrowicz to her purpose. The marvel of Hepburn's mesmerizing performance, and what so completely obliterates her co-stars, is her love of Williams' words, the way she savors every syllable. Listen to the gorgeous things she does with words like "Dementia Praecox" or "Hong Kong" or "debris" (accent on the first syllable). No matter how rapidly she speaks, every meaning is articulated, every transition is fluid, and every subject change becomes a deft maneuver. It is a beautifully spoken performance. The emotional swings, the blatant lies, and the simmering layers of protective delusion make Violet a warm-up for Hepburn's next (and greatest) performance as Mary Tyrone in *Long Day's Journey Into Night* (1962). She clasps Dr. Cukrowicz's arm in a warmly conspiratorial manner, ingratiating herself as they walk through Sebastian's garden, a backyard tropical forest, an unexpected jungle. It is a voluptuous visual, Sebastian's "dawn of creation" in all its beauty and horror, a microcosm of the world's savagery. Hepburn, an exotic flower herself, is properly eccentric and fanciful, but she has flickers of both

Not a Full Monty

Three years after his horrific car accident, Montgomery Clift appears shakier than ever, further depleted by his dependency on drugs and alcohol. Taylor, out of devotion to their friendship, was instrumental in his being in the movie (and *staying* in the movie), despite his absurd casting. Obviously weak and fragile, he's the last person in the world to whom you would entrust an experimental surgery. Clift is six years past his peak achievement, *From Here to Eternity* (1953), in which he gave an emotionally transparent and quietly riveting performance. By 1959, he was an entirely different presence, a comatose shell of the gifted and beautiful actor he had been. (Too bad Clift didn't play Tom in the 1950 *Glass Menagerie*, a role that suited his sensitive and troubled persona perfectly.)

imperious coldness and shattering frailty. You might say that this was Hepburn's only true villain role, even though that categorization diminishes the breadth of her performance. Her devious powers of persuasion would be even more impressive if she were acting with someone who showed some resistance to her finesse. With Clift such a wet blanket, her polished efforts hardly seem worth the trouble.

Hepburn glows especially when talking about Sebastian, who emerges as an aesthete, a poet who produced one work per year, each poem inspired by a summer vacation with Violet. When Violet speaks of Sebastian's desire to remain unknown, unpolluted by fame, her unintended implication is that he was a bad poet who was wealthy enough to indulge his pretensions. She says, "We were a famous couple" and "We needed no one but one another." There's no politically correct way to say this: Violet Venable is a fag hag. She reveled in her son's erudite company, which made her feel sophisticated and altogether "fabulous," rather than just rich, vain, and snobbish. Violet saw herself as a poet's muse, and she is now devoted to preserving his name, or, rather, creating his name, determined to delete sexual orientation from his story (with the help of Catherine's lobotomy). A stereotype of the gay son's clinging mother (and as overbearing as *The Glass Menagerie*'s Amanda), she of course knew that her son was gay but chose not to see it. In his studio, there's a painting of a naked male

(from behind) and a sculpture of a male torso, but we can presume Sebastian was fairly discreet about his sexual activities. Violet may describe him as "fastidious," or with other euphemistic adjectives, but Sebastian was still a son who had sex with men. She is disturbed by her niece's "babbling" and her "hideous attacks" on Sebastian's "moral character." Hepburn's performance is fiendishly shrewd but not altogether unsympathetic because her conniving, however ugly and selfish, comes from Violet's psychological desperation and unfathomable sadness. Hepburn has stolen a movie that has only begun, and she will show up periodically to put the rest of the cast in its place.

When Taylor at last appears, she is deglamorized by her standards, though her plain dress is tight-fitting enough to put the focus on her breasts. Things get off to a good start when a nun at St. Mary's reprimands her for smoking, which results in Catherine putting out the cigarette in the nun's hand. It appears that Taylor is going to be bold and feisty, like Barbara Stanwyck in one of her prison stays. Since this is supposedly 1937, and Catherine is a maltreated woman with some fight in her (plus a constant craving for a smoke), you can also imagine a young Bette Davis or Ida Lupino in the role. But there's no such excitement in Taylor, who doesn't have a flair for jittery, jangled emotions. The level of concentration that she sustained as Maggie the Cat, in both character and accent, is nowhere evident. Here her Southern accent is occasional, as if she is still testing dialect variations without having made any final decision. Her monologue about being raped, prior to "last summer," has little impact. (Imagine what the

A Jungle Out There

The key monologue in the first part of the film is Hepburn's to Clift in which Violet remembers her trip with Sebastian to the Galapagos Islands ("the Encantadas"). Sebastian wanted to see the great sea turtles deposit their eggs in the sand. More importantly, he then wanted to return for the eggs' hatching. As all those baby turtles raced to the sea, birds swooped down and tore hungrily into their flesh, leaving few survivors. Hammering his theme of the cruelty of God and nature, Williams also foreshadows Sebastian's own gruesome death. "The killers inherited the earth," Violet says, "but then they always do, don't they?"

Stand back everyone, Ms. Taylor is about to scream in **Suddenly, Last Summer**.

1937 Davis or Lupino could have done with such a meaty speech.) After Hepburn's "aria" in the garden, Taylor's complementary "aria" in the asylum is a letdown. She cannot get a handle on Catherine or surmount the obvious pitfall of the role's victimization. Catherine is a target: Aunt Violet is conspiring for her lobotomy; the hospital is willing to satisfy Violet to get the Venable money; even Catherine's family is ready to ensure their fair share by following Violet's orders. Dr. Cukrowicz is her only ally, though he is not yet sure about Catherine's mental state. Taylor's performance might have been more intriguing if the character's sanity was ever really in doubt. Flawed as the role is, it is still more interesting than Taylor plays it. After all, you could do worse than playing a woman unjustly incarcerated in a mental institution while suffering with an amnesiac block (added for the film) regarding her cousin's death. Taylor and Clift, teamed unromantically (in their third and final film together), generate nothing on-screen, not even glimmers of their great off-screen friendship. As she

keeps straining to coerce herself into emotional frenzies, he looks on passively, hardly providing the kind of partnering that might have lifted her performance. Clift unconsciously makes the plot scarier because it's so hard to have any faith in him as her protector.

Once situated at Lions View, Catherine has been glamorized (at the doctor's orders), having had her hair done and now wearing a tasteful black dress from last summer's stop in Paris. (Let's not forget that moviegoers came to see Elizabeth Taylor!) Catherine has a reunion with her foolish and gabby mother (Mercedes McCambridge) and her brother, George (Gary Raymond), both very Southern in their speech. Mrs. Holly and George fill the Gooper and Mae slots from *Cat on a Hot Tin Roof*, the greedy relatives looking out for themselves. (Whereas Madeleine Sherwood consummately made Mae three-dimensional, watch McCambridge utterly condescend to her character, telegraphing that she is only play-acting at being a horrid woman.) And there's no mother-daughter connection, good or bad, between Taylor and McCambridge (who played Taylor's sister-in-law in *Giant*). The Hollys not only want Catherine to allow herself to be committed (so that Violet will not block George's share of Sebastian's money), but they also reveal to her the surprising news of her impending lobotomy. Whenever riled, as she so often is here, Taylor reveals a mannerism undetected in previous performances, a halting delivery. She utters her lines in staccato blasts, suggesting poor breath control more than harrowing emotion. This is consistently irritating and ineffective, and it happens throughout the movie. It is the kind of mannerism that Bette Davis was able to use to startling effect, but it just seems to exhaust Taylor. Her voice grates as she wails, "You can't let them!" She runs out of the room and directly into one of the film's invented scenes. Although the play is entirely situated at the Venable home, the screenplay managed to use nearly all of the play's text by moving some of the dialogue to new scenes in different locations. Though Williams shares screen credit with Gore Vidal for adapting his one-act drama to feature-film length, Vidal states in his autobiography, *Palimpsest*, that he wrote the screenplay by himself and that Williams' credit was merely a perk provided by producer Sam Spiegel. (If I were Vidal I wouldn't be bragging.) The new scene is another mental-institution exploitation moment, with Taylor accidentally entering the men's day room (on a bridge above the inmates). As she contemplates her lobotomized future, some aroused fellows paw at her ankles. The movie has tried to break up all the talk with some purely visual action, however silly.

Taylor and Hepburn at last meet, seventy-two minutes into the movie, for a highly anticipated showdown. Along with Violet's misery over her son's death is her seething jealousy over Catherine, who took Violet's place last summer. Sebastian's invitation to Catherine was a painful rejection for Violet, but it now allows her to blame Catherine for the tragic results. Before their shared moments, Hepburn has a scene at the hospital with Clift in which she tells him that Sebastian was "chaste," above mere carnality, which sounds like a motherly excuse for why her precious boy never found the right girl, or *any* girl besides her. (Sebastian was hardly a boy who found everything he needed in dear old mother.) Hepburn detects the duality in Violet's nature, both her blind conviction in her rewrite of history and her thinly

disguised awareness of who Sebastian really was and how he lived. When Catherine, coming out of sedation, confronts Violet, watch Hepburn underplay, instinctively knowing that this is the way to out-act the easily overexerted Taylor. Now the facts start coming out. Sebastian replaced Violet with Catherine for a specific function, though it is hard to imagine any circumstance in which Elizabeth Taylor and Katharine Hepburn might be interchangeable. Catherine refers to herself and her aunt as "decoys" and "bait," and then explicitly states, "We procured for him." Then comes the lie in Williams' conceit: "Sebastian was shy with people." It is not plausible that Sebastian, a very rich, high-living, and fashionable gay man, by all accounts charming and attractive, would have relied on eye-catching women to draw potential lovers to him. This is an absurdly convoluted and questionable strategy, his use of women to lure men who would then sleep with him. Was Violet his "Auntie Mame," getting all the gay boys to worship at her feet so that he could then pounce? Where in the text is an example of Sebastian's so-called shyness? "We both made contacts for him," Catherine continues, as if he required the services of a delusional mother and a naïve cousin. (Though Violet would have figured out Sebastian's tactics, they certainly never discussed them.) Sebastian isn't afforded much dignity, but couldn't Williams at least have given him the ability to find sex on his own? As Taylor gets louder and shriller and starts talking about the truth being cut out of her brain, you, too, may be rooting for Catherine's silence.

The second invented scary-movie sequence is Catherine's far-fetched suicide attempt, following the run-in with her aunt. This is another ploy to "open up" a talky script. With a blank expression, Taylor enters the women's ward on a raised level, high atop the patients. She climbs over the rail to the accompanying giggles of the *Snake Pit* extras. Catherine is supposedly hopeless, but when exactly did she give up? Wasn't she, moments before, declaring the truth in a most lucid and spirited fashion? This unsuspenseful scene is gratuitous; no one could imagine that she would really jump. The scene worsens when Taylor improbably starts screaming her head off when rescued by an intern. Why is she suddenly so hysterically desperate to end it all? Neither the screenplay nor Taylor is able to connect the dots in Catherine's thinking, advancing the impression that she is a hollow creation and that Taylor needed more help than she got in fleshing her out. But this is all leading to the climactic stunt that will crack open her memory and release her demons. And it must be staged at Sebastian's garden, according to Cukrowicz. Why? Because it's the best set in the movie and such a display ought to be staged in a theatrical setting, right? (In the play, this is Violet's idea.) Clift administers truth serum to Taylor (which doesn't make her acting more truthful) in a scene with intimations, oblivious to Clift, of a possible future romance. He asks her to give him all her "resistance," an odd request since Clift appears so much limper than Taylor. All his character needs to be is solid and smart, but Clift is simply too inconsequential a presence. Her passionate kiss and sexual need aren't reciprocated by him. (Clift would later score in more intentionally vulnerable roles in *Wild River* [1960] and *The Misfits* [1961].)

Taylor's overwritten monologue is treated like an exorcism, with the rest of the principals gathered around for the big show. (I assume Hepburn wasn't present for any moment in which she's not actually seen, sparing herself much of this spectacle.) The scene and its revelations are positioned in the manner of an old-time witness-stand mad scene, again invoking Davis and Lupino, but its effectiveness is derailed by Taylor's inability to make Williams' words sound as if they would actually come from her lips. The writing is filled with repetitions, including many descriptions of white light, and it all sounds, in Taylor's reading, like words on a page with no special resonance for the actress saying them. When characters recall past incidents in the film versions of *Streetcar* and *Cat*, there are no flashbacks, but that's not the case here. And it's easy to see why. This is the film's chance to deliver sex (Taylor in her bathing suit) and violence (Sebastian's death), but, more importantly, the flashback takes the pressure off Taylor to hold the screen for such an extended time, something of which she wasn't capable. The images are smoothly edited to allow her to share the screen with the flashback, narrating at the sidelines. But here the literal nature of the film is at its most damaging. Williams wrote this monologue to be performed on a stage, offering an actress the opportunity to evoke his audacious imagery through her fierce commitment to his words. Audiences could either accept her story or take into

"Sebastian and Violet, Violet and Sebastian"

Suddenly, Last Summer is filled with recurrent Williams themes (though often taken to extremes): deliberate cruelty (from *Streetcar*), here seen in Violet's cold-blooded attempt to destroy Catherine, but also in the complicity of Catherine's family in Violet's plot, as well as the violence of God and nature, ultimately reflected in Sebastian's murder; living in delusion (again from *Streetcar*), here depicted in Violet's need to sustain her myths about herself and her son, and her mental snapping when that's no longer possible, resulting in a "kindness of strangers" kind of exit; the inability to face homosexuality (from *Cat*), again a trait of Violet, who cannot openly accept the sexual orientation of her son. It is interesting that most of what is compelling about the piece is to be found in the two Venables, mother and son, with Catherine a mere prop in their story. This is another reason the deck was so stacked against Taylor. Catherine's plight, an injured party fighting the odds, feels generic, mired in melodramatic pain as she is tossed haphazardly from crisis to crisis.

account possible tricks of memory and perspective and comprehension. But the film *shows* what happened, on realistic locations, including moments that couldn't have been observed by Catherine, specifically much of the climactic chase (which moves far ahead of her). What had been a fevered recollection of a nightmarish event is now a filmed record, less plausible thanks to the "realism."

Sebastian, who is seen from behind or in long shot (though his face remains obscured), is bent on a form of sacrificial suicide, obsessed as he is with the cruelty of God, nature, and humanity. Taylor is seen in "decoy" mode, coming out of the water in the white swimsuit (and bathing cap) and driving wild the beach boys of Spain's Cabeza de Lobo. This was "to attract attention," allowing Sebastian to approach a group of males. In no way suggesting shyness, Sebastian is later holding court on the beach. But, unlike in the jet-set locales he frequented with Violet, Sebastian was now dealing with hungry youths. Maybe his tastes had gotten rougher, or his self-destructive impulses more pronounced, or both, and he now craved the excitement that came with danger. Sebastian had heart trouble and he did pop pills, but his horrible death is orchestrated by a death-wish mentality, an acceptance of life's cruelty, perhaps augmented by the boredom of always having anything he wanted, and the realization that he had no talent for anything beyond pleasure. In increasing numbers, dirty boys and young men (described as naked in the play) chase him up a hill. Even after Sebastian throws money at them, they persist. Many of his pursuers are playing makeshift instruments, turning the sequence into a formalized ritual, which on-screen looks too perfectly organized and choreographed. Bosoms heaving, Taylor is seen racing up the hill to Sebastian. As she hyperventilates her way through the words, an already taxing speech becomes increasingly unwieldy; it is hooey of an especially literate and gory nature. Williams, assisted by Vidal, goes over the top. How do you account for a line as bad as this one, when Catherine describes the sun as "a great white bone of a giant beast that had caught on fire in the sky." Awful, yes; now imagine Taylor saying it, making it worse. As Sebastian climbs higher, so does Taylor's voice. He is overtaken, with only one of his arms emerging from the cluster of bodies surrounding him. Taylor backs up in revulsion, finally unleashing three blood-curdling (and rather hilarious) screams of "Help!"

The flashback has ended but the monologue continues, with Taylor sobbing. Catherine found Sebastian's naked body, which looked as though parts of it had been "devoured." Taylor collapses onto the ground, still bawling as she speaks in the tinny, toneless timbre of a child. Finally, it's over. Hepburn has the right response; she promptly goes mad. (Violet does not go mad in the play, so, thanks to Vidal, Hepburn has a graceful and happily mad send-off.) After mistaking Cukrowicz for Sebastian, Violet makes her way to her elevator, off to fantasy land. (Maybe that proposed lobotomy won't go to waste after all.) Again, in one swift move, Hepburn steals the show from Taylor, who had been acting up a storm for an interminable length of time. Taylor has the final scene, though, an acknowledgment that Catherine's catharsis has healed her. She will be fine, perhaps marrying the doctor. Who could have expected, or wanted, such a simplistic, convenient, and conventionally happy ending?

Taylor might have been better as Catherine if she had been more carefully guided by Mankie-

wicz, a man who had directed some spectacular performances, including Bette Davis in *All About Eve* (1950), James Mason in *5 Fingers* (1952), Michael Redgrave in *The Quiet American* (1958), not to mention Hepburn's Violet Venable. So why was he of no help to Taylor? Most of her scenes feel like unfocused first takes that merited further tries. Mankiewicz didn't shape her performance, leaving her to fend and flail for herself, especially in her inability to modulate her voice. Mankiewicz's gift as a director was in making witty material scintillate on-screen, as in the best sections of *A Letter to Three Wives* (1949) and *all* of *All About Eve*. He also was skilled at making fascinating, introspective character studies, such as the aforementioned *5 Fingers* and *The Quiet American*. The nutty and baroque affectations of *Suddenly, Last Summer* were beyond Mankiewicz's lean, understated sensibility. Though talky films were Mankiewicz's specialty, Williams and Vidal didn't provide his *kind* of talk. It is doubtful that there was a way for anyone to make a great film from this play. The material isn't first-rate and it required a delicate hyper-real tone. Perhaps Elia Kazan could have pulled it off, and maybe a more versatile actress than Taylor, such as Jean Simmons, could have made Catherine a whole being. In *Memoirs*, Williams says of the film, "The profits were as good as the movie was bad." This Columbia production was filmed in England, though the flashback was staged in Spain. Clift is second-billed in the opening credits while Hepburn is billed third, but they switch places in the closing credits. And, for anyone keeping track of such things, Hepburn and Taylor each say the title twice, and "Catherine" had been "Catharine" in the play.

Taylor won the Golden Globe for Best Actress (Drama) for *Suddenly, Last Summer* and received her third consecutive Oscar nomination, with Hepburn alongside her as one of the other nominees. This marked the second time in Oscar history that two actresses from the same film competed in the lead category. Coincidentally, the first instance was also for a Mankiewicz film, when Bette Davis and Anne Baxter were recognized (and lost) for *All About Eve*. *Suddenly, Last Summer*'s third Oscar nomination was for black-and-white art direction, a nod to the lushly overwhelming Venable garden.

Taylor was at the height of her popularity and acclaim, while also the darling and/or devil of the tab-

And the Oscar Goes to...

Taylor and Hepburn lost the 1959 Best Actress Oscar to Simone Signoret for her exquisite performance as the married woman in an affair with younger Laurence Harvey in the excellent (if a bit bludgeoning) *Room at the Top.* Signoret's soulful and restrained performance is the kind of intimately wrought achievement that Oscar rarely notices. However, the award that year truly belonged to Audrey Hepburn for *The Nun's Story,* a brilliantly developed and luminous piece of acting, the beloved Audrey's finest hour.

loids. Since Mike Todd's death, she made headlines for the following: stealing Eddie Fisher from wife Debbie Reynolds; marrying Fisher right before beginning work on *Suddenly, Last Summer;* having a near-death bout with pneumonia; winning the Best Actress Oscar for *Butterfield 8* (1960), a movie she hated and made only to end her ties to MGM. Her Oscar was one of those sympathy awards: expressing appreciation that she hadn't died; forgiving her for hurting Debbie; and as consolation for her three previous losses. *Butterfield 8* is glossy trash, a surprisingly old-fashioned and moralizing soap opera, like a racy pre-Code "woman's picture" defanged for 1960. Though Taylor did not deserve the Oscar, the movie at least restored the likably blunt and wisecracking Taylor reminiscent of *Giant* and *Cat.* Directed by *The Rose Tattoo*'s Daniel Mann, *Butterfield 8* is the movie in which Taylor, as a "model," writes "No Sale" in lipstick on lover Laurence Harvey's mirror after she finds $250 in her purse. (She then promptly steals his wife's fur coat.) Eddie Fisher plays her best pal, a supporting role (in which he's dreadful). In *Room at the Top* and *Butterfield 8*—back-to-back "Best Actress" Oscar-winning movies co-starring Laurence Harvey—Simone Signoret and Elizabeth Taylor both die in climactic car accidents.

Taylor reteamed with Mankiewicz on a little something called *Cleopatra* (1963), a movie so unbearably dull that it makes you regret every bad thing you ever said about Cecil B. DeMille. It became most famous for its behind-the-scenes drama in which Taylor, via co-star Richard Burton (as her Marc Antony), did to Eddie Fisher what Fisher had done to Debbie Reynolds. Taylor and Burton's off-screen affair must have

sapped all their energy because they have little on-screen chemistry. Aside from some impressive production values, and a classy performance from Rex Harrison as Julius Caesar, *Cleopatra* is four hours of wide-screen anesthesia, yet it actually feels rushed, hurtling to get to the next boring scene, all too enervating and rudderless to be any fun. Under Mankiewicz's direction, Taylor was again at her worst. If George Stevens was the man who got the finest results out of Taylor, then Mankiewicz was the man who didn't have a clue how to tap her talent. Her Cleopatra lacks wit and command, coming off as no more than a pretty face in a foul mood. Compared to Vivien Leigh's 1945 Cleopatra, Taylor is graceless, tacky, and devoid of any queenly style or physical panache. She also doesn't rate alongside Claudette Colbert's borderline tongue-in-cheek siren of DeMille's *Cleopatra* (1934), but I'll give Taylor this: she surpassed Rhonda Fleming's vapid, Halloween-party Cleo of *Serpent of the Nile* (1953).

Before their marriage in 1964, the soon-to-be Burtons were quickly reteamed in the shiny sterility of *The V.I.P.s* (1963), taking advantage of all that *Cleopatra* publicity and bringing their high glamour quotient to an ensemble soap opera centered in a fog-bound London airport. As the disenchanted wife of Burton's self-made tycoon, Taylor is about to run off with playboy Louis Jourdan. But Burton intends to fight for her. Since it's a foregone conclusion that she will return to him, it is made explicit that her "affair" has not been consummated. Taylor, with hair tightly wrapped in a bun, keeps whining and moaning about needing to feel needed. Though Jourdan makes a hopeless attempt to come between the stars, his performance has considerably more verve than either of theirs. But the film fulfilled its sole function—to make a profit—as did *The Sandpiper* (1965), the first Taylor-Burton picture released after their marriage, proving that the duo remained a box-office draw even without the lure of their unwedded bliss. Like *The V.I.P.s, The Sandpiper* is high-minded trash, an overlong and humorless yawn directed by Vincente Minnelli. This reunion for Taylor and Minnelli came a decade and a half after their pair of *Father of the Bride* pictures, which had depicted Taylor as America's prettiest embodiment of young womanhood and eager domesticity. In keeping with her much-altered persona of the mid-sixties, *The Sandpiper* has Taylor playing a rule-breaking, sexually free grown-up, specifically an unwed bohemian painter who home-schools her nine-year-old son. With no real income, she is somehow the kind of bohemian with an extensive Irene Sharaff wardrobe and a fabulous "shack" on the ocean at Big Sur. Her affair with Burton, a married minister, results in one of her worst performances, either too shrill or too soft-spoken, with rarely any modulations in between. *The Sandpiper* may have been the last hurrah for a certain brand of MGM gloss, the type of lustrous rubbish (which would include *Butterfield 8* and *The V.I.P.s*) that was more concerned with costume changes than character development. It would be hard to imagine a squarer film about nonconformity, despite all its blather about religion, sex, and women's roles. Isn't it ultimately just *Back Street* all over again?

After establishing serious-actress credentials in the late 1950s, which culminated in her 1960 Oscar win, the post-*Cleopatra* Taylor seemed determined to undo all of her hard work. This dispiriting trend was reversed when the Burtons starred in *Who's Afraid of Virginia Woolf?* (1966), an impressive and uncompromising rendering of Edward Albee's shattering 1962 Broadway play, an examination of a marriage which addresses what tears its central couple apart, what holds them together, and how they absorb life's disappointments and keep on going. The material is somewhat diminished by the film's understandable inclusion of scenes set outside the play's living-room pressure cooker. Even so, Haskell Wexler's black-and-white cinematography is extraordinary, and the direction by first-time filmmaker Mike Nichols is unfailingly intelligent. At thirty-three, Taylor is clearly not old enough to be playing Martha, a blowsy middle-aged wreck, but she committed to the role as she hadn't to any other since Maggie the Cat. In spite of her noticeable age makeup and essential miscasting, she is remarkable, especially in her quieter moments in the second half. Taylor displays considerable guts and abandon, which can sometimes lead to an obvious straining for desired effects, particularly when she's cackling. But the film contains much of her most powerful work, and she certainly comes through in the most important scenes. Taylor's unexpected casting provides an undeniable charge, but the movie still belongs to Burton. After three embarrassing pairings, the Burtons delivered an artistic triumph *and* a sen-

sational box-office success, a film whose sexual content and explicit language helped move the industry into a new era of permissiveness. And who better to help ease that transition than two mainstream movie stars? Taylor won her second Best Actress Oscar, and this time no one derided her award as being unmerited or as payback for former slights.

Having tackled Albee victoriously, why not take a stab at Shakespeare? After all, Taylor was currently married to one of the most respected Shakespeareans in the business. *The Taming of the Shrew* (1967) was a logical choice for the Burtons, a robust comedy that permitted them to engage in lively verbal brawls not so far removed from those they had performed so effectively in *Virginia Woolf*. (Actually, Taylor turned just about every subsequent major role she played into yet another variation of loud, bad-tempered Martha.) Mounted lavishly by director Franco Zeffirelli, *Shrew* is a boisterous Shakespeare film, though it's marred by Zeffirelli's exhausting determination never to be boring, making the comedy more relentlessly overactive than actually funny. Ironically, the Burtons continued to display little in the way of on-screen sexual chemistry, the kind that would have brought a sensible and enlivening subtext to the warring couple at *Shrew*'s center. As in *Virginia Woolf,* Taylor is game and fearless, putting on a brazen good show and meeting the challenge ably, despite her apparent "classical" limitations. (As was usually the case in Taylor's films of the 1960s, *Shrew* places an inescapable emphasis on her breasts, often making them the screen's focal point.) Taking a break from Burton, Taylor starred in *Reflections in a Golden Eye* (1967), opposite Marlon Brando as her military-officer husband, a latent homosexual. Directed by John Huston (who had directed Burton so superbly in *The Night of the Iguana*), *Reflections* certainly had the potential to be something special. The outcome, however, is portentous claptrap, with Taylor quite awful, starting with her overdone Southern accent. Again channeling *Virginia Woolf*'s Martha, Taylor is horny and crass, but her acting is amateurish. She does get to whip Brando's face with a riding crop at a party, and, in a classic camp moment, she removes her blouse and then flings her bra in his face (a moment guaranteed to accelerate his coming-out process).

Taylor was back with Burton for *The Comedians* (1967), a misleading title for a political thriller set in Haiti, especially with funnymen Alec Guinness and Peter Ustinov in the cast. Like *Virginia Woolf* and *Shrew*, *The Comedians* was at least another prestige picture for the Burtons, rather than one of their tinseled melodramas, yet it is strangely uninvolving and forgettable. Switching their adulterous positions from *The Sandpiper*, this time it is Taylor who is married (to Ustinov) and Burton who is single. In a role secondary to the main action (which involves Burton), Taylor is saddled with the soapiest elements of a serious-minded film. She uses an occasional and wholly unidentifiable accent, eventually revealed to be German (even though that may not be one of your guesses). She appears uncomfortable throughout, even when, go figure, making love to Burton. *Doctor Faustus*, released in England in 1967 but not in the States until early 1968, made 1967 Taylor's most productive screen year since 1954, which also saw four Taylor releases. Continuing the Burtons' attraction to Elizabethan drama (begun with *Shrew*), *Doctor Faustus* is a true oddity, a cheap and misguided version of Christopher Marlowe's play. Its sole pleasures are the visuals of a wordless Taylor, stunningly showcased as Helen of Troy. Over the course of the movie, her hair is alternately dark, blond, redheaded, and spray-painted silver, making the whole enterprise more valuable as a photo shoot than a motion picture.

Considering the Burtons' individual successes in the Tennessee Williams films—*Cat on a Hot Tin Roof* and *Suddenly, Last Summer* for her, and *The Night of the Iguana* (1964) for him—it made sense to pair them on a Williams project. But there had been no recent hit plays from Williams, none successful enough for an inevitable trip to the movies. *The Milk Train Doesn't Stop Here Anymore* had perhaps the strangest trajectory of any Williams play, even more so than *Orpheus Descending*. After a 1962 festival premiere in Spoleto, Italy, which was well received, *Milk Train* had the misfortune of opening on Broadway during a 1963 newspaper strike. The play's star, Hermione Baddeley (who created her role in Spoleto), was again highly praised (and got a Tony nomination), but there was far less enthusiasm for the play itself, which closed after sixty-nine performances. In an unusual twist, the play returned to Broadway the following season in a new production with bigger names attached: director Tony Richardson and stars Tallulah Bankhead

After Kate's Mrs. Venable, Why Not Bette's Mrs. Goforth?

The role of Mrs. Goforth might have been the occasion for a serious comeback by Bette Davis (who had already swiped for herself other Tallulah stage vehicles: *Dark Victory* and *The Little Foxes*). A potential Davis triumph became an opportunity wasted on Taylor.

(in Baddeley's role) and Tab Hunter. Reopening in early 1964, *Milk Train* closed after just five performances, confirming the previous season's response to the play without duplicating the raves for its lead actress. Though Tallulah, at sixty-one, was ideal for the role of Flora "Sissy" Goforth—a wealthy, near-death American widow living atop an Italian mountain—she was long past her theatrical prime, depleted by hard living and beyond the disciplines of such a large and demanding role. When reading the play, it is easy to imagine Tallulah as Mrs. Goforth, a former Follies girl and self-proclaimed "old Georgia swamp-bitch," even to hear Tallulah's throaty voice and witty inflections on Williams' words. One actress you don't conjure while reading *Milk Train* is Elizabeth Taylor. But, wait, hadn't Taylor seemed incomprehensible casting as *Virginia Woolf*'s Martha? Look how that turned out! Since she had defied the odds as Martha, couldn't she do it again? Besides, the character would be reconceived as a much younger woman, a "taylor"-made Mrs. Goforth requiring no age makeup, thus making the role less of an acting stretch for her. She would be co-starring with her husband in material written by a playwright with whom her two previous collaborations had netted her Oscar nominations. And Williams himself would be writing the screenplay. How much more surefire could this thing get?

Milk Train became *Boom* (1968) for the screen, directed by Joseph Losey, an American director who first made his mark with the allegorical "cult" film *The Boy with Green Hair* (1948), an anti-war message picture aimed at children. When he was blacklisted in the early 1950s during Hollywood's shameful purge of suspected communists, Losey moved to England and worked his way to prominence in the British film industry. His most notable and fascinating English movie is *The Servant* (1963), with its devious cat-and-mouse game of class warfare between a privileged young man (James Fox) and his manservant (Dirk Bogarde). Written by Harold Pinter with an elegant creepiness, *The Servant* is steeped in mysterious, unsettling behavior, and it remains a bold, subversive, and immoderate drama. The Losey who made *The Servant* would seem a fine choice to direct *Boom,* another bizarre but deeply human story. Though reteamed with *The Servant*'s ace cinematographer, Douglas Slocombe, Losey still made a bomb out of *Boom,* the worst Williams film yet made. It has nothing to recommend except its breathtaking Sardinian location and its pleasurable supporting performance from Noël Coward. Since the material is lesser Williams to begin with, the film cannot even occasionally rest on the shoulders of its source material's greatness, which even the pallid 1950 *Glass Menagerie* sometimes could. Nor can it coast on the strength of a lead performance, the way the unexceptional *Period of Adjustment* is buoyantly lifted by Jane Fonda. Plus, *both* Taylor and Burton are miscast: she is too young; he is too old. Nonetheless, *Boom* made Taylor the only person ever to star in three Williams films.

As with her Cleopatra, Taylor is useless in what might be called a style role, one requiring physically graceful extravagance, vocal stamina, and emotional flamboyance. The best that Taylor can do is to make Mrs. Goforth a splotchy imitation of her braying Martha, though a much wealthier and more expensively clad bitch than *Virginia Woolf*'s. By now, Taylor seemed to equate giving a great performance with high decibel levels and crude behavior, whether it was appropriate to the character or not. The role cries out for a grand presence who can dominate the piece, yet all Taylor evokes is a Hollywood brat having tantrums on the set, overreacting to the slightest infractions. Much of *Boom* feels like a behind-the-scenes documentary in which you can watch Elizabeth Taylor screech at underlings and strike fear into their hearts. But she is never the formidable creature whose horrid demeanor derives from deep-seated fears, physical pain, and loneliness, a woman willfully isolated (in her white modernistic fortress) against the world and her own impending death. Without access to the character's terror of encroaching mortality, Taylor is a glamorous cipher, offering the role

nothing but incessant shrieking and panting. Aside from the chance to gaze upon that magnificent face in color, there is nothing in Taylor's performance worth anyone's time. Her acting quickly becomes tediously repetitive, all used up after her first few scenes. Her knockout fashions (by Tiziani of Rome) and jewels (by Bulgari) have more variety and natural dazzle than she does.

Much of the blame falls to Williams, who seems to have abandoned his film audience. At his best, Williams had been able to prod moviegoers into darker, truer places because he unlocked his characters' palpitating humanity, however unusual their lives or circumstances. *Boom* does explore familiar Williams themes of emotional panic and the fight against aging, but they are buried under ostentatious and flagrantly weird trappings, alienating those interested in getting close to the characters. And Losey, unlike the best of the Williams film directors—Elia Kazan, John Huston, and Sidney Lumet—is unable to make Mrs. Goforth's recognizable struggles either sympathetic or compelling. Losey's sleepwalking direction treats a heightened dramatic situation—an encounter between a dying woman and her Angel of Death—as dull and confounding realism, making the offbeat goings-on seem even more peculiar than necessary (which had also been true of *Suddenly, Last Summer,* if not quite as disastrously). The juxtaposition of a fatally dark fairy tale and a palpably authentic physical location makes for an uncomfortable fit, with the splendorous natural setting the clear winner. (The play is set on the Amalfi coast, but *Boom* is set on a tiny private island nearby.) The activities atop Mrs. Goforth's mountain play like absurd incidents at an overproduced costume party in the lair of a James Bond villain. (The interiors were shot in a Rome studio.) The overall effect is that of watching a really bad Fellini movie or a particularly sluggish science-fiction film. If Losey had been able to guide Taylor as painstakingly as Mike Nichols had in *Virginia Woolf,* then she might have found some range within her interpretation and been better able to sustain interest. But Taylor delivers not a single interesting or memorable line reading, carelessly throwing away good lines and bellowing the nuances out of others.

Taylor is first seen from behind, in bed on her stomach, getting a massage and a manicure. After sipping a drink handed to her, she goes into a con-

*I'd love to know what Noël Coward was thinking when Taylor went Kabuki in **Boom**.*

vulsion, clutching her sheets and then calling on her intercom for one of her life-sustaining injections. Though her face is only partially seen, her diamond bracelet and ring are prominently featured. When she later emerges, she is most becoming in her white caftan and matching head scarf. Nearly all of Taylor's costumes, most of them gowns, are white (as are her accessories, including an unforgettable pair of sunglasses), perfect for the Mediterranean locale but evoking a Grecian high priestess more than a dying dowager. Most of her scenes stress the character as a petty, impatient, and materialistic woman with a nasty tongue, but it's all on the surface with Taylor. Mrs. Goforth shouldn't be soft, but she should make sense as someone dealing badly with terminal illness, kicking and screaming her way to the grave. Dictating page-turning memoirs (titled *Facts and a Figure* in the play), Taylor is devoid of captivating grandeur or any tingles of haunting emotional residue. She recollects six dead husbands, five of them wealthy ("a pyramid of tycoons"). Husband number six was

a poet and her great love, yet Taylor recalls him without any honest feeling or lingering grief. (With five husbands by 1968, Taylor was gaining on Mrs. Goforth and would eventually surpass her.) The character's past, elaborated upon in the play, is skimpy in Williams' screenplay, presumably because Taylor was too young to carry much "past." The play's Mrs. Goforth had been a poor-born Georgia girl who entered showbiz at fifteen and went on to become a Follies star, marrying for the first time in her teens. She has a daughter and three grandchildren; on-screen, she has no family. It is appropriate to play Mrs. Goforth as a brassy broad, which appears to be Taylor's inclination, but absent from her characterization are the studied manners of a once-poor/now-rich person who has acquired an upper-class bearing, a "show" of grace and sophistication. Taylor has no finesse. She is harsh, more like a truck driver in drag couture than a mock royal. Taylor resorts to tiresome petulance, lacking any fascination or mystique. Even her pangs of physical pain are implausible. In the play, it's clear that Williams' sense of humor has not abandoned him in the way that Taylor's screen performance suggests, wherein she substitutes loud sarcasm for genuine humor. Her many run-ins with her secretary, "Blackie" (Joanna Shimkus, later Mrs. Sidney Poitier), have the potential for laughs, as they do in the play, but are merely unpleasant.

Jaded, tired, and deliberately secluded, Mrs. Goforth is both unnerved and sparked by the intriguing arrival of Chris Flanders (Burton), a poet claiming to have met her before. Will he be a new lover to help her out of depression this summer? Curious to discover more about him before seeing him, she calls on the Witch of Capri (Noël Coward), actually Bill Ridgeway but evidently nicknamed for his flair with gossip and bitchery. He reveals to her Chris' reputation as an Angel of Death to women. The Witch was played by females in the play's two Broadway incarnations, so it was a freshening twist to make the witch male. The friendship between a cultured older gay man and a young and beautiful woman is easily acceptable. Nearing seventy, Coward is treated more as an unthreatening eunuch than as a sexual being (unlike the baron in *The Roman Spring of Mrs. Stone)*, and is therefore an exceedingly discreet gay creation by Williams. The only overt acknowledgment of the Witch's sexuality (aside from his moniker) is Mrs. Goforth's comment to Blackie about him "putting the make on the poet." The Witch was a worthwhile late-career opportunity for Coward, and he gives the film its only bona fide humor, intelligence, and charisma. (He is billed above the title, following Taylor and Burton.) Unlike Taylor, who plows through the text, Coward makes every line count, crafting the words beautifully and wringing them for every savored ounce of flavor. In dinner clothes, of course, Coward amusingly enters the film being carried from the shore to a funicular: he is sitting upon the shoulders of a boatman. On his first line, he refers to "Sissy" as a "bitch." How's that for an entrance, both visually and aurally? Coward is, thank heaven, very much the Noël Coward he usually played, such as when he says, "I've heard some very disturbing rumors about you, Sissy," rolling the first "r" in "rumors" indefinitely, and then, smiling, "I love you too much to repeat them." It would not be unreasonable to imagine Coward in Taylor's role, as a gay *Mister* Goforth, with his appropriate age, showbiz background, and colorful sexual history (a fairly "out" gay man in closeted

times). More of Noël Coward, however it might have been achieved, would have served *Boom* extremely well. He makes his final exit escorted by the same handsome boatman who first deposited him. Too bad the camera doesn't ditch the Burtons and follow Coward back to Capri.

Mrs. Goforth's elaborate intercom system allows her to start dictating her memoirs whenever and wherever the spirit moves her. That night, on loudspeakers heard throughout the complex, she recounts the death of Mr. Goforth, her first husband. The sequence is shot overhead and somewhat behind Taylor as she lies in bed in a white nightgown, spreading her legs as she unfavorably recalls their sex life. Then, out of bed and in close-up, she speaks of the terror in his eyes when he faced death and how she fled the room in panic. Taylor continues with the camera now behind her, eventually making her way onto the terrace. It appears as though Losey is haphazardly trying various shots and angles in a doomed quest to make Taylor look good, as if hoping he might accidentally stumble onto a winning formula. Showing no control over her voice or body, her performance lodges in her throat (*Suddenly, Last Summer* all over again), preventing any connection between her gut and her brain. When she and Burton finally have their first dialogue scene together, fifty-two minutes into the movie, it then falls to him to be the main recipient of her strident tirades. Chris reminds her that they met years ago at the Waldorf Astoria and that she had told him to drop by, an invitation she deems expired. There's a repeated bit concerning her fear of falling down the mountain at the part of her terrace where the balustrade ends, providing more occasions for Taylor's squealing.

Why are we watching this irritating harridan and this male nonentity? Aside from her runway show of fashions, especially a jaw-dropping Kabuki get-up, and her spacious and art-filled living quarters, what about Taylor's Mrs. Goforth deserves our attention? Her most memorable moment comes when she's perfuming herself and dabs a little cologne on her tongue, which feels more like a glimpse into the beauty secrets of Elizabeth Taylor than anything connected to *Boom*. She loses sight of the character's consistent motivation of self-preservation, the fragile belief that she can control death the way she thinks she has been able to control everything else. She describes the island as her summer retreat, a place

Long Before It Went Boom

Milk Train began as a 1953 short story by Williams titled *Man Bring This Up Road*, which reads as a framework for the eventual play. In the story (not published until 1959), Mrs. Goforth is seventy-one years old, and Chris (called Jimmy Dobyne) is a poet. At the end, Mrs. Goforth doesn't die. She presents her naked body to Jimmy, who balks at his chance to sleep with her. Soon after, she asks him to leave. The name Jimmy Dobyne was also used by Williams later that decade for the leading male character in his screenplay *The Loss of a Teardrop Diamond.*

where she can do whatever she likes, even though it's hard to imagine that she behaves otherwise anywhere else. Drawn to Chris physically, she is rightly cynical about his intentions. He kisses her but she pulls away. When they go down to the sea, his skinny-dipping alarms her, but is that sufficient reason for Taylor to *scream* her demand for him to put his robe back on? Chris is a variation on the homeless young man in *The Roman Spring of Mrs. Stone,* another Angel of Death seemingly summoned by a victim fearful of him yet drawn to him. Chris' mission is to help people make peace with imminent death, but Mrs. Goforth is unable to trust anyone or expose her vulnerabilities. As death nears, she must come to terms with this reality, but, because Taylor looks so gorgeous, there's really no connection between the story and what we're looking at. She does cough her way through an entire scene (coughing always signifies incurable illness at the movies) and her coughing, if not her acting, is impressive and sustained.

She eventually invites him into her bedroom, but he refuses to join her, citing his all-day hunger and resentment over the inhospitable treatment he has received. Outside the bedroom, she telephones the kitchen for a meal (another wearying chance for Taylor to act riled and testy with the help), but it's too late. He has decided to leave. Though unwilling to accept his help in her passage out of life, she finally acknowledges that her time has come. But she wants to go through it alone, refusing to admit need, saying, "You miscalculated with this one, the milk train doesn't stop here anymore." Suddenly (and ridiculously) at death's door, she asks for his assistance

in returning to her bed. Once under the covers, she asks him to stay, knowing it's the end. Moments before she dies, she says, "Be here when I wake up." This sequence isn't moving or disturbing because Taylor, not merely unbelievable as someone expiring, reveals nothing nakedly personal or emotionally revelatory in Mrs. Goforth's confrontation with dreaded inevitability. Though the character has often behaved nightmarishly, she still might have been enormously affecting, warts and all, if acted by someone who was imaginatively and intimately invested.

Referring to *Milk Train* in *Memoirs,* Williams states that the play was "really only successful, scriptwise, as the movie *Boom,*" and he goes on to call the film (despite "miscasting") "an artistic success," adding that "eventually it will be received with acclaim." (Williams did, after all, write the screenplay.) The play's stylization—its use of two stage assistants unnoticed by the characters except when assuming tiny roles—made its allegorical pretentions easier to take. For *Boom,* Williams deleted some of the play's best speeches, which might have, heaven forbid, taken screen time away from the film's crashing waves and gown changes. More indistinct than the play (which isn't given screen credit until the film's end), *Boom* has considerably less feeling, humor, and character detail. Unconcerned with connecting to an audience, *Boom* is, worst of all, *boring,* settling into a draggy groove, a shocking fate for a Williams film. It unsurprisingly died at the box office and was dismissed by the critics. After more than forty years, Williams' folly has yet to receive the critical acclaim that he predicted would be its destiny.

Gluttons for punishment, Taylor and Losey quickly reteamed on *Secret Ceremony* (1968), in which two women foster their twisted relationship in a fabulous English home, making the film a more obvious companion piece to *The Servant* (Losey's most famous picture) than to *Boom.* Taylor plays a prostitute grieving the death of her young daughter, while Mia Farrow (at her freakiest) is an heiress grieving the loss of her mother. They assume the roles of parent and child, yet the movie is never anywhere near as interesting as its premise suggests, lacking *The Servant*'s crisp, riveting arc and seductive power. *Secret Ceremony* is ultimately a baffling and miserable movie, a groggy ordeal worsened by barren psychology. Though its domestic deceptions have shades of *Virginia Woolf,* the end result feels more like one of those 1960s horror pictures with two big-name dames battling for supremacy. In *Boom*, Taylor revels in her badness, smashing her way through the movie, but in *Secret Ceremony* she behaves indifferently, giving a barely adequate performance, which leaves you wondering why she bothered at all. The Taylor in the Losey films could never be confused with a major screen actress, and she fares even worse on purely movie-star terms, seeming to be deliberately driving away her audience. Though it was yet another fashion-parade opportunity for her, *Secret Ceremony* fails there, too. Taylor may still have had the most beautiful face in the world, but she hadn't looked good in clothes since *Butterfield 8*.

If Taylor had never again worked with George Stevens, I could have stood by my claim that no other director handled her as effectively as he did. Stevens' final film, *The Only Game in Town* (1970), from a failed Broadway play, broke the spell: not only *not a Place in the Sun* or a *Giant*, it's a dreary affair about two losers falling in love after a one-night stand. The odd tone is that of a romantic comedy played as a dirge, with Taylor a Las Vegas dancer and Warren Beatty a lounge pianist with a gambling addiction. At least Beatty's performance is lightweight, unlike the manufactured-feeling and constricted emoting in his co-star's acting. With her harsh, push-pull technique, she seems unable simply to *be* on-screen, with Stevens having lost his knack to coax wonderful things from her, or even control her excesses. (I presume she was no longer as malleable as she had been in her pre-Oscar-winning teens and early twenties.) The film, set in Vegas but filmed in Paris, offers nothing to care about, a situation exacerbated by a complete lack of fireworks between the stars. Taylor's days as a box-office draw were irretrievably over (and had been since *Virginia Woolf*), but she wasn't quite finished as an actress.

X Y & Zee (1972) was her last stand as a first-class performer, the final example of her approaching filmmaking with utmost seriousness and refined skill. The movie is essentially soapy junk, but it is entertaining and adult, with Taylor struggling to hold on to husband Michael Caine and derail his affair with widow Susannah York. Though the film did nothing for her career, it proved that Taylor wasn't utterly passé in 1972, that she had the potential to be a valuable player in 1970s cinema. Entering her early forties, she was also facing

an industry that was about to erase women from American movies for virtually the first half of the new decade. But in the British *X Y & Zee* she momentarily reclaimed her position as a high-voltage star, reminding moviegoers (the few who *saw* the movie) why they loved her, just in case, through no fault of theirs, they had forgotten. It had been a long time since Taylor looked as happy in her work as she does here, as if she were rediscovering a love of acting. Refashioning *Virginia Woolf*'s Martha once again, Taylor is loosely relaxed, raucous and abrasive, and irresistibly bitchy fun, all the while maneuvering a turbulent and childless marriage. She is at her funniest and most likable, by turns playful and fiery, believably suppressing her vulnerabilities. Still gorgeous from the neck up, and wearing all the blue eye shadow in London, Taylor turned in her best post-*Virginia Woolf* acting job. The movie itself isn't much, but it's driven by the magnetism and, dare I say it, *talent,* of Elizabeth Taylor.

When the Burtons joined professional forces again, it became apparent how quickly times had changed. The Taylor-Burton combination was still of enormous interest to magazine readers, but it no longer carried any weight with film-ticket buyers. Despite having proven their New-Hollywood prowess in *Virginia Woolf*, the Burtons had quickly become irrelevant, fixed in the public's perception as cultural icons of the previous decade. And they had certainly accelerated their decline with most of their choices of co-ventures. Not only were their final two films dismissed, they were non-events. *Under Milk Wood* (released in 1971 in the U.K. but not until 1973 in the U.S.) isn't really even a Taylor-Burton picture because the duo shares no scenes within it. Her role is basically one scene (with Peter O'Toole), and, despite her charming Welsh accent, the effect is that of a show-stopping personal appearance rather than a performance, akin to her Helen of Troy in *Doctor Faustus* (and only slightly more significant). Even closer to *Doctor Faustus* is *Hammersmith Is Out* (1972), the final Taylor-Burton feature, a 1970s "comic" update of the Faust legend. Directed by, and co-starring, Peter Ustinov (the Burtons' *Comedians* colleague), *Hammersmith* is a vulgar disaster, a fitting end to the predominantly awful movies that had teamed Taylor with Burton. She plays a blond waitress who becomes the girlfriend of the Faust figure (Beau Bridges); Burton is the film's Mephistopheles. The most interest-

Maggie the Cat Is "Live"

I saw Taylor onstage in her two Broadway ventures, both revivals: *The Little Foxes* in 1981, for which she received a Tony nomination, and *Private Lives* in 1983, a chance to see the twice-divorced Burtons make love and war in a comedy written by their late *Boom* co-star Noël Coward. As Regina in *The Little Foxes,* she acquitted herself ably, less so in *Private Lives,* which I recall mostly for its interminably long intermissions.

ing thing about Taylor's stumbling performance is watching her hair darken as the movie proceeds. She and Burton have scenes together but each has more to do with Bridges (whose loopy performance provides the only enjoyment). The funniest thing about *Hammersmith* is that it won Taylor the Best Actress prize at the Berlin Film Festival.

Good roles dried up for Taylor, though she kept busy by divorcing Burton in 1974, remarrying him in 1975, and re-divorcing him in 1976. It seemed like a new start when she was cast in the screen version of the sublime Stephen Sondheim musical *A Little Night Music* (1977). Nevertheless, the outcome is a minor catastrophe, bad enough to make me doubt the merits of a musical-theatre piece that I love. Taylor's tuneless rendition of "Send in the Clowns" is unacceptable, a low point in the history of recorded sound. As a stage actress who rekindles a past romance, Taylor gives a foggy performance, lacking the requisite ability to enchant. To be fair, no one comes off well, not even the members of the original Broadway cast. Directed by Harold Prince, who directed it onstage, *Night Music* provides not a shiver of pleasure, turning theatre magic into celluloid dross. The film ends with a curtain call: if ever a film *didn't* warrant a curtain call, this is it. Taylor also plays an actress in *The Mirror Crack'd* (1980), which feels like a television movie, a pre-*Murder, She Wrote* warm-up for a murder-solving Angela Lansbury (here as Miss Marple). Though it's sub-par Agatha Christie, the film is a pleasing gathering of former box-office favorites, with Taylor acting alongside Tony Curtis, Kim Novak, and her *Giant* co-star Rock Hudson. Again cast as husband and wife, Hudson and Taylor are unable to reignite their *Giant*-sized chemistry from a quarter century ago. (Taylor and Lansbury had been sisters in *National Velvet* but barely cross paths here.) Two-time Oscar winner Taylor gives a proficient performance as a two-time Oscar-winning star, and she's also a good sport about being on the receiving end of Novak's fat jokes. Taylor and Novak (who was rarely, if ever, this animated) have a high old time sparring comically as aging Hollywood rivals, providing the brightest moments in a workmanlike and undemanding murder mystery (whose plot parallels the real-life tragedy of Gene Tierney).

There would be two more husbands for Taylor (John Warner and Larry Fortensky), as well as television work, activism on behalf of AIDS, and a phenomenally successful perfume enterprise, with film projects becoming increasingly sparse. Her final big-screen appearance to date can be seen in *The Flintstones* (1994), a pointless and wastefully overproduced live-action cartoon. In the supporting role of John Goodman's meddling mother-in-law, Taylor is ostensibly present to show the world how fabulous she looks past sixty, slimmed-down and glamorously rejuvenated. However ludicrous her presence seems here, she takes lighthearted pleasure in her goofy surroundings. But will something as marginal as *The Flintstones* really be the final feature film in the half-century screen career of a star as enduring and adored as Elizabeth Taylor?

She had a fourth professional encounter with Tennessee Williams when she starred with Mark Harmon in a television movie of *Sweet Bird of Youth* (1989). In her late fifties, Taylor was too old to be playing Alexandra Del Lago, a movie star in the midst of making her leading-lady comeback. Taylor's Alexandra should worry less about her close-ups than her weight, which is simply too zaftig for a character with hopes of regaining her stardom. This might be overlooked if Taylor's performance wasn't so lifeless and half-hearted. Most surprising of all is how unconvincing she is as a great star, even botching the climactic phone call with a humorless delivery, a sequence further hampered by the teleplay's foolish alteration of having Taylor intercut with two actors on the call's other end. Thus, a classic Williams scene goes by without notice. Taylor's track record with Williams is a case of one base hit (her strong and tantalizing Maggie the Cat) followed by three strike-outs (*Suddenly, Last Summer; Boom;* and *Sweet Bird of Youth*). She should have quit once she got Brick back into her bed.

Joanne Woodward

*Three outsiders in **The Fugitive Kind**: Magnani's Lady, Brando's Val, and Woodward's Carol.*

Joanne Woodward: Filmography

- *Count Three and Pray (1955)*
- *A Kiss Before Dying (1956)*
- *The Three Faces of Eve (1957)*
- *No Down Payment (1957)*
- *The Long, Hot Summer (1958)*
- *Rally 'Round the Flag, Boys! (1958)*
- *The Sound and the Fury (1959)*
- *The Fugitive Kind (1960)*
- *From the Terrace (1960)*
- *Paris Blues (1961)*
- *The Stripper (1963)*
- *A New Kind of Love (1963)*
- *Signpost to Murder (1964)*
- *A Big Hand for the Little Lady (1966)*
- *A Fine Madness (1966)*
- *Rachel, Rachel (1968)*
- *Winning (1969)*
- *WUSA (1970)*
- *They Might Be Giants (1971)*
- *The Effect of Gamma Rays on Man-in-the-Moon Marigolds (1972)*
- *Summer Wishes, Winter Dreams (1973)*
- *The Drowning Pool (1975)*
- *The End (1978)*
- *Harry and Son (1984)*
- *The Glass Menagerie (1987)*
- *Mr. and Mrs. Bridge (1990)*
- *The Age of Innocence (1993) (as narrator)*
- *Philadelphia (1993)*

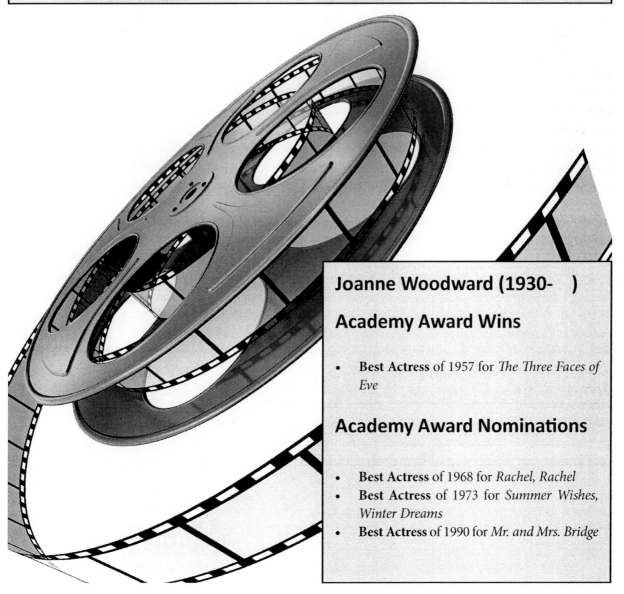

Joanne Woodward (1930-)

Academy Award Wins

- **Best Actress** of 1957 for *The Three Faces of Eve*

Academy Award Nominations

- **Best Actress** of 1968 for *Rachel, Rachel*
- **Best Actress** of 1973 for *Summer Wishes, Winter Dreams*
- **Best Actress** of 1990 for *Mr. and Mrs. Bridge*

Carol Cutrere in *The Fugitive Kind* (1960)
Amanda Wingfield in *The Glass Menagerie* (1987)

Joanne Woodward has been a highly respected and unstintingly intelligent actress for over fifty years, and she made it all on her own. However, I don't think it's too indelicate to suggest that her career would not have had its longevity, nor her name its staying power, had she not married Paul Newman in 1958. They were on equal footing career-wise when they wed; Woodward was actually a bit ahead, having won an Oscar for *The Three Faces of Eve* just a few weeks after becoming Mrs. Newman. Over the next few years it grew clear that, despite her talent, Woodward was not movie-star material and was never going to be a box-office attraction, something that was becoming obvious at about the same time her sexy and charismatic husband was bursting into superstar status. Though Woodward's career had slumped by the mid-sixties, Newman would always be there to give her a boost, notably when he directed her on-screen, but also by continuing to play opposite her occasionally (though their track record as a screen team was hardly enviable). Woodward could wait out any lulls, knowing that opportunities via Newman would eventually present themselves.

Born in Georgia on February 27, 1930, Woodward paid her acting dues and honed her camera skills on "live" television in New York, appearing in dozens of programs between 1952 and 1958. She studied at the Neighborhood Playhouse and the Actors Studio and was an understudy in the original Broadway production of *Picnic* (1953), in which Newman had a featured role. Though Newman would famously flop in his debut screen entry, *The Silver Chalice* (1954),

Woodward did rather well with her first Hollywood foray. The picture was *Count Three and Pray* (1955), a post-Civil War semi-western starring Van Heflin, fresh from *Shane* (1953), as a wannabe preacher. Woodward, looking like she could be the kid sister of *Shane*'s Jean Arthur, is this modest film's chief asset. The role is an orphaned tomboy, and an animated Woodward brings to it a scruffy appeal and sassy humor. She's a female Davy Crockett, a butch and barefoot moppet with short blond hair and boys' clothes. Though she is eighteen, Heflin's character thinks she's younger, rendering this one of those now uncomfortable-making films—similar to *Susan Slept Here* (1954), *Daddy Long Legs* (1955), and, of course, *Gigi* (1958)—in which an adult male befriends a girl, comes to know her *as* a girl, and then suddenly sees her as a woman and winds up with her. But even before Woodward exposes any overt femininity, you just know she's headed for a makeover (and she gets one from the local prostitute.)

Next up was a smaller role in *A Kiss Before Dying* (1956), opposite a never-better Robert Wagner as a preppy dreamboat and homicidal maniac. Colorful and trashy, it certainly keeps you watching, and Woodward is memorably fragile and clinging as Wagner's wealthy pregnant girlfriend. Sitting on a rooftop ledge, she is pushed backward by him to her death, as shocking a mid-picture demise as Janet Leigh's four years later in *Psycho*. (Both films shift their focus to the truth-seeking sisters of the dead girls.) But then came the big break, *The Three Faces of Eve* (1957), the film that gave Woodward a part

Hope Marie Woodward?

Without Paul Newman, Woodward's movie career might have been closer to those of Eva Marie Saint and Hope Lange, too other blond and attractive (but not beautiful) "serious actresses" who, like Woodward, emerged in Hollywood in the mid-fifties, had a brush with Oscar (Saint won for 1954's *On the Waterfront;* Lange was nominated for 1957's *Peyton Place*), and then began to slide in the early 1960s. While Woodward would receive three Oscar nominations (two for projects with Newman) after 1967, the year the New Hollywood officially began with *Bonnie and Clyde* and *The Graduate,* Saint and Lange would never again occupy that high a profile in the industry. But in the late 1950s, this trio of actresses was nearly interchangeable, making it easy to imagine them in each other's roles: Woodward in Lange's role in *Bus Stop* (1956); Lange in Saint's role in *Raintree County* (1957); or Saint in Woodward's role in *The Long, Hot Summer* (1958).

showy enough to win her the Best Actress Oscar. A small black-and-white drama about "multiple personality," it is simplistic, unbearably dated, and implausible in its revelations. But it is saved by Woodward's admirably restrained tour de force in which she never overdoes anything, despite the role's almost irresistible potential for overacting. "Eve White" is a sad and drably ordinary person, and Woodward, instead of being dull herself, personalizes the drabness, making it interesting and touching. "Eve Black" is the fun-loving slut, and Woodward completely gives herself over to the role's unbridled sexuality, creating a likable sexpot. Unfortunately, the third "face," the stable end result, is a blandly perfect nobody. (Eve Beige?) This Georgia-set film is static, glum, and false, and both its male leads (David Wayne and Lee J. Cobb) are miscast. But Woodward seized her make-or-break chance and carted home the Oscar (beating her future *Fugitive Kind* co-star, Anna Magnani, nominated for *Wild Is the Wind*).

No Down Payment (1957), her first of four films for director Martin Ritt, is a suburban-California soap with an ensemble cast. Though it addresses bigotry, rape, and religion, the treatment is more banal and overwrought than probing. Mostly it's a tale of sex, booze, and money, revolving around four couples, with Woodward paired off with Cameron Mitchell as a brutish war hero. She rehashes Eve Black, again playing a cheap and lusty Southern gal, but it wasn't worth the effort, unlike her next film. *The Long, Hot Summer* (1958), in addition to pairing her on-screen with Newman for the first time, was her first major box-office success. Set in Mississippi and based on William Faulkner stories, this second of her films for director Ritt is more entertaining than *No Down Payment* but just about as penetrating. A superficial "steamy" melodrama, *The Long, Hot Summer* casts Woodward as a lonely but rich and strong-willed schoolteacher headed for spinsterhood, as repressed as suggested by her tightly pulled-back hair. She is ready to explode when, luckily, Newman's bad-boy drifter comes to town. Woodward has her most affecting moment when he kisses her for the first time and she impulsively wraps her arms tightly around his middle. Newman radiates sexuality, while Woodward, here and in all their romantic pairings, seems, ironically, not quite sexy enough to be plausibly linked with him. Their first film together after their real-life wedding was *Rally 'Round the Flag, Boys!*

(1958), a broad and witless comedy that proved director Leo McCarey's days as a comic master *(Ruggles of Red Gap, The Awful Truth)* were long behind him. And Newman and Woodward showed no signs of being Cary Grant and Irene Dunne. As a married suburban couple, the Newmans telegraph their "comic" moments, gesticulating madly, and pitching just about every moment too high. They are not ace farceurs, with Woodward especially flat, charmless, and unfunny. Her recent Oscar had elevated her to the top, yet it was already apparent that she was never going to be a "personality" star, the kind who could rely on charm and looks as well as skill, like, say, Paul Newman.

The Sound and the Fury (1959), impersonally directed by Ritt, plays like a too-soon replay of bits from previous Woodward dramas. Not only another adaptation of Faulkner set in Mississippi, it has Woodward playing a restless teenager (only seventeen) and contains an eventual romance between her and an older man. The film is almost a parody of Southern Gothic, yet how could anything this strident, overblown, and florid be so boring? You can feel it striving to be Tennessee Williams (even though Faulkner's novel was published in 1929), most blatantly in the performance of Margaret Leighton as Woodward's scandalous mother who abandoned her at birth. Leighton is done up as Vivien Leigh in *Streetcar,* and the impact of Leighton's character, who is flamboyant and aging and worn out, is that of a Blanche DuBois knockoff, merely serving, by comparison, to underline the failure of the film, which is extremely unfaithful to Faulkner. Woodward earnestly tries but fails to break your heart; her ache to be loved is more irritating than sympathetic. And she cannot forge any connection with the distant and wooden Yul Brynner as her Cajun father-figure. (Is he stifled by all that brown hair atop his head?) With her string of Southern girls, somewhat tediously familiar in their yearnings, Woodward was the Sissy Spacek of the 1950s. It was about time that she had a shot at an actual Tennessee Williams character after her handful of also-rans.

Of all the players featured in this book, Woodward is the only Southerner, the only one seemingly born for the words and milieu of Tennessee Williams. Whether or not being a Georgian gave her an edge, Woodward connected with Williams' work in ways that went far beyond her real-deal

Southern accent. *The Fugitive Kind* (1960), based on Williams' play *Orpheus Descending,* caused not a stir on its release, ending a streak of screen hits for the playwright, but that is no blight on Woodward. She was never better than she is in *The Fugitive Kind,* and it remains her most underrated and overlooked film performance. Her role is not even the female lead, which is played by Anna Magnani. It was an interesting career move for Woodward, an Oscar winner and not yet thirty years old, to accept a secondary role, peripheral to the main action. This speaks to the quality of the character, Carol Cutrere, and just how worthy she was of Woodward's time and talent. I guess you could dismiss Carol, like Woodward's role in *No Down Payment,* as another rerun of Eve Black, but, whereas the *No Down Payment* character feels like a diminishing of what Woodward had done in *The Three Faces of Eve,* Carol Cutrere is a more fully dimensional and richly imagined Eve Black. Even though no one noticed at the time, Woodward had not yet appeared in a film anywhere near as good as *The Fugitive Kind,* which isn't thin or synthetic or outdated like her films of the fifties. She is genuinely provocative here, both a hoot and a horror, a black-sheep family member laughing her way to self-destruction. This isn't like watching Shirley Jones play-act her hooker role in *Elmer Gantry* (that same year) because Woodward delves inside the character, not only her sexuality, recklessness, and loose physicality, but also the pain and isolation that inform her behavior. Like the other main characters, Magnani's Lady and Marlon Brando's Val, Carol can't fit into this small Mississippi town. Instead of taking her disillusionment elsewhere and starting over, she is too hopeless to do anything but go extravagantly down in flames, and, in the process, punish her privileged family. Her more intimate feelings will surface in her relationship with Val, but most people see nothing but the train-wreck spectacle of her bedraggled hedonism.

Woodward roars into the movie in a beat-up convertible, shouting "Snakeskin!" at the sight of Brando outside Magnani's store. (He is nicknamed "Snakeskin" because of his snakeskin jacket.) She falls out of her car before we can even get a good look at her. Wrapped in a raincoat, her most striking feature is her dark, raccoon-like eye makeup, further accentuated by her blond hair. Woodward is costumed in whites, even a white cap, in contrast to her blackened lifestyle but also suggestive of an essential innocence and purity in Carol, a good soul with a good heart no matter how hard she tries to degrade herself. Carol is the kind of person who, knowing her power to shock and appall, can't wait to offend gossipy, upstanding types. She has clearly decided to be as awful as everyone thinks she is, and to revel in her awfulness. Often noisy and cackling, Woodward discerns that Carol has become someone used to getting attention solely through negative means, such as offensive behavior. Ordered out of the county, she is also being paid by her wealthy brother to stay away. She remembers Val from last New Year's Eve, but he doesn't remember her (or won't admit that he does). Val is looking for work in Lady's dry-goods store, having left behind a rowdy life in New Orleans in which he sang and played guitar and got into trouble. (Val and Carol are both hard-living eternal innocents.) She likes Val and recognizes him as a kindred spirit, but he ignores her. Carol is not allowed to drive in this county, so Val offers to drive her (and her car) out of town. Woodward moves from the driver's seat to the passenger side but leaves her feet by the gas pedal, with her dress above her knees. When he asks her to move her legs, she moves only the right one, thereby spreading her legs. Asked to move her other leg, she giggles as she brings her legs together, then raises her right foot to glove-compartment level. Eve Black would blush.

They stop at Ruby's Bar-B-Q, a dive off the Dixie Highway, and Carol makes a pay-phone call. Woodward, turning every public action of Carol's into a display, talks too loudly, squeals with delight, and keeps herself planted outside the phone booth as she carries on. Then comes one of Woodward's peak moments, her "jooking" monologue. Asked by a bar patron what she means by "jooking," she details her idea of a great night out, an alternating program of driving around, drinking, and dancing to jukebox tunes, with drinking the longest-lasting of the night's trio of pleasures. She insinuates that sex is the proper end of a successful evening of "jooking." ("Jooking" is how Williams spells the word in the play, but shouldn't it be "juking"?) In one uninterrupted take, Woodward delivers this speech while flouncing around the establishment, all floppy and clownish and using expansive gestures. As the camera follows her around the room, she drinks from a stranger's bottle and dances briefly with a couple.

Her buoyant exhibitionism, almost as vibrant and unbound as if she were performing a musical number, eventually leads her, when seated, to flinging a liquor bottle and hoisting her legs in the air. It is a likably free-spirited romp, broken by a slap from her drunken brother, who just happens to be in attendance. But she slaps him back, and Woodward's is the harder-hitting of the smacks.

In the car again, she opens up to Val, though he still barely contributes. (Brando seems to be watching Woodward's performance rather than acting alongside her.) She tells him, "I want people to know I'm alive" and be "noticed and seen and heard and felt." Woodward conveys that on some level Carol's outrageous behavior satisfies those feelings, a preferable existence to those well-mannered but suffocated lives around her (like Lady's). But she also bares the sadness of an aimless life, a useless wallowing in a battered, circular reality. Carol talks about her past, fighting for the equal treatment of blacks by making speeches and writing letters and marching in protest, eventually getting arrested for "lewd vagrancy." Though Woodward laughs about all this, her subtext is anything but comical. With Carol's good and unselfish impulses discouraged and stifled by the community, she now pours her energy into excessive escapades of numbing the pain, showing just "how lewd a lewd vagrant can be when she puts her whole heart into it." She has been spitefully committed to her particularly flagrant brand of social revenge, rather than just leaving for good. She and Val stop at the darkened cemetery, the "bone orchard" she calls it. On her knees, she whispers, looking directly at his crotch, that the dead are telling us to live. She then moves closer to him and reaches for his belt, an unambiguous attempt to perform oral sex, which isn't in the play. (This *must* be the first time such a moment occurs in an American feature film.) When he takes her hands away, she whispers, "Please let me, let me." Whether it's Carol's use of sex as a way to blot things out, or as the most intense way to feel alive, or just another means of debasing herself further, or merely a pathetic attempt to get him to like her, all these flickering possibilities come through in Woodward, who plays the scene with more vulnerability than lust or aggression. Another interesting shading in her performance is the possibility that Carol isn't as promiscuous as she pretends, overplaying her repu-

tation for effect, but rarely, if ever, going as far as she suggests. Val is a catalyst for her to rethink her life, including the prospect of love. The longing to connect in Woodward's Carol is raw and exposed, and very much in need of a helping hand. She reaches out to him, physically and emotionally, but doesn't get much in return, just as Woodward gets little from Brando. Woodward has been vocal about how much she hated acting with Brando, but his remote behavior apparently affected her creativity beautifully, whether or not this was his intention.

Woodward isn't seen again till much later, after the Brando-Magnani relationship has taken center stage. Carol causes a disturbance at the gas station across the street from Lady's store, getting slapped by a fellow before being rescued by Val. She has returned just to see him again. (By now, both Lady and Carol are besotted with Val, and both see him as the way out of their dead-end lives.) Her nose bloodied, Woodward has a scene with Brando at the side of the store. Still playful, and still sure they have compatible souls, she tells him, in a lovely and piercing moment, that she would love to hold something the way he holds his guitar, "with such tender protection." It is the basic craving not just to *be* loved but to love fully. As suspected, Carol is a more thoughtful and sensitive person than indicated by the floor shows she puts on for gaping viewers. (If, as "Orpheus," Val has come to rescue Lady from her hell, he may also have come for Carol, unintentionally instigating her move out of stagnation.) She wants Val, but he presumably still avoids her because she represents a kind of life he never wants again. Yet shouldn't he be sensitive enough to see that she, too, is seeking a way out? Whereas Carol and Lady always achieve dramatic logic, further enhanced by the contributions of Woodward and Magnani, Val seldom makes basic sense and Brando finds few illuminating moments. Though Val continues to discourage Carol's attentions, his very presence helps transform her. In him, she sees a future, and, whether she gets him or not, is now at least able to think in those terms.

Near the end, Carol returns after hearing that Val is leaving (because of threats made on his life by the sheriff). She wants to go with him. Carol has also been offered big bucks by her family to go as far as Europe. Woodward is by now more lucid and levelheaded than the gal who first slammed into the movie. In a scene with Lady (who also sees Val as

The Trouble with *Angels*

In *Battle of Angels,* Williams' original 1940 version of what became *Orpheus Descending,* Carol is named Cassandra, a rather pointed reference to her as the bearer of warnings to Val regarding his imminent death. Cassandra dies off-stage, driving her car off a bridge during a storm. Revising Cassandra into Carol was a definite improvement, and her promising ending is a bittersweet coda after a tragic climax. Carol now has the potential to find a mate far more interesting than two-dimensional Val. But no one cared when the film was released, and, despite its trio of Oscar-winning stars, *The Fugitive Kind* tanked at the box office and received scant praise.

her future), Carol recognizes her as a "sister" because "you've found out what I know," that, in life, catch all you can "with both your hands till your fingers are broken." This touching reflection, regarding both women's transitions in response to Val, reveals Carol as someone profoundly changed after so much wasted time, ready again to believe in things and move forward and "live" (as the dead once urged her to). Courtesy of Lady's vengeful husband (Victor Jory), Val will shortly die in a fire and Lady will be shot dead. The next morning, Uncle Pleasant (Emory Richardson), known as "the Conjure Man," a silent and mystical black man, finds Val's snake-skin jacket among the wreckage. Woodward holds it to her face and says, "Wild things leave skins behind them," as well as teeth and bones "so that the fugitive kind can follow their kind." Woodward savors this moment, with Carol treasuring the jacket, her connection to Val and their kind. She puts it on, gets in her car, and drives off. After the especially heartbreaking death of the pregnant Lady, the last moments are hopeful. Carol seems headed *to* something, something better, and ready to go after it with both hands, till her fingers are broken.

Woodward hooked up again with Newman for *From the Terrace* (1960), a glossy soap along the lines of *The Long, Hot Summer* though downright awful. Why wasn't *From the Terrace*'s director, Mark Robson, able to bring to this John O'Hara adaptation some of the textures and feeling he culled from his comparably trashy *Peyton Place* (1957)? Woodward, as a society girl, has platinum-blond hair and

an array of Travilla fashions (including a sky-blue wedding gown), all of which proves one thing inadvertently: Woodward could not pull off a glamour role. Devoid of any stylish allure, she seems like an uncomfortable mannequin, as if glamorized against her will. Both Newmans come off as vapid presences in their portrait of a wealthy and miserable marriage, which includes extramarital affairs for both. (Newman opts for someone other than Woodward at the end: nice girl Ina Balin.) For Woodward, *From the Terrace* was the antithesis of *The Fugitive Kind* in terms of her role's value and her own effectiveness, as well as the overall quality of the movie. Add to this the fact that *From the Terrace*, numbing and plasticized though it may be, was a roaring box-office hit while *The Fugitive Kind* went virtually unseen. Woodward never again starred in a movie as financially successful as *From the Terrace*, but even its high grosses, directly attributable to Newman's soaring stature as a popular draw, couldn't turn her into a free-standing movie star.

Their next match-up, *Paris Blues* (1961), Woodward's fourth and final film for director Martin Ritt, was the first box-office loser for the Newman-Woodward team, not even generating critical enthusiasm. In this romanticized hokum (presented under the guise of "cool"), Woodward, a tourist in Paris, chases musician Newman, sleeps with him, and then loses him. *The Stripper* (1963), however, gave her one of her better roles, a failed starlet (touring with a magic troupe) who finds herself stranded in a Midwestern town where she had lived as a youth. In this adaptation of a lesser William Inge play *(A Loss of Roses),* Woodward conjures Marilyn Monroe emotionally (with a bruised vulnerability) and physically (in her flouncy walk and tight clothes), as well as in Monroe's final "look," with her cotton-candy puff of platinum hair. A variation on the whore-with-a-heart-of-gold, Woodward is a sweet, none-too-bright doormat where men are concerned, falling for (and being hurt by) younger-man Richard Beymer. Woodward never overplays or caricatures a potentially clichéd role, performing with an affecting softness and honest simplicity. She's a tramp with soul. Though Woodward couldn't pull off the old-style Hollywood glamour required of *From the Terrace,* she handled the sad, tawdry glamour of *The Stripper* superbly. Despite her exceptional and undervalued performance, one of the all-time best she ever gave, the film is an insignificant and dismissible drama. Yet it does provide the unique sight of Woodward performing a strip to "Something's Gotta Give," bursting the balloons that constitute her costume.

Back with Newman, and apparently determined to have another go at generating laughs (after the unencouraging results of *Rally 'Round the Flag, Boys!*), the duo starred in the even worse comedy *A New Kind of Love* (1963). If *Rally 'Round* had proven that they weren't Cary Grant and Irene Dunne, then this smarmy and childish sex comedy (in the typical early-sixties manner) proved that they weren't Rock Hudson and Doris Day either, who had naturally high spirits. This sparkle-free romp has Woodward as a mannish employee of the fashion industry, with her dark glasses and brown hair calling to mind Edith Head, the film's costume designer. Woodward's "semi-virgin" comes up against Newman's womanizing newspaper columnist. (Their roles aren't dissimilar to the ones they played in *The Long, Hot Summer*.) After her requisite makeover, Woodward, in a blond wig and couture fashions, looks like a drag queen, more Jack Lemmon than Marilyn Monroe. When Newman thinks she's a high-class whore, it's the moment when hilarity is supposed to ensue. In a role, however lame, that offered her the comic mileage of two identities (à la 1936's bright Irene Dunne vehicle *Theodora Goes Wild*), Woodward isn't funny or even any fun. A misogynistic misfire, *A New Kind of Love* gave Woodward the bizarrely unexpected chance to be sung to by Maurice Chevalier, a rather repellent prospect by 1963.

After a short-lived return to the stage, opposite Newman in Broadway's *Baby Want a Kiss* (1964), and a "B" screen thriller, *Signpost to Murder* (1964), Woodward seemed primed for a return to form with two major 1966 releases: *A Big Hand for the Little Lady*, a western opposite Henry Fonda, and *A Fine Madness*, a "zany" farce opposite Sean Connery. The former, based on a television play, can't shake its limited small-screen feeling, though it is clever and does sustain interest. All about a once-a-year poker game among high-rollers, the film is most memorable for its surprise twist. *A Fine Madness* is more ambitious but less satisfying, both scattered and stupefyingly unfunny. It deservedly flopped for being so irritating, a portrait of the artist as a total creep. Connery, underwhelming and confused-looking as

an obnoxious and abusive poet, is just as miscast as Woodward, who, conversely, overacts as his waitress wife, gratingly unconvincing in her forced New York accent and discordant vocal inflections. The stars have no chemistry, and the outcome is strained and mirthless and ultimately baffling.

But then came one of those instances when Newman came to Woodward's rescue and rehabilitated her career. Best Picture Oscar nominee *Rachel, Rachel* (1968), helmed by Newman in his debut as a screen director, garnered Woodward her second nomination, though it may now leave you wondering what all the fuss was about. Essentially an earnest, simply told "old-maid schoolteacher" drama (marked by masochism), I suspect that this minor and unmemorable film was over-praised because of Newman's selfless restraint and sensitivity, which never called attention to *Paul Newman*. Woodward is open and sincere as a thirty-five-year-old virgin playing servant to her selfish, pampered mother, but the repressed, closed-off Rachel is a bore. Though the character evokes some of Eve White's dullness (as well as Eve's flashback concerning childhood and death), Woodward's drabness isn't all that interesting this time around. Rachel may not add up to much yet Woodward won the New York Film Critics' Best Actress honor in the year of Barbra Streisand in *Funny Girl*, Mia Farrow in *Rosemary's Baby*, and Vanessa Redgrave in *Isadora*.

Winning (1969) and *WUSA* (1970), two hugely disappointing films with Newman, put the final box-office whammy on the Newmans as a screen team (while he continued to have big hits on his own). A very slight car-racing drama, *Winning* at least reunited Woodward with Robert Wagner (thirteen years after he pushed her off the roof in *A Kiss Before Dying*), cast as Newman's rival on and off the track. In *WUSA*, more ambitious than *Winning* but no better, Woodward plays a secondary Shirley MacLaine-ish doormat role, while Newman and Anthony Perkins are at odds in the center of the film's overcooked political paranoia. Better for Woodward was a moderately enchanting bit of contemporary whimsy called *They Might Be Giants* (1971), in which co-star George C. Scott, showcasing his post-*Patton* versatility, believes he is Sherlock Holmes. Woodward is his Dr. Watson, a homely, glasses-wearing analyst who tries to cure him but inevitably succumbs to his fantasy world. (Having stolen *The Hustler* from Paul Newman, Scott steals *They Might Be Giants* from Woodward.) Though it doesn't really progress beyond its delightful conceit, the film is a charmer with a cult following, having generated little business when first released. Aiming to be an ugly-duckling love story in the *African Queen* mold, *They Might Be Giants* lacks stars with the sufficient compatibility. It is another Katharine Hepburn movie that is called to mind: *Bringing Up Baby* (1938), in which another loon (Hepburn) awakens an uptight nerd (Cary Grant) when they share a madcap adventure.

Newman directed *The Effect of Gamma Rays on Man-in-the-Moon Marigolds* (1972), another movie that nobody saw (and they didn't miss much), though it snagged Woodward the Best Actress prize at Cannes. A shabby domestic drama adapted from Paul Zindel's Pulitzer Prize-winning play, *Gamma Rays* makes little impact, with a brown-haired Woodward less than comfortably cast. There's no denying her commitment, but her blowsy, bitter character feels effortfully put on, as if she were suddenly replacing Shelley Winters. Despite her miscasting, Woodward's performance is of interest as a forerunner to her Amanda Wingfield in *The Glass Menagerie* (1987), since both characters, women of unfulfilled dreams, are domineering mothers of two, abandoned by their husbands and living in financial distress. (The Newmans' daughter, Nell Potts, plays one of Woodward's two girls in *Gamma Rays*.) She got a third Oscar nomination, and a second award from the New York critics, for *Summer Wishes, Winter Dreams* (1973), a dismal drama made at a time when opportunities for women in American film were at their nadir. (To those who cite the early 1970s as the second Golden Age of Hollywood, I ask: how can an era be labeled *golden* when it virtually erased—aside from a few good hooker roles—an entire gender from the screen?) Brown-haired again, which apparently signifies she's in a serious film, Woodward plays an upper-class New York matron, a cold and unpleasant wife who drove away her gay son. Straining to be an Ingmar Bergman chamber drama (utilizing dreams and flashbacks), the film is more like that same year's *Save the Tiger*, another ponderous, self-important, and unilluminating drama of middle-aged angst, regret, and self-pity. Written by Stewart Stern (who wrote *Rachel, Rachel*), the film maroons Woodward, who tries valiantly to flesh out an unformed character.

In between two more roles, which relegated her to supporting-player status, in Newman vehicles—*The Drowning Pool* (1975) and *Harry & Son* (1984), the latter of which he also directed—Woodward became one of the queens of movies made for television, returning to the medium in which she had been discovered twenty years before. The most famous of these projects is *Sybil* (1976), with the full-circle casting of Woodward as the psychiatrist of a young woman (Sally Field) with many more "faces" than Eve. (*Sybil* did for Field what *Eve* had done for Woodward.) Woodward went on to win Emmys for *See How She Runs* (1978) and *Do You Remember Love* (1985), also starring in, among others, *Come Back, Little Sheba* (1978), opposite her childhood idol Laurence Olivier, *Crisis at Central High* (1981), and *Breathing Lessons* (1994). She also made a tepidly received return to Broadway in George Bernard Shaw's *Candida* (1981). But would she ever again star in a feature film?

In 1985, Woodward played Amanda Wingfield in Tennessee Williams' career-making play *The Glass Menagerie* at the Williamstown Theatre Festival in Massachusetts, reprising the role soon after at the Long Wharf Theatre in Connecticut. Both productions were directed by Nikos Psacharopoulos and costarred Karen Allen as Laura Wingfield and James Naughton as the Gentleman Caller. In Massachusetts, John Sayles played Tom Wingfield; in Connecticut, Treat Williams was Tom. Paul Newman was so impressed with his wife's performance that he was determined to preserve it on film. It would become a very low-budget venture, bringing along Karen Allen and James Naughton, and adding John Malkovich's Tom as the new ingredient. Malkovich had played Tom onstage in a 1979 Steppenwolf production in Chicago, which means that the set-up for this movie was similar to that of the film of *A Streetcar Named Desire*, which also starred three actors from one stage production (Marlon Brando, Karl Malden, and Kim Hunter) and a fourth player (Vivien Leigh) from a different stage production. In both cases, the quartet of stars was intimately familiar with the text, but the question mark was how the newcomer would affect, and be affected by, the other three. In both cases, it was a healthy shake-up, preventing mere transfers of what had occurred on stages, forcing the actors to rethink scenes and discover new creative answers. But weren't the 1980s a bit late to be filming a play, however classic, as familiar as *The Glass Menagerie*? Wouldn't anyone inclined to go to the movie have already read and/or seen the play countless times since its 1945 Broadway premiere? In its favor was the fact that Newman would actually be doing a service to the play, reducing the bad taste left behind by the painfully compromised and disrespectful 1950 film version, which had sentimentalized the material to disastrous effect. It had been the first film made from a Williams text, an inauspicious start to the playwright's future in movies. Newman's remake, which made *The Glass Menagerie* the only Williams play filmed twice for the big screen, automatically gets points for faithfulness. Despite its integrity, this *Glass Menagerie* isn't much of a movie, more solid and reverent than living and breathing, and not especially affecting. Though it lacks the invigoration of an interesting interpretation, or an overall vitality as a film, I'm still glad that it exists. Williams never saw Newman's 1987 film, having died four years before its release.

Abandoned by her husband sixteen years ago, and now living meagerly with her two grown children, Amanda Wingfield is a role that great actresses attempt when they move into middle age and beyond. People may argue about who was the greatest Blanche DuBois or Maggie the Cat, but you never hear such talk applied to Amanda. The role's creator, Laurette Taylor, apparently set an unattainably high standard in what remains one of Broadway's most acclaimed performances. Taylor's legend has been burnished by the fact that there is no filmed or aural record of her performance, nothing to challenge its daunting reputation. No Amanda of the last sixty-five years has been perceived as coming close to Taylor's achievement. And it's not as though prominent actresses have shied away: Maureen Stapleton, Jessica Tandy, Julie Harris, and Jessica Lange were subsequent Broadway Amandas; Shirley Booth and Katharine Hepburn played the role on television; and Helen Hayes was Amanda in London. All lofty figures, yet none put a stamp on the role to rival Taylor's, nor are any of them spoken about in the same breath with her. On stage and then on film, Woodward joined this illustrious company and, following her predecessors, did not budge Taylor from her pedestal. (Taylor's handling of Amanda's two phone conversations, selling magazine subscriptions, were reported revelations of her performance, whereas Woodward's telephone scenes,

though skillfully done, will hardly leave you raving.) Woodward is good throughout, but it's not a performance that I suspect anyone beyond her husband thought merited preservation. My main criticism is that she's never quite enough in portraying any of Amanda's facets, not annoying, funny, pathetic, embarrassing, or selfish *enough*. She hits all of these and other character traits, but the performance feels more safe than risky, and a role as famous as this one requires some boldness and a high-stakes commitment. You might credit Woodward for making Amanda more mundanely real than theatrically larger-than-life, but the material isn't as moving or haunting if Amanda isn't rendered in go-for-broke terms; Woodward doesn't fill the part's *size*. In striving to make Amanda a sadly unexceptional figure, Woodward diminishes the character's uncommon verve and will. Her everyday approach appears to be an intentional safeguard against Amanda ever coming across as a campy grand dame, which wouldn't be such a bad thing in small doses. Always intelligent and always connected, Woodward, however, doesn't bring much imagination to the fore. She was more artistically suited to the role of Laura and might have been excellent in that role if the first film version had been made in 1955 instead of 1950; Amanda is more of a strain on her natural abilities.

The film opens with Malkovich's Tom on the street of the now oddly decrepit and vacant apartment building where he once lived with his mother and sister. As Tom looks back, exactly how much time has passed in this version? It appears to be decades, based on the neighborhood's desertion, yet Tom is still a young man. He addresses the film audience, establishing the device of having Malkovich speak Tom's stage monologues (intended for the theatre audience) directly into the camera, delivered from the now-rotting apartment. Malkovich is least effective in these sequences, mostly because of his signature tonal monotony. It would have been more natural to turn all these passages into voice-overs (which Newman does only briefly), rather than having photographed monologues serve as reminders that this is just barely a movie. (It is also strange to have retained Tom's references to this being a "play," instead of changing "play" to "film.") He tells us what *The Glass Menagerie* is all about: "the long-delayed but always expected something that we live for." The scene flashes back to 1930s St. Louis and the dinner table

*In **The Glass Menagerie**, Woodward's Amanda grills Malkovich's Tom about tomorrow night's Gentleman Caller.*

of Amanda, Tom, and Laura. Gray and frizzy-haired, Woodward is a matron chattering on about the proper, leisurely way to digest a meal, with talk of "salivary glands" and "mastication." Predating Blanche DuBois by two years, Amanda is another belle trapped in a decisively grim setting while trying to maintain a semblance of a more genteel past. Amusing as Woodward is here, this speech is indicative of what's wrong with her entire performance. Amanda is someone who does everything full-out, but Woodward is no more than a mildly pestering frump. She speaks too softly, perhaps consciously reining in her stage performance, but more sound is demanded by Williams' words. Woodward's bland, reedy voice, often a detriment in her films, is inadequate to the task. Amanda's voice should be irksome in the way that Shirley Booth's cuts through everything in *Come Back, Little Sheba*, but, instead, it's annoying for its thinness. Woodward's voice is too much in her head; it needs more weight, tone, and crackle. (No complaints, though, about her Deep-Southern accent.)

Woodward soon launches into Amanda's reverie of her Mississippi youth and its peak moment, the afternoon she was attended by seventeen gentleman callers. (This would become a ludicrous moment in the 1950 film, a startling flashback in which Gertrude Lawrence cavorts with suitors in what looks like the antebellum South. This is especially hilarious because, instead of an ingénue stand-in, there's Lawrence herself, past fifty, looking like a crazed grandmother.) This is Woodward's chance to indulge some Scarlett O'Hara charm as Amanda explains how she maneuvered so many men with "the art of conversation." Woodward, again, is capable enough, but you can't imagine that all those boys were entranced by her. If one believes that Amanda is wildly exaggerating, Woodward isn't a good enough bewitcher to come close to convincing me of things that I suspect are untrue, nor does she have the pitiable poignancy of a harmless liar. In a coincidental aside, two of Amanda's gentleman callers were the Cutrere brothers (perhaps relatives of Carol?). Woodward's Amanda lacks the kind of self-absorption and ravaged grandeur that would justify the eye-rollings she receives from Tom. When Woodward asks Karen Allen's Laura how many gentleman callers they are expecting tonight, it makes little sense because this Amanda never seems extravagant enough to be the kind of personality who would ever suggest the possibility of something so ridiculous.

Broken *Glass*

Of the 1950 film version of *The Glass Menagerie,* Williams says, in *Memoirs,* that it was "awful" and "the most unfortunate film ever made of my work." (The screenplay was co-credited to him and Peter Berneis.) Considering the ruthless distortions to the play (specifically the revised ending) and the questionable casting, it is not difficult to understand Williams' assessment. As Amanda, a tattered Southern belle steeped in her former glory days, why cast British Gertrude Lawrence? (Warner Brothers must have been hoping for a repeat of the sensation caused by British Vivien Leigh as the Southern belle of *Gone With the Wind*.) Despite renown as a sophisticated theatre star, Lawrence hadn't found success in her few forays into film, far more at home on Broadway and London stages. She makes an honest try as Amanda, but she dallies on the role's externals and is unable to give the character an inner life. (The next year, 1951, she starred on Broadway as Anna in *The King and I* and then died the following year.) Fresh from her Oscar-winning performance in *Johnny Belinda* (1948), Jane Wyman was cast as Laura, Amanda's fragile daughter, turning in a dim, simplistic performance, a one-dimensional attenuation of the vulnerability and delicacy she had brought to *Johnny Belinda.* Talented Arthur Kennedy seemed good casting as Tom, Amanda's son, but proved not to be a strong or varied enough presence to hold the screen for so long without becoming tiresome. Kirk Douglas had the opposite problem, too much

of a magnetic star to be acceptable as the Gentleman Caller, an ordinary-guy role more suited to Kennedy. (One asset of the film is the easy camaraderie between Kennedy and Douglas, who had just played brothers to Oscar-nominated effect in 1949's *Champion*.) Despite their genuine efforts, the cast was unable to probe beneath the surface of the text, further undermined by Irving Rapper's prosaic direction. The material merited a first-class director, someone adept at bringing plays to the screen. Rapper, who occasionally rose to first-class heights (1942's *Now, Voyager*) more often churned out professional if uninspired pictures. In the book *A Look at Tennessee Williams,* Rapper tells author Mike Steen that Williams was "most eager, too eager, to transfer all authority and all know-how to everybody entrusted with the picture," implying that if Williams had simply been present more often he might have rescued the film from the worst of its studio-imposed alterations, though Rapper does say that Williams "added a few scenes" himself. Maybe If William Wyler, who had just brought *The Heiress* (1949) to the screen superbly, had directed *Menagerie* and forbidden any tampering with the play, then it might have become the screen classic it had the potential of being. A 1950 dream cast might have included Irene Dunne as Amanda, Montgomery Clift as Tom, and, for Laura, maybe Betsy Blair (who had understudied the role on Broadway) or Barbara Bel Geddes or Wyler favorites Teresa Wright and Cathy O'Donnell.

Amanda learns that Laura secretly dropped out of business college, effectively ending Laura's prospects for making her own way in life. With a disability that has left her walking with a limp, in addition to her crushing shyness, Laura is a challenge to a mother desperate to find ways to help a daughter who won't help herself. Laura escapes into her glass menagerie, her collection of small animals. (The Wingfields, too, are a glass menagerie of breakable human beings living in a confined space.) Tom, harboring thoughts of adventure, is saddled with supporting his mother and sister by working in a dead-end job at a shoe warehouse, resenting every moment of his servitude but anchored by his affection for his sister and steady doses of guilt dispensed by Amanda. The long-ago departure of Mr.

Wingfield ("a telephone man who fell in love with long distance") instantly made Tom the man of the house, severely limiting his options. *The Glass Menagerie* is about three desperate people: Amanda, fearful for her family's future, specifically with regard to finances; Tom, yearning to leave but helpless to do so; and Laura, a young woman terrified of engaging with the outside world.

Like Blanche, Amanda is another Williams female able to drop her Southern-belle shtick when it's time to get down to business. (Both are dependent on others, with Blanche the open-ended visiting relation and Amanda reliant on Tom's slim paycheck.) Woodward scores in these reality-check scenes because naturalism comes easier to her than grandiosity. In chastising Laura for her "deception" about her

Not the Marrying Kind

Much has been written about the three main characters and their correlations to Williams' own life, with Amanda and Laura substituting for his real mother and sister, and Tom being a version of himself. The play is not autobiography, though the characters could aptly be called autobiographically inspired, which brings up an interesting question for any actor playing Tom. There is no overt suggestion that Tom is gay, so if an actor decides to play him as such it could be only through inference. Tom is an amateur poet, a young man without a girlfriend or any mention of going out on dates. He never sufficiently explains what he does every night, though he can't disguise the fact that he likes to get drunk, an escape from the drudgery of his life and perhaps his suppressed sexual desires. (He may need to drink to work up the courage to find bedmates, then drink some more to drown the resulting guilt.) This is a perfectly reasonable subtext for Tom as a gay man living in a hopelessly closeted world in which companionship is difficult to come by. The film adds a winking touch by having Tom listen to opera on the radio. Later, Malkovich displays a complete lack of interest in the sports pages. In his final speech, he makes an ambiguous reference to "companions." An actor might be able to hint at something unspoken in Tom's arguments with Amanda over his staying out late, further clarifying his touchiness about being interrogated. She taunts him in her disbelief that he goes to the movies every night, or

that that's all he does. (I don't believe him either.) One way for an actor to spotlight Tom's gayness is in his relationship with co-worker Jim O'Connor, the gentleman caller. Tom satisfies his mother's craving for a visitor (for Laura's sake) by inviting Jim to dinner, though Jim's hoped-for interest in Laura would seem a decided long shot. But it affords Tom the opportunity to spend time with Jim outside of work. Jim is affable, athletic (and usually played by a handsome actor), and it makes sense that Tom could have a crush on his only friend at the warehouse, the guy who affectionately calls him "Shakespeare." Tom says, in one of his monologues, that the other guys at work regarded him with "suspicious hostility" (which sounds like a reaction to a guy who isn't exactly one of the boys) until Jim befriended him. Even though Tom would know that Jim was straight, he could still take pleasure in Jim's attention. (Tom and Laura both knew Jim in high school, where he was a star onstage and on the basketball court.) Whether or not any of this is detected by an audience, it is nonetheless a fascinating and defensible subtext, and I imagine it has been utilized often in recent years. Malkovich's natural androgyny, slight effeminacy, and sometimes flamboyant physicality suggest the definite possibility that he's decided Tom is gay. The tensions in his confrontations with Amanda imply secrets that are never to be shared and that will always stand between them. Malkovich's Tom doesn't, however, show any special interest in James Naughton's Jim, too consumed with leaving town by that point to focus much on anything else.

school attendance, Woodward wields Amanda's gift for instilling guilt, her major tool for controlling her children (and probably what drove Mr. Wingfield away). Amanda warns Laura of ending up as one of those "barely tolerated spinsters" living off relatives, "bird-like women without any nests." (A character such as this would be played wondrously by Mildred Dunnock in the 1956 Williams picture *Baby Doll*.) You should never doubt that Amanda loves her children, and Woodward is believably as loving as Amanda claims to be. But the character's ways of expressing that love, and her attempts at bending her children toward what she believes is best for them (and her), leave much to be desired. Though Woodward is fine at conveying Amanda's anger and frustration, she never reaches the depths of her bit-

terness regarding how her life turned out, thanks to her husband, and worse, her own foolishness.

Amanda has never learned that in trying to control her men she has actually pushed them away. (Her daily "Rise and shine!" makes Tom think "how lucky dead people are.") Every accusation of selfishness she levels at Tom is an insult to his self-sacrifice and an ungrateful response to his daily grind. She thinks she's merely shoring up his sense of responsibility, but she's actually gnawing at his soul. Williams makes the Tom-Amanda quarrels play as assumed repeats of scenes Amanda would have played with her husband, as her nagging is met with mounting disgust. Tom's bravura speech about going out every night to "opium dens" and being known in the underworld as "Killer" and "El Diablo" is a funny and exhilarating release of his pent-up fury against Amanda's incessant harassment. (The colorful details attest to the fact that, yes, Tom has definitely seen a lot of movies.) He climaxes with "You ugly babbling old witch!" to which Woodward simultaneously reacts with high dudgeon (at his unwarranted cruelty) and hurt feelings (expressed through tears), exiting to her bedroom. As the story proceeds, Woodward makes plain that Amanda knows Tom has all the power. If he becomes immune to her needling, then how will she keep him in St. Louis? Amanda is no villain; she is deeply frightened, feeling that only through Tom can she and Laura survive. She is someone who has experienced hard knocks and knows she must do everything in her power to prevent any more. Woodward carries the burden of sixteen years of making ends meet, and she knows that, even at her most highfalutin, Amanda must always be striving to stay on top of things. Her Amanda is least effective and plausible whenever she resorts to being dotty and oblivious.

Woodward embodies Amanda's total lack of self-examination, never seeing her own wheedling of Tom as selfishness or thoughtlessness on her part. Sacrifices are part of life, and Tom will have to accept this like everyone else. She, too, was a dreamer, in her case imagining a life of sustained privilege. Maybe Amanda was foolish to think she was meant for better things than she got, or perhaps she really was as unlucky as she says, simply falling for the wrong guy. But since her own dreams were dashed, she seems not to have much interest, or put much stock, in Tom's. Woodward also captures Amanda's prevailing impatience with Tom's restlessness, something she hasn't the time to consider except with regard to how it affects her and Laura. Like Blanche, Amanda champions the mind and the spirit above baser things, and she's suspicious of any of Tom's needs beyond his family, all of which she perceives as threats. Their battles continue to sound more like husband-wife squabbles than those of mother and son. She at last agrees that he may leave, but only after he helps secure a husband for Laura. Enter Jim, the gentleman caller.

Jim's acceptance of Tom's dinner invitation is an actual sign of hope in a home without any. When Tom tells Amanda that Jim will be coming *tomorrow*, it affords Woodward one of Williams' most delightful comic sequences, which becomes one of her own best scenes. Her delirious fantasy about completely redoing the apartment in twenty-four hours reaches its first comic peak with a dead-serious "I wish I had time to paper the walls." Woodward nimbly shifts back and forth from giddiness at her answered prayer to misery over their dowdy rooms, an unfit location for such a magical event. With every realization of just how dreary the apartment is, Woodward soon snaps back, glowing with another quick-fix inspiration bound to transform the place. The scene is a beautiful representation of the two sides of Amanda's nature, her clear-eyed reality and her flair for illusion. Woodward is funniest as Amanda grills Tom about Jim's background, including her disappointment that he is Irish on both sides, which implies to her a drinking man. How quickly beggars become choosers! But she continues to turn every problem into an opportunity for victory, such as her salmon loaf being the answer of what to serve to a Catholic on a Friday night. The scene is also a vivid contrast between Malkovich's sarcastic, bored demeanor and Woodward's high-flying take on a situation in which she sees all challenges as springboards to a happy ending. Reality returns when she states to Tom her hard-learned outlook on life, about how "the future becomes the present, the present the past, and the past turns into everlasting regret unless you plan for it." Amanda confesses that she was taken in by her husband's good looks ("that face fooled everybody"), but the only reason to keep his portrait on the wall is because she continues to await his return.

When the night arrives and Laura is consumed with terror (because she had a crush on Jim in high school), it soon becomes clear that tonight is just as much about Amanda as Laura. It is Amanda's chance to relive her girlhood, including her wearing a long white dress from that time. Woodward gives glimmers of the scene's potential—Amanda's shaggy radiance, her mortifying attempt to recreate her youth, her uncontained gaiety all aflutter—but it's not the all-out exquisite moment it should be. Yes, many an Amanda has overplayed the part, and while Woodward's control is often admirable it seems, in this sequence, more like timidity than discernment, a natural unwillingness to go all the way. Williams provides Amanda with an unconsciously cruel moment, reliving her dancing days and swirling about the room while her disabled daughter watches and listens. Laura is fading into the background, even though this is supposedly *her* night. Woodward's rendition of the subsequent speech, about how the young Amanda's malaria fever didn't get in the way of her social calendar, is executed in too whispery a fashion, minimizing its impact. Young Amanda's mad, insatiable desire to be surrounded by jonquils was an expression of an overflowing desire for life, which was soon stymied by her marriage. Woodward induces the right mood of nostalgic longing but falls short on magic and poetry, never really re-entering that world, never making this one of those ravishing Williams moments when an actress melds indelibly with his words.

As Amanda tries to prevent Laura's pending panic attack, Woodward cannily stresses an essential frustration within Amanda, that neither of her children is much help to her unless coerced, making Amanda feel as though she's doing all the heavy lifting in keeping this family afloat. If Tom and Laura could only meet her standards of enthusiasm and discipline! After all these preparations, this dinner is going to happen, even if without the girl for whom it was intended. Woodward displays the backbone in Amanda, making visible the woman who raised two children on her own. She orders Laura to answer the door. Tom and Jim are somewhat stunned by Amanda's dress, as if no one told them it was a costume party. Here is Woodward's chance to give us her Scarlett O'Hara at the barbecue. A touch of temporary madness would be welcome in Woodward's Amanda, as the character loses her sense of proportion and behaves as if Jim is paying *her* a call. She chatters and flirts, but Woodward isn't devastating, neither as an actual charmer nor as an embarrassing excuse for one. Southern charm isn't all that rare a trait, and it's reasonable to expect Amanda to be darned good at it. Woodward is only adequate, far better at inhabiting the Amanda who gets lost in telling her life story (in too revealing terms) to Jim, a complete stranger. Laura's collapse at the dinner table is only a momentary hurdle, leaving Amanda in full charge of keeping Jim in their grasp. At the meal's end, the lights go out (because Tom paid his merchant-seamen union dues instead of the electric bill). Woodward adds a nice touch to the pleasant banter by playing the scene slightly tipsily, the results of dandelion wine. When Jim leaves the room and crashes into something on his way to check the

fuse box, Amanda, fearing Jim's untimely demise, says to Tom (in Woodward's hilariously humorless line reading), "Wouldn't it be awful if we lost him?"

Before she and Tom do the dishes, Amanda sends Jim to Laura in the living room, aided by a lighted candelabrum, leading to the famed "gentleman caller" scene, the play's centerpiece, which in this version plays for twenty-nine minutes, surefire as ever. (Has this scene ever not worked *anywhere*?) Jim is a nice guy being kind to a shy girl, helping to draw her out and doing so quite successfully, as much out of sympathy as from his self-satisfying knack for figuring out people. His analysis of her "inferiority complex" is both simplistic and accurate, and the scene becomes richer as they reminisce about their high-school days, particularly her reminder that he used to call her "Blue Roses" because that's what he thought she said when she told him the reason—pleurosis—for her extended absence. Laura should be played by a mildly pretty actress because an audience must be filled with a sense of hope and possibility during this scene, but Karen Allen is more strikingly attractive than pleasingly plain. As an actress, though, she has the proper fragility and the halting confidence as her Laura tentatively opens up. In her recollection of his youthful exploits, she finds a way out of her self-consciousness, and it's lovely to watch her discover her own budding charm, utterly unlike her mother's. Jim is a guy who likes to hear himself talk, perfect for a girl who wants *never* to talk. James Naughton's Jim is very likable and nicely energized, an appealing blend of puffed-up and innocent. He's the high-school star still waiting for his life to start and for all his promise to begin paying off. Though their ages aren't mentioned in the film, they are twenty-three years old in the play (Tom is two years younger). While Tom yearns for the adventures he has seen at the movies, Jim dreams about the practical pleasures of a successful career. Jim is a man of untapped potential, a bit sad beneath his bravado. But he has a lot going for him, including an interest in the future of television. There's no guarantee he'll succeed, which is why the role works best with a non-name actor (someone not already marked by success). Laura shows him her glass collection, particularly her treasured unicorn, the most personal thing she could share. (For all her mental and physical woes, Laura does remarkably well in her first outing with a man.) As music wafts in from the dance hall across the way, Jim teaches Laura to dance. They move rather well together until they bump into a table, causing the unicorn to fall and break his horn. The symbolism is straightforward but nonetheless touching: the unicorn and Laura have been normalized, no longer freaks. Jim tells her she's pretty and kisses her, partly out of genuine feeling, partly out of knowing how much she needs this. (In the 1950 film, even the gentleman-caller scene is dampened, first by being intercut with added scenes of Amanda and Tom in the kitchen, but worse by Jim and Laura actually *going* to the dance hall and her receiving his kiss there.) The final revelation that Jim is engaged is a blow, but why should it be? Did anyone actually believe it could be this easy, that the first gentleman caller would want to marry her? Was tonight her only shot at meeting someone? And who could have imagined that Laura would have handled herself so well, alone with a man? Isn't the evening a small victory for Laura, a good practice run? (Williams treats Jim more like Mitch in *Streetcar*, as a last-chance prospect, but Mitch really *is* one.) Bad as the 1950 film is, it does allow Laura the feeling of a breakthrough, of having made a significant first step.

Amanda, still on her high, interrupts Jim and Laura with lemonade. When he mentions "Betty," Woodward's face goes slack with the agonizing feeling that the name means exactly what Amanda fears it does. But she holds herself together until he exits. Woodward is astutely subdued because Amanda is shaken to her core. When she says to Laura, "Things have a way of turning out so badly," all of Amanda's dreaming has evaporated. In assuming that Tom deliberately made fools of them by inviting an engaged man to dinner, Woodward makes Amanda's anger appropriately impulsive rather than considered (Tom, of course, didn't know of Jim's engagement), driving him further away, irreparably. In humiliation, Amanda resorts to her foremost tactic: guilt. (Unlike Blanche DuBois or Brick Pollitt, both consumed with guilt, Amanda feels guilt-free as she inflicts guilt on others.) Referring to herself as a "deserted" mother and Laura as Tom's "crippled" sister, she crosses a line. Until now, Amanda has been incensed when either Tom or Laura used the word "crippled," yet here she is using it to manipulate Tom. It is a chilling, brilliant moment in the text, but the scene should be uglier and more stinging than Woodward plays it, amplifying the impression

Who the Hell Is Richard?

Though the 1950 film acknowledges that the visit from Jim had its bright side, the movie then goes way overboard, with Laura asking Jim to come see them again *with Betty,* followed by Laura giving Tom her permission to leave, and, in the final moments, Laura greeting "Richard," her new beau! Worse than this cheap cop-out of a tacked-on happy ending is the total betrayal of the play's lingering strains of guilt, regret, loss, and disappointment, as well as its struggles between reality and dreams and between obligation and self-actualization. All the thoughts and feelings so achingly dramatized by Williams were washed away in one fell swoop of slop, with every character getting what he/she wants.

that Amanda, stripped emotionally bare, has nothing left to lose as she makes her way to her famous final line: "Go to the moon you selfish dreamer!"

What might have been a promising start to more evenings of gentleman callers (with men perhaps less desirable than Jim) has quickly ended in a war of words too harsh to take back. During narrator Tom's final speech, Amanda is glimpsed consoling Laura. In the play, one cannot know what became of Amanda and Laura, a situation worsened in the 1987 film because the abandoned apartment building leaves you hopeless. (They were more likely evicted than rescued, no?) This imagery goes too far in defining, even obliquely, what should remain entirely unknown. When Tom left, he forfeited his right to know the resolution of his family's story, just as his father had. Tom made his choice, a terribly unfair choice, knowing that neither of his options would be easy to live with.

Newman's direction is attentive and unobtrusive, but at 134 minutes this is, to its disadvantage, the longest of the Williams pictures. Though the camerawork (by Michael Ballhaus) isn't static, the movie has the feeling of filmed theatre because it is so obviously underpopulated (there's not even an extra in the street). Karen Allen played Laura after already having had big success in film as the female leads in *Raiders of the Lost Ark* (1981) and *Starman* (1984). Laura isn't as fully developed as Amanda or Tom, and she can even be a little unsympathetic in her unwillingness to help herself, but Allen handles

Everything *Including* the Kitchen Sink

The 1950 film also added several small speaking roles and included new scenes: Tom at sea and at the warehouse; Laura at business college and at the zoo and with her mother at a department store; and Amanda selling subscriptions door to door. Paul Newman chose not to open up the play at all.

the role with sensitivity and grace, though she and John Malkovich do not share a sufficiently intimate sibling bond, which would have heightened Tom's struggle and furthered the emotional impact of his ultimate choice. Malkovich, who had been a recent Oscar nominee for *Places in the Heart* (1984), is one of many actors of his generation who bore the obvious influence of Marlon Brando in his work, notably in his startling outbursts, his penchant for uninflected line readings, and his strange unpredictability. Malkovich's Tom, especially when acerbic or in foul moods or seeming possibly gay, is the film's most original performance. His Tom is unlikely to remind you of someone else's, whereas the other three stars, more than able, manage to blend into all the well-acted Amandas, Lauras, and Jims we've seen.

The only subsequent film role of note for Woodward came in the Merchant-Ivory production of *Mr. and Mrs. Bridge* (1990), nabbing her a third prize from the New York critics and a fourth Oscar nomination. Playing spouses, she and Newman make for consistently unpleasant company, enacting two old-fashioned lives up against changing times (1937 to mid-war). Rendered without illumination, and episodic (in the bad way), this slow movie, despite nice moments, has you wondering if it's ever going to start. Woodward does an upscale variation of Lola in *Come Back, Little Sheba,* an ineffectual and tiresome matron, dim and unloved. By now, Mrs. Bridge seemed all too typically a Woodward role. In 1993, she turned up on the periphery of two high-profile pictures, as the narrator of *The Age of Innocence* and as Tom Hanks' mother in *Philadelphia*.

For all the ups and downs of her career, in Newman and non-Newman projects, Woodward never appeared in a better film than *The Fugitive Kind.* And despite three faces of Eve and two shouts of Rachel, I'll take just one Carol Cutrere.

Geraldine Page

*Dr. John (Laurence Harvey) seeks to find what ails Miss Alma (Page) in **Summer and Smoke**.*

Geraldine Page: Filmography

- *Out of the Night (1947)*
- *Taxi (1953)*
- *Hondo (1953)*
- *Summer and Smoke (1961)*
- *Sweet Bird of Youth (1962)*
- *Toys in the Attic (1963)*
- *Dear Heart (1964)*
- *You're a Big Boy Now (1966)*
- *The Happiest Millionaire (1967)*
- *Monday's Child (1967)*
- *Trilogy (1969)*
- *What Ever Happened to Aunt Alice? (1969)*
- *The Beguiled (1971)*
- *J. W. Coop (1972)*
- *Pete 'n' Tillie (1972)*
- *Happy As the Grass Was Green (1973)*
- *The Day of the Locust (1975)*
- *Nasty Habits (1977)*
- *The Rescuers (1977) (voice only)*
- *Interiors (1978)*
- *Harry's War (1981)*
- *Honky Tonk Freeway (1981)*
- *I'm Dancing As Fast As I Can (1982)*
- *The Pope of Greenwich Village (1984)*
- *The Bride (1985)*
- *Walls of Glass (1985)*
- *White Nights (1985)*
- *The Trip to Bountiful (1985)*
- *My Little Girl (1986)*
- *Native Son (1986)*
- *Riders to the Sea (1987)*

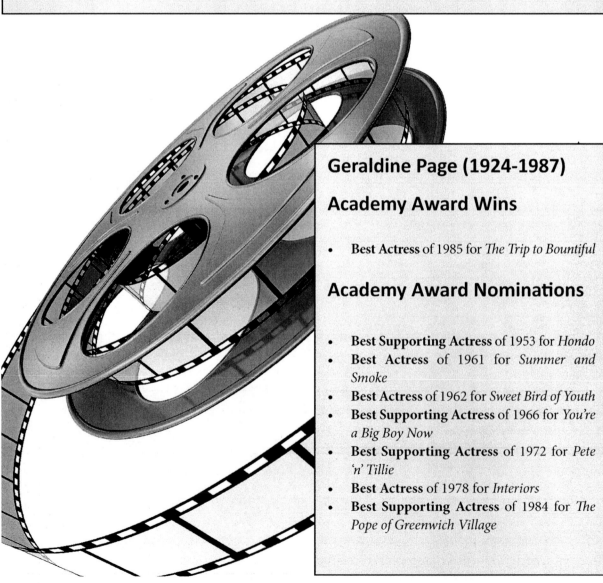

Geraldine Page (1924-1987)

Academy Award Wins

- **Best Actress** of 1985 for *The Trip to Bountiful*

Academy Award Nominations

- **Best Supporting Actress** of 1953 for *Hondo*
- **Best Actress** of 1961 for *Summer and Smoke*
- **Best Actress** of 1962 for *Sweet Bird of Youth*
- **Best Supporting Actress** of 1966 for *You're a Big Boy Now*
- **Best Supporting Actress** of 1972 for *Pete 'n' Tillie*
- **Best Actress** of 1978 for *Interiors*
- **Best Supporting Actress** of 1984 for *The Pope of Greenwich Village*

Alma Winemiller in *Summer and Smoke* (1961)
Alexandra Del Lago in *Sweet Bird of Youth* (1962)

If Marlon Brando is the actor most identified with Tennessee Williams' work, then Geraldine Page is the corresponding actress, and she has an overall edge by having collaborated on Williams projects more often than Brando did. Page, like Brando, owed her theatre stardom to Williams, making her mark in a 1952 revival of his play *Summer and Smoke* at the Circle in the Square, among several esteemed productions (including a 1956 restaging of Eugene O'Neill's drama *The Iceman Cometh*) that are credited with turning Off-Broadway into a vital force within the New York theatre. Page and Brando were model examples of post-war America's new breed of actor, with their concentrated intensity, thrilling spontaneity, and keenly observed attention to human behavior. Both stars merged so intuitively with their characters that, at their best, they were incapable of making wrong moves. Page is the only performer featured in this book to have recreated on-screen two performances she gave in major Williams roles on New York stages, as Alma Winemiller in *Summer and Smoke* and Alexandra Del Lago in *Sweet Bird of Youth,* characters who couldn't be more different from each other, rendering Page's back-to-back film performances all the more impressive. She was barely recognizable as the same actress.

Page was born in Missouri on November 22, 1924, and raised in Chicago, where she later attended the prestigious Goodman Theatre School. As an aspiring New York actress, she studied with Uta Hagen and worked Off-Broadway, on radio and television, and in stock (where she played Blanche in *Streetcar*), eventually joining the Actors Studio like many of the up-and-coming east-coast actors of the 1950s. The original 1948 New York production of *Summer and Smoke,* with Margaret Phillips as Alma, was not a success, despite a rave from Brooks Atkinson in the New York Times, becoming Williams' first Broadway failure. (After the high of *A Streetcar Named Desire,* what next play would *not* have been a disappointment?) Four years later, *Summer and Smoke* found new life when an unknown Page became an overnight sensation in the more intimate downtown production directed by

José Quintero. In his autobiography, Quintero says that Page "gave the greatest performance outside of Laurette Taylor in *The Glass Menagerie* that I have ever seen." The Times' Atkinson raved again, going so far as to rate the play higher than *Streetcar,* an assessment that now seems absurd. *Summer and Smoke* explores its themes with blatantly obvious strokes, seeming more the creation of a novice writer than that of an accomplished playwright with two important efforts behind him. In *Memoirs,* Williams states that Alma "may very well be the best female portrait I have drawn in a play," a flabbergasting determination until you remember that he also thought *The Roman Spring of Mrs. Stone* was the finest film version of one of his works.

Hondo (1953), a typically action-fueled John Wayne western, was most unlikely territory for Page's big break into the movies. If *Hondo* is traditional fare, almost kids' stuff, then Page is its most refreshing element. Cast as a pioneer woman deserted by her rotten husband and single-handedly raising their six-year-old boy, Page imbues the role with an emotional core of loneliness and need, elevating a standard script. She was surely one of the

The Female Brando (Almost)

If Page's talent, invention, and daring were of Brando's caliber, then why is she barely remembered today? Why did major roles in film dry up so quickly for Page, relegating her to offbeat supporting turns and only the occasional lead role? The answer is no great surprise. Brando's artistic skills were magnified by his remarkable beauty and sexual appeal; Page was not a beauty. It was (and is) exceedingly difficult for gifted actresses as ordinary-looking as Page to sustain movie stardom. No one can say that it was anything but sheer, undeniable talent that got Page to the top of the acting profession, and, for a brief streak in the early sixties, she was actually starring in motion pictures. Without those two Williams roles, though, her short span as a leading lady of the screen would probably never have happened.

more unexpected love interests encountered by Wayne in his lengthy career, yet her non-Hollywood look feels authentic in these surroundings. She actually describes herself to Wayne as "homely," making their eventual coming together that much more special and satisfying. Though her Oscar nomination (in the supporting category) now seems an excessive gesture, I believe it was a testament to just how unusual Page seemed at the time. Following the film's enormous popularity, what kinds of movie roles would there be for the "homely" Page? It was a problem encountered by many of Broadway's notable actresses—Helen Hayes, Shirley Booth, Julie Harris—who, despite having found some success on the screen, were less than sexy and photogenic.

On Broadway, Page appeared opposite Louis Jourdan and James Dean in *The Immoralist* (1954), and then later that year in *The Rainmaker*, as old-maid Lizzie, a high point of her stage career though she unfairly lost the role in the movie version to a too-old Katharine Hepburn, who was also too magnetic for such a plain-Jane character. In 1957, Page replaced Margaret Leighton on Broadway in *Separate Tables* (directed by Peter Glenville, the Englishman who would direct the film of *Summer and Smoke*), and she capped an extraordinary decade in the New York theatre by creating the role of Alexandra in Williams' *Sweet Bird of Youth* (1959). It was about time for her to return to the screen. Hal Wallis, who produced the admired and profitable film adaptation of *The Rose Tattoo* (1955) for Paramount, had the rights to *Summer and Smoke,* anticipating another Williams success for the studio. The screenplay for *Summer and Smoke* was penned by James Poe and Meade Roberts, without involvement from Williams. Poe had been co-credited for the *Cat on a Hot Tin Roof* screenplay, while Roberts had co-written *The Fugitive Kind,* the former a commercial success and artistic fiasco, the latter a box-office tragedy but a peak Williams picture. The screen's *Summer and Smoke,* very faithful to the play, has its virtues but is not very good, marred not just by its inadequate male lead but by the source material itself. However adult in its sexual discussions and activities, *Summer and Smoke* came too late to the screen. After the previous seven Williams pictures, and sexually preoccupied potboilers like *Peyton Place* (1957) and *A Summer Place* (1959), why would filmgoers be transfixed by a talky and

Joe & Gerry & Pete & Viv

It is bizarre that José Quintero, the man who guided Page's stage performance as Alma to plaudits, would make his film-directing debut in the same year that *Summer and Smoke* came to the screen, but with another Williams property, *The Roman Spring of Mrs. Stone.* Though the two films were made for different studios, wouldn't it have been more logical to find a way for Quintero to continue with *Summer and Smoke* and perhaps have Peter Glenville direct *Roman Spring,* which would star his British compatriot Vivien Leigh? Yes, Glenville had directed *Summer and Smoke* on the London stage in 1951 (with Margaret Johnson), but Quintero was the man who had shaped Page's Alma. Perhaps there would have been nothing left for Page and Quintero to explore ***together*** with this material, while Glenville and Page had the potential to find new inspiration in each other's ideas about Alma. Ultimately, it was Vivien Leigh who lucked out: Quintero's *Roman Spring* turned out to be the superior picture.

wispy period piece about a repressed virgin? (Set on the eve of our entry into World War I, *Summer and Smoke* was the only Williams film, until the recent 1923-set *Loss of a Teardrop Diamond,* to be situated before the Depression.) The play is weakened by its mounting masochism and overexplicit announcements of its themes. Instead of being moved by what befalls Alma, I feel dispirited by the spectacle of her degradation in the name of drama. Williams gives Alma ample opportunities to be victimized and humiliated, and he crowns the piece with overblown and unconvincing ironies presumably intended to give it an air of adding up to something. This is one of the unsexiest movies about sex, partially because of the lack of chemistry between Page and top-billed (but second-rate) Laurence Harvey, whose career was hot at the time even though his talent extended little beyond the memorization of his lines. His character, John Buchanan, is as important as Alma, yet Harvey draws a blank, coasting on his dark, slick handsomeness and moody bluster, forgetting to confront John's inner turmoil or make sense of his baffling connection to Alma.

Alma, daughter of a minister (Malcolm Atterbury), is a young woman who has taken on the public duties of a clergyman's wife because her mother (Una Merkel) hasn't been well since her nervous breakdown a decade ago. Alma sings at local functions and teaches music at the rectory. She is also a bit of a joke in the community for being so affected, with her broad-A speech and lack of a Southern accent in the Deep South. (The play is set in Mississippi but the movie refers only to the Delta and to Glorious Hill, the town.) Alma loves John, the boy next door, pining for him since childhood. John is home from medical school, following in his physician father's footsteps yet lacking in dedication, idling his time with women, gambling, and alcohol. The drama is the clash of opposites, a rather heavy-handed battle between the body and the soul as represented by John and Alma. (It is said one too many times that Alma is "Spanish for soul"; Blanche DuBois mentions what her name means only *once*.) The play and the film rarely surmount their thematic pretensions, pitting animal urges against loftier aspirations, never approaching the subtlety or complexity of Stanley versus Blanche in *Streetcar* despite the obvious similarities. Everything about *Summer and Smoke* feels schematic, tricked for its switcheroo climax, with Alma getting the long-suffering old-time "woman's picture" treatment. Blanche may be pathetic but she's a fighter, and she's shrewd, bold, funny, and electric; Alma is a whiny drip and not good company (whether you're in the movie or just watching it). The film unsurprisingly fared poorly at the box office.

Page brings enormous delicacy to the part, but nothing she does can make an emotional wipeout out of a fallacious drama. The film's chief value is its preservation of her theatre performance. If she is a bit stagy, that's okay because Alma is a woman who puts on airs with her rarefied speech, quaint manners, and religious propriety. Page's mannered gestures and overall oddness are perfect for someone as uncomfortable in her own skin as Alma. Though Page is a fancy actress playing a fancy-acting woman, she, at thirty-seven, looks old for the movie, already too much the spinster. (She played the role onstage at twenty-eight.) But this is forgivable in light of her talent and the fact that Alma, prematurely taking on her mother's role, has grown older before her time. Page's lack of prettiness is more of an issue. Like Laura in *The Glass Menagerie*, Alma should be plain but not unattractive, making more plausible the possibility of a happy romantic ending for her with good-look-

ing John. Page is blonder than usual and very thin, which inadvertently emphasizes her lack of a pretty face. She wears lovely long dresses (designed by Edith Head), often with hats featuring fat and wholesome-looking bows, but mostly in pale colors, as if Alma were slowly fading away. Page often has a hand at her collar or is waving a fan, nervous habits of Alma's but also useless attempts to tamp down feelings rising in her chest. Her unbridled laughter rightly sounds more like releases of roiling anxieties than outbursts of pleasure. Page is always interesting to watch, even after Alma no longer is.

The movie unfortunately retains Williams' prologue, featuring the ten-year-old Alma and John at the park fountain, with its statue of an angel named "Eternity," the location for many of the drama's more significant scenes. A girl refers to Alma as "that priss," setting up the character as the self-consciously cultured creature she will grow up to be. The scene establishes Alma's adoration of John and his bad-boy streak; she calls him "beautiful" and he exits laughing after getting her to kiss him. This forced, artificial scene offers nothing that won't be easily conveyed in the main body of the film. The action picks up about fifteen years later at a Fourth of July celebration. Page is first seen at the rectory, getting ready to attend the holiday festivities with her parents. Alma is experiencing her usual terror of singing in public, and so Page begins the film in a state of controlled panic, a prim yet rattled presence.

John, home for the summer, has an accidental reunion with Alma after her song on the bandstand, a scene near the angel statue. (Their relationship is as it was in the prologue.) John has studied to be a bacteriologist, suggestively steeping himself in the world of germs. He sees Alma as having a "doppelganger," two selves warring within her. Though he doesn't say so, he is afflicted by the same duality. When he tells Alma of some woman's unkind imitation of her, Page, mixing pride with vulnerability, tries to conceal a thin skin, declaring herself "mystified" by "unprovoked malice" (similar to *Streetcar*'s "deliberate cruelty"), yet she is wounded nonetheless. Page reveals the Alma often mocked, the woman trying to radiate decorum through an outwardly superior nature. As in the prologue, and in just about every scene between them that follows, Alma is left feeling demeaned by John. But she keeps coming back for more. Page musters some spine when Alma admonishes John for his debauched lifestyle, which disrespects his talent and worth. Both in her criticisms (acutely enhanced by her whiff of vindictive anger regarding his telling her about the imitation) and in her envy of his ennobling profession, Page is an Alma with a passion suitable for her father's pulpit. Her impact is also that of a scolding aunt, with some glimmers of an inspiring lover, all of which seems just right. To Alma's credit, she isn't shy about her feelings once she gets going. But her suppressed sexual feelings are generic, unsurprising coming from a proper Christian virgin. And there's little excitement in the Alma-John encounters, never a sense that their repetitive arguments have erotic tension or even much intellectual tension. Her happier moments with him are merely set-ups for later letdowns, like his casual invitation for a hypothetical car ride, which delights her no end but is soon forgotten by him. Movies about unattainable love can be punishing to sit through unless there's something riveting about their psychology, as in watching the formidable Scarlett O'Hara relentlessly fixated on weakling Ashley Wilkes.

Mrs. Winemiller is a showy but rather one-note role, giving actress Una Merkel the chance to be outspoken and outrageous but hardly three-dimensional. The best aspect of her performance is the character's enjoyment in being troublesome, whether at home needling Alma or, in public, stealing a hat or having a bratty flare-up about ice cream. Ever since her breakdown released her from obeying society's rules, Mrs. Winemiller no longer edits herself, expressing her thoughts as fully and inappropriately as she likes. A source of continual discomfort for the emotionally clenched Alma, Mrs. Winemiller is one of those "crazies" who invariably spouts the truth, causing unrest in and outside the home. Maybe she snapped, as Alma might, from being so reined in by the strictures of a minister's household. But the

Merkel Rides Again

Una Merkel is best remembered for her wisecracking dames of the 1930s, like the sassiest of the chorines in *42nd Street* (1933). She capped that decade with her great barroom brawl with Marlene Dietrich in *Destry Rides Again* (1939), a showstopper of slapping, hair-pulling, dress-ripping, and floor-rolling.

character is afforded little specificity. There's a notably clumsy moment when she, in her attempt to do a puzzle, cries, "The pieces don't fit!" (This kind of hammering symbolism is beneath Williams' talent.)

What does make sense is a wife and mother's resentment of the daughter who has taken her place as lady of the house, whether she wants the title back or not. Page plays Alma with a burdened attitude toward her rectory responsibilities, but this is pronounced enough to suggest that she secretly enjoys her position, simply projecting otherwise to disguise her private satisfaction. Mrs. Winemiller exists dramatically to antagonize Alma, such as when she shrieks "Alma's in love!" in front of one of her daughter's pupils, or when she talks openly of Alma's spying on John. "You have a devil in you," Alma tells her in their big confrontation. Wouldn't it be *enough* for Alma to be lonely, repressed, and unloved by John? Yet Williams almost revels in debasing her, not just romantically and socially but even in the privacy of her own home. The mother and child roles have been reversed, but Mrs. Winemiller is also Alma's crutch, an excuse for the lacks in her life. Here Page gets to rip into Merkel about how "tied down here" Alma is, and how she's thought of as an "old maid" before her time. It is gratifying to hear Page verbally attack her, breaking from Alma's saintly patience. "You have taken my youth away from me!" she declares, followed by the gentler "If you were just *kind*," allowing Page to articulate not just pent-up anger but also Alma's ongoing struggle to understand her mother's inexplicably heartless behavior. Page's Alma never loses sympathy for her mother, accepting the situation as one of the crosses she must bear (with some degree of righteous self-pity). Part of her frustration is the fact that everything Mrs. Winemiller says, though often unkind and improper, is accurate. And, though often at odds, the women share a perhaps genetic predilection for hysteria and an ultimate inability to live within the boundaries set before them.

Nothing Laurence Harvey does makes it clear why John toys with Alma. After she good-naturedly reprimands him for never taking her on that car ride, she invites him to a meeting of her "cultural group" at the rectory, an evening of "readings and refreshments," the kind of occasion that might send anyone in search of a bar, and certainly the antithesis of one of John's nights out. Page is delighted when

Flavor of the Moment

Laurence Harvey had made an international splash as the star of the British *Room at the Top* (1959), a very fine angry-young-man drama in which he was ideally cast as a cold-blooded civil servant wreaking romantic anguish during his social-climbing quest. Though effective, and an eventual Oscar nominee, Harvey also exposed his limitations; he bared no depths, no range of emotion. But the film's success brought him to Hollywood where he was actively employed for the next few years. *The Alamo* (1960), in which Harvey plays the garrison's strict and disliked commander, is so laboriously long that it actually makes you eager for the massacre. Though Harvey seems as out of place as his character, he comes closer to giving an actual performance than anyone else in this John Wayne-directed blunder. In *Butterfield 8* (1960), as Elizabeth Taylor's wealthy married lover (another coupling sans chemistry), Harvey is charmless and robotic, barely human even when his shoe is being memorably grinded by Taylor's high heel. Incapable of nuance, and with a penchant for scenery-chewing, he's pretty awful opposite Shirley MacLaine in *Two Loves* (1961) and Jane Fonda in *Walk on the Wild Side* (1962). But Harvey has a secure place in film history for his role in director John Frankenheimer's magnificent piece of Cold War paranoia, *The Manchurian Candidate* (1962), one of the great films of the 1960s, both an ingenious black comedy and a harrowing thriller. With his naturally alien presence, Harvey is perfection as a brainwash victim. Despite this bull's-eye performance, Harvey's Hollywood career understandably petered out by the end of the decade. He died of cancer at only forty-five in 1973.

he agrees to come, indulging Alma's fantasy that she can somehow lead him from darkness to light. The arrogance in her mission also comes through in Page, who is never hampered by trying to make Alma especially lovable. In the play, John attends the rectory gathering, but in the movie he telephones his regrets, telling Alma that he is visiting a patient (when actually he's been sidetracked by gambling). Page responds with a haughty indifference meant to minimize her disappointment, but Alma isn't fooling anyone. Other Williams females—Blanche DuBois, Amanda Wingfield, Violet Venable, among them—also prop themselves up with unrealistic expectations. But whereas their delusions are rooted in the deepest recesses of their characters, allowing them to keep on going and avoid the things they cannot face, Alma appears to be confronting imposed obstacles (some melodramatic, others symbolic) flung at her by an overeager playwright. Even when he presents her with an honest-to-goodness matrimonial option, Williams doesn't make the fellow a viable choice, but, rather, a somewhat comical nerd to whom she reacts with expected indifference.

Much of the problem with the movie stems from Laurence Harvey's inability to convey anything beyond what's in the dialogue, not even seeming to take any pleasure in John's decadence. There is plenty here for an actor to dissect, particularly John's self-destructive bent, tied to his resentment of his perfect father, a man he believes he can never equal personally or professionally. Feeling that he has always been a disappointment, John has now embraced that role and revels in it. He apparently sees something of value in his exchanges with Alma—an alluring spiritual contrast to the sensations of booze and sex and gambling—but Harvey doesn't appear to make this connection. Why would Harvey's John, a smoothie with the ladies, spend ten minutes with Page's Alma? This question is compounded by the stars' lack of emotional intimacy. There must be a perceptible struggle in John between his flesh and his spirit, something that would draw him to Alma, which would also make her seem less foolish in her yearning for him. If his conflicted interest in her was evident, then she wouldn't seem quite the martyr that she does. But without any percolating subtexts, John merely manipulates Alma thoughtlessly, which makes their major scenes perplexing and all the more cruel because Alma appears to mean so little to him. The remote possibility of them as a couple seems not just impossible but not even something to root for. Harvey, a British star (though Lithuanian-born), sustains his Southern accent but would have served the film better had he not consistently skimmed over his character's inner rumblings.

Hours after John's lame phone call about missing the rectory meeting, Alma shows up at his house in the middle of the night, claiming she needs to see his father professionally because of her nerves. She is actually there to disrupt John's evening with the sexually available Rosa (Rita Moreno) and *save* him. As acted by Page, Alma's fragility is pushy, as is her aura of sadness, resulting in a characterization discerningly more passive-aggressive than merely passive. John's diagnosis of her heartbeat is that "Miss Alma's lonesome," offending her and continuing their tiresome cycle of his insults and her wounded pride. Alma's persistent romantic hopes are exhausting to witness, as is John's leading her on. He makes an actual date with her for Saturday night, but why? Where is the vital bond somehow linking this apparent mismatch? In its absence, Alma and John appear to be victims of Williams and the screenwriters, thrust toward and away from each other at regular intervals without sufficient reason. Page exits the scene aglow, looking ahead to Saturday, but Alma is yet again being set up for a fall. If she truly speaks to the buried soul inside John, then why does he insensitively take her to the club where Rosa is dancing? Unless his motive is to scare Alma away for good, why does he bring her to a cockfight? Though the scene is implausible (Alma doesn't attend the cockfight in the play), it offers Page one thrilling moment when two spurts of blood land on her blouse and she emits a nightmarish scream, covering her face theatrically with one hand. This release is a horrified reaction to the violence, yes, but Page makes it so much more, a primal cry stemming from all the frustrations whirling within Alma.

Outside, in what looks like an enchanted forest, Page delivers a lovely rendition of Alma's speech about Gothic cathedrals, an encapsulation of her lofty outlook. Everything about those cathedrals "reaches up," and Page again speaks Alma's words with the heartfelt zeal of a true-believing preacher's daughter. "Look up, John," she encourages, confident in his potential. (Her blind faith in him may be what draws John to her, though Harvey doesn't connect those dots.) John is Alma's cause as well as her love. After she opens up about her failed courtships (her heart was never in them), John says that he senses excitement in her, but there isn't any visible in Page (nor does Harvey really seem excited by her). The talk moves to "conjugal relations," still a bit racy for 1961, even within the seemingly safe confines of a period piece. Eventually flat on her back and kissing him, Page fails to generate any real fire in Alma, either willingly or instinctually.

Even Alma's lifelong love for John has to be taken on faith. It looks as if Page, uninspired by Harvey, is trying to see past him to the John in her imagination, yet this only widens their divide. Until Alma panics and removes herself, this is one of the chattier seductions in movie history. Why must Alma be treated as such a prig? Is it so strange that a young woman of the 1910s would be protecting her virginity until marriage? And if John feels anything at all for her, why would he want to deflower her this way, treating her like all the others? Is he so overcome with lust? That seems unlikely. Is he trying to prove that the soul is no match for the body? Is a sexual response all that he can offer any woman? Harvey's performance brings no insights or revelations to any of these questions.

In response to her father's news that John is going to marry Rosa (as a means of settling his debt to her casino-owning father), Alma phones John's father (John McIntire), away at a fever clinic, to come home and stop the wedding (as much for herself as John). Meanwhile, there is an apparent orgy going on in John's house, a celebration of his imminent marriage. All this leads to the film's most flagrant melodrama, when John's father is shot by Rosa's father (Thomas Gomez) after the two men meet the following morning amid all the sleeping bodies strewn about the house. John speaks to Alma about "some meddlesome fool" being responsible, and she at least has the courage to confess her interference. Both share responsibility for what happened yet each blames the other. John calls Alma a "white-blooded spinster" and then laughably forces her to look at his anatomy chart. As he refers to the hungers of the brain and the belly, the camera stays on the chart, but, as he starts to aim lower, the camera angle changes and the chart is out of plain sight. Instead of describing the next of our hungers as "the sex" (as he does in the play), all John says is "here… hungry for love," though "here" is blocked by Page's head, making this a particularly timid moment in a supposedly steamy film. Alma naturally brings up the soul, nowhere on his chart. Their ongoing discussion of body versus soul remains an intellectual exercise, a literary conceit, and a tedious debate.

The death of his father alters John completely, ridiculously so, but exactly as Alma would have hoped. Though inadvertently tragic, the incident, engineered by Alma, achieved the desired effect of setting John on the path for which he was meant. He leaves town to finish his father's work at the clinic, a noble plot turn right out of a "B" jungle picture. John becomes his sainted father, curing the fever and returning home in glory. This is so neatly worked out as to be completely unconvincing. Meanwhile, Alma has become reclusive since John left town still angry with her. She has dropped her music students and spends her days in her bathrobe. Alma may have become a drudge but she goes out at night when she can't sleep, perhaps already pondering a straying from the path on which she lost her precious John. In response to her father's displeasure and lack of compassion, Page makes Alma evasive, sarcastic, and edgier, a welcome contrast to her usual fluttery gentility. (Is she on the road to becoming her mother?) As John and Alma move toward switching places, *Summer and Smoke* becomes a puzzle in which the pieces fit together all too well. Though heartened by his return and change of life, Alma isn't through with her pursuit of romantic degradation. John stops by to apologize, only to be turned away by her father, who tells Alma that John didn't even ask about her. (This scene is not in the play.) More melodrama, more perpetual victimization.

There are three women who want to marry John: Alma, Rosa, and Nellie (Pamela Tiffin). This trio is almost a case of three faces of Eve, with uptight Alma, sexually accommodating Rosa, and the in-between Nellie, a beautiful and genial virgin devoid of sexual fears or hang-ups. Of course, Nellie, both innocent and flirtatious, will be the winner. Tiffin, who received "introducing" billing, is fresh and bubbly (Page and Moreno don't stand a chance), and she brightens the picture considerably at just about the point it needs it most. Page and Tiffin share a chance meeting at the fountain beneath the angel, with Page in a black scarf around her head, as if in mourning for her loss of John. Alma seems much older, having been through an ordeal that left its mark, but Nellie revitalizes her with the news of John's gratitude. A luminous, if incidental, moment in Page's performance occurs when Tiffin gives her a Christmas present, a scented handkerchief. Page inhales the gift so fully and gratefully, eyes closed, that you can almost smell its transporting, mood-altering aroma. The fact that it's from John makes it all the more treasured. So, once again, Alma's false hopes are revived. The item Nellie conveniently

doesn't get to mention is her engagement to John, all the better to be saved for a big, fat humiliation at the climax.

Alma arrives at John's office more colorfully attired than usual, wearing a blue outfit with a feathered hat. Though she tells him that she believes in dreaming big but expecting nothing, she clearly hasn't taken her own advice. Page's light, energized quality contrasts appropriately with Harvey's subdued demeanor, which should be a tip-off to Alma about where the scene is headed. There are several explanations for the inclusion of "smoke" in the title, none of which are especially enlightening, the most lucid attempt being that the old Alma, of last summer, suffocated from the smoke of the fire inside her. The new Alma unbuttons her blouse for his stethoscope, no longer the terrified creature she was the last time she endured this professional intimacy. Page tingles at his touch, strokes his hair, and kisses his forehead. "We were so close we almost breathed together," she tells him, making her seem somewhat off-balance. When was there ever such a moment between them? Even in romantic delirium, how can Alma utter such a thing? It sounds like self-laceration thrust upon a character increasingly deprived of dignity by her creator. Despite my reservations, I cannot imagine anyone acting this scene as beautifully as Page does, baring Alma's feelings with a soft-spoken intensity and expanding candor. She says that the old Alma told her not to die empty-handed, to "make sure that your hands have something in them," a poignant line followed by, "Forget about pride whenever it stands between you and what you *must* have," which sounds more like Norma Shearer than Tennessee Williams.

John acknowledges that she has been right all along, at exactly the moment she would rather hear otherwise. Not wanting a "spiritual relationship," Alma confesses her "affliction of love," while John speaks floridly of her "flame, mistaken for ice," a case of Williams straining for poetry. "The tables have turned with a vengeance," Page asserts in laughter tinged with anger, but the vengeance feels like it's coming from Williams rather than fate, with the playwright wallowing in his protagonist's downfall. "Your being a gentleman isn't *important* to me anymore," is her most naked admission of all. Alma eventually asks for "those little white tablets," the temporary cure-all she has come to rely on ever since

John first prescribed them. Nellie's arrival answers any remaining questions. When Alma sees the girl's ring, a solitaire, she says that it is wrongly named because the ring "means two," on which Page looks achingly at Harvey. She then brilliantly stresses the word "blinding" when examining the ring, a symbol of Alma's dashed dreams, and then all-too honestly states that "it hurts my eyes," momentary examples of first-rate Williams. The final blow comes when Nellie asks Alma to sing at the wedding.

Alma isn't quite through being dragged about. Back at the fountain, still in her blue outfit, she initiates small talk with a traveling salesman (Earl Holliman). When he admits he's lonely, she says, "All rooms are lonely when there's only one person." Alma has turned a corner, spurred by the finality of losing John. With the character's nerves calmed by a pill, Page is relaxed and forward in a way we haven't seen before, with Alma offering the salesman the seat next to her on the bench. She tells him Alma is "Spanish for soul," and they engage in some limited Spanish, laughing together easily. When he asks about what there is to do at night around here, she speaks of "all kinds of after-dark entertainment." She takes his hand. Before they exit in search of a taxi, Page gives a meaningful glance to the angel, the figure she previously described this way: "Her body is stone and her blood is mineral water." Alma, no angel, or at least no longer one, is about to embrace her flesh and blood. Again, Page's playing cannot be faulted, even if the scene is so pointedly ironic as to be borderline campy. It wouldn't be so bad if the scene suggested even the tiniest possibility that Alma might find some pleasure and satisfaction in exploring her sexuality and breaking out of a shut-in life, but the tone is bleak and "shocking," all too obvious and fraudulent in its weighty tone. Last seen picking up a one-night stand, Alma may be on her way to prostitution as well as drug addiction, perhaps arriving at an untimely oblivion, planned or accidental, but doomed nonetheless. She is now in Blanche DuBois territory, seeking out strangers, but, unlike Blanche, Alma feels like a pawn at Williams' mercy.

Summer and Smoke received four Oscar nominations, including merited nods for color art direction and score (by Elmer Bernstein). Merkel was nominated for Best Supporting Actress, competing against Rita Moreno, who was nominated not for *Summer and Smoke* but for *West Side Story.* Joining

Where Have I Seen That Before?

Summer and Smoke reminds me of several *better* movies: *Kings Row* (1942), another period drama consumed with sex and doctors; *Meet Me in St. Louis* (1944), with its female lead longing for the boy next door; *Stars in My Crown* (1950), dealing with father-son doctors at odds in a post-Civil War small town; and *East of Eden* (1955), with its rigid, righteous father and his rebellious son.

them was Lotte Lenya in *The Roman Spring of Mrs. Stone,* making this the only time that two performers from two different Williams pictures competed in the same Oscar category. Of the three, Lenya was the most deserving, but Moreno was the winner. In her stereotypical role as *Summer and Smoke*'s fiery Latina, Moreno did a solid job, especially in her deep-seated craving for a better life (exemplified by Harvey's John). Page's Alma resulted in her first Best Actress Oscar nomination. In her favor on Oscar night was the fact that the two previous winners—Simone Signoret in *Room at the Top* and Elizabeth Taylor in *Butterfield 8*—won for roles in which they appeared opposite Harvey. Why did Page break the streak? Well, both Signoret and Taylor ended their performances in fatal car crashes. Was Page's survival her mistake? She lost the Oscar to Sophia Loren in *Two Women,* a powerhouse of rage and guts, though the performance hits the same limited chords repeatedly. Page received consolation with a Golden Globe and the best-actress citation from the National Board of Review. (The standout lead-actress performance of the year came from unnominated Deborah Kerr in *The Innocents.*)

The most award-worthy contributor to *Summer and Smoke* was cinematographer Charles Lang, Jr., an Oscar winner for *A Farewell to Arms* (1932) and an eighteen-time nominee for such films as *The Ghost and Mrs. Muir* (1947) and *Some Like It Hot* (1959). Lang's work on *Summer and Smoke* is infused with a gauzy nostalgia, enhanced by his striking color sense and imaginative lighting effects, including, yes, occasional puffs of "smoke." Director Peter Glenville, a theatre man with only two films to his credit, assumedly left the visuals to master craftsman Lang and concentrated on the text and the cast. However, Glenville was unable to

Alma Revisited

Williams rewrote *Summer and Smoke* (similarly to the way he rewrote *Battle of Angels* into *Orpheus Descending*) as *The Eccentricities of a Nightingale* (published in 1964), using the same main characters and setting, but altering the drama appreciably. After wisely cutting the children's prologue, Williams deleted the characters of John's father, Rosa, and Ellie, and added the character of John's controlling mother. (Alma's parents were retained.) Identified as an eccentric, Alma is now more peculiar and openly neurotic, more of an outcast, while John is a much milder fellow, nicer and duller. Gone is the oppressive masochism and victimization, with Alma more aggressive, eventually consummating her love for John in a hotel room. The story still ends with Alma and the salesman, a scene now set indefinitely in the future and clearly not the first such encounter for her. *Eccentricities* overall isn't that much better a play than *Summer and Smoke,* but it is certainly more of a character study, with Alma searching for identity and fulfillment, and less of a sad soap about a put-upon virgin.

enrich the material or even embellish its strengths or build any dramatic momentum. The screenplay by Poe and Roberts made no attempt to fine-tune Williams' overwritten play, keeping it mired in its heavy symbols and enervating trajectory. The emotions are pasted on the characters rather than rising from within them, making *Summer and Smoke* a deficient and anemic prestige picture.

Before she brought Alma to the screen, Page had spent 1959-60 on Broadway in Williams' brand-new *Sweet Bird of Youth,* opposite recently crowned movie star Paul Newman. Page was not obvious casting as Alexandra Del Lago, an aging film actress ("a star before big taxes") and once-great beauty dealing with the unendurable fact of a failed comeback. At thirty-five, Page was too young to play a woman returning to the screen after fifteen years in retirement. The role also called for a bravura theatricality for which Page was not known, having made and sustained her name in a series of aching portrayals of spinsters. Alexandra is a self-proclaimed monster, and the play's director, Elia Kazan, reports in his autobiography that he convinced a skeptical Page that she could stretch herself accordingly and pull it off. It turned out to be a personal triumph, but that wouldn't automatically ensure her casting in the movie version, especially since Kazan would not be its director. (Richard Brooks, who would write the screenplay and direct the film, appropriately deleted the play's more stylized elements, notably the scenes in which Alexandra addresses the audience directly.) Page would be even less "right" for the movie, where her actual age would be more readily apparent. (In bringing her Williams roles to the screen, she was technically too old for Alma and too young for Alexandra.) It would also be that much harder on the

screen to convince audiences that Page's Alexandra had once been gorgeous. To Page's advantage was the fact that Paul Newman would be repeating his role in the film, making the rest of the cast almost immaterial with regard to marquee value. Newman was a huge box-office attraction, and he didn't need a major female co-star to help him deliver an audience, thus paving the way for Page to recreate her role and give one of the key performances in the Williams filmography. In the presence of her artistry, it doesn't seem to matter that she isn't beautiful enough or old enough. The film is vague about Alexandra's timeline, which is best ignored since the on-screen Page, not even forty, couldn't possibly be a star who retreated fifteen years ago. (Did she retire at twenty-five because of premature wrinkles?) Page's magnificence trumps any of the sound reasons why she *shouldn't* be in the movie. In fact, she *is* the movie, and, without her, it would be an exceedingly minor Williams film. Page makes Alexandra *her* role through sheer force of will and presence. Even though she was more evidently suited to play Alma Winemiller, Page is far more memorable and striking as Alexandra. Among the eleven actors who are this book's subjects, none played Williams characters as contrasting as Page's Alma and Alexandra. The only thing the characters share is a cultivated mid-Atlantic speech, utilized by Alma to seem more cultured than she is, and by Alexandra as the learned affectation of a Golden Age film star.

Page's redheaded Alexandra is first seen slumped in the backseat of her white Cadillac convertible as Newman's Chance Wayne drives her somewhere along the Gulf Coast. In sunglasses, she rises to shout, "Hey you!" to the apparent stranger ("whoever you are") manning her car, demanding a drink before she slumps back down, out of sight. It can be presumed that this isn't a particularly unusual situation for Alexandra; Page seems in no way unnerved by the clueless circumstances, barking orders and expecting her requests to be handled immediately, focused solely on her need for alcohol. The resulting bottle of vodka washes down a pill, just before she descends once again. Chance plops her unconscious body onto the bed of their suite at the Regal Palms Hotel in St. Cloud (Chance's hometown). Her alias is the Princess Kosmonopolis, not exactly Jane Doe and every bit as attention-getting as her real name (which can't possibly *be* real). In the play, she speaks of a husband who was "a great merchant prince," allowing for the possibility that she became actual royalty in the manner of Rita Hayworth and Grace Kelly. But in the movie it appears that her princess "tag" is entirely a ruse. For a while, Page is little more than a writhing creature spread across the bed, still in her sunglasses, high heels, and tailored white suit until undressed by Newman and slipped under the sheets. But she emits a wonderfully italicized variety of loud and unpleasant noises, all manner of gasps and coughs, moans and groans. Even in sleep, Page's Alexandra commands notice and puts on quite a show.

When Chance awakens her, Page's sudden terror reveals that Alexandra, now mostly recovered from her drunken stupor, has no memory of the considerable time (a few days, at least) spent with this latest trick. Page looks off and, in a foghorn tone, calls, "Help!" even though there is no one else there. She appears to be playing a scene from one of her old movies. This somewhat sober Alexandra is unmoored by not knowing where she is, the panic of which instigates her need of oxygen. Chance gets her cylinder of oxygen and its accompanying mask, and she clutches them hungrily. When she childishly hits him with a fancy pillow, a painless reprimand for his delay, it is a small sign of how much pleasure Page is going to bring to the movie, never doing the expected thing and always adding little touches worth watching. Alexandra is next disturbed by Chance when she hears the sound of his rewinding tape recorder. Page at last has her first completely lucid scene, first wondering if he is "one of those male nurses." Chance explains their situation, all of which is news to her, including his recent addition to her employ, which, again, elicits no great surprise. Alexandra plays by her own rules, or, rather, the rules

of superstars, a select breed whose penchant for imbalance derives from the pressures of their position, the *toll* of such stardom. Though Alexandra has been shaken by her perceived fall from her pedestal, she retains her ruthless self-possession.

In his book, *A Look at Tennessee Williams,* Mike Steen, who appears in this movie as a deputy, discusses with Page the difference between her stage and screen Alexandras. She remarks that the film's conception of the character was tilted more comically and then admits her preference for what she did onstage. That is immensely interesting because the humor Page unlocks on-screen is the key element in what makes the performance so remarkable and unpredictable. In a film that nearly collapses under the weight of its sweaty political melodrama and fire-breathing theatrics (the sections of the film that Page barely brushes up against), she offers *Sweet Bird* the creative wit otherwise sorely lacking, elevating the movie each time she grabs hold of it. This isn't to imply that she inappropriately takes it upon herself to insert laughs or try to lighten inten-

The Casting Game

The role of Alexandra Del Lago should have been coveted by every middle-aged actress in Hollywood, a category known for its paucity of great parts. Bigger names than Page, such as Patricia Neal, Ava Gardner, Eleanor Parker, and Susan Hayward were obvious possibilities, each a *real* movie star and all of them beauties. But Neal was even younger than Page, and Gardner would have been a risk, dramatically speaking, though she had proven her acting chops when given a real chance, as in *On the Beach* (1959). And Gardner was certainly a beauty past her prime. Would Eleanor Parker have been *too* actressy and Susan Hayward *too* down to earth? Vivien Leigh was another logical choice, though she had just made *The Roman Spring of Mrs. Stone* (1961), the *other* Williams film about an aging actress who has a sexual relationship with a young stud. Leigh might have been marvelous as Alexandra, a role with a far more expansive temperament than the muted Mrs. Stone, and therefore unlikely to have engendered a repeat performance. Nearly fifty, Leigh looked the right age, though Williams never reveals Alexandra's exact number of years.

tionally dark material. What Page does brilliantly is to find the genuine humor inherent in moments or lines of dialogue that most actresses might be too timid or unimaginative to explore. Alexandra's high drama is built into the piece, but Page's instinctive comic gifts humanize the character and make her a more fully dimensional creation. Yes, Williams' words are often funny on their own, and Page never misses a beat, but her talent finds comic grace notes beyond Williams' intentions, through her offbeat line readings or unexpected pauses, all of which reaches its astonishing peak in her climactic phone-call monologue. (Paul Newman's "correct" line readings are always sensible yet unmemorable and rarely enlightening.) Alexandra is a flamboyant character, demanding size and color and excess, and Page's comic flair prevents her from being just another Hollywood dragon or campy bitch.

Alexandra is committed to keeping her mind incapable of remembering her recent and disastrous comeback, proving she is not quite the fantasist one might suspect. Despite her make-believe world, she is a realist, so cognizant of the truths about her life that she must pollute herself lavishly to forget the things she knows to be so. It is an exhausting, dangerous business, fending off all those thoughts that cannot wait to race back into her consciousness (as soon as the latest diversion wears off). Alexandra has smarts, too much for her own good. She is *too* aware of things as they are, and is therefore recklessly self-destructive in her determination to blot out any pain. For all the humor residing in Page's performance, this ongoing undercurrent, this subtext of avoiding unfaceable failure, is her motivating pulse, the through-line that makes her so riveting. Alexandra is a jaded, imperious queen who recently put her self-worth into the hands of the public, which, it appears, has turned its back on her. Of course, she continues to treat everyone as servants, needing to feel like *somebody* more than ever. Ordering people around comes naturally to her, and she apparently has the money to continue the lifestyle to which she became accustomed. There's no doubt that she worked hard to get where she got, and that she knew she had the stuff of which few people are made: "I was *born* a monster." (That line is a fitting addition by writer-director Richard Brooks.) Page has an old-school star's dazzling panache and magnetic pull, as well as the rock-hard grit to have

once wrestled the movie industry to its knees. Alexandra's ego has been fed by her insatiable need for attention, acclaim, and love. Page beautifully intertwines inner steel and insecurity, cannily conceived as two sides of the same coin. Beneath Page's flourishes of self-centered bravado is the more fragile Alexandra, the woman mired in the indulgences of self-pity and self-gratification. None of this is especially unique in a portrait of a fictional actress, but rarely has it been executed so spellbindingly, a worthy peer of Bette Davis in *All About Eve* (1950) and Gloria Swanson in *Sunset Boulevard* (1950).

As Alexandra tells Chance of her need to forget, via drugs and vodka, Page occasionally lets loose with a ballsy, guttural laugh, the sound of a woman who has held her own in the presence of cigar-chomping studio bosses. When Chance tells her, "I like you, you are a nice monster," it is Williams' apt acknowledgment of his identifiably human yet larger-than-life creation, by turns good company and a holy hell. Her sexual appetite is of a voracity rarely expressed by a woman in movies of this era (except in other Williams films). Chance gives Alexandra the eyeglasses she damaged in a drunken spill, and she at last gets a good look at him, ogling his body as the connoisseur of the male form she undoubtedly is. Page appreciates Newman's physique as if ready to make a meal of him, wryly adding, "I may have done better, but God knows I have done worse," a neat Williams trick of complimenting Chance while still keeping him in his place. Sprawled out on the bed together, she admires the "silky smooth hard gold" of his bare chest, yet they have not as yet had sex. Though the implication is that of an older woman and a younger man, in reality Page was just two months older than Newman.

The event that Alexandra is trying to forget is seen in flashback; in the play, Page recounted the experience in monologue. The flashback begins with a Brooks-invented scene in Alexandra's on-set dressing room on a soundstage. Seated, she is attended by a make-up woman and a male hair stylist (Sydney Guilaroff himself, the ubiquitously credited MGM hairdresser) who fluffs her swept-up "do." Elaborately gowned, Page looks at herself in a hand mirror while a studio executive rambles on about her comeback, adding to the pressure as she puffs nervously on a cigarette. Her apprehensions derive from the fear that her fans are "devoted to the way I used to be, the way I used to *look*," a reasonable anxiety for anyone making a comeback. But the executive's assessment that Alexandra is "the sex symbol of America" seems decidedly *un*reasonable. The flashback is halted by her inability to continue reliving it, with Page collapsing under the weight of the lingering humiliation Alexandra works so hard to keep at bay. This leads to her demand for the Moroccan hashish she has stashed away, upping the distancing factor beyond mere liquor and tablets. Page amusingly imagines a drug arrest and subsequent incarceration in a prison for "distinguished addicts," a clever Williams phrase that foreshadows all those high-profile rehab visits by stars in the decades to come. "There is no place to retire to when you retire from the movies," she notes, adding that there is only oblivion. "I wasn't old. I just wasn't young," she admits, and today it's hard to accept that not that long ago age thirty-five was considered "mature" for a movie actress, meaning that Page's seeming youth in the role was less questionable in 1962 than it appears today. Though Alexandra knows she still has the will and the talent, she also knows that "the camera doesn't know how to lie" (a Brooks line) and that "the screen is a very clear mirror" (a Williams line). Though Williams' line is much the finer of the two, it is nonetheless interesting for both to be uttered *within* a movie.

Mention of the dreaded "close-up" reignites the flashback. Page is seen on a grand staircase in what looks like the set for some Russian Revolution epic (and not a good one). She leans over the staircase's side to have her cigarette lighted by a bald, monocled man in uniform. The camera moves in and "all your terrible history screams while you smile," a stinging Williams line that Page delivers accordingly (in voice-over). It is hard to detect the horror the camera is picking up (Page has rarely looked this *good*), but Alexandra's confidence starts to fray. The scene cuts to preview night and a throng of adoring fans greeting her arrival at the theatre. When the close-up elicits whispers and murmured chatter, Page exits in a panic, creating a scene more embarrassing than if Alexandra had stayed and endured the audience's reactions. Dodging a fan outside, she takes a tumble and angrily fights off crowding onlookers. The flashback is distinctly over the top, which is appropriate since it is the probably exaggerated memory of someone prone to overreacting.

She has been running ever since. The incident is referred to as "last month" in the play.

Her latest distraction is one of Chance's papaya-cream rubs, which had so entranced her in Palm Beach, when he, a hired beach boy, visited her private cabaña. At his touch, Page purrs, "I don't remember your face but your hands are familiar," very much the words of someone more conscious of her own pleasure than the person at the other end of it. (This is another line that proves Brooks was better at writing Williams-sounding lines than he had been on *Cat on a Hot Tin Roof*.) Chance's delay in offering sexual gratification, a ploy to sustain her interest, may backfire, as she reveals, "My interest always increases with satisfaction," another Williams clarification of Alexandra's need for getting what she wants at the exact moment she wants it. When Chance reveals that he has taped their conversation about her drug use—his way of ensuring that she will honor the contract they signed—it amuses her, partially because she no longer believes she *has* a career to worry about. Page flashes delight that this nobody thinks he can outwit *the* Alexandra Del Lago, then adds forcefully, "When monster meets monster, one monster has to give way, and it will *never be me!*" Williams gave Alexandra the core of a lion, and Page proudly roars whenever anyone needs to be reminded of who and what she is, however diminished she may be by controlled substances. She still calls the shots, such as her current desire for lovemaking, "the only dependable distraction." Her needs and desires must always come first, perhaps especially now that her insecurity has reached new depths. Later, as Chance pushes to be her new discovery, she is straight with him: "My only interest in life is me." This line by Brooks is stated by Page as a simple, hard fact. Her morning-after bliss (a movie staple in the days when you couldn't show the sex itself) is expressed through Page's tingling pleasure at her first glimpse of Newman and the way she caresses his smooth back, plus her slinky movements beneath the sheets and, of course, the requisite cigarette. She affirms the obvious this Easter Sunday, that she feels reborn. The rapport between Page and Newman derives from their characters connecting as cold-blooded strivers, she with great success, he on the fringes, but joined by their mutual quests and struggles. And there is also their supposed shared beauty: "I had it," she says, "and I say it with pride."

Geraldine Page was never better than when on the phone with Walter Winchell in **Sweet Bird of Youth**.

Page married actor Rip Torn a year after this film was released. Both members of the Actors Studio, they had appeared together onstage in *Sweet Bird* before making the film. As Tom Junior, the brother of Chance's great love, Heavenly (Shirley Knight), Torn shares one scene with Page, warning Alexandra to get out of town and to take Chance with her. Tom Junior is a violent, vindictive good old boy who despises Chance over Heavenly's pregnancy and subsequent abortion. Page treats him with immediate disdain, the way Alexandra treats anybody who doesn't do what she wants, until she realizes that he's dangerous. The Torn-Page (can you believe it?) combination is highly charged (just think of all the extra rehearsal their personal relationship afforded the scene), and Page uses the moment to jolt Alexandra, alerting her to a world outside herself, something she absorbs as a considerable surprise. The scene alarms her enough to reach for her distractions, rendering her a drunken mess when she locates Chance in the bar downstairs. Page cleverly sustains a star's vanity even in debasement, putting on her unflattering glasses just long enough to take a few short glances in search of him. However, director Brooks went too far here, having Page fall to the ground not once but twice, first when a fan knocks off her glasses, then when she sees Chance and crashes into a table. (Add her fall at the film preview and Page spends too much time toppling over, and always with her mink stole. Then add the two private-beach spills in the water taken by Shirley Knight's Heavenly, in an argument with her father, and you may start to wonder about Brooks' penchant for knocking down actresses.) Page is completely in Alexandra's needy, helpless mode, fearful and limp. But she also conveys Alexandra's childlike trust in public, as if she knows that a star of her stature will always be taken care of by somebody, picked up off the floor, or carried to her room, even if such strangers usually want something from her.

This leads to Page's most poignant scene, a conversation with Chance outside the hotel as he is about to rush off to see Heavenly. Shaken by her encounter with Tom Junior, she begs him to leave St. Cloud, coming across with genuine affection for him, nicely modulated by Page amid the pollutants swirling in Alexandra's system. She tells him that her revelation about their failed comebacks (her new film and his return home) has triggered a startling pang of compassion inside her. "I felt something for somebody besides myself," she confesses, as if another aspect of herself has been reborn, even if, as is Alexandra's wont, her feelings are fleeting, intense while they're happening but unlikely to be recalled a short while later. But there's a softness in Page here nowhere else in the film, an access to emotion that can assumedly be connected to the sensitivity that made Alexandra a beloved actress. Page is full-out in inhabiting whatever the ever-changing, undependable Alexandra happens to be at any given moment. She means everything she says… until she doesn't. After Chance leaves her calling after him, Brooks gives her an exit line delivered to Miss Lucy (Madeleine Sherwood), the mistress of Heavenly's father. In the kindness-of-strangers tradition, regarding her approaching entrance into the hotel lobby, Page grandly intones, "The public and I have always enjoyed the very *best* of relations."

When Chance returns that evening, Alexandra is packing furiously. Cold and hardened, Page is no longer the weakened Alexandra he left stranded outside the hotel. Chance is ready to go with her now, but she's made other arrangements. Then the phone rings, answered by Chance. Columnist Walter Winchell is calling from Hollywood, the assumed next chapter in Alexandra's waking nightmare. Page's face fills with dread; Alexandra is being asked to look into the heart of everything she cannot face. "Tell him that I am *dying* and I just *might*," Page says before fortifying herself, calling on all Alexandra's reserves of strength. She revives the outwardly confident movie star she was at her peak and has transformed completely by the time she trumpets into the phone, "Well, is that *really* you, Waldo?" What happens in the next few minutes is the *true* resurrection of Alexandra Del Lago into full and glorious monster mode. Winchell's voice is never heard, but Page listens intently enough to make it seem as though both sides of the conversation are audible. She begins in charming self-deprecation, talking to a trusted old pal about "that monstrous CinemaScope" and her mad dash out of the theatre, as well as her subsequent avoidance of any press reports. Winchell's compliments please her, but she accepts them as the flattery of a staunch supporter. Page's virtuosity takes hold once the world around Alexandra starts to fade, in direct proportion to Winchell's increasingly positive spin on her career. Like any self-absorbed artist, nothing else exists for her when, as now, praise is being offered. Chance becomes an annoying insect whose buzzing is impairing her total immersion in the adulation being tossed her way. No one but Page would pause between the last two words of her line to Newman, "Stick your head under cold water," focused back on Winchell even before getting to the end of her sentence. Now she's pumping him for more, luxuriating in each new tidbit: "Grown, did you say… more depth…more power?" Sprawled across the bed, Page continues to loom larger, with Alexandra stunned by Winchell's words yet accepting them as the natural order of things, returning her to her rightful place. This is a surging display of actorly ego and narcissism, and arguably the greatest scene of Page's film career. And there's more to come.

"They want me…they really want… me?" is her transition between reveling in Winchell's approval and the realization that actual employment awaits her. Another inspired choice by Page is her looseness with the phone. The more obvious option would be to stay unerringly focused on the phone, holding it tightly to her ear. But Page becomes so transported by the news coming through it that she cannot contain herself, letting the phone drift away from her as she relishes this turnabout, sometimes looking as though she's forgotten that the phone is the source of her newfound ecstasy. Page also gives off the delicious sensation that, as Alexandra reclaims her prominence, she expects, even more than usual, for everything (even telephones and their disembodied voices) to operate at her whims and wait indefinitely for *her*. She has blotted out Chance, and even Winchell is starting to fade, now that her future has opened wide. The best bit is when she jabs her foot in Newman's chest as Chance makes yet another feeble attempt to get her to mention him to Winchell. The contrast between her great-lady phone voice and this slapstick kick is a perfect representation of the two sides of a great star, the classy idol of millions and the grasping creature lurking within. And we haven't even gotten to the reviews! Of course she didn't read them, but by now she can suspect they were better than anticipated. In another hilarious line reading, Page, with barely a breath at the comma, asks, "Who cares what the newspapers say, what did they say?" Then on to "Tell me, tell me, word for word," laughing, beaming, soaring. The phone monologue is longer in the movie than the play and Brooks was wise to embellish it, staying true to Williams' intent and making it that much more to savor. However, it was wrong of Brooks to cut away mid-phone call to the political rally downstairs, even though it doesn't hamper Page's impact. Her staggering self-involvement reaches its fitting peak on the final sentence, "Walter, I'll have to call you back later," a seemingly throwaway line that Page makes the perfect capper to her transcontinental aria. What she does is hang up the phone before saying the final two words, and then she pauses *between* those words, by now detached from everything but herself, even behaving rudely (though unintentionally) to the messenger. In the play, Alexandra participates more in the making of the call, feeling that it's time to face the music; the call is to Sally Powers, a fictional columnist, rather than the real-life Winchell. (Another very funny phone-call scene by Williams occurs when Jane Fonda delightfully bawls her way through one in the same year's screen adaptation of *Period of Adjustment*.)

Alexandra announces, not to Chance but to the room at large, "My picture has broken box-office records in New York and L.A.," standing up and pointing high on "L.A." Page creates for Alexandra a state of enclosed euphoria, oblivious to all else. She then, at heightened speed, launches into a list of all that must get done immediately, from covering her recent tracks ("these past few weeks in Hell") to checking into a clinic. No longer vulnerable ("Now I need *nobody*!"), she is still able to acknowledge the "gold-plated Hell" to which she is returning, another sign of Alexandra's essential hold on reality beneath her emotional extravagance. Brooks embroiders this scene, too, knowing a thing or two himself about Hollywood, adding Williams-worthy lines to augment the situation, such as that "gold-plated Hell" reference. When Chance forces her to look at herself in a mirror, thinking he will shock her back to the truth of her advancing years, he is way off. Page says, adoringly, "I see *me*, Alexandra Del Lago, artist and star!" She then blisteringly confronts *his* reality, recalling another aging stud, Franz Albertzart, who pitifully ended up escorting a seventy-year-old woman around Europe and "his eyes were older than hers" (one of Williams' best lines in all of *Sweet Bird*). Packing up, Page adroitly uses props, throwing individual items into her handbag with a staccato snap, accentuating her words. She asks Chance if he can face his own truth, inviting him to join her only as her chauffeur or butler. He refuses, not even accepting her unusually unselfish final gesture of securing his safe getaway from Tom Junior's wrath.

She exits but returns instantly, almost sheepishly, remembering to retrieve those incriminating audio tapes, now of monumental value. In a scene not in the play, Page enters poised to do some wheedling and groveling, ready to open her purse as well. (In the play, she has already packed the tapes.) They laugh together easily before he hands the tapes over "on the house," with both stars extending the unforeseen fondness they forged between the characters. After he kisses her hand in response to her further offerings of a ride to safety, there's nothing left for her to do but make a grand exit, even out of public view. Page blows Newman a kiss, tosses her head theatrically, and, best of all, flings her mink stole around her neck, clanking it against the door, sounding a comically percussive coda. (She exits before Brooks distorts the play's disturbing inevitability with his young-love-triumphant phoniness.) In his stage directions, Williams stresses the temporary nature of Alexandra's latest upswing, but the film avoids such intimations, even though Page instills her with a readiness for all that lies ahead, lustily grabbing at the good times because she knows they do not last. Alexandra is the rare female winner in the Williams films. The agonies she suffers in the play and the film are self-inflicted, despite the truth of her accelerating age in a cruel business. But if she had waited for the reviews, then she would have known quickly about her success and need not have embarked on such a reckless spree. She is not a victim, not defeated like Blanche DuBois or Karen Stone (who fled from a legitimate show-business failure). Alexandra may be a drama queen but overall she is a survivor. It feels good to watch her walk out that door like a diva about to take a curtain call, ready to devour Hollywood once more.

Award junkies may find it fascinating to track Page's mostly empty-handed journey with this role. She was nominated for a Tony in 1960, losing to Anne Bancroft in *The Miracle Worker*. At Oscar time, Page was again a nominee, losing to, you guessed it, Bancroft in *The Miracle Worker*. Though *The Miracle Worker* is a far superior film to *Sweet Bird*, I prefer Page's innovative work to Bancroft's admirable, physically demanding performance, which I think could have been duplicated by any number of seasoned actresses. Page's work is indelible, not to be replicated by anyone. This is a moot comparison because the finest achievement by an actress that year was Katharine Hepburn's performance in *Long Day's Journey into Night*. (More to come on the Page-Bancroft award rivalry two decades ahead.) Page did get another Golden Globe, though, to match the one she had gotten for her Alma the previous year. *Sweet Bird*, despite Newman's pres-

Broadway Becomes Her

Sweet Bird showed up on the big screen again, sort of, in the comedy *Death Becomes Her* (1992), when a glamorized Meryl Streep, as an age-obsessed Broadway star, is seen in a flop musical version of *Sweet Bird* titled *Songbird!* Streep enthusiastically headlines a tacky, Vegas-style production number overpopulated with chorus boys dressed as movie ushers.

ence, was not the box-office sensation that *Cat on a Hot Tin Roof* had been, which may come down to the simple fact that opposite him were two leading ladies—Page and Shirley Knight—who could not compete with the advertising imagery of Elizabeth Taylor in a slip. (Taylor would go on to play Alexandra in a 1989 TV-movie.)

Page followed the critical acclaim of her two Williams screen roles with another prestige picture, the 1963 adaptation of Lillian Hellman's 1960 Broadway play *Toys in the Attic*, assuming the role created by Maureen Stapleton, another favorite Williams actress. Hellman's play can be classified as Southern-fried hooey, with its painfully spelled-out drama of family dysfunction and its straining for a Williams-style complexity. The film version plays as overwrought twaddle, with everything rammed at you and nothing to be discovered. Page and Wendy Hiller play unmarried sisters residing in their decaying New Orleans mansion, awaiting a visit from their prodigal baby brother Dean Martin. (How's that for a bizarre trio of siblings?) The drama's dirty secret is Page's incestuous love for Martin. As she sets out to destroy his marriage to sweet and insecure Yvette Mimieux, Page succumbs to the role's excesses and descends to her worst habits, resulting in an overly mannered and rather shameless performance, right up to its *Little Foxes* ending. Director George Roy Hill, whose first film was Williams' *Period of Adjustment*, falls prey to the obviousness of it all, a whole lot of fevered acting devoid of any underlying honesty. *Toys in the Attic* evokes sub-par Eugene O'Neill more than it does Tennessee Williams, and the film is as unconvincing as the 1961 screen adaptation of Hellman's 1934 success *The Children's Hour*.

Dear Heart (1964), Page's next starring vehicle, was a complete departure, an old-fashioned romantic comedy, the kind of ugly-duckling charmer that might have been conceived for Jean Arthur in the early 1940s. Considering her serious-actress background and Actors Studio ties, Page did remarkably well in what was merely a personality role in a conventional picture. Though her character is (yet again) sad and lonely and single, she is also friendly and outgoing, lightening and freshening a familiar Page persona. As an Ohio postmaster in New York City for a convention, Page is childlike and a bit of a kook, but she invests the role with reserves of warmth and yearning and a heretofore unseen charm. Within the genre's confines, she manages to give a truly touching and exposed performance sparked by spasms of joy, endearing humor, and an eccentric radiance. (Her character is the kind who likes to have herself paged in hotel lobbies, merely for the thrill of hearing her name called.) A competent but resistible Glenn Ford is her traveling-salesman love interest, but his half of the plot is far less interesting than hers. Delbert Mann's direction is reliably dull, so it falls entirely to Page to make *Dear Heart* so immensely pleasing and likable, seeming better than it really is. Despite her ingratiating skill at projecting infectious good cheer, Page wasn't exactly Doris Day at the box office.

There would be no leading film roles for a while, but Page continued to work on the stage and on television. On Broadway, she starred in revivals of *Strange Interlude* (1963), which featured Jane Fonda, and *The Three Sisters* (1964), an Actors Studio production (of which there is a 1966 filmed record) directed by Lee Strasberg himself and co-starring Kim Stanley and *Sweet Bird*'s Shirley Knight (though Sandy Dennis stepped in for Knight when it was filmed). The later sixties landed Page in a hit Broadway comedy, Peter Shaffer's *Black Comedy/White Lies* (1967), and two heartwarming small-screen adaptations of Truman Capote stories, *A Christmas Memory* (1966) and *The Thanksgiving Visitor* (1967), each winning her an Emmy. Page got a fourth Oscar nomination, in the supporting category, as an overbearing mother in Francis Ford Coppola's determinedly quirky *You're a Big Boy Now* (1966), overdirected in a chaotic and tiring fashion. More irritating than funny, *You're a Big Boy Now* is a pre-*Graduate* coming-of-age tale aligned with the cultural upheaval of its era. Sharing the screen with Rip Torn as Peter Kastner's parents, a dark-haired Page is broadly amusing, prone to maternal

smothering, but it's not an especially memorable effort. (You know a movie is trying too hard to be wacky when Karen Black is its most stable element.) More unexpected was Page's appearance in a Walt Disney musical, *The Happiest Millionaire* (1967), an ungainly and inflated entry in the decade's series of three-hour musicals, those with usually unjustified perks of overtures, intermissions, and exit music. As unoriginal and charmless as it is spotlessly wholesome, *The Happiest Millionaire* stars Fred MacMurray and features easy-to-hate songs with titles like "Fortuosity" and "I'll Always Be Irish." The only reason to suffer through this 1916-set misfortune is the musical duet ("There Are Those") between Page and the great Gladys Cooper, a bitchy "challenge" song that briefly enlivens things. A blond Page plays the snob mother of young John Davidson, yet she doesn't seem at ease, perhaps uncomfortable at being merely a cog in this synthetically engineered ten-ton piece of so-called whimsy.

It took Bette Davis thirty years to be reduced to starring in schlock horror movies, but Page got there in a mere eight years after her first leading role. *What Ever Happened to Aunt Alice?* (1969) may have given Page a major role, but it was hack work in the murderous-old-broad genre (as unoriginal as its title suggests). Page plays a rich matron rendered destitute by widowhood, thus embarking on a wealth-restoring spree of killing her housekeepers for their savings. When Ruth Gordon arrives as the latest victim, the film becomes a battle of the scene stealers. Page gives it her all, to no avail. It is *not* campy fun to see beloved old actresses—Ruth Gordon and Mildred Dunnock—beaten and killed brutally by Page. It was another horror tale, *The Beguiled* (1971), that provided Page with her best dramatic screen role since Alexandra Del Lago, the headmistress of a Southern girls' school during the Civil War. Stability is disrupted when she and her houseful of females tend to a wounded Union soldier (Clint Eastwood). Don Siegel's film, released the same year as his *Dirty Harry*, is a riveting multi-genre picture, part war movie, part battle of the sexes, and part chiller, surprisingly character-driven and marked by continual power shifts. With its tangible period flavor and menacing mood, *The Beguiled* works as both male sexual fantasy and female revenge fantasy, pitting one hot stud (trying to survive by any means necessary) against nine lonely and isolated females. Page, back in her incestuous mode from *Toys in the Attic* but taking it further, is a proper lady with a dark secret about her former relationship with her brother. And that's not all. She also lusts after Clint and has a lesbian desire for teacher Elizabeth Hartman, leading to the strangest scene in Page's film career, a sex dream in which she shares a bed with Eastwood and Hartman, kissing them both. Frightening and enjoyable, *The Beguiled* affords Page the opportunity to play a woman scorned (by Clint) whose payback astounds Dirty Harry himself. She gives a formidable performance, luxuriating in a large role amply suited to her. The film profits enormously from her theatricality and command, as well as her craftiness, sensuality, and single-minded flair for vengeance. Most shocking of all was the film's fate as a rare box-office failure for Eastwood. How surprising that Page could count among her leading men both Clint Eastwood and John Wayne!

But it was back to featured roles in support of other stars. Page got another supporting Oscar nomination as Carol Burnett's best friend in Martin Ritt's *Pete 'n' Tillie* (1972), a very bad film that moves from banal romantic-comedy courtship (between Burnett and Walter Matthau), evoking Neil Simon at his worst, to bathetic tearjerker. Untarnished by the sludge around her, Page, blond again, plays an extravagant and fashionable matron, making her friendship with secretary Burnett a tad ludicrous. Page's character won't tell anyone how old she is, and, in the scene for which she merited her nomination, she is asked by a policeman to state her age. She starts to emit an "F" sound but is unable to get past it to say "forty" (or "fifty"?), executing this extended bit with inspired timing, sustaining her stammering on the "F" sound until she finally collapses, toppling backward. But the scene is immediately followed by a ghastly girlfight between her and Burnett, a mean and ugly piece of slapstick involving garbage pails and a water hose, all too hurtful and grotesque to be diverting, capped by Burnett pulling Page's wig off. Even worse is John Schlesinger's loathsome film version of *The Day of the Locust* (1975), in which Page has a cameo as a radio evangelist ("Big Sister"), healing people, booming her voice, and steering clear of the wreckage around her. This vision of 1930s Hollywood as Hell, which Schlesinger conceives as having no connection to the real world, is beyond heavy-handed and self-important, an unrelenting freak show. There are no ups and downs, just downs and downs, with nothing quite as low as the film itself.

In her fifties, Page nabbed a high-profile leading screen role from an unlikely source. Woody Allen's *Interiors* (1978), the writer-director's first drama, was an unmistakable stab at making an American "Ingmar Bergman" movie, but the result is the antithesis of Bergman. Allen devised his characters in overexplicit psychological terms, a painfully self-conscious approach, whereas Bergman usually left audiences to figure his films out for themselves. *Interiors* is a chore to sit through, tedious in its visual tastefulness while wallowing in the self-absorbed bores who populate it. Old-pros Page and Maureen Stapleton are its only assets, both of whom rise above the full-of-itself atmosphere. Page plays an interior decorator, a cold and controlling mother of three daughters. Dumped by husband E.G. Marshall, she is irrationally obsessed with reconciliation, but Marshall marries the upbeat Stapleton. Page's performance is interesting because *Page* is interesting. She brings surprises of her own to an underwritten role, though the film is almost constantly borderline laughable. Page is actually miscast; the way she's talked about (as a beautiful perfectionist) makes you expect Deborah Kerr to walk into the room. She ends up like Norman Maine, a beach suicide, a logical response to her option of spending any more time with her whiny, selfish, and unbearable daughters and their mates. Allen essentially rewrote his three-sistered *Interiors,* improving it as a comedy and inserting himself into the plot. The result, *Hannah and Her Sisters* (1986), became one of his more popular and acclaimed movies.

Page elevated another terrible movie, *I'm Dancing As Fast As I Can* (1982), a simplistically undeveloped and pitifully unpersuasive true story of Valium addiction and mental illness, a best-intentioned misfire that features a startling number of bad performances from name actors (especially Nicol Williamson). Star Jill Clayburgh makes an attempt at a full-scale Susan Hayward role and comes up empty, despite all that screaming. But there's one bit of greatness here, from Page as a poet dying of cancer, the subject of a documentary being made by Clayburgh. In her anger and quiet conviction, Page shames everyone around her in a performance of bare and scorching truth, particularly in the scene when she tells off Clayburgh about what sanitized pablum her film is (like the film we're watching). Prickly and complicated, Page is much too good for this movie and probably would have been Oscar-nominated again if anyone had seen her in it. She did get another supporting Oscar nomination for a smaller role in *The Pope of Greenwich Village* (1984), which stars Mickey Rourke (lifeless) and Eric Roberts (overacting repulsively) as distant cousins and small-time hoods, a relationship seemingly inspired by *Of Mice and Men*. It is an undistinguished movie, but it gets an eight-minute bolt of electricity from Page's two scenes as an Irish cop's mother, unconnected to the main plot or characters. Cast against type, with a cigarette in one hand and a whiskey in the other, Page is tough, shrewd, and resilient, a former cleaning lady who likes to read the racing forms. She looks as if she could be running her own mob, like, say, Ma Barker. And she has a whopper of a New Yawk accent. It is a lively, showy turn, allowing Page the chance to say "pricks" and "assholes," yet her acting transcends caricature, primarily because of the strong love she conveys for her son (Jack Kehoe), both in her first scene (with him) and in her second scene (with other cops after the son's death). It is an unsentimental cameo, injecting zip and weight into a film that could use a lot more of her.

But then, just like Jessica Tandy being handed Miss Daisy, Page got a late-career present when she starred in the 1985 film version of Horton Foote's 1953 teleplay and subsequent Broadway drama *The Trip to Bountiful*, a lovely piece and a major event in Page's career, her finest screen work since *Sweet Bird of Youth*. At its best, this Truman-era story feels universal and primal, all about the yearning for home and one's roots, with Page giving an extraordinary performance as an unhappy old woman aching to see her childhood home in Bountiful, Texas, just one more time before she dies. Escaping from her uselessness in the Houston household of her son and horrid daughter-in-law, she runs away *to* home, on a bus headed for the place she hasn't seen in twenty years. (It is not exactly Tara, but it is the place from which she derives her strength and identity.) Page is a wonder, funny and surprising, fiercely determined

yet often heartbreaking, a steady flow of spontaneous feeling. She is lovable yet never saintly. Through the course of the movie, she becomes so much more than the little old lady she at first appears to be, with Page especially poignant in her unsuspected revelations of the loves and losses of a seemingly uneventful life. The overall film isn't much, looking like an inexpensive television production, but director Peter Masterson wisely keeps the focus on Page. With her front and center, how could anyone complain? The climax, after many tribulations, is Page's exquisite, profoundly satisfying scene at her serene destination. Lillian Gish created the role on television and on Broadway, but now it is forever Page's, especially since it was the part that finally brought her the elusive Best Actress Academy Award (on her eighth overall nomination). One of the actresses she beat that year was Anne Bancroft, the woman who made a habit of snatching awards away from Page in the early sixties. Not only did Page best Bancroft this time around, but Bancroft was nominated for *Agnes of God* in a role that Page created on Broadway. (I saw Page in *Agnes of God*; Bancroft was not her equal in the Mother Superior role.)

Page never did receive a Tony Award, despite nominations for *Sweet Bird, Absurd Person Singular* (1974), *Agnes of God* (1982), and the 1987 revival of *Blithe Spirit* in which she played Madame Arcati. She originated one other Williams role, Zelda Fitzgerald in *Clothes for a Summer Hotel* (1980), a Broadway flop directed by José Quintero, bringing Page full circle with the two men who made her a star in *Summer and Smoke* nearly thirty years prior. Page died of a heart attack at only sixty-two in 1987, during her run in *Blithe Spirit*. I fear she is not as well remembered as warranted by the breadth of her talent and achievements. But I also have no doubt that her glorious triumph in *The Trip to Bountiful* will stand the test of time, as will her on-screen association with Williams in her two "Al" roles, Alma in *Summer and Smoke* and Alexandra in *Sweet Bird of Youth,* the virgin and the tramp, the nobody and the somebody.

Richard Burton

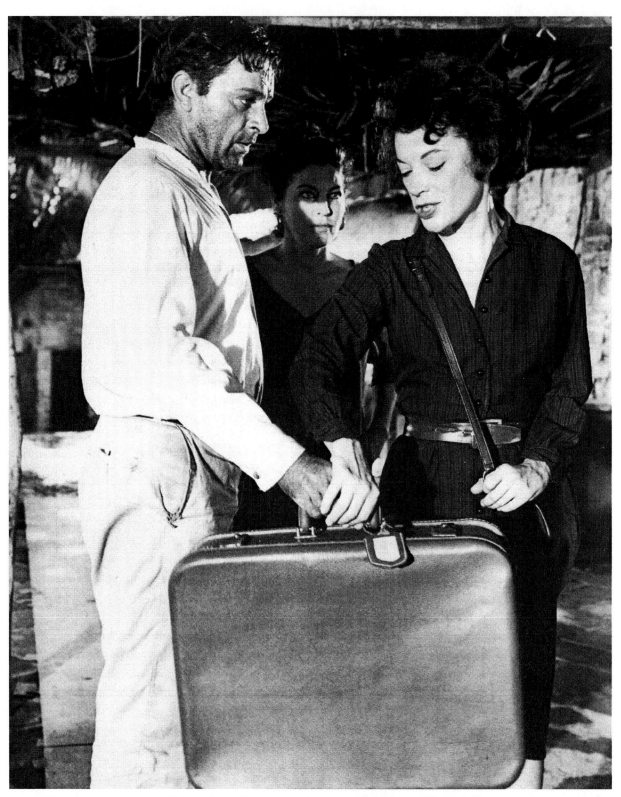

*Richard Burton versus Grayson Hall, with Ava Gardner looking on, in **The Night of the Iguana**.*

Richard Burton: Filmography

- *The Last Days of Dolwyn (1949)*
- *Now Barabbas Was a Robber (1949)*
- *Waterfront (1950)*
- *The Woman With No Name (1950)*
- *Green Grow the Rushes (1951)*
- *My Cousin Rachel (1952)*
- *The Desert Rats (1953)*
- *The Robe (1953)*
- *Prince of Players (1955)*
- *The Rains of Ranchipur (1955)*
- *Alexander the Great (1956)*
- *Bitter Victory (1957)*
- *Sea Wife (1957)*
- *Look Back in Anger (1959)*
- *Ice Palace (1960)*
- *The Bramble Bush (1960)*
- *The Longest Day (1962)*
- *Cleopatra (1963)*
- *The V.I.P.s (1963)*
- *Becket (1964)*
- *The Night of the Iguana (1964)*
- *Zulu (1964) (as narrator)*
- *What's New Pussycat? (1965)*
- *The Sandpiper (1965)*
- *The Spy Who Came in from the Cold (1965)*
- *Who's Afraid of Virginia Woolf? (1966)*
- *The Taming of the Shrew (1967)*
- *Doctor Faustus (1967) (also co-director)*
- *The Comedians (1967)*
- *Boom (1968)*
- *Candy (1968)*
- *Where Eagles Dare (1968)*
- *Staircase (1969)*
- *Anne of the Thousand Days (1969)*
- *Raid on Rommel (1971)*
- *Villain (1971)*
- *Under Milk Wood (1971)*
- *The Assassination of Trotsky (1972)*
- *Hammersmith Is Out (1972)*
- *Bluebeard (1972)*
- *The Battle of Sutjeska (1973)*
- *Massacre in Rome (1973)*
- *The Klansman (1974)*
- *The Voyage (1974)*
- *Jackpot (1975)*
- *Exorcist II: The Heretic (1977)*
- *Equus (1977)*
- *The Medusa Touch (1978)*
- *The Wild Geese (1978)*
- *Absolution (1978)*
- *Breakthrough (1979)*
- *Circle of Two (1980)*
- *Lovespell (1981)*
- *Nineteen Eighty-Four (1984)*

Richard Burton (1925-1984)

Academy Award Nominations

- **Best Supporting Actor** of 1952 for *My Cousin Rachel*
- **Best Actor** of 1953 for *The Robe*
- **Best Actor** of 1964 for *Becket*
- **Best Actor** of 1965 for *The Spy Who Came in from the Cold*
- **Best Actor** of 1966 for *Who's Afraid of Virginia Woolf?*
- **Best Actor** of 1969 for *Anne of the Thousand Days*
- **Best Actor** of 1977 for *Equus*

T. Lawrence Shannon in *The Night of the Iguana* (1964)
Chris Flanders in *Boom* (1968)

Just as Joanne Woodward followed Paul Newman, Richard Burton began his association with Williams after his real-life partner (but not yet wife) Elizabeth Taylor had already been a much-touted success in Williams material on-screen. By 1964, the Williams movies had produced a remarkable array of sterling female performances in leading roles (most notably from Vivien Leigh, Anna Magnani, and Geraldine Page), but there had been only one great performance from a leading male, Marlon Brando's Stanley Kowalski in *Streetcar*. A second great male-star performance, ultimately the *only* other one in the Williams films, finally arrived when Burton played Reverend T. Lawrence Shannon in *The Night of the Iguana*. The set-up looked like a familiar Williams trap, that of a male star, in the film's largest role, ground to dust by two female co-stars, which had been the case in *Suddenly, Last Summer* and *The Fugitive Kind*. But this time it was the male who dominated the proceedings, giving the standout performance in the movie's best role. Despite Burton's physical appeal and the character's substantial sexuality, Shannon is not an eye-candy role akin to the Williams film roles played by Burt Lancaster (Mangiacavallo), Warren Beatty (Paolo di Leo), or, of course, the two roles apiece played by Brando and Newman. Shannon is the rare Williams male to be overtly teetering on an emotional and mental precipice. Like Blanche DuBois, he finds himself in what appears to be a last-chance situation propelled by sexual activities (but in his case there is ultimately hope). On the episode of television's *American Masters* devoted to Williams, you can hear the playwright himself call Shannon "the best male part I had written" and "a male equivalent almost of Blanche DuBois." I agree, particularly with his modifying "almost." Burton's Shannon is a study in jagged nerves, acid wit, and naughty mischief, marked by elastically supple transitions and inventive comic instincts in serio-comic situations. With his classical English-theatre background—he was neither a Method actor nor a product of the New York stage, unlike the other male stars featured in this book—Burton was as unexpected a Williams collaborator as Magnani or Leigh. His swift yet incisive delivery of Williams' words (as deft as Leigh in *Streetcar* or Katharine Hepburn in *Suddenly, Last Summer*) never misses a beat, nor any occasion for a splash of humor amid the turmoil. Add Burton's natural elegance and immaculate diction and the effect is a bit like watching Cary Grant lose his mind.

Born Richard Jenkins in Wales on November 10, 1925, Burton was the twelfth of thirteen children. He studied at Oxford, served in the Royal Air Force, and got his big breaks, on both stage and screen, in 1949, making his first film, *The Last Days of Dolwyn* with Edith Evans, and receiving notice on the London stage in *The Lady's Not for Burning* (starring and directed by John Gielgud), a production that traveled to Broadway in 1950, marking Burton's New York bow. He built up his Shakespearean credentials in England and made four other British movies before making his American screen debut opposite two-time Oscar winner Olivia de Havilland in *My Cousin Rachel* (1952). Directed by Henry Koster, the film gave Burton a brooding Heathcliff-like opportunity, a showcase for his considerable handsomeness, exquisite vocal resonance, and facility with love-and-hate passions. A nineteenth-century costume picture set in Cornwall, *My Cousin Rachel* is an enjoyably moody though fairly shallow mystery, with de Havilland particularly reined in by a character who must keep us guessing. With his obvious star quality and commanding presence, Burton snagged a supporting-actor Oscar nomination, even though he had the leading role. *The Desert Rats* (1953), Burton's next film, is a gritty and exciting combat-heavy World War II picture set in the Libyan desert. Directed by Robert Wise, and concerned more with warfare than character development, *The Desert Rats* was a good career move for Burton, proving that he needn't be trapped in elocutionary period pictures. As an all-business British colonel on his way to becoming more human, he leads an Australian infantry unit to defend Tobruk from Rommel (James Mason). Burton is dry and clipped, occasionally arch and stagy, but his potential is undeniable.

In all its pandering religiosity, *The Robe* (1953) was the first film made in Twentieth Century-Fox's new wide-screen CinemaScope process and a winner of five Oscar nominations, including best picture and Burton's as best actor. Again directed by *My Cousin Rachel*'s Henry Koster, Burton was cast as the Roman tribune who crucifies Christ and is haunted by the experience (and Christ's red robe), leading to his religious conversion and new life of purpose, meaning, and unselfishness. But you could hardly tell any of that from Burton's bored and lifeless performance, mostly stone-faced despite occasional spasms of overacting. Alongside him, in the film's most heartfelt portrayal, is lovely Jean Simmons, plus a lethargic Victor Mature as the slave Demetrius, and a queeny and memorably terrible Jay Robinson as Caligula (determined to outdo Peter Ustinov's Nero from *Quo Vadis*). It was the biggest hit of 1953, yet it didn't interfere with Burton's commitment to Shakespeare back home, including a post-*Robe* season at the Old Vic theatre. Though poised to be one of the major Hollywood actors of the decade, Burton sank in a trio of lavish losers: *Prince of Players* (1955), worthy subject matter (stage actor Edwin Booth) handled superficially and far too briskly, though it provided Burton with a generous forum in which to display his Shakespearean abilities, making the film better "onstage" than "off"; *The Rains of Ranchipur* (1955), an inferior remake of *The Rains Came* (1939), with Burton in the old Tyrone Power role, the Indian doctor, paired numbingly with Lana Turner and acting as if he would rather be anywhere else, though he looks good in turbans of assorted colors; and *Alexander the Great* (1956), a talky drone in which he is far too uninspiring to be followed by legions. Maybe he was stymied by his unflattering blond wig.

He retreated back to the Old Vic and Shakespeare, and a decidedly un-Hollywood film for director Nicholas Ray, another black-and-white WWII picture set in the Libyan desert, a situation that had served him well in *The Desert Rats*. *Bitter Victory* (1957) is about war in general, dealing with courage and ego, rather than WWII specifically. This pulsing psychological drama is a battle of wills between Burton's Welsh captain (a fatalistic archaeologist) and his cowardly superior (Curt Jürgens). Both actors are extremely good, with Burton wryly cynical and pessimistic while Jürgens bristles with anger

and guilt. Similar in theme and content to that same year's *Paths of Glory, Bitter Victory* shows director Ray in a restrained mode, unlike his more feverish work on *Johnny Guitar* (1954) or *Rebel without a Cause* (1955). But the film is missing a basic excitement that would energize its drama into high emotional gear. More admirable than visceral, it is nonetheless a layered and ironic work, a proper vehicle for Burton that went virtually unseen. He was also seen that year, again in WWII, in *Sea Wife* (1957), an inflatable raft/deserted island picture in which he doesn't know that the woman he loves is a nun. (With *Heaven Knows, Mr. Allison* also in release, 1957 was the year to be stranded with a "sister"!). Mired in romance-novel territory, Burton gives his most dour and unengaged performance, the probable consequence of his own embarrassment at starring with top-billed Joan Collins in such a one-idea melodrama. *Sea Wife* maroons Collins, who tries to be simultaneously sexy and holy, and renders Burton as depressing as he is depressed.

Burton, the presumed Shakespearean heir to Laurence Olivier, had a brush with the contemporary theatre movement when he starred in the 1959 film version of John Osborne's 1956 theatre-shaking play *Look Back in Anger,* the quintessential angry-young-man drama of England's gloomy post-empire period. A landmark that shows its age, *Look Back in Anger* lacks the force and resonance it is said to have had (or was it always overrated?). Directed by Tony Richardson, who had directed it onstage, the film isn't stagy, shot in a smoky black and white, but its characters feel like rigged devices, and they don't evoke much sympathy. As aimless Jimmy Porter, Burton displays a seething bite and crisp lucidity, but there's no disguising the tiresome nature of his self-pitying rants. The movie was, however, a well-received prestige project, unlike his next American films, *Ice Palace* and *The Bramble Bush,* two bombs from 1960 that did nothing to rescue him from his prolonged Hollywood slump. Burton was having far more success on Broadway than in American movie houses, first with Helen Hayes in Jean Anouilh's comedy *Time Remembered* (1957), for which he got his first Tony nomination, and then, in a career benchmark, as King Arthur in the Lerner-and-Loewe musical *Camelot* (1960), co-starring a pre-Hollywood Julie Andrews. Burton's sonorous talk-singing won him a Tony Award, following in the footsteps of Rex

Looking Back at *Streetcar*

Look Back in Anger was Britain's answer to *A Streetcar Named Desire,* which it steals from unashamedly: Burton plays a low-class and abusive fellow; Mary Ure is his socially superior but sexually compatible (and pregnant) wife; and third-party Claire Bloom is Ure's friend and Burton's foe. Here the "Stanley" and "Blanche," after all their open bitterness, fall into bed and then into love, creating a soapy triangle before Burton reunites with Ure.

Harrison in *My Fair Lady* (1956), the previous Lerner-and-Loewe musical starring Andrews. But could anyone have foreseen just how famous Burton was to become in the next few years, not just on stages and screens but as a tabloid cover boy?

Joseph L. Mankiewicz's *Cleopatra* (1963) is, among many things, a film featuring Julie Andrews' two non-singing leading men, Burton (Marc Antony) and Harrison (Julius Caesar), yet both are billed below the title, with only Cleopatra herself, Elizabeth Taylor, billed above it. Burton enters the movie, which is longer than *Gone With the Wind,* at the one-hour mark, giving a half-committed and often distracted-looking performance prone to attacks of hammy tirades (a method he had been falling back on since *The Robe,* presumably whenever he took a gig for the money and didn't think much of the script, as if forgetting that the films were actually going to be seen, not to mention last into posterity.) Of course, the real fireworks were taking place off-screen, with the internationally covered affair between *adulterers* Taylor and Burton. Imagine the disappointment when audiences finally saw them together on-screen, acting badly and generating few sparks. Where was the sexy and magnetic Burton when needed most? *Cleopatra* is too deadly to be campy fun, finally a lumbering testament to how incapacitating a star-studded and bank-breaking blockbuster can be. Though still not married to each other, but very much the couple of the moment, Burton and Taylor next made *The V.I.P.s* (1963), a *Grand Hotel*-type ensemble picture set in an airport. It is hard to believe that such antiseptic schlock was crafted by the classy team of writer Terence Rattigan and director Anthony Asquith, the pair who made the moving and subdued drama

The Browning Version (1951). Nowhere in evidence is Burton's assumed pleasure at working on-screen with his off-screen love, and he is again tight, stiff, and unconnected.

The year 1964 was a turning point for Burton. He not only gave a Tony-nominated performance as Hamlet in a bare-boned Broadway production directed by Gielgud, but was also on screens in two lauded appearances in prestigious projects with theatre origins. *Becket,* unsurely directed by *Summer and Smoke*'s Peter Glenville, has top-billed Burton in the title role opposite Peter O'Toole's Henry II. In this clash between the church and the monarchy, the central dramatic idea is Becket's unexpected transformation when his friend Henry, in a calculating political prank, makes him Archbishop of Canterbury. Unfortunately, Edward Anhalt's Oscar-winning adaptation of Jean Anouilh's play is so schematic that Burton's transition is instantaneous, with Becket suddenly a self-righteous pain. Burton succumbs to the role's dullness, while O'Toole, though he yells too much, comes off better in the more fiery role, which includes a homosexual subtext that turns unrequited love into anger and spite. (The movie overdoes the two men's "wenching" out of fear the movie might seem too gay.) Though it's apparent that Henry found in his relationship with Becket what Becket found in his devotion to God, the drama's emphasis isn't where it belongs: on Becket's gradual conversion and Henry's frustrated sexuality. Both a high-minded snob hit and a flabby historical pageant, *Becket* is as unimaginative as it is stately. Both its stars were in the Oscar race, along with Anthony Quinn (*Becket*'s Henry II on Broadway) for *Zorba the Greek,* with all of them losing to—small world, isn't it?—Rex Harrison in *My Fair Lady.* Burton deserved to be nominated that year but for *The Night of the Iguana* rather than *Becket.* Though the films appear to have nothing in common, they both cast Burton as men of God, but, while Becket was moving closer and closer *to* God, Reverend Shannon appeared to be beating a hasty retreat.

Tennessee Williams' play *The Night of the Iguana* opened on Broadway in 1961 and received a Tony nomination for Best Play, as well as winning Margaret Leighton the Best Actress Tony for her portrayal of wandering artist Hannah Jelkes. The other central female, hotel owner Maxine Faulk, was played by Bette Davis, and the role of Shannon went to Patrick

O'Neal, not quite the "name" his co-stars were. (Aren't you glad you weren't backstage the night Davis found out that Leighton was nominated for a Tony and she wasn't?) Coming soon after the success of *Sweet Bird of Youth* (1959), *The Night of the Iguana* sustained Williams' high level of prominence in the New York theatre and it remains a fine play, though not one of his all-time best. Yet it did become one of the top Williams films, not of the caliber of *Streetcar,* but of comparable quality with *Baby Doll* and *The Fugitive Kind.* (The four best Williams films are all in black and white.) Directed and co-written by the esteemed John Huston—the man who made *The Maltese Falcon* (1941), *The Treasure of the Sierra Madre* (1948), and *The African Queen* (1951), as well as underrated works such as *The Red Badge of Courage* (1951), *The Roots of Heaven* (1958), and *Freud* (1962)—the film of *Iguana* provides the right balance of humor and poignancy, passion and reflection. Faithful to Williams' spirit but tweaked for greater emotional impact, the film surpasses the play. With its vivid depictions of scenes only referred to onstage, the screen *Iguana* takes palpable advantage of its Mexican location, making this the first Williams film not set in either the U.S. or Italy. Much credit goes to the deep-focus and multi-textured cinematography of Gabriel Figueroa, a major Mexican film artist whose credits include Luis Buñuel's *Nazarin* (1958), as well as John Ford's drama *The Fugitive* (1947). With Ava Gardner (Maxine) and Deborah Kerr (Hannah) alongside Burton, the three leads are close in age, a wise choice that eradicates the play's ten-year age gap between Shannon and Maxine and thus allows for increased romantic potential within this trio.

In a remarkable feat of adaptation, Huston's film, co-written with frequent collaborator Anthony Veiller, doesn't reach the play's opening scene until twenty-seven minutes into the movie. And yet nothing that happens in the first half hour is a significant departure from Williams, simply a smart and intoxicating visualization and embellishment of events merely spoken of in the play. In Reverend Shannon, Williams finally gave audiences a male character unraveling as extravagantly as some of his female creations, not just Blanche, but also, among others, Catherine Holly, Carol Cutrere, and Karen Stone. And the film gets right to it. In a superb pre-credits sequence, opening on a church exterior during a downpour and then joining the action within,

Shannon, an Episcopal pastor, is about to give his sermon, but, before he mounts the pulpit, as parishioners sing, he's plainly troubled. Burton begins the scene softly, in a state of humbled seriousness, speaking of "he that hath no rule over his own spirit." It is clear that something bad happened recently: Burton, looking shaken and distraught, starts to stumble over words. Judgmental and unsympathetic churchgoers are soon whispering. In response, Burton introduces a raw anger into his delivery, suddenly raising his voice, then crumpling his sermon and tossing it aside. Reacting to the unnamed scandal of which he is the obvious center, Burton's Shannon snaps and comes fabulously undone, wailing bitterly at the congregation. Reminding them he's "the grandson of two bishops," and then raising the issue of human "appetites," Shannon is a man in pain who foolishly hoped for some understanding regarding his human frailty. With none forthcoming, he marches down the central aisle as he speaks, terrorizing his worshippers as they flee hurriedly into the rain. This is a shocking opening even by Williams' standards, but highly pleasurable because of Burton's outrageous transition and his ferocious verbal satisfaction. The incongruity of a routine Sunday service and Burton's blazing assault makes this an especially funny (though not laugh-out-loud) sequence. An initially meek and insecure Shannon has descended into fire-and-brimstone rage, and it's a great start to Burton's performance, already a thrilling and unpredictable combination of vulnerability, fury, and humor, a release of all that is pent up inside Shannon. Risking offending moviegoers as well as his on-screen flock, in what is still the first scene, Burton hollers about the "cruel, senile delinquent" God embraced by humanity in favor of "the God of love and compassion." Savoring the liberating sensations of telling off his parish, he isn't considering how he'll have to pay for this later.

After the credits, Burton is seen sitting on the grounds of a Mexican cathedral, a newspaper over his head and a beer bottle at his side. Shannon is now a tour guide for a less than first-rate company, a pathetically demeaning (for him) and monstrously comic (for us) situation. He must charm people he loathes, all the while trying to curb his desire for pretty young things. Blond Sue Lyon, evoking Carroll Baker's Baby Doll, as well as Lolita (the role that shot Lyon to prominence two years before), plays the teasing and aggressive Charlotte Goodall, a hormone-raging teenager of sixteen or seventeen. With his verbal dexterity and a thinly concealed superior air, Burton is perfection at trying to tamp down his self-pitying resentments and play gracious host to his latest batch of tourists, not only Charlotte but about a dozen faculty members from Baptist Female College in Texas. (Burton is playing an American, and no one ever questions his British accent, which somehow suits Shannon's vocal eloquence.) As his mostly middle-aged charges launch into "Happy Days Are Here Again" while their steamy tour bus chugs along, Burton mutters his first "Fantastic," his frequent utterance whenever something seems positively unreal to him, or when he suddenly realizes just how low he has sunk, more Hell on Earth than "Happy Days." In a scene invented for the film, Shannon asks Hank (James Ward), the driver, to stop the bus so the ladies can see Mexican women beating their laundry at the river while children are splashing about, a sight intended to make them absorb something real and innocent and beautiful. Despite his unappreciative tourists, the moment reveals Shannon's humanistic feeling beyond his own woes, a soulful man trapped in a body he can't always control. Burton's Shannon is in a state of emotional dishevelment and barely holding himself together. He finds a nemesis in Judith Fellowes (Grayson Hall), the leader of the tourist ladies and Charlotte's chaperone. Charlotte becomes the object over which all the difficulties between Shannon and Miss Fellowes arise. He is not a pedophile; he's a nonpracticing reverend with a strong sexual urge and trying *not* to have unsanctified intercourse. It just so happens that right now the stakes have been raised by Charlotte's being underage, not just a temptation but unlawful. (Williams is never more politically incorrect than when Shannon describes statutory rape to Maxine as "when a man is seduced by a girl under twenty.")

Grayson Hall's Miss Fellowes is appropriately over the top. She is a repressed lesbian, the largest unambiguously gay role in any Williams film, though so closeted as not to know the truth herself. Her possessiveness and jealousy over Charlotte are enacted on the scale of Greek tragedy. Not since Mercedes McCambridge in *Johnny Guitar* (1954) had there been such a sexually turbulent and furiously frustrated female in an American movie. Hall suggests a ravaged evil queen; she is dark, haggard,

and rail-thin, but always fiercely energized. (Shannon refers to her as "a butch vocal teacher.") Though she's the emotionally neurotic villain of the piece, the treatment of her is ultimately more sympathetic than cruel. But for most of the picture she's the lady you love to hate. And it is great fun to watch an actress tear into a role in which every moment is played as life or death. Best known for television's horror soap opera *Dark Shadows* and its two big-screen outings (all of which came between 1967 and 1971), Hall brings to Miss Fellowes a decided vampiric quality. Burton and Hall have wonderful clashes, with his mood-lightening comments falling flat against her humorless rectitude. But more dangerous for Shannon is Charlotte's blond adorability and carnal eagerness. Burton recognizes the bedroom-farce elements of the plot, bringing delicious humor to his encounters with Lyon, mostly consisting of his strenuously resisting her at all costs, acting as if being tested by the Devil himself. Whenever Shannon's sexual antennae are raised, Burton melds arousal and despair into one and the same, trying hard to remain a man of God and still hoping one day to return to the fold. Shannon is neither a womanizing sleaze nor a studly seducer; he's a hapless fellow with an identity problem, a man futilely on the run from himself. Though it has its absurdly funny aspects, his torment is no joke. Women throw themselves at him and he can resist only for so long.

A flat tire is an excuse for him to disappear and take a dip in the sea, soon finding Charlotte beside him in the water. When they emerge, Burton, not buff by today's standards, has a moment equivalent to Elizabeth Taylor's in *Suddenly, Last Summer,* appearing in a wet white bathing suit, which in Burton's case is his underwear, revealing an outline of his manhood (provocative by 1964 standards). When Charlotte appears in his hotel room that night, he begs her to leave. A perspiring Burton, fully in bedroom-farce mode as he tries to get rid of her before she is discovered, plays the age-old conflict of trying to say "no" when you want to say "yes." Again combining humor with desolation, he appears as though his sanity might truly be on the brink. Charlotte is as relentless as Miss Fellowes, who eventually finds them out, interrupting their make-out session. At the center of all these heated confrontations is the very real drama of what's to become of Shannon if he loses this job. Burton's charm may go a long way in sustaining Shannon's tenuous hold over the group, but he looks increasingly like someone who can't keep it going much longer. Miss Fellowes wires her powerful brother (a Texas judge) to look into her tour guide's past, which unnerves Shannon. When the bus arrives in Puerto Vallarta, Shannon is in the driver's seat, barreling through town and beyond, terrifying the women with his reckless speeding and unknown intentions. The scene is a perfect match to the opening, another instance in which Burton's Shannon behaves carelessly, deciding that there's only one way to battle the danger about to overtake him: to go on the attack himself. His desperate acts of self-preservation are mere delays of the inevitable. The heart-racing ride out of town is a purely cinematic illustration of the moments that precede the opening scene of the play: Shannon's arrival at Maxine's hilltop hotel. As nonchalantly as possible, Burton grabs his suitcase and hops off the bus, then removes the engine's distributor head (which makes Hank and the women his prisoners) and bounds up the hill, all the while spewing his tour-guide spiel about their current (and unscheduled) destination.

At the top of the hill is Ava Gardner's Maxine, a far more believable loose-living lady than the 1961 Bette Davis could possibly have been, too far gone by then in her mannered ways. Gardner, of course, was never a talent of Davis' caliber, but she had a natural gift for the screen, and, when used properly and directed with care, she could be marvelous, as she was in John Ford's *Mogambo* (1953) and Stanley Kramer's *On the Beach* (1959). Though the screenwriters, Huston and Anthony Veiller, had scripted *The Killers* (1946), the seminal film noir that made the astonishingly beautiful Gardner a star, Huston had never directed her before *Iguana*. At age forty during the filming, Gardner was by now well-known as a wild-living and hard-drinking playgirl, making her ideal for Maxine, a widow who amuses herself with two young beach boys (and employees) who are incessantly shirtless and shaking maracas. (Her mostly sexless marriage had been to a man twenty-eight years her senior.) In addition to Maxine's eyebrow-raising lifestyle and smoldering sensuality, Gardner also shared the character's no-nonsense likability. When Deborah Kerr's Hannah admits that she's pushing forty, Gardner blasts back with "Well, who the hell isn't?" (a line not in the play). When Grayson Hall's Miss Fellowes makes a crack about

Maxine being Shannon's "paramour," Gardner strikes back with a smile: "You're gambling with your front teeth!" (also not in the play). She tells Hannah about knowing the difference between love and "just going to bed." Huston clearly tilted the role to Gardner's acting strengths and most comfortable persona, recognizing her essence as a tough but warmhearted broad with a barely protected vulnerability, allowing the actress and the character to merge seamlessly. A big plus is her sprinkling most of her lines with "baby" or "honey," enhancing Maxine's relaxed and playful nature. Gardner also makes casual use of her bona fide Southern accent, something she had worked so hard to get rid of twenty years prior.

Gardner's performance, undeniably effective, is admittedly hit or miss. Without any technique to depend on, she *feels* her way through; sometimes she's glorious and sometimes she's effortful, pushing her body and voice (especially her laugh) unnaturally. She occasionally seems to be a drunk actress rather than a laid-back character. Despite her limitations and erratic impact, the film would be much less without her humor and earthiness, both of which trump her pangs of discomfort. She's got guts and presence, notably in her fully-clothed three-way foreplay with her beach boys on the shore at night, an important moment created for the film in which she, unable to get Shannon and his recriminations from her thoughts, flings the boys off her, done with all of that, and heads down the beach alone (one of several hints in the film as to where it is headed romantically). Gardner displays special feeling for Burton early on, setting up Maxine's unrequited amatory interest in Shannon. First seen barefoot, in tight pants and a loose blouse, the hands-on-hips Gardner should be on every pamphlet for how to unwind in Mexico. Widowed less than a month ago, Maxine is the welcoming light at the end of Shannon's seemingly unending tunnel. Gardner's easygoing and ostensibly grounded Maxine is a blatant contrast to Burton's restless and tattered Shannon. At the sight of him, she shrieks his name and bellows a laugh.

As a favor to old-pal Shannon, Maxine opens up her isolated inn of bungalows (usually closed in August) to him and his resentful party. He is already on probation with the touring company, and now he's stalling for time, knowing that one more complaint will finish him. Despite few amenities, Maxine's place is a breathtaking perch overlooking the sea. Shannon hopes to show the ladies a grand time before it's too late, with Burton again *working* Shannon's charm, wit, and full smile, all of which are at increasing odds with his mounting dread. Burton has a wicked glint in his eye whenever Shannon momentarily thinks that things are going his way, but mostly what he conveys is a quick mind struggling to keep up, racing from tactic to tactic in anticipation of the next disaster. Maxine calms this savage beast somewhat when she shaves his face, forcing him to be still in her hammock and dissipate some of his mad-dog energy. Plagued by the "spook" of his panic, Shannon hasn't been of use to anyone, including himself, for a long time, trapped in spiraling self-absorption and, according to Maxine, cracking up regularly. He wants to return to the church but Maxine knows that would be a mistake, a clue that she would be good for him (more foreshadowing of the revised ending). With more than enough already going on, the third main character, Hannah Jelkes, enters at thirty-nine minutes into the movie. Hannah, unlike Shannon or Maxine, never seems three-dimensional, feeling like a playwright's device. She is given the most self-consciously poetic lines to say, and nothing about her is easily believed. Arriving with her nearly deaf and cane-bearing 97-year-old grandfather, Nonno (Cyril Delevanti), Deborah Kerr's Hannah looks fresh and cool under a sun-shielding umbrella, improbably clad in a spotless and tasteful outfit and white gloves, with her scarved head under a hat. She is a water-color painter and quick-sketch artist; Nonno is Jonathan Coffin, the world's oldest practicing poet. (Williams and his names: a 97-year-old named Coffin, a lesbian named Fellowes, a free-love advocate named Faulk.) This duo travels the world as roving artists, making their way humbly by selling her sketches and his recitations. Thanks to Shannon's intervention, Maxine lets Hannah and Nonno stay for one night without paying. Williams has suddenly turned Maxine's hotel into a refuge for a conspicuously offbeat assortment of individuals.

Several sources claim that Williams originally envisioned Katharine Hepburn as Hannah, no doubt influenced by her recent artistic dominance of the film version of his *Suddenly, Last Summer*. Like Hepburn, Hannah is a New Englander (from Nantucket) and an odd duck. Kerr doesn't seem rarefied or unusual enough to be Hannah, who arrives like an apparition to help Shannon and then moves on once she's done. However beautifully Kerr speaks the text or glows with spirituality, there is nothing eccentric about her; she isn't plausible or even imaginable as someone living outside the realm of conventional society. Without a striking nonconformity, Kerr's Hannah seems a playwright's construct. (It is ironic that the more "real" Hannah seems, the less believable she is.) Hepburn was too old for the part by 1964, but she certainly had proven in the past that she could be effortlessly peculiar enough to make Hannah come alive on-screen, much as she so bewitchingly had done with her grandly strange Mrs. Venable in *Sud-*

Heavenly Deborah Kerr

By 1964, Deborah Kerr had long been one of Hollywood's foremost actresses, having arrived at MGM in 1947 after making her name in British films, most notably the magnificent *Black Narcissus* (1947) in which she played a nun. After being stifled by MGM, who used her primarily as an ornamentally pretty redhead in hits like *King Solomon's Mines* (1950) and *Quo Vadis* (1951), she was rescued from banality by her cheating-wife role in Columbia's *From Here to Eternity* (1953) and was thereafter one of the more sought-after and versatile actresses in the business, appearing in *The King and I* (1956), *An Affair to Remember* (1957), and, eventually, *The Sundowners* (1960) and *The Innocents* (1961), which contain her two greatest performances. She racked up six nominations but never won the Best Actress Oscar, losing to Elizabeth Taylor in *Butterfield 8* the year she merited the prize for *The Sundowners*. Kerr had one of her biggest hits when she worked with John Huston previously in the WWII-set *Heaven Knows, Mr. Allison* (1957), in which she gives a lovely, understated performance, again playing a nun, stranded on an island with marine Robert Mitchum, a successful variation of Huston's own *African Queen* with another mug and religious lady thrown together unexpectedly (though this time the affection can go only so far). Another Kerr film with an *Iguana* connection is *Separate Tables* (1958): both vehicles starred Margaret Leighton on Broadway in Tony-winning virgin roles assumed on film by Kerr.

denly, Last Summer. (If Williams *had* gotten Hepburn for Hannah, alongside Bette Davis' Maxine, it would have been too overpowering for the play, like seeing a musical starring both Ethel Merman and Mary Martin.) With her customary grace, Kerr still comes off rather well, but the role's challenges (or deficiencies) make her less successful than Burton or Gardner (who wasn't close to being in Kerr's league as an actress). Kerr and Gardner had appeared together once before, in just one scene in Kerr's first American film, *The Hucksters* (1947), an earnest, too well-behaved Clark Gable picture about the advertising world. The women were cast as they would be in *Iguana,* with Kerr the proper lady and Gardner the good-time gal, setting up a triangle in which Gable opts for the lady. In *Iguana,* the women share much more screen time and their characters are strong in different ways, creating another Williams contrast of body and soul (as in *Streetcar* or *Summer and Smoke*), representing two very different ways of being alive, with Shannon somewhere in the middle. Both women are here to listen to Shannon and do what they can for him. A triangular conflict emerges through Maxine's jealousy of Shannon's attentiveness to Hannah and their sudden emotional intimacy.

Though Williams did not co-write the screenplay, and received credit only as the play's author, he was in Mexico for some of the filming and was courted by Huston to add input and make contributions. One scene that John Huston's biographer, Lawrence Grobel, credits to Williams is one of the best additions to the movie, the broken-glass scene. This comes directly after the sequence in which Miss Fellowes confronts Shannon theatrically with "Seducer!" and announces his "career of seducing young girls," thanks to her phone conversation with her brother. Stammering with fear, Burton suggests a child cornered. Later, drunk in his room and now wearing his clerical collar, he is yet again visited by Charlotte. At the sight and sound of her, Burton leaps up in horror and knocks his liquor bottle crashing to the floor. Standing on the broken glass, Burton plays Shannon as too drunk to know better, too drunk to feel the shards of glass and far more troubled by his vulnerability to the dangers Charlotte represents. He tells her his "emotional bank balance" has run out, visible in Burton as the persistent toll of Shannon's perpetual self-loathing and self-destruction. Speaking of their mutually un-

stable conditions and "destructive potential"—she wants to marry him—he paces over the glass. Burton delivers a shivering mad scene, with Shannon so intent on explaining himself that he's oblivious to the cuts bloodying his feet. Williams provides instant physical, vein-opening penance for a man wracked by perceived sinfulness, trying to maintain his sanity while simultaneously martyring his body. Burton's rapid speech amplifies the comic quotient in Shannon's sexual torment. When Charlotte, too, walks on the glass, and Shannon immediately lifts her and carries her out kicking and screaming, the scene is a voluptuous exhibition of emotional flamboyance from two overdramatizing characters.

"Hell and damnation" is how he describes the incident to Hannah, who has become Shannon's ever-present witness. As she tends to his bloodied feet, Burton launches into one of *Iguana*'s key speeches, about how people live life on two planes, "the fantastic level" and "the realistic level." He's been living more and more in the "fantastic" while struggling to survive in the "realistic." His awareness of his "spooked" condition only makes it worse. Shannon responds to Hannah's generosity of spirit, and he opens up to her about his one year active in the clergy, recalling the film's opening scene (at the point in the play when those details are revealed). Even though the film dramatized his career-bursting breakdown, it doesn't feel repetitive to have him recount it to Hannah, especially because he includes details about the initial scandal, his "fornication" with a young Sunday-school teacher who pursued him. Portraying himself as the victim (just as he sees himself with Charlotte), he recalls how their kneeling in prayer together unintentionally gave way to a more reclining position. The woman's subsequent suicide attempt erupted the scandal. He insists he's still "a frocked minister," just one locked out of his church. Unseen was his stint in an institution and emergence as a tour guide. Shannon continues to unburden himself, and Burton's performance is particularly probing and thoughtful when Shannon ponders man's inhumanity to God, including our destruction of His planet and our misconception of who He truly is.

If the church and the tour company both abandon him, there's nothing left but suicide, "the long swim" to China. At dinner that evening, he is very drunk. (By now, the fickle Charlotte has shifted her attentions to Hank, the bus driver.) A phone call from Shannon's tour-company boss gives Burton another comic set-up in an unfunny situation. With alcohol-infused grandeur, and feeling as if it is he who holds all the power, Burton is expansively entertaining while on the telephone, delusionally declaring his position as the equivalent of the captain of a ship. Unaware of the extent of his drunkenness, and still imagining himself cool and collected, Burton's Shannon is more "high" than mighty. He is fired, even losing the pocketed distributor head when Hank and Charlotte overtake him. It is an expert drunk scene, as pathetic as it is amusing, with Shannon losing his final toehold in the realistic world. For his grand farewell gesture to the ladies of the tour, he pees (off-screen) on Miss Fellowes' suitcase, horrifying the group but delighting Maxine. Burton is a smiling, self-satisfied prankster here, a vindictive clown. Miss Fellowes makes threats about a blacklisting and an arrest, but Burton sustains Shannon's still-blotto merriment.

Coming to his defense, Maxine addresses Miss Fellowes as "butch old gal" and makes a "dykes" reference, referring as well to Charlotte's "natural preference for men." This is Grayson Hall's key moment, played with astounding bafflement. Miss Fellowes is either feigning obliviousness or genuinely dumbstruck by the implications, or perhaps caught somewhere in a subconscious middle ground. Her true and unadmittable feelings for Charlotte are buried deeply, sealed beyond consciousness. When Shannon intervenes it is not in the way expected. Refusing to stomp upon his enemy's vulnerability, he protects her by stifling Maxine. He then quietly suggests Miss Fellowes' immediate exit. After she is gone, Shannon insightfully states, "If she ever recognized the truth about herself, it would destroy her." (This essential sequence is not in the play.) Miss Fellowes is not a carnivorous sexual predator waiting to pounce on her object of desire. She is a confused and unhappy woman, who, like Shannon, is not living a natural life, one to which she is emotionally suited. Despite their mutual animosity, he recognizes another soul in pain and frustration, and, even in his inebriation and self-disgust, he is able to extend empathy, instinctively exposing some of what drew him to become a man of God in the first place. Burton appreciates the moment for what it is, an important revelation of Shannon's interior life, an acknowledgment that he isn't yet too far gone.

Burton plays the scene in a hushed manner, pooling Shannon's resources and mustering whatever it takes to be temporarily sober at a crucial moment.

In a fitting companion piece to the broken-glass scene, Shannon, alone with Hannah, handles the cross around his neck, rubbing its chain repeatedly across the back of his neck, another occasion to draw blood. (This moment *is* in the play.) More suffering, more penance, and an obvious expression of painful emotional constriction. Shannon understands punishment and self-abuse but is helplessly unable to effect positive change or find peace. He dives into the sea in a rash suicide attempt but is quickly rescued by the beach boys. The scene is now set for the film's titular "night." The metaphor of the iguana is handled so blatantly by Williams that I'm not sure it can even be labeled as such. Shannon is tied up in a hammock to protect him from self-harm. Nearby is another wild thing, a tied-up iguana captured by the beach boys for fattening and eventual eating, also at "the end of his rope." Burton at first suggests the strait-jacketed patient of an asylum movie, howling and raving and flailing, encased like a sausage. Hannah, his administering nurse, astutely accuses him of reveling in this latest misery, more atonement for his sins. Burton's touches of masochistic pleasure—Shannon's well-honed ability to gain attention through negative means (like Carol Cutrere in *The Fugitive Kind*)—are reflections of a man who has been railing against everything for so long that he doesn't seem able (or has forgotten how) to live any other way. His downfall has become a way of life (connecting him further with Ms. Cutrere). Can Shannon get past himself, as he did so nobly in his final encounter with Miss Fellowes, or is "the long swim to China" all that's really left? After Maxine straddles Shannon in an effort to quiet him, he offends her with a zinger about her night swims with the beach boys, forcing her to face her own aimless life. Played by Burton with a smirking glee, this moment—more groundwork for the new ending—may be interpreted as an unconscious indication of Shannon's spiteful jealousy regarding Maxine's love life. After her hurt and angry exit, he tells Hannah that Maxine is "indestructible," unlike poor Miss Fellowes, making him able to treat her as such, blindly missing the sensitivity in Maxine so apparent to Hannah.

The final half hour of the movie basically belongs to Hannah, who does most of the talking. Her somewhat smug wisdom is of questionable value, though Williams evidently thinks she has much to offer Shannon. This extended scene is the film's stagiest, both physically and in its dialogue. Hannah speaks of her "unbearable torments," and you have to wonder what she can possibly be talking about, particularly since she doesn't elaborate. She pontificates on a range of subjects: "the need to believe in someone or something"; her belief in "broken barriers between people" and "one-night communications" (as opposed to one-night stands); and the creation of "home" with other people rather than in places. Some of what she says is lovely, though not necessarily believable coming from someone who has lived such an alien existence. Hannah is a lofty conception of the nomadic artist, an intuitive observer of life rather than a participant, coolly and purposefully apart. Hannah appears to have lived only on "the fantastic level," remotely dabbling in the real world, yet Williams endows her with special vision on earthly matters, arriving out of nowhere as Shannon's fairy godmother and vanishing almost as suddenly. When he prods her on the subject of sex, she says that there are worse things than chastity. Burton snaps back, "Lunacy and death," the two things Shannon has been boldly courting of late. She reveals her two so-called "love experiences": the unwanted attentions of a movie-theatre masher when she was sixteen (and recently orphaned); and a more recent incident with a salesman who wished for her to remove one piece of clothing for him to hold briefly. (She doesn't state which garment she gave him, nor did she look to see what he did with it.) When Shannon asks if she was disgusted by the salesman's behavior, she says, in the play's big line, "Nothing human disgusts me, Mr. Shannon, unless it's unkind or violent," as perfect a summation as exists of Williams' life work and of which variations appear throughout his plays.

When he's sufficiently calmed, she unties him (he unties himself in the play) and launches into a speech about her "crack-up" and the "blue devil" who taunted her. Again, it is very hard to believe her, especially since she offers no details. Shannon is affected by her advice, that it all comes down to endurance. She takes it further, condoning whatever it takes to endure, including alcohol, without regard for the obvious dangers (another politically incorrect point for Williams). This is the script's most high-flown passage, uneasily absorbed in a film whose melding of its aural and visual elements has up to this point been faultless. (Even in the less realistic domain of the stage, Hannah is a challenge to accept as an actual person.) Once freed, Burton's Shannon is no longer a roiling mass of despair, nor is he metaphorically tied too tightly. He frees the iguana, his kindred sufferer. This night of freedom continues when Nonno calls out to announce that he has finished his long-gestating final poem. (Williams' poets, Nonno and *Suddenly, Last Summer*'s Sebastian, are not exactly prolific.) After dictating his poem to Hannah, he, too, can be freed, in his case by death.

After Nonno's body is buried, Hannah is ready to head down the hill and into Puerto Vallarta, continuing her life as a roaming and virtually penniless artist, suddenly without the "home" she shared with Nonno. (If there was ever a time for her to crack up, it should be now, when she is literally *and* figuratively homeless.) Williams utilizes her as an unearthly tool, similar to his use of Val Xavier in *Orpheus Descending*, with both characters—so-called artists and members of the fugitive kind—having a strange power to drift through, change people's lives, and move on (though Val is destroyed when he becomes too involved). As the ending approaches, the film appropriately feels as if it could finish in several ways. Shannon asks Hannah if they might travel together, platonically, having not yet realized that it is definitely time for him to stop running. She refuses his offer, as well as Maxine's impulsive proposal (not in the play) that Shannon and Hannah run the place for her while she returns to the States. When Shannon gives Hannah his cross, it is his acceptance of the end of his struggles.

The play ends with Shannon opting to stay at Maxine's, partially as her plaything, in companionship rather than love. The final image is Nonno's death, Hannah beside him. The film's alterations are a considerable improvement, rearranging the events intelligently and romanticizing the ending without making it a compromise. It is dramatically stronger in the film to see Shannon and Maxine reaching out to each other and choosing to take a chance on a life together. According to Lawrence Grobel, author of *The Hustons*, Williams wasn't pleased with Huston's new ending, but it isn't a *damaging* happy ending like those in the preceding films of *The Glass Menagerie*, *Cat on a Hot Tin Roof*, or *Sweet Bird of Youth*.

Despite Williams' objections, Huston was insistent, providing the logical emotional conclusion that the film demands and has been establishing from the start. Shannon approaches Maxine, who is angrily packing in her room. Playing the new proprietor, he offers her a rum coco. She assumes Hannah will be staying on with him until he tells her that she has gone, making his intentions clear. In the intensely satisfying final moments, Gardner goes to the window in tears and Burton follows, both of them facing the glorious view before them. She suggests that they go down to the beach. Burton unguardedly speaks Shannon's line about being able to get down the hill okay but not so sure about making it back up. Gardner turns to him and says tenderly, "I'll get you back up, baby, I'll always get you back up," making this the most touching happy ending in the Williams films. In the play, Maxine says only, "I'll get you back up the hill," then continues with lines about their running the place. It isn't poignant or memorable, unlike the shared vulnerability of Burton and Gardner, augmented by the enveloping warmth of her line reading. This is a restrained and unsentimental finish, with no Hollywood kiss to seal it. He puts down the rum coco and starts to loosen his tie (no longer "tied up"), and she quite naturally assists him. It isn't happily-ever-after but it's a start, with both characters already breathing easier.

The play is set in 1940, allowing for some Nazi-sympathizing Germans to be staying at Maxine's, giving the play more of a historical moral context, which it doesn't need. There is plenty enough going on without the addition of Nazis. Huston was wise to cut those characters and contemporize the action. In the play, Shannon has been conducting tours for as long as ten years, and he and Charlotte have definitely had sex. Shannon also has a post-sex violent streak, a response to his sexual guilt, a trait that would have unfortunately marred Shannon's likability and humor had it been carried over to the movie. The *Iguana* film is so well done that its few missteps glare, like the dumb and overlong new scene of Hank's comically choreographed fistfight with the beach boys, which he loses (though it wins him Charlotte). Mostly, Huston and Williams seem ideally suited, with their free-spirited, nonjudgmental, and humorously offbeat sensibilities meshing rather nicely. The director's vibrant filmmaking perfectly matches the author's vibrant characters, making *Iguana* a gift to

First *Night*

The Night of the Iguana first began life as a 1948 Williams short story, focused on Edith Jelkes, a Southern spinster and painter who taught art until she suffered a nervous breakdown. She travels, but, unlike Hannah, has a modest inheritance to pay her way. The plot includes a Mexican hotel and a tied-up iguana but little else that ended up in the play. The story's plot centers on Edith's inability to befriend a gay male couple.

a playwright often bruised by Hollywood. A good play had become a very good film, one of the finest released in a very fine screen year. (Huston had also recently done well with Arthur Miller, Broadway's other playwrighting luminary of that era, directing Miller's 1961 original screenplay *The Misfits*, another piercing and literate black-and-white beauty, but, unlike *Iguana*, a box-office lemon.)

Produced for MGM by Ray Stark, *The Night of the Iguana* was filmed on location in Puerto Vallarta, at the time a remote and difficult locale but worth the trouble. (Huston had a special feeling for Mexico, as attested by his classic *The Treasure of the Sierra Madre*.) Elizabeth Taylor was present for the entire shoot, keeping her eye on Burton and his three leading ladies while bringing the film considerable and welcome publicity. The film turned out to be Williams' final box-office winner, just as the play was his last major Broadway success (aside from revivals). A fascinating companion to this gorgeous black-and-white movie is a promotional short titled *On the Trail of the Iguana*, a thirteen-minute making-of documentary shot in color, which ultimately proves that black and white was the right choice for the material. Even so, it's a treat to glimpse the cast, as well as their costumes and the settings, in varied colors. *Iguana* received four Oscar nominations, for supporting actress Grayson Hall and for black-and-white cinematography, art direction, and costume design. Dorothy Jeakins' costumes were the only winner, with the other nominees losing to *Zorba the Greek*. (Hall lost to *Zorba*'s Lila Kedrova for her unbeatable performance in a surefire aging-courtesan role.)

Marking a trilogy of consecutive clergyman vehicles (following *Becket* and *Iguana*), Burton next starred, far less distinguishedly, in *The Sandpiper*

Huston, We Have Several Problems

Ava Gardner made two more films with John Huston, both of them stinkers: *The Bible* (1966), long as the book itself, with Huston the wrong director for material without sufficient ambiguity, humor, or cynicism, and Gardner used merely decoratively as Sarah, Abraham's barren wife; and *The Life and Times of Judge Roy Bean* (1972), in which she has a final-scene cameo as actress Lily Langtry, a graceful and beautiful goddess wafting through a film that otherwise leaves a bad taste. Deborah Kerr later appeared in Huston's *Casino Royale* (1967), a disjointed and rather disastrous James Bond spoof helmed by *five* directors, with Kerr broadly comic in her lustiness and thick Scottish burr. For Gardner and Kerr, *Iguana* marked their final major screen performances and last high-quality film. Burton was top-billed, followed by Gardner, then Kerr. Incidentally, all three stars had been nominees on the same decade-ago Oscar night, with Burton in contention for *The Robe,* Gardner for *Mogambo,* and Kerr for *From Here to Eternity.* They all lost.

(1965), his first film with Taylor since they became husband and wife in 1964. (Burton divorced Sybil Williams, his wife since 1949.) He plays a minister who is headmaster of a boys' school. Though married to Eva Marie Saint, he begins an affair with Taylor, a self-proclaimed "naturalist" and atheist. The script is the kind of pap in which the lovers conveniently make each other better persons: she recharges his misplaced idealism; he endows her with faith in man-woman relationships. After a supposedly tearjerking farewell, Burton heads nobly alone to Bolivia to do good work. More a Pacific Coast travelogue than a legitimate drama, *The Sandpiper* serves Burton better than Taylor. He has the more restrained role, and, silly as it is, he at least stays connected, even though he usually tuned out when faced with such unworthy material. Aided by its Oscar-winning song, "The Shadow of Your Smile," *The Sandpiper* was a big fat hit.

The Spy Who Came in from the Cold (1965), adapted from John Le Carré's Cold War novel and ingeniously directed by Martin Ritt, is the best film Burton ever made and it contains, fittingly, his greatest performance. Fusing intensity and intelligence in a most riveting fashion, Burton plays a longtime British agent thrust into an elaborate defection scheme intended to bring down an East German agent. A grim antidote to the James Bond films, this is the tautest and most believable spy picture I've ever seen, with Burton giving an unforgettable portrait of the painful isolation and emotional sacrifices that can accompany a life in espionage. Heading to the stunning climax at the Berlin Wall, Burton brings rumbling depths to the role, fascinatingly blurring the line between the character's professional and personal lives. His rigor-

ous concentration and attention to detail make his immersion into the character complete. This peerless performance merited him the Oscar, but he lost the prize to Lee Marvin for his go-for-broke comic turn in *Cat Ballou,* an entertaining but negligible achievement compared to Burton's.

Based on playwright Edward Albee's masterpiece, Mike Nichols' *Who's Afraid of Virginia Woolf?* (1966) sustained Burton's mid-decade career high, while offering the first creative justification for the ongoing presence of Burton and Taylor as a screen team. For this dissection of a marriage in which mutual self-deception is a balm against anguished reality, the casting of a too-young Taylor was a risk, but Burton was ideally suited to play her husband, an associate history professor. With stinging wit, unsettling humor, and the toll of an aching sadness, Burton gives a phenomenal performance, another of his masterful displays of character delineation sculpted with utmost clarity. George Segal and an extraordinary Sandy Dennis play the guests, serving as the main characters' much-needed audience for their long night's journey into day. Taylor won her second Oscar, but Burton's work was more award-worthy. Even so, he was robbed again, this time losing to Paul Scofield's impeccably worked-out Thomas More in *A Man for All Seasons,* an irritatingly smug performance that had been "perfected" onstage. Burton's performance has greater variety and complexity, and his artistry is deployed more invisibly.

Though there is a filmed record of a "live" performance of Burton's 1964 Hamlet, his only Shakespearean feature film is the Franco Zeffirelli production of *The Taming of the Shrew* (1967), with Taylor playing Kate to his bearded Petruchio. A frenetic film that strains for hilarity, it's a reasonably entertaining try at bringing the Bard to the screen, though *Shrew* is hardly one of his funnier comedies. Burton is skillful but inexplicably muted, lacking the all-out panache and vigor expected, perhaps an instinctive attempt to compensate for Zeffirelli's unrestrained direction. *The Comedians* (1967), helmed by *Becket*'s Peter Glenville and written by Graham Greene, plays like an emotionally distant and overlong update of *Casablanca* set in Haiti, with Burton a cynical English hotelkeeper detached from the nation's violent unrest and preoccupied with his affair with a married woman (Taylor). This unwieldy though admirable drama never quite ignites. A bit too mopey, Burton nonetheless underplays expertly, and, as Bogie did, ultimately becomes a part of something bigger than himself. *Doctor Faustus* (1967), like *Shrew* another classical pairing for the Burtons, is a film version of Christopher Marlowe's play co-directed by Burton and Nevill Coghill, based on their 1966 Oxford theatre production in which Burton played the title role. Released in the U.S. in early 1968, months after its U.K. release, *Doctor Faustus* is as uninvolving a vision of *Faust* as can be imagined, with Burton acting up a storm to no avail. Colorful but stagy and dull, the film is an all-around embarrassment.

Spouses Paul Newman and Joanne Woodward had both appeared in Tennessee Williams movies, and by now so had Burton and Taylor. But the Burtons pulled ahead of the Newmans by starring *together* in *Boom* (1968), a Joseph Losey-directed adaptation of Williams' unsuccessful Broadway play *The Milk Train Doesn't Stop Here Anymore* (1963), one of Williams' dramas with a showy and sizable central role for an actress around whom everyone else revolves. Taylor had played parts secondary to Burton's in *The Comedians* and *Doctor Faustus,* but in *Boom* it would be Burton in the subordinate role. His character, Chris Flanders, was created by Paul Roebling, then revived by Tab Hunter in the play's second failed Broadway outing in back-to-back seasons. Who could have imagined that Richard Burton would bring to the screen a stage role previously played by Tab Hunter? Chris is another of Williams' spiritually and artistically gifted wanderers arriving out of nowhere, putting Burton in the Hannah Jelkes slot (even though he was far more comfortable playing the flawed and struggling Shannons of the

King Richard...Harris

One 1967 film in which Burton did **not** star was *Camelot.* Though Joshua Logan's screen version turned out rather badly, it still seems a grave shame that Burton and Julie Andrews didn't get the chance to preserve their Broadway performances on film, especially since they were currently among the world's most popular and acclaimed movie stars. Richard Harris and Vanessa Redgrave became the screen's Arthur and Guenevere.

world). If *Iguana*'s Hannah and *Fugitive Kind*'s Val aren't wholly convincing in their functions as human angels, they are far more believable than Chris Flanders, a role Burton never should have accepted, even if only to hang out with his wife on a glorious Sardinian location. Chris is also another Williams poet, but, unlike *Iguana*'s Nonno, his work is never spoken on-screen. His main purpose is as a flesh-and-blood Angel of Death who appears at the homes of dying wealthy women and helps them through their transition out of life. Purely in service to the female lead (Taylor's terminally ill Mrs. Goforth), Chris is an essentially unactable role to which Burton responds by not acting at all. His non-performance, in which he delivers his lines fragrantly and proficiently, seems more suited to radio than film. Without a hint of any interpretive grasp of his character, Burton makes no apparent choices and never seems to be anyone specific. Depriving the role of a personal imprint, he drifts through the film and never draws focus, as if protecting himself from stepping into the quicksand of the disastrous movie surrounding him. Risking zero, he offers nothing, merely playing witness to Taylor's hysterics. Is Chris a living saint, a crackpot do-gooder, or a scheming charlatan? Don't ask Burton. For all Taylor's sloppy overacting, at least she is in there trying, unlike the noncommittal Burton, safely on the sidelines.

After hitching a boat ride to Mrs. Goforth's private island, Chris swims to shore with his two canvas bags. He chooses to ignore her "Private Property—Keep Out" sign (in three languages). They met years ago briefly, yet he seeks her company with urgency. Just as in *The Night of the Iguana*, Burton must climb a steep hill to get to the main setting of the drama. This Angel of Death is clad in a black long-sleeved shirt and black trousers, an unusual outfit for summer in the Mediterranean. He keeps shouting her name as he gets closer to the top, as if she will emerge at the recognized sound of his voice. Against an authentic and scene-stealing Sardinian landscape, everything about this arduously mystical set-up feels phony rather than stimulatingly bizarre. Vicious guard dogs attack, wounding him and shredding his clothes. His subsequent shout of "Mrs. *Bloody* Goforth!" feels like Burton Anglicizing the dialogue on impulse (and out of boredom). Through a servant, he sends Mrs. Goforth his book of poetry as his calling card and means of re-introduction. Sent to her pink villa, he bathes and rests and hopes to be fed. Replacing his tattered clothes, Mrs. Goforth sends him a black samurai robe, complete with heavy sword, as once worn by her beloved sixth husband, who, like Chris, was a poet. Burton spends the rest of the movie in the robe, not to be confused with *The Robe* (which was red). He has several increasingly mystifying scenes with Joanna Shimkus as Blackie, Mrs. Goforth's recently widowed secretary. Initially, he shows her one of his metal mobiles that he has brought along with him, making a case for himself as an artist as well as a poet, though he tells her he's "a professional houseguest." Later, he begins to seduce her and they share a kissing scene, perhaps because of his instinct for giving people whatever they need, which in her case might be affection. However, Burton comes off as a veteran seducer, not a healer. He looks too impure to suggest such selflessness, primed more for a nightcap than a therapeutic encounter. The next morning it looks as though he might rape Blackie, further confusing the character and his objectives. Not one aspect of Chris is credible in the form of Richard Burton.

The Witch of Capri (Noël Coward), Mrs. Goforth's dinner guest, invites Chris for a visit, encouraging him to leave here before another death furthers his fearsome reputation. Though Chris is a man with a mission, he gives mixed signals, a bewildering combination. As he did with Blackie, he uses his sexuality to try to reach Mrs. Goforth. Struck by his physical appeal, she notices that he keeps "fiddling" with his sword. He provokes a violent verbal outburst from her when he skinny-dips in her presence. Perhaps Chris does whatever he thinks will spark the attention of those he yearns to help, yet he never seems like a character who thinks and then makes

decisions. Despite the blatant opportunities and the drama's outright demands, Burton seems oblivious to the subtextual possibilities in Chris' use of sex. He simply goes through the motions. Though the character has a definite function—to be present at Mrs. Goforth's demise—Burton's Chris is too amorphous, unconvincing on either mortal or spiritual levels. If he wants to help her and presumably go on to the next soul in need, why does he inquire about taking up residence in her beachside grass hut? He occasionally utters, "Boom," signifying "the shock of each moment…of still being alive," the opposite of death, the I'm-still-here feeling that remains until the final breath. Chris uses "boom" similarly to the way *Iguana*'s Shannon said "fantastic," as a way to express the unfathomable essence of being alive. But whereas "fantastic" was a gut response from Burton's Shannon, "boom" feels pasted onto his Chris.

When Mrs. Goforth invites him into her bedroom, he declines. Frozen in her doorway, he's resentful of her continual refusal to provide him with any food. What happened to his selfless mission? Why pout now? He tells her he's off to visit a woman whose mother just died. Before leaving, he says that he came here to show Mrs. Goforth that she will "need someone or something that'll mean God" to her before she dies, perhaps a hand or a voice but *something*. How exactly can he do this? And when was he going to start? If he does, in fact, presume to offer dying women whatever they need—understanding, tenderness, even sex—he hasn't made a persuasive case for his talents. (Many of the perplexities in Chris might have been corrected if Burton had simply engaged himself and decided who *his* Chris was going to be.) When she later allows him to help her into bed, he tells her the story of how he came to his vocation: by assisting in the drowning suicide of a dying old man. As he speaks, he removes all of the glittering jewelry she is wearing—earrings, several bracelets, a ring—and he examines the pieces, as if appraising them, before setting them down on the bed. It is difficult to pay attention to his monologue because the scene's unavoidable focus becomes the issue of whether or not Chris is going to fleece her, as he may have intended all along. Or he may simply be helping to free her from her materialism, preparing her properly for the other side. He leaves the jewelry on the bed, all except the ring. If he never intended to take

If not for her coughing, Taylor would be put to sleep by Burton's performance in **Boom***, like the rest of us.*

it all, then why did he examine each piece? Adding to the overriding emptiness and sustained unsatisfaction, Burton, now on the terrace, drinks a glass of red wine, flinging the wine bottle off the terrace. He again considers the meaning of "boom" aloud, then looks at the ring and smiles, dropping it into his wine glass ritualistically. He intentionally releases the glass to fall down the mountain. Smiling once more, he laughs and exits. We hear his final "boom" on the soundtrack as the film fades on crashing waves. *Boom* appears to have run out of everything by the end, as if throwing up its hands in the hope that something or other will stick in its nonsensical finale. The ending is a rush of moments fraught with the kind of meaning and significance that can mean and signify anything you want.

Chris is the worst leading male role in the Tennessee Williams films. Though Williams wrote the screenplay, he managed to excise the vulnerability that Chris bares in the play. However, nothing in Burton's performance suggests that he was open to exploring this character's potential. As a man assisting the dying, Burton simply played dead. He actually leaves me wondering what Tab Hunter might have brought to *Boom*, presumably, at the very least, some enthusiasm. Chris is thirty-five in the play, but Burton was past forty and looked every day of it. Whereas the tinkering with the leading characters' ages had been a bonus to the screen version of *Iguana*, it was a mistake in *Boom*. Not only was Taylor much too young and healthy to be Mrs. Goforth, but Burton looked far more worn out than she did. In the two years since *Virginia Woolf*, the Burtons, as a screen team, had declined from artistic and commercial prominence to critical dismissal and box-office poison.

Boom wasn't helped by its emphasis on Taylor's scene-stealing jewelry, a blatant reminder of the Burtons' off-screen extravagance. It was clearly time to take a well-earned professional break from his wife, and so Burton was next seen in *Where Eagles Dare* (1968), a purely action-oriented, *Dirty Dozen*-style WWII picture co-starring Clint Eastwood. Unfortunately, there isn't enough plot or character to make any of the action *matter*. A juvenile comic book, *Where Eagles Dare* is repetitive and blaring, happiest whenever something is exploding. Though a reunion for Burton with *Look Back in Anger*'s Mary Ure, the film made no demands on his abilities. Negligible as it is, *Where Eagles Dare* proved to be a big hit, coming at a time when Burton sorely needed one, especially in light of the embarrassing flop that followed it. In Stanley Donen's *Staircase*, Burton and Rex Harrison play a pitiable gay couple. (Oh boy, Marc Antony and Julius Caesar shacking up!) They live above their shared beauty salon, together for thirty years in what appears to be a homosexual production of *Virginia Woolf*. It is an unkind, witless film, with the stars equally ineffective and removed from their roles. As they mince about, the message is plain: we are not really *like that*. Despite a real issue lurking—the mistreatment of gay men in London—the film is misguided muck, too

poor to resonate on behalf of its cause. Can *Sunday, Bloody Sunday* (1971), with its magnificent, fully dimensional performance by Peter Finch as a gay doctor, really be just two years away from the false and cowardly *Staircase*?

While Taylor's career continued its decline, Burton was still in the game, receiving his sixth Oscar nomination for *Anne of the Thousand Days* (1969), which became both a popular movie and Oscar catnip. In a role coincidentally originated on Broadway by Rex Harrison, Burton stars as Henry VIII opposite a lovely and strong Genevieve Bujold as his Anne Boleyn. The film is a good historical drama, literate and clear and well-mounted, but, like most films of its kind from this era, too long, talky, and pristine-looking (positively spotless). A bearded Burton is durable and emotionally connected, yet he offers no fresh interpretation of Henry. He can't compete with Charles Laughton in *The Private Life of Henry VIII* (1933) or Robert Shaw in *A Man for All Seasons* (1966), but he doesn't even try, bringing neither originality nor a personal stamp to his work. Call it a fine, thoughtful, and immensely forgettable performance, outshone by Bujold's electricity. Burton's acting matches the film's admirable sturdiness and restraint, as well as its overall lack of inspiration. When his Henry has Thomas More beheaded, it strikes me as sly payback for when Paul Scofield's Thomas More beat Burton in the 1966 Oscar race.

Just as Taylor made the mistake of reteaming with director Joseph Losey after *Boom* (in his *Secret Ceremony*), Burton did the same, assuming the title role in an excruciating Losey mess called *The Assassination of Trotsky* (1972), one of those international affairs with a host of actors in a hopeless collision of accents. Hiding behind glasses and a white beard and mustache, Burton's Trotsky is a pontificating

Ten Is More than Enough

Like Paul Newman and Joanne Woodward, the Burtons made ten feature films together, and, as with the Newmans, most of their joint efforts aren't very good. Nor does either couple have thrilling chemistry. Go figure. Born the same year, Burton and Newman were among the more acclaimed and popular male stars of the 1960s, but only Newman was able to sustain his stardom into the 1970s.

snooze. If he seems to be walking through this incoherent movie, well, he *literally* walks through *Under Milk Wood* (1971), serving as the narrator on the soundtrack while strolling through a Welsh town. An adaptation of Dylan Thomas' radio play, in which Burton had appeared in the original 1954 production, this *Under Milk Wood* is a gallant misfire, lovingly attempted but a disservice to anyone experiencing Thomas' piece for the first time. It is hardly a film at all, more a perplexing hybrid, a failed melding of words and visuals. Burton has scenes with neither Peter O'Toole (his *Becket* co-star) nor Taylor, who breezes through in a small role as a whore. Not content with one bad "Faust" movie (*Doctor Faustus*), the Burtons headlined *Hammersmith Is Out* (1972), their final big-screen venture, with Burton having moved from the Faust role to that of Satan. In a broadly conceived and supposedly hilarious modern-dress version (featuring a nose-picking Beau Bridges in the Faust slot), Burton is a sternly straight-faced Devil, an escaped mental patient who remains expressionless. His is a rigidly uninventive performance, creepy and nothing else, though Taylor is no better as Bridges' trashy love interest.

After more off-screen drama with Taylor—divorce, remarriage, divorce—Burton returned to Broadway in triumph, taking over the leading role of the psychiatrist in the long-running original New York production of Peter Shaffer's *Equus,* winning himself a special 1976 Tony Award. The inevitable film version, directed by Sidney Lumet in 1977, garnered Burton his seventh Oscar nomination. As was the case when he lost the statuette to Lee Marvin in *Cat Ballou,* Burton was sidestepped for a lightweight comic turn, with the Academy cuddling up to Richard Dreyfuss in *The Goodbye Girl.* Burton's performance, though, isn't among his finest. Despite his intense concentration and properly burned-out look, he gives an unexciting performance in an admittedly limited role. The film's impact is both pretentious and simplistic as Burton treats a teenage boy (Peter Firth) who has blinded six horses with a metal spike. The story evolves into an examination of passion, with the passionless Burton coming to envy the boy he must regretfully neutralize. It was a prestige project, all right, but Burton's work wasn't quite crowning enough to nab him the elusive Oscar, even though his win would have gone unquestioned as compensation for previously unjust losses, specifically those for *The Spy Who Came in from the Cold* and *Who's Afraid of Virginia Woolf?* He is the only one of the nine leading-role subjects in this book who never won an Oscar.

Burton made his final big-screen appearance in *Nineteen Eighty-Four,* an uncoincidentally 1984 adaptation of George Orwell's 1949 novel of futuristic miseries. The star is a pale and scrawny John Hurt, with Burton in the supporting role of O'Brien, a man of softspoken and gently administered evil, providing a glimpse of what Burton might have been like as Hannibal Lecter. The film is too relentlessly bleak and punishing to be effective, or even watchable. But it had more integrity than many of Burton's film choices in the latter part of his career: remember *Bluebeard* (1972) or *Exorcist II: The Heretic* (1977)? There would be two more wives after Taylor, as Burton's lifetime of hard drinking was increasingly taking its toll. He died from a cerebral hemorrhage at only fifty-eight in 1984.

Like Marlon Brando, Burton had a strikingly inconsistent film career. The two men shared staggering talent and less than the utmost respect for their craft, as witnessed by their choices of material and erratic commitment levels. Despite their markedly different professional backgrounds and on-screen personalities, both were transcendent portrayers of Tennessee Williams characters. Unlike the Williams associations of the other ten performers examined in this book, Burton's two Williams pictures decisively represent him at his best and worst, perfectly elucidating Burton's conflicting sides: in *Iguana,* he is the consummate artist and professional, delivering a revelatory characterization; in *Boom,* he is the lazy celebrity taking the money and running. Put them together and you have a portrait of the incredible yet maddening Richard Burton, actor and star.

Mildred Dunnock

*Mildred Dunnock's finest hour in the movies, as **Baby Doll's** dotty Aunt Rose Comfort, alongside Karl Malden's Archie Lee.*

Mildred Dunnock: Filmography

- *The Corn Is Green (1945)*
- *Kiss of Death (1947)*
- *Death of a Salesman (1951)*
- *I Want You (1951)*
- *Viva Zapata! (1952)*
- *The Girl in White (1952)*
- *The Jazz Singer (1953)*
- *Bad for Each Other (1953)*
- *Hansel and Gretel (1954) (voice only)*
- *The Trouble with Harry (1955)*
- *Love Me Tender (1956)*
- *Baby Doll (1956)*
- *Peyton Place (1957)*
- *The Nun's Story (1959)*
- *The Story on Page One (1959)*
- *Butterfield 8 (1960)*
- *Something Wild (1961)*
- *Sweet Bird of Youth (1962)*
- *Behold a Pale Horse (1964)*
- *Youngblood Hawke (1964)*
- *7 Women (1966)*
- *What Ever Happened to Aunt Alice? (1969)*
- *The Spiral Staircase (1975)*
- *Dragonfly (1976)*
- *The Pick-up Artist (1987)*

Mildred Dunnock (1901-1991)

Academy Award Nominations

- **Best Supporting Actress** of 1951 for *Death of a Salesman*
- **Best Supporting Actress** of 1956 for *Baby Doll*

Aunt Rose Comfort in *Baby Doll* (1956)
Aunt Nonnie in *Sweet Bird of Youth* (1962)

wheelchair-bound woman with an Italian accent is visited by a homicidal maniac in her second-floor apartment. The man is looking for the woman's son, a criminal mistakenly believed to be a squealer. The woman lies about her son's whereabouts. The madman then ties her to the chair, wheels her into the hallway (despite her screams), and then pushes her down the flight of stairs to a crashing death. It is one of the screen's more shocking and brutal murders. The film is *Kiss of Death* (1947), the giggling killer is Richard Widmark (in his screen debut), and the woman is Mildred Dunnock. Her brief, unbilled role may not have offered much of an acting challenge, but the scene became a classic. Movie audiences would thankfully have plenty of time in the next two decades to appreciate Dunnock's talent.

Born on January 25, 1901, Mildred Dunnock came late to acting and didn't have her break until the 1940 Broadway opening of *The Corn Is Green,* in which she supported the legendary Ethel Barrymore. After further New York appearances opposite Tallulah Bankhead in *Foolish Notion* (1945) and Mary Martin and Yul Brynner in *Lute Song* (1946), Dunnock finished the decade in two notable Broadway successes: Lillian Hellman's *Another Part of the Forest* in 1946 and 1947, and then, in one of the American theatre's landmark events, the 1949 premiere of Arthur Miller's *Death of a Salesman,* featuring Dunnock's highly praised performance as Linda, wife of Lee J. Cobb's Willy Loman. She now had a place in theatre history as well as film history, though creating Linda Loman was far more impressive than being flung down a staircase.

Dunnock had made her screen debut in a competent film version of *The Corn Is Green* (1945), repeating her Broadway role as a silly well-off spinster

Everything Old Is New Again

The Corn is Green plays like an 1895 version of *Billy Elliot,* with its talented and impoverished young man, a devoted teacher, and a big test/audition at its climax.

who assists with the new school run by Miss Moffat (Bette Davis). Dunnock gives a pleasing light-comic turn; her character eventually becomes a teacher. Despite being too young, Davis, still at the peak of her stardom, snatched Ethel Barrymore's coveted role as the unmarried British teacher who nurtures the intellect of a gifted Welsh coal miner (John Dall). Davis is forcibly restrained yet still so mannered in what turned out to be her final prestige picture (even though it looks cheap) for Warner Brothers, her home studio. The film is a stagy celebration of literacy, never quite the emotional winner it aims to be, too melodramatic and strenuously "inspiring." But it was a good start for Dunnock.

When she repeated her stage role in the screen version of *Death of a Salesman* (1951), with Fredric March ably filling Cobb's part, Dunnock received a supporting-actress Oscar nomination, losing to *A Streetcar Named Desire*'s Kim Hunter. Another (like *The Corn is Green*) stagy screen adaptation of a hit play, *Death of a Salesman* didn't quite come off, but it was an honorable try and it does preserve the integrity of Dunnock's admired theatre performance. As the 1950s wore on, Dunnock developed a screen persona that, at its worst, could be described as having a saintly smugness, an attitude that could actually make you want to trip her. With her delicate frame and large doe eyes, she positively *screamed* "victim," which was only compounded by bravely long-suffering roles. The quintessential Dunnock role of this kind is the dignified old-maid schoolteacher in the sudsy sensation *Peyton Place* (1957), a woman too good and docile to make a fuss when passed over for the principal's job that is rightly hers. Her masochism, mistaken for wisdom and grace, has an air of virtuous superiority. Another typical Dunnock role is Elizabeth Taylor's doormat mother in *Butterfield 8* (1960), in which she is on the receiving end of one of the great camp lines: "Mama, face it, I was the slut of all time." Dunnock's acting is perfectly fine in both of these trash spectaculars, but for a truly irritating example of Dunnock at her passive-aggressive worst you have to go to the altogether lousy *Bad for Each Other* (1953), in which she plays Charlton Heston's mother. Heston is improbably cast as a brilliant surgeon who sells out for a café-society clientele, lured there by the robotic charms of Bacall-wannabe Lizabeth Scott. Dunnock wants Heston to serve the coal miners (another Dunnock movie about coal miners!), and she can't even show a glimmer of gladness at his personal success, insufferably self-righteous and sanctimonious.

Dunnock had one of her best screen roles in a surprisingly good and virtually unknown biopic, *The Girl in White* (1952), about Emily Dunning, the first woman doctor to practice in a New York hospital (at the turn of the last century). June Allyson plays Emily, and, as dismal as that sounds, she is serviceable in a film that stays true to its feminist impulses right to the end, with Allyson breaking down barriers one person at a time. In this winning and absorbing film, directed with care by John Sturges, Dunnock plays Allyson's inspiration and mentor, a certified M.D. who has been treated like "a glorified midwife" her whole career. It may be yet another hard-knocks spinster role, but Dunnock is strong, dedicated, and perceptive. She is playing a gentle pioneer rather than a victim, and a thrilled supporter of Allyson's strides. The Dunnock-Allyson friendship is one of the loveliest elements in a real sleeper. But film roles for Dunnock in the 1950s were typically less rewarding. She plays the wife of Robert Keith and the mother of Dana Andrews and Farley Granger (all of them unimaginatively cast to type) in *I Want You* (1951), Samuel Goldwyn's Korean War answer to his own WWII-themed blockbuster *The Best Years of Our Lives* (1946), but it lacked the former picture's dramatic verve and vivid characters. *Love Me Tender* (1956) gave Dunnock the distinction (?) of playing the mother of Elvis Presley in his strangely chosen debut vehicle, a derivative post-Civil War western. Grayed and speaking with a country accent, Dunnock was unchallenged dramatically and positioned firmly in the film's background. However, she unexpectedly found herself having some of the title tune sung directly to her by you-know-who.

In 1955, Dunnock created a second unforgettable role on the Broadway stage when she played Big Mama in Tennessee Williams' *Cat on a Hot Tin Roof,* directed by Elia Kazan (who had also directed Dunnock in the stage version of *Death of a Salesman*). She had already appeared in one Kazan film, *Viva Zapata!* (1952), in the insignificant role of Jean Peters' mother, a demure and respectable Mexican lady, barely figuring in the proceedings. Her circumstances were much improved in her second Kazan film, in which actress and director joined forces with Williams on *Baby Doll.* Among the many pleasures and perks of this daring little venture was the inspired casting of Dunnock *against type* as the delightfully dotty Aunt Rose Comfort, complete with a thick and impeccable Southern accent. Gone is the plain and sensible Dunnock and in her place is an eccentric comedienne, a joy to encounter. Her role may be small, but her performance is flawless.

Aunt Rose Comfort is a white-haired granny type, scurrying around a deteriorating mansion in her apron and cap, and sometimes a shawl, almost a nursery-rhyme figure somehow transplanted into much more adult fare. In her first appearance, she is afraid to answer the telephone, a mystifying contraption, then forced to do so at the insistence of Archie Lee (Karl Malden), husband of her niece Baby Doll (Carroll Baker), daughter of Aunt Rose's deceased brother. Essentially playing servant, particularly to her spoiled and beautiful niece, Aunt Rose has been living with the couple for several months, with the filthy kitchen as her domain. She is the kind of maiden-aunt poor relation passed from house to house within a family, never having a place to call her own. Unfortunately, Rose is hard of hearing and she cannot cook. If she were easier to communicate with, or was whipping up fabulous Southern dinners, her presence would be less of a strain on Archie Lee. Dunnock, assisted by her character's convenient deafness, plays much of the film with incessant pleasantness and smiling warmth, in the manner of someone who has always had to be accommodating and easygoing in order to maintain the good will of those hosting her and on whom she is dependent.

Williams gave Aunt Rose a deliciously nonchalant capacity for macabre whimsy. A sweet tooth in an older person is nothing new, but Aunt Rose's taste for chocolate candies goes a bit further. It is her habit to check the newspapers to see if anyone she knows is registered at the county hospital, an institution known for distributing chocolates to its patients. Aunt Rose (off-screen) visits sick friends so she can eat up all their chocolate candies, even when those friends are dying. All we get to see of this is a long-shot image of Dunnock rushing out of the house on her way to the hospital, eager with anticipation for all those satisfying (and free) chocolates. Later, we see her dash out of the house into the rain with a piece of newspaper on her head, no explanation given. Not even bad weather will stop her. The mental picture of Dunnock's Aunt Rose, such a harmless old creature, giddily making her way through hospital hallways on one of her chocolate sprees, is enough to induce broad smiles.

The role would be little more to the film than a charming grace note without her climactic confrontation with Archie Lee. He is steaming because of his suspicions that Baby Doll has been unfaithful to him with Silva Vacarro (Eli Wallach), the man whose thriving business has caused the decline of Archie Lee's cotton gin. A bullying weakling, Archie Lee has taken out many of his frustrations on helpless Aunt Rose, and once again he chooses her as his punching bag. Silva has accepted an invitation to join them for a tense dinner. Though Aunt Rose appears to be a sprite, she can react quickly and carefully when something is important. Walking in on a make-out session between Baby Doll and Silva, her instinctive concern is for her niece's safety, prompting her to hum loudly and turn on a light, warnings about Archie Lee's nearness. And why not? Archie Lee has never been kind or respectful to Aunt Rose, merely (and barely) tolerating her. She goes on to serve the meal in her gracious Southern fashion. "Archie Lee dotes on greens," Dunnock says merrily while Malden considers an unappetizing spoonful of the undercooked vegetable. It turns out that Archie Lee *doesn't* like greens; Aunt Rose has confused him with another relative. He thrusts the greens-filled tureen back into her hands. She giggles about having forgotten to light the stove early enough, her explanation for the less than mouth-watering results. Dunnock remains a sweet and lovable flake, perhaps Aunt Rose's tried-and-true technique for staying in the good graces (and sympathies) of the households in which she has spent her life. But the scene takes a turn when Archie Lee asks her to sit down. Still holding the heavy tureen of greens, Dunnock, wide-eyed and unblinking, obeys with the sense that something bad is about to happen, something that cannot be laughed off. As he speaks about Aunt Rose's future and her past, Dunnock's lips start to tremble. Malden's Archie Lee, in a flash of Stanley Kowalski-style "deliberate cruelty," makes a seemingly feeble individual his target.

But Archie Lee loses out, yet again, even to an apparent ninny like Aunt Rose. Dunnock rises to the occasion of Rose's big serious moment, a proud defense of her life. Fighting back tears, she stands up for herself, speaking of being a help to her relatives, caring for new babies and sick people, always ready to be of aid, "sometimes begged to come." Archie Lee's mean attack is parried without any of her former foolishness, and it becomes an unexpected and touching moment, allowing Aunt Rose to claim her dignity and no longer be dismissed as a joke. "Nobody ever had to put me out," she tells him, and then, without self-pity or hesitancy, "I'll run up and pack." Silva offers her a job and a place to stay, which she accepts. (Silva has stolen Archie Lee's business, his wife's affections, and now even Aunt Rose!) Williams gave Rose this wonderful pay-off, and Dunnock afforded the character the depth and strength to declare herself nobody's victim. The pain of her lonely life also comes through, the acknowledgment that, yes, on some level, she knows she has been a burden, but overriding all of that is the value she knows she brought to those who needed her. She strives to make herself worthy of whatever home she occupies and never wear out her welcome. After all, she wasn't always deaf and forgetful. Archie Lee may have pushed her out but she is the ostensible victor in this battle, the one with self-respect intact. It is a privilege to watch a superlative actress give her underestimated character her due.

At the end, all packed and ready to go, Aunt Rose, looking like Mother Goose, is left behind by Silva. With Archie Lee hauled off by the cops for a drunken shotgun-wielding outburst, and Baby Doll wondering what tomorrow will bring, the film ends with Aunt Rose following her niece back into the house. The final line is Dunnock's sigh of "Oh my, oh my." Rose's future will depend on Baby Doll's next move. Will the young beauty remain with Archie Lee, go off with Silva, or make a completely new start (with Aunt Rose in tow)? *Baby Doll* ends not with a feeling of what comes next, but with the tingle of our *never* knowing what the future holds. In addition to Williams' short play *27 Wagons Full of Cotton*, *Baby Doll* is also based on a second short Williams play, *The Unsatisfactory Supper* (also known as *The Long Stay Cut Short*), which deals exclusively with the Aunt Rose subplot. In the play, both Baby Doll (large and dark-haired) and Archie Lee want to be

Aunt Rose Gets Robbed

Dunnock told author Mike Steen, in *A Look at Tennessee Williams,* that while on location in Mississippi she questioned Williams about Aunt Rose, to which he replied, "Honey, I'm so sick of that old woman! You know more about her than I do anyhow, so do anything you want to do with her." Though what she did got her an Oscar nomination, Dunnock lost the 1956 Best Supporting Actress Academy Award to Dorothy Malone in the color-drenched *Written on the Wind,* the most fully realized of Douglas Sirk's overrated and meticulously orchestrated melodramas. Malone's lively and game turn as the trampy daughter in an oil-rich (but miserable) Texas family resorts to nose-flaring, bosom-heaving, and eye-rolling effects. Though she does a mean mambo, it was hardly award-worthy, nor was the final image of her stroking the phallic model of an oil derrick. Nominees Dunnock or Eileen Heckart *(The Bad Seed)* would have been more deserving Oscar recipients, as well as un-nominated Debbie Reynolds *(The Catered Affair)* or Marie Windsor *(The Killing).*

rid of her. The title refers to that last-straw meal of inedible greens. This sad little play offers Aunt Rose no moment of triumph and no viable alternatives.

Between her two appearances in Williams films, Dunnock was part of the amazing ensemble that supported Audrey Hepburn in Fred Zinnemann's magnificent drama *The Nun's Story,* the finest film in which Dunnock ever appeared, though it is woefully underappreciated today. (I assume its title scares away those expecting something saccharine and sentimental.) Among the many great actresses playing older nuns, Dunnock is the Mistress of Postulants, fundamentally another selfless-teacher role, training Hepburn and her fellow novices in the rituals of the life ahead of them. With her face framed by her habit, Dunnock's prominent eyes have never looked larger. She is gentle but firm, adding both delicacy and weight to a major motion picture. Less memorable appearances include her graciously intimidating mother (of Gig Young) in the barely passable courtroom drama *The Story on Page One* (1959). As the villain of the piece, concealing her machinations under her Southern accent and gentility, Dunnock is undone by an obvious role, a

sweet little killer shark implausibly conceived by writer-director Clifford Odets. The movie is a low-rent *Anatomy of a Murder* (also 1959), aiming to be sexually provocative adult fare but really just a tawdry and lifeless affair starring a narcotized Rita Hayworth struggling in Barbara Stanwyck territory. Dunnock was reteamed with Carroll Baker on the no-budget *Something Wild* (1961), this time as Baker's mother rather than her aunt. A weird, slow drama, it begins promisingly as an exploration of the emotional trauma brought on by Baker's rape, but goes awry when it becomes an awful, offensive hostage thriller. (The film's prime distinction may be its casting of Jean Stapleton as a prostitute.) Directed by Jack Garfein, Baker's husband, this empty movie is occasionally brought to life by an elegant Dunnock as another selfish mother. Her big scene is her fierce and pained meltdown when finally reunited with Baker.

Though Dunnock didn't get to recreate her Big Mama for the movies, she did get the opportunity to bring a Williams role to the screen originated by another actress (Martine Bartlett). Aunt Nonnie in *Sweet Bird of Youth* is miles from Aunt Rose Comfort. Though both characters are Southern spinster ladies taken in by relatives and attached to their pretty blond nieces, Aunt Nonnie is a disappointingly typical Dunnock role, playing into all of the actress' most predictable on-screen qualities: submissive comportment, dewy-eyed stoicism, noble goodness. Nonnie is virtually indistinguishable from many a Dunnock role, but it was also a featured part in a high-profile adaptation of a Williams hit, so why not? In the play, Aunt Nonnie lives with the guilt and hopelessness of having encouraged the relationship between her wealthy niece, Heavenly, and poor-boy Chance Wayne, a union that inadvertently led to a sexually transmitted disease and Heavenly's hysterectomy. The film's adjustment, replacing disease and sterilization with pregnancy and abortion, led to a sentimentalizing of Aunt Nonnie as an old maid who valiantly believes in true love. She functions as a treasured go-between, abetting her Romeo and Juliet in their fight against family opposition. The love story becomes idealized enough to resemble a fairy tale, with a blatantly evil king and his maniacal prince, a saintly princess and her motherly aunt, and a commoner Prince Charming.

In **Sweet Bird of Youth**, Dunnock's Aunt Nonnie warns Paul Newman's Chance to leave St. Cloud for his own safety.

Aunt Nonnie is the sister-in-law of Boss Finley (Ed Begley), head of a powerful and vicious political machine. As the unmarried sister of Finley's deceased wife, Nonnie resides in the Finley mansion, serving as chaperone to her sweet niece, Heavenly (Shirley Knight), while trying to avoid her rotten nephew, Tom Junior (Rip Torn). Dunnock first appears, unselfishly of course, handing out soft drinks to patrolmen outside the mansion. To the Finley men, Nonnie's romantic sympathies brand her as a family traitor, and she probably has been allowed to remain in the house only out of respect for the late Mrs. Finley's assumed affection for her kindly sister. Dunnock emanates Nonnie's quiet pleasure in being a thorn in the sides of her brother-in-law and nephew, while outwardly projecting a presence that seems entirely ineffectual. Though a happy ending seems an impossibility, Nonnie has steadfastly believed in the coupling of Heavenly and Chance (Paul Newman). But when Chance returns home from his

latest dream-chasing adventures, Nonnie tries to keep him from seeing Heavenly out of fear for his safety. Chance doesn't know about the pregnancy or the abortion, and so he is unaware of Boss Finley's impending vengeance. Nonnie rightly believes that Chance could never knowingly harm Heavenly, and she acts accordingly. In Chance's flashbacks to better days, there's Nonnie attending to him with tender affection. Along with Heavenly, they form a loving threesome in the vile world encircling them. Nonnie waits on them, unerringly available for whatever they might need, even if it's just some lemonade. Without them as her purpose, her life would be unendurable loneliness and invisibility.

One of Dunnock's few important moments is her scene with Newman at the tombstone of Chance's mother, just before the start of Easter services. After putting flowers on the grave, she pleads with him to leave town, though she cannot tell him the whole story, knowing that the facts of Heavenly's recent ordeal would only make him want to stay more. Besides, the details are too indelicate to be spoken aloud by someone as mild and modest as Nonnie. Dunnock easily exudes maternal concern and worry as she furtively whispers that she's afraid for him. Later, she will become active in trying to bring the couple together, distracting Heavenly's bodyguard with a picnic basket of fried chicken, which allows Heavenly to take her speedboat to meet Chance at their secret hideaway. At the climactic televised political rally, to which Boss Finley has forced Heavenly's (and therefore Nonnie's) attendance, there is Dunnock dutifully perched with the family on a platform. When the event turns into a riot, sparked by a heckler's question about Heavenly's "illegal operation," Boss Finley's moral-values stance is in jeopardy. But the film dispenses with the play's grim ending, permitting the young lovers to escape by car from Finley's clutches once and for all. Dunnock, as if in hushed prayer, murmurs, "Go," as Ed Begley's Boss Finley calls out to his daughter. The bad guy loses, and the underestimated little-old-lady (like Aunt Rose Comfort before her) has a center-stage moment of triumph, which appears to have made her whole life worth living. Writer-director Richard Brooks gave Dunnock the new closing line, aimed squarely at Begley: "You can go straight to Hell." Reminiscent of "Frankly, my dear…," it is one of those longtime-coming thoughts that is finally expressed out loud. Dunnock delivers the line with a buoyant smile; Nonnie's victory is so beautifully complete.

Though the role offered Dunnock nothing she hadn't done before, she handled it with unqualified professionalism and grace, and at least had the final zinger, the best justification for having accepted such an undemanding part. Another Williams role quickly came her way, back on Broadway, as the Witch of Capri opposite Hermione Baddeley in *The Milk Train Doesn't Stop Here Anymore* (1963). (Dunnock's role would be played by none other than Noël Coward in the 1968 film version known as *Boom*). The play was neither a critical nor commercial success, but film roles continued to come her way. Director Fred Zinnemann (*The Nun's Story*) hired Dunnock again for his *Behold a Pale Horse* (1964), in the small role of the Spanish mother of an absurdly cast Gregory Peck as a famed freedom fighter of the Spanish Civil War. Dunnock's hospital-deathbed performance is tensely concentrated

as she half-whispers her lines to priest Omar Sharif, seeking the clergyman's aid in saving Peck from Anthony Quinn, the military captain using news of Dunnock's imminent demise to lure Peck from France to Spain. (Quinn should be playing Peck's role.) The plot is promising, but the film is turgid and drawn-out, missing its mark.

Dunnock was among the *7 Women* (1966), the final film of John Ford, who apparently saved his worst for last. (Patricia Neal's three strokes necessitated her being replaced by Anne Bancroft as the main "woman.") Set at a mission in 1935 China, the film is an unmitigated debacle, despite one of the best collections of actresses since *The Nun's Story*, including Margaret Leighton and Betty Field. Yet just about all of them are terrible, while the hopelessly dated script plays like parody, with plotting reminiscent of *The Bitter Tea of General Yen* (1933). You're never quite sure how to take it. Played on an obvious studio set, and devoid of period flavor, it is an ugly, flat, and confounding movie. Bancroft plays a butch doctor, and Leighton is the lesbian head of the mission, with Dunnock her assistant. Unlike most of the others, Dunnock avoids embarrassment mostly because she was called upon to play "Mildred Dunnock," staying on safe and unexciting ground while campy hell breaks loose around her. It wasn't much of an improvement to see her in *What Ever Happened to Aunt Alice?* (1969), wherein she is bashed in the head with a shovel by *Sweet Bird's* Geraldine Page. Again in sweet-little-granny mode, Dunnock appears briefly, though her death prompts the main action, the arrival of Ruth Gordon to solve the mystery of her disappearance. But it was more campy rubbish, beneath the actresses carrying it.

Dunnock appeared in a well-received television production of *Death of a Saleman* (1966), reuniting her with Lee J. Cobb seventeen years after they had originated their roles on Broadway. She never again did anything as celebrated on the small screen, though she continued to work in made-for-television movies throughout the 1970s and up to 1982, including an appearance in *The Patricia Neal Story* (1981) in which she played herself. In her mid-eighties, she gave her final big-screen performance in *The Pick-up Artist* (1987), a curiously poor and half-formed romantic comedy. In three short scenes, Dunnock is seen as the diabetic grandmother of the annoying jerk played by Robert Downey, Jr.

Mildred Dunnock died from natural causes at age ninety in 1991. She is best remembered by theatre people as *Death of a Salesman*'s Linda Loman, demanding that "attention must be paid" to her dead husband. To filmgoers, she is the helpless victim of a deranged Richard Widmark, the self-effacing teacher in *Peyton Place,* and just about *everybody's* mother or aunt. In association with Tennessee Williams, she straddled both worlds, the stage and the camera, creating two of his roles on Broadway and committing two of his characters to film. Two of those outings, the film of *Sweet Bird* and the onstage *Milk Train,* are outshone by the other two, the ones directed by Elia Kazan. Though Dunnock's Big Mama in *Cat on a Hot Tin Roof* is lost to all but those who witnessed it, her Aunt Rose Comfort can readily be appreciated as one of the great supporting performances in the Williams films, as well as the finest screen performance the estimable Mildred Dunnock ever gave.

Madeleine Sherwood

In **Cat on a Hot Tin Roof**, there's Madeleine Sherwood's Mae Pollitt, always ready to foist her "no-neck monsters" on Big Daddy, with Big Mama (Judith Anderson) and Gooper (Jack Carson) behind her.

Madeleine Sherwood Filmography

- *Baby Doll (1956)*
- *Cat on a Hot Tin Roof (1958)*
- *Parrish (1961)*
- *Sweet Bird of Youth (1962)*
- *Hurry Sundown (1967)*
- *Pendulum (1969)*
- *Wicked, Wicked (1973)*
- *The Changeling (1980)*
- *Resurrection (1980)*
- *Teachers (1984)*
- *Zwei Frauen (1989)*
- *An Unremarkable Life (1989)*

Madeleine Sherwood (1922-   )

Mae Pollitt in *Cat on a Hot Tin Roof* (1958)
Miss Lucy in *Sweet Bird of Youth* (1962)

*I*f, like me, you were a TV-watching child of the 1960s, or maybe a later devotee of syndicated sitcoms, then your main familiarity with the work of actress Madeleine Sherwood is probably as the dignified Reverend Mother to Sally Field's Sister Bertrille in the one-of-a-kind series *The Flying Nun* (1967-70). In a television decade of domesticated monsters and witches, as well as a Martian, a genie, a talking car and a talking horse, perhaps a ninety-pound airborne nun was the most bizarre notion of them all. Playing straight man to Field's relentlessly upbeat and resourceful antics, Sherwood was the show's backbone, a firm and disciplined (though essentially warmhearted) "boss" who was literally powerless in keeping the feet of the aerodynamically gifted Field on the ground. The San Juan-set series was yet another sixties metaphor (like *Bewitched*) for the burgeoning women's movement, a subversive, if overly cute and cheerful, comedy that showed unbound female power "taking wing." Sherwood has her piece of TV-land immortality, though let's hope that *The Flying Nun* never overshadows her distinguished legacy with Tennessee Williams, onstage and on film. Sherwood is the only subject in this book to have repeated on film two Williams roles that she created on Broadway. She never had much of a film career, but her two Williams movies ensure that she will continue to be watched and admired. Neither role is large, but Sherwood is unforgettable as both characters, making me grateful that she wasn't bypassed in favor of some less deserving actress who just happened to be under contract.

Born Madeleine Thornton in Canada on November 13, 1922, Sherwood came to New York to pursue a theatre career, making her Broadway debut as Kim Stanley's replacement in *The Chase* (1952). Sherwood made her mark in 1953, originating the role of Abigail in *The Crucible*, Arthur Miller's Tony Award-winning allegory about the McCarthy years, set during the Salem witch trials. Sherwood's character was the brazen teenager who instigates all the furor, the jilted lover of the married lead character played by Arthur Kennedy. Her third Broadway show was Williams' *Cat on a Hot Tin Roof* (1955), directed by Elia Kazan. Sherwood and Burl Ives were the only members of the original cast who repeated their roles in the 1958 film. While Ives' performance as Big Daddy seems worn out, too pooped to explode on the movie screen, Sherwood's Mae Pollitt is utterly fresh and vibrant. In between the stage and film versions, Sherwood made her screen debut in a tiny role in Williams' *Baby Doll* (1956), also directed by Kazan. As a blunt receptionist-nurse in a small-town doctor's office, a dark-haired Sherwood deadpans her lines, arms folded. She has only a few words to say, seeming simultaneously nosy and detached, devoid of a bedside manner and decidedly bored. She is a molasses version of Thelma Ritter.

It is easy to see why Sherwood would be asked to repeat the role of Mae in *Cat*: she is perfection in the part. It is, primarily, a comic role, played with utter seriousness. Also known as "Sister Woman," Mae is a light-brown-haired iron butterfly, extremely amusing because she doesn't know she's funny. Sherwood's concentration is staggering; Mae, her mind always spinning furiously, never seems able to relax. She has always played by the rules and done everything right, marrying well by wedding wealthy Gooper Pollitt (Jack Carson), a successful lawyer and the eldest son (and obvious heir) to Big Daddy. Mae has dutifully supplied the family with five offspring and there's one more on the way. She is one of those women who seems to be perpetually pregnant and always healthy as a horse. Her brown maternity dress has a big fat bow on her chest, making her fertility look as though it has been wrapped as a large present for Big Daddy's birthday. Everything should be nice and easy for Mae and Gooper, but they smell trouble. Big Daddy and Big Mama (Judith Anderson) have a second son, Brick (Paul Newman), something of a screw-up but clearly the family favorite. Like Mae, Gooper has lived his life doing what was expected of him, all the while forgetting to acquire a likable personality. With Big Daddy near death, and Brick an unemployed alcoholic with a childless wife, Maggie (Elizabeth Taylor), Mae and Gooper shouldn't have to be working this hard to get attention. With no certainty that Big Daddy is going to leave Gooper in charge, Mae is in an ongoing state of pro-active panic. Could Big Daddy be thinking of leaving his estate to the favored but incompetent Brick? Is it Mae and Gooper's fault that they are not naturally lovable? Mae may be a schemer, but she's so fallible as to be almost endearing. Her great flaw, so perceptively captured in Sherwood's performance, is that she tries too hard at everything she does.

Mae cannot compete with Maggie in the beauty and charm departments, but her ace in the hole is those kids, which she shamelessly trots out at every opportunity, parading them before Big Daddy like sandwich boards announcing that his name will be carried on (thanks to her). But the ornery Big Daddy cannot stand his grandchildren, so snidely described by Maggie as "no-neck monsters." Sherwood is first seen, whistle in her mouth, stalwartly conducting her brood's rehearsal of "Dixie," with each child playing a different instrument. (One boy carries a Confederate flag.) At the airport, greeting Big Daddy's return from a clinic, the kiddies deliver their "Dixie" performance, but Big Daddy doesn't care. Sherwood tells the kids to "Hush up," as if they've failed her, which, to Mae's way of thinking, they have. Instead of allowing the children to offer their grandfather spontaneous merriment, Mae has created her own little army of wind-up horrors. Sherwood plays Mae like the fly you swat away who returns a second later determined as ever to annoy you. Though easily hurt, she heals rapidly. Sherwood stays focused on Burl Ives, as Mae makes her persistent appeals for Big Daddy's love and attention, not realizing that her sledgehammer tactics are never going to work, especially that repertoire of sickening songs she has taught the children. Sherwood makes a big show of naming all the immunization shots the kids have received, another of Mae's pronouncements of how damned fertile she is. It is Mae who takes center stage to carry Big Daddy's enormous candle-lit cake as "Happy Birthday" is

Oops!

For those who like to catch movie mistakes, watch for the following mismatched shots: Sherwood first appears in a long shot, leading her children's marching band, then is immediately seen in a medium shot and suddenly *behind* the kids.

sung, again anticipating recognition and appreciation that do not come. She "acts" warm and daughterly because, try though she might, those attributes simply do not come naturally to her.

In one of Maggie's monologues to Brick, she speaks of Mae's past. Born Mae Flynn, of the "Memphis Flynns," she was later "Queen of the Cotton Carnival." It is no surprise that Mae was a pageant winner, however small-time, since Sherwood's performance approaches each scene with the objective of something to be won, evoking the pageant-girl mix of proper manners and killer instincts. Sherwood, more often than not on the offensive, plays Mae like a Southern barracuda. Notice her skulking around, trying to overhear bits of information as she zips through the background of a scene. Her accent is thick and syrupy, a reminder that there's no one as Southern as she is, no one more appropriate to become the next great lady of the Pollitt plantation. Big Mama appears to be the person Mae is trying to emulate; both women seem to be clueless when it matters most, and both manage to irritate their husbands regularly. Like Big Mama, Mae has a big mouth that is often abruptly stifled by her husband, yet both women tend to push things as far as they can before succumbing to wifely obedience. Add Brick's disgust for Maggie, and no Pollitt man seems able to stand his wife. Maggie and Mae share little, aside from distaste for each other, but Big Daddy notices that "they don't look peaceful." They are both fighting for their men, and both appear more primed for the fight than their husbands do.

In the makeshift birthday-party scene in Brick and Maggie's bedroom, Mae makes a point of catching Maggie in a lie about the gift Brick supposedly picked out for Big Daddy. A salesgirl told Mae that it was Maggie who bought the present. Sherwood smugly scores a point, even though no one takes notice, making it pathetically plain that Mae never seems to understand which points count and which don't. Big Daddy dismisses everyone so he can have a private conversation with Brick, his troubled boy. Before long, Big Daddy catches Mae eavesdropping and confronts her. She wants to know why he's so hurtful to "those that really love you." And she means it, in her way. She has done nothing but the right things, the expected things, the planned things. She is on far less secure ground when trying to decipher feelings and emotions, elements that can't be easily measured or tallied. With Big Daddy's cancer death imminent, Gooper and Mae start circling Big Mama, seeking her support. Sherwood gives Mae her due, battling unwaveringly for her neglected husband against his drunken baby brother (and lying wife). Williams has been somewhat unfair to Mae and Gooper, making them the too-easy flat-out villains of Act III, encouraging the viewer to abhor them. But why shouldn't Gooper be given more responsibility than Brick at this particular moment? And why is Gooper so poorly regarded by his parents? Mae and Gooper's crime is more about style than content. Along with not being amiable and charismatic, they are aggressive and inappropriate, particularly now when openly addressing the Pollitt family future while Big Daddy is still very much alive.

Sherwood lets go of what little grace and tact Mae had, showing more steely confidence and sarcasm away from Big Daddy (who is now in the basement with Brick). It is juicy fun to watch Sherwood once Mae really gets going and can't quite turn herself off, such as when she's equating Brick's experience with footballs and highballs. Her best crack is the one about Brick's big athletic success in "The Punch Bowl." She is now the viperous and grasping pageant girl unmasked. But she does get a moment of speechless mortification when she runs into Brick at the stairs and he corrects her: "It was the Cotton Bowl." Another blow arrives when Elizabeth Taylor delivers Maggie's lie about being pregnant. Sherwood, after the initial shock, closes her eyes; Mae knows temporary defeat when she hears it. As Big Daddy and Big Mama make peace, and even Brick and Gooper have a friendly moment, Mae is unjustly left dangling as the person everyone can dislike. She is correct in shouting that Maggie's lie *is* a lie, but even her husband turns on her. Again, the writing seems unfairly tilted against Mae, overeager to put her in her place. She continues grilling Brick about Maggie's nightly sexual pleas and his refusals, but Sherwood's performance eventually comes to a vanquished end, looking for support from her mate which never comes. Instead, Gooper gives her one last "Shut up!" (which isn't in the play), reducing Mae to an almost comic villain, someone we can laugh at as Brick and Maggie go to their bedroom for the happy-ending fornication. But Sherwood has made Mae too interesting and complicated to be dispatched so casually, despite her unflattering behavior. It is hard to dislike Mae

because Sherwood never plays her as the caricature she might easily become in lesser hands. When a character is this inadvertently amusing, touchingly misguided, and truly doing the best that she can, it is no pleasure to witness her as she is finally seen, sitting at the bottom of the stairs and absorbing her crushing loss. But for Sherwood's Mae let's just call it a setback because we know she will soon be counting the months until Maggie's due date, hoping against hope that there won't be any baby. Mae ought to be on to number seven by then.

After not receiving the Oscar nomination she deserved for *Cat,* Sherwood took her next film role in the lavishly mounted and colorful piece of crap known as *Parrish* (1961), a family epic intended to do for tobacco what *Giant* had done for cattle and oil. While the star was the handsome dead weight known as Troy Donahue, Sherwood was no more than a glorified extra, a tobacco-farm field hand, sassy and loose but vanishing before ever emerging. What a sight: our Mae Pollitt, no longer trying to seize control of a plantation, reduced to working one! Far better for Sherwood, an Actors Studio member, was her time on Broadway. Before appearing with Jane Fonda, Eileen Heckart, and Celeste Holm (what a cast!) in Arthur Laurents' *Invitation to a March* (1960), she created the role of Miss Lucy in Williams' *Sweet Bird of Youth* (1959). With fellow cast members Paul Newman, Geraldine Page, and Rip Torn, Sherwood went on to appear in the 1962 film version. Though her role is fairly small, it's no wonder that Sherwood was brought along with the others. The film's writer-director was *Cat's* Richard Brooks, and, after her performance for him as Mae, how could he *not* want to work with her again? And how gratifying for Sherwood to be able to commit to film two such disparate stage characters, little-miss-perfect Mae and kept-woman Lucy. The only similarity is their dripping Southern accents.

The first reference to Miss Lucy comes when Heavenly (Shirley Knight) mentions the name to her cruel big-shot father, Boss Finley (Ed Begley), knowing full well that Lucy is daddy's longtime mistress. He denies knowing such a person, even though *everyone* knows about Miss Lucy, his paid lover since before his wife's death. Heavenly speaks of Lucy's fifty-dollar-a-day suite of rooms at the Regal Palms Hotel, plus her array of expense accounts. She then can't resist repeating the gossip about what Miss Lucy wrote in lipstick on the ladies-room mirror in the hotel bar: "Boss Finley can't cut the mustard." This is an unusually enticing build-up to a character's entrance, while also setting Boss Finley's inevitable revenge into motion. When he enters Lucy's suite, there's Sherwood, sitting half-dressed, enjoying the clichés of a blond bimbo, manicuring her toenails and eating candy as two televisions blare in two untidy rooms. After so many years of prostituting herself to an old, fat fellow whom she probably loathes, Lucy has gotten a bit lazy. She still enjoys the perks of their arrangement but the rest is simple endurance. His foul mood must be addressed, requiring Lucy to stir from her slumber and shift gears. Sherwood shrewdly, and quite entertainingly, goes into automatic pilot, launching Lucy's presumably usual show of titillating effects. She puts on a new negligee (her Easter present for him) and re-emerges with a "Ta-da!" Swirling about the room like Ginger Rogers, she then literally barks at him as if starting a bout of foreplay, but everything she does, however energized, feels like the rote routine of a bored hooker's umpteenth performance. (Lucy isn't one of those mistresses delusionally waiting for, or even wanting, a wedding ring.) Considering her "cut the mustard" comment, it must be hard work keeping a flaccid coot feeling like a great lover. His gold-boxed gift delights her (it is, after all, a present), and she girlishly continues to play dumber than she clearly is. Inside an elegant Fabergé Easter egg is a piece of glittering jewelry. He bangs the egg closed on her finger, eliciting two howls from Sherwood that seem to come as much from surprise as pain. Then he slaps her across the face, sending her into a frozen amazement, which eventually leads to tears and more screams. Telling her off with a smile, he tears her new negligee, trashes the room a bit, and then exits. She didn't play fair with him and should have known the viciousness of which he was capable, but Lucy, mired in her materialistic rut, apparently thought she could amuse herself by mocking him and still get away with it. Boredom was her undoing. Lucy may end up regretting the loss of Boss Finley's financial support, but she plainly needed to do something mischievous or bust. In the play, Sherwood merely got to recount this incident, instead of acting it out in all its gaudy display of sex and violence.

If Lucy underestimated Finley, well, he does the same with her. With her finger now bandaged, Sherwood is next seen entering a phone booth, as Lucy places an anonymous call to Finley's political opposition. Into the phone, she says deviously, "It takes a hillbilly to cut down a hillbilly, and that's *me*," all the while looking pointedly at her damaged finger. Plotting to disrupt Finley's televised political rally that evening, she instructs her would-be heckler to ask, "Why did Boss Finley make Dr. Scudder chief of staff at the hospital?" (The answer is that Scudder performed Heavenly's abortion.) When the expelled Lucy is later told at the hotel desk that her bill is paid in full, Sherwood insinuatingly replies, "That's what you think."

Miss Lucy is a character who presents a new facet of her personality each time she appears. After her role-playing as a dim-witted sex kitten, followed by her cool malice on the telephone, Sherwood then appears as what might be called the *real* Lucy, the good-natured, no-bull gal. When she spots Chance Wayne (Paul Newman) in the hotel lobby, she calls out, open-armed, "Chance High-Stepping Wayne!" Hugging him, she continues, "Honey, you used to be so attractive I couldn't stand it…now I can…*almost* stand it," which moves gracefully from compliment to friendly jab and back to compliment. She comfortably relates to him as a fellow whore, though it's unclear how much Lucy knows about Chance's exploits outside the South. It is a happy reunion, the intimation being that they had been good friends, perhaps because they were both from the wrong side of the tracks. Now they also share a sense of being aging players in a young person's market. (It's gratifying to see Sherwood and Newman getting along so well after all their Mae-Brick tensions in *Cat*.) Here Sherwood is a loose, likable, and relaxed broad with a breezy self-deprecating side. When Chance tells her she looks like a million dollars, she alters that by adding, "Confederate money." Boss Finley has by now cancelled all her perks, providing only a one-way ticket to New Orleans. (It's a nice touch that Sherwood holds up her lone injured finger, a tangible reminder of the incident, when she says "one-way.") When Chance takes a pill, which he says increases his feeling of fun, a skeptical Lucy replies, "Honey, I'm an expert at pretending to have fun," a nifty new line that allows Sherwood again to deepen our sense of Lucy as a clear-eyed, seen-it-all dame. Maybe in New Orleans Miss Lucy won't have to pretend anymore, or maybe she will just end up pretending anew for another sugar daddy.

*Moments before Miss Lucy (Sherwood) receives her comeuppance from Boss Finley (Ed Begley) in **Sweet Bird of Youth**.*

Miss Lucy comes to the rescue of Chance's current "employer," the film star Alexandra Del Lago (Geraldine Page), when Alexandra is temporarily abandoned by him at the hotel. Lucy offers Southern Comfort, literally and figuratively, potentially bonding with another woman who knows about hard knocks and the inevitability of losing one's youth. Too bad Sherwood and Page don't have a full-scale scene together, perhaps laughing over cocktails while comparing their extensive sexual histories (even though they currently work opposite sides of the prostitute-client relationship). Alexandra later tells Chance that she has secured Miss Lucy to drive her as far as New Orleans. That's the sequel I want to see, the road trip of Alexandra and Lucy. (In the play, Boss Finley's son, Tom, arranges for a trooper to chauffeur Alexandra out of town.) All that's left of Sherwood's performance are reaction shots at the rally. Following the heckler's riotous disruption, she smiles to herself before disappearing into the crowd. Her screen time may be minimal, but each of Sher-

wood's three major scenes is memorable, and the development of her character is a pleasure to watch. Instead of the traditional whore with a heart of gold, which she has definite traces of, Miss Lucy is more the whore with a heart of vengeance.

Not long after completing the *Sweet Bird* film, Sherwood tackled another Williams role, this time a lead. She was among the actresses, including Bette Davis and Shelley Winters, who played Maxine Faulk (a character closer to Miss Lucy than to Mae) on Broadway in the original production of *The Night of the Iguana*. Other Broadway credits for Sherwood include the musical *Do I Hear a Waltz?* (1965), written by Richard Rodgers, Stephen Sondheim, and Arthur Laurents, in which she played one of the Americans abroad in Venice. On the recording, she acquits herself more than ably in three group numbers. She spent the following season in John Osborne's hit play *Inadmissible Evidence*. After her *Flying Nun* years, she returned to Broadway, along with Jessica Tandy and Colleen Dewhurst, in

Edward Albee's *All Over* (1971), directed by no less than John Gielgud. In the 1970s, she worked primarily on the small screen, doing guest shots on series, stints on soap operas, and featured roles in made-for-television movies.

Nothing in Sherwood's film career ever came close to the quality of her appearances in her Williams pictures, with most of her other films barely meriting even passing mentions. She is part of a big-name ensemble cast, led by Jane Fonda and Michael Caine, in Otto Preminger's deplorable Southern drama *Hurry Sundown* (1967), a positively laughable travesty. Sherwood plays the society-conscious wife of a racist Georgian judge (hammy Burgess Meredith) and easily walks off with the movie with just a few scenes. Unlike most of her co-players, she is able to be larger than life yet still convey a real person, filling each moment with witty details and imaginative bits of business that ground her horror of a character. Fonda and Caine may be hilarious but Sherwood is *intentionally* funny. Overly battered and then fried to a crisp, *Hurry Sundown* exhibits the downside of Tennessee Williams' influence, the tasteless imitations his work spawned.

Pendulum (1969) is a TV-style thriller with serious pretensions, with star George Peppard underplaying to the point of unconsciousness and Jean Seberg getting killed off early (in the tradition of *Psycho's* Janet Leigh). Sherwood's role is showy—the blowsy, boozy mother of a killer—but the film is so poorly written that not even she can rise above it. Later films of hers include *The Changeling* (1980), *Resurrection* (1980), and *Teachers* (1984), all of which cast her in incidental roles. She made her final pre-retirement big-screen appearance in *An Unremarkable Life* (1989), a *Whales of August*-type endeavor, this time starring Patricia Neal and Shelley Winters as sisters. Though the film is clumsy and slow-going, the actresses fill in many of the blanks, while Sherwood has only a teensy part as a bingo player in one scene with Winters.

If Sherwood hadn't repeated her stage roles of Mae Pollitt and Miss Lucy on film, would there be enough evidence available of her singular talent? Without those screen performances, she might now be little more than a name in old *Playbills*. Television made her a familiar face, especially to those partial to sitcom nuns, but her most enduring work remains the film versions of *Cat on a Hot Tin Roof* and *Sweet Bird of Youth*. There is much to complain about in both those pictures, but, when their virtues are considered, chief among them is Sherwood, who rejuvenates both films whenever she appears, dispensing some of the presumed excitement that each play aroused in the theatre.

Selected Bibliography

Brando, Marlon (with Robert Lindsey). *Songs My Mother Taught Me*. Random House, 1994.

Bragg, Melvyn. *Richard Burton: A Life*. Little, Brown and Company, 1988.

Edwards, Anne. *Vivien Leigh*. Simon and Schuster, 1977.

Grobel, Lawrence. *The Hustons*. Charles Scribner's Sons, 1989.

Hirsch, Foster. *Elizabeth Taylor*. Pyramid Publications, 1973.

Jordan, Rene. *Marlon Brando*. Pyramid Publications, 1973.

Kazan, Elia. *A Life*. Alfred A. Knopf, 1988.

Kerbel, Michael. *Paul Newman*. Pyramid Publications, 1974.

Leverich, Lyle. *Tom: The Unknown Tennessee Williams*. Crown Publishers, Inc., 1995.

Lumet, Sidney. *Making Movies*. Alfred A. Knopf, 1995.

Malden, Karl (with Carla Malden). *When Do I Start?* Simon and Schuster, 1997.

Manso, Peter. *Brando: The Biography*. Hyperion, 1994.

McGilligan, Pat. *Backstory 2: Interviews with Screenwriters of the 1940s and 1950s*. University of California Press, 1991.

Parish, James Robert. *Hollywood's Great Love Teams*. Arlington House Publishers, 1974.

Phillips, Gene D. *The Films of Tennessee Williams*. Associated University Presses, Inc., 1980.

Pistagnesi, Patrizia. *Anna Magnani*. Fabbri Editori, 1988.

Quintero, José. *If You Don't Dance They Beat You*. Little, Brown and Company, 1974.

Shipman, David. *The Great Movie Stars: The International Years*. St. Martin's Press, 1972.

Staggs, Sam. *When Blanche Met Brando: The Scandalous Story of "A Streetcar Named Desire."* St. Martin's Press, 2005.

Steen, Mike. *A Look at Tennessee Williams*. Hawthorn Books, Inc., 1969.

Thomas, Tony. *The Films of Marlon Brando*. Citadel Press, 1973.

Thornton, Margaret Bradham. *Notebooks*. Yale University Press, 2006.

Vermilye, Jerry and Mark Ricci. *The Films of Elizabeth Taylor*. Citadel Press, 1976.

Williams, Tennessee. *Collected Stories*. New Directions, 1985.

Williams, Tennessee. *Memoirs*. Doubleday and Company, Inc., 1975.

Yacowar, Maurice. *Tennessee Williams and Film*. Frederick Ungar Publishing Company, 1977.

The Tennessee Williams Filmography

The Glass Menagerie (1950, Warner Brothers). Director: Irving Rapper; Producers: Charles K. Feldman and Jerry Wald; Screenplay: Tennessee Williams and Peter Berneis, based on the play by Williams; Cinematography: Robert Burks; Art Direction: Robert Haas; Editing: David Weisbart; Costume Design: Milo Anderson; Original Score: Max Steiner. 107 minutes. CAST: Gertrude Lawrence (Amanda Wingfield), Arthur Kennedy (Tom Wingfield), Jane Wyman (Laura Wingfield), Kirk Douglas (Jim O'Connor).

A Streetcar Named Desire (1951, Warner Brothers). Director: Elia Kazan; Producer: Charles K. Feldman; Screenplay: Tennessee Williams (adaptation by Oscar Saul), based on the play by Williams; Cinematography: Harry Stradling; Art Direction: Richard Day; Editing: David Weisbart; Costume Design: Lucinda Ballard; Original Score: Alex North. 125 minutes. CAST: Vivien Leigh (Blanche DuBois), Marlon Brando (Stanley Kowalski), Kim Hunter (Stella Kowalski), Karl Malden (Harold Mitchell). Academy Awards for Actress (Leigh), Supporting Actor (Malden), Supporting Actress (Hunter), and Art Direction (black and white). Academy Award nominations for Picture, Actor (Brando), Director, Screenplay, Cinematography (black and white), Costume Design (black and white), Sound, and Score.

Senso (1954, Lux). Director: Luchino Visconti; Producer: Domenico Forges Davanzati; Screenplay: Luchino Visconti and Suso Cecchi D'Amico, with additional dialogue by Tennessee Williams and Paul Bowles, based on the novella by Camillo Boito; Cinematography: G. R. Aldo and Robert Krasker; Art Direction: Ottavio Scotti and Gino Brosio; Editing: Mario Serandrei; Costume Design: Marcel Escoffier and Piero Tosi. 116 minutes. CAST: Alida Valli (Countess Livia Serpieri), Farley Granger (Lt. Franz Mahler), Massino Girotti (Marquis Roberto Ussoni).

The Rose Tattoo (1955, Paramount). Director: Daniel Mann; Producer: Hal B. Wallis; Screenplay: Tennessee Williams (adaptation by Hal Kanter), based on the play by Williams; Cinematography: James Wong Howe; Art Direction: Hal Pereira and Tambi Larsen; Editing: Warren Low; Costume Design: Edith Head; Original Score: Alex North. 117 minutes. CAST: Anna Magnani (Serafina delle Rose), Burt Lancaster (Alvaro Mangiacavallo), Marisa Pavan (Rosa delle Rose), Ben Cooper (Jack Hunter), Virginia Grey (Estelle), Jo Van Fleet (Bessie), Sandro Giglio (Father De Leo). Academy Awards for Actress (Magnani), Cinematography (black and white), Art Direction (black and white). Academy Award nominations for Picture, Supporting Actress (Pavan), Editing, Costume Design (black and white), and Score.

Baby Doll (1956, Warner Brothers). Director and Producer: Elia Kazan; Screenplay: Tennessee Williams, based on his plays *27 Wagons Full of Cotton* and *The Unsatisfactory Supper*; Cinematography: Boris Kaufman; Art Direction: Richard Sylbert; Editing: Gene Milford; Costume Design: Anna Hill Johnstone; Original Score: Kenyon Hopkins. 115 minutes. CAST: Karl Malden (Archie Lee Meighan), Carroll Baker (Baby Doll Meighan), Eli Wallach (Silva Vacarro), Mildred Dunnock (Aunt Rose Comfort), Madeleine Sherwood (Nurse), Rip Torn (Dentist). Academy Award nominations for Adapted Screenplay, Actress (Baker), Supporting Actress (Dunnock), and Cinematography (black and white).

Cat on a Hot Tin Roof (1958, MGM). Director: Richard Brooks; Producer: Lawrence Weingarten; Screenplay: Richard Brooks and James Poe, based on the play by Tennessee Williams; Cinematography: William Daniels; Art Direction: William A. Horning and Urie McCleary; Editing: Ferris Webster; Costume Design: Helen Rose. 108 minutes. CAST: Elizabeth Taylor (Maggie Pollitt), Paul Newman (Brick Pollitt), Burl Ives (Big Daddy), Jack Carson (Gooper), Judith Anderson (Big Mama), Madeleine Sherwood (Mae), Larry Gates (Doc Baugh).

Academy Award nominations for Picture, Actor (Newman), Actress (Taylor), Director, Adapted Screenplay, and Cinematography (color).

Suddenly, Last Summer (1959, Columbia). Director: Joseph L. Mankiewicz; Producer: Sam Spiegel; Screenplay: Gore Vidal and Tennessee Williams, based on the play by Williams; Cinematography: Jack Hildyard; Production Design: Oliver Messel; Art Direction: William Kellner; Editing: Thomas G. Stanford; Original Score: Malcolm Arnold and Buxton Orr. 114 minutes. CAST: Elizabeth Taylor (Catherine Holly), Katharine Hepburn (Violet Venable), Montgomery Clift (Dr. Cukrowicz), Albert Dekker (Dr. Hockstader), Mercedes McCambridge (Mrs. Holly), Gary Raymond (George Holly). Academy Award nominations for Actress (both Taylor and Hepburn) and Art Direction (black and white).

The Fugitive Kind (1960, United Artists). Director: Sidney Lumet; Producers: Martin Jurow and Richard A. Shepherd; Screenplay by Tennessee Williams and Meade Roberts, based on the play *Orpheus Descending* by Williams; Cinematography: Boris Kaufman; Art Direction: Richard Sylbert; Editing: Carl Lerner; Costume Design: Frank Thompson; Original Score: Kenyon Hopkins. 121 minutes. CAST: Marlon Brando (Val Xavier), Anna Magnani (Lady Torrance), Joanne Woodward (Carol Cutrere), Victor Jory (Jabe Torrance), Maureen Stapleton (Vee Talbott), R. G. Armstrong (Sheriff Talbott), John Baragrey (David Cutrere), Virgilia Chew (Nurse), Emory Richardson (Uncle Pleasant).

Summer and Smoke (1961, Paramount). Director: Peter Glenville; Producer: Hal B. Wallis; Screenplay: James Poe and Meade Roberts, based on the play by Tennessee Williams; Cinematography: Charles Lang, Jr.; Art Direction: Hal Pereira and Walter Tyler; Editing: Warren Low; Costume Design: Edith Head; Original Score: Elmer Bernstein. 118 minutes. CAST: Geraldine Page (Alma Winemiller), Laurence Harvey (John Buchanan), Rita Moreno (Rosa Zacharias), Una Merkel (Mrs. Winemiller), John McIntire (Dr. Buchanan), Thomas Gomez (Papa Zacharias), Pamela Tiffin (Nellie Ewell), Malcolm Atterbury (Reverend Winemiller), Earl Holliman (Traveling Salesman), Lee Patrick (Mrs. Ewell), Casey Adams (Roger Doremus). Academy Award nominations for Actress (Page), Supporting Actress (Merkel), Art Direction (color), and Score.

The Roman Spring of Mrs. Stone (1961, Warner Brothers). Director: José Quintero; Producer: Louis de Rochemont; Screenplay: Gavin Lambert, based on the novella by Tennessee Williams; Cinematography: Harry Waxman; Production Design: Roger Furse; Art Direction: Herbert Smith; Editing: Ralph Kemplen; Costume Design: Beatrice Dawson and Balmain of Paris; Original Score: Richard Addinsell. 104 minutes. CAST: Vivien Leigh (Karen Stone), Warren Beatty (Paolo di Leo), Lotte Lenya (the Contessa), Coral Browne (Meg Bishop), Jill St. John (Barbara Bingham), Jeremy Spenser (the Young Man). Academy Award nomination for Supporting Actress (Lenya).

Sweet Bird of Youth (1962, MGM). Director: Richard Brooks; Producer: Pandro S. Berman; Screenplay: Richard Brooks, based on the play by Tennessee Williams; Cinematographer: Milton Krasner; Art Direction: George W. Davis and Urie McCleary; Editing: Henry Berman; Costume Design: Orry-Kelly. 120 minutes. CAST: Paul Newman (Chance Wayne), Geraldine Page (Alexandra Del Lago), Shirley Knight (Heavenly Finley), Ed Begley (Boss Finley), Rip Torn (Tom Finley, Jr.), Mildred Dunnock (Aunt Nonnie), Madeleine Sherwood (Miss Lucy). Academy Award for Supporting Actor (Begley). Academy Award nominations for Actress (Page) and Supporting Actress (Knight).

Period of Adjustment (1962, MGM). Director: George Roy Hill; Producer: Lawrence Weingarten; Screenplay: Isobel Lennart, based on the play by Tennessee Williams; Cinematography: Paul C. Vogel; Art Direction: George W. Davis and Edward Carfagno; Editing: Fredric Steinkamp; Original Score: Lyn Murray. 111 minutes. CAST: Jane Fonda (Isabel Haverstick), Tony Franciosa (Ralph Bates), Jim Hutton (George Haverstick), Lois Nettleton (Dorothea Bates), John McGiver (Stewart P. McGill), Mabel Albertson (Alice McGill). Academy Award nomination for Art Direction (black and white).

The Night of the Iguana (1964, MGM). Director: John Huston; Producer: Ray Stark; Screenplay: John Huston and Anthony Veiller, based on the play by Tennessee Williams; Cinematography: Gabriel Figueroa; Art Direction: Stephen Grimes; Editing: Ralph Kemplen; Costume Design: Dorothy Jeakins; Original Score: Benjamin Frankel. 118 minutes. CAST: Richard Burton (Reverend T. Lawrence Shannon), Ava Gardner (Maxine Faulk), Deborah

Kerr (Hannah Jelkes), Sue Lyon (Charlotte Goodall), Grayson Hall (Judith Fellowes), James Ward (Hank), Cyril Delevanti (Nonno). Academy Award for Costume Design (black and white). Academy Award nominations for Supporting Actress (Hall), Cinematography (black and white), and Art Direction (black and white).

This Property Is Condemned (1966, Paramount). Director: Sydney Pollack; Producer: John Houseman; Screenplay: Francis Coppola, Fred Coe, and Edith Sommer, based on a short play by Tennessee Williams; Cinematography: James Wong Howe; Production Design: Stephen Grimes; Art Direction: Phil Jefferies; Editing: Adrienne Fazan; Costume Design: Edith Head; Original Score: Kenyon Hopkins. 110 minutes. CAST: Natalie Wood (Alva Starr), Robert Redford (Owen Legate), Kate Reid (Hazel Starr), Mary Badham (Willie Starr), Charles Bronson (J. J. Nichols), Robert Blake (Sidney), Dabney Coleman (Salesman).

Boom (1968, Universal). Director: Joseph Losey; Producers: John Heyman and Norman Priggen; Screenplay: Tennessee Williams, based on his play *The Milk Train Doesn't Stop Here Anymore*; Cinematography: Douglas Slocombe; Production Design: Richard MacDonald; Editing: Reginald Beck; Costume Design: Tiziani of Rome; Original Score: John Barry. 113 minutes. CAST: Elizabeth Taylor (Flora Goforth), Richard Burton (Chris Flanders), Noël Coward (The Witch of Capri), Joanna Shimkus (Blackie), Michael Dunn (Rudy).

The Last of the Mobile Hotshots (1970, Warner Brothers). Director and Producer: Sidney Lumet; Screenplay: Gore Vidal, based on the play *The Seven Descents of Myrtle* by Tennessee Williams; Cinematography: James Wong Howe; Production Design:

Gene Callahan; Editing: Alan Heim; Costume Design: Patricia Zipprodt; Music: Quincy Jones. 108 minutes. CAST: James Coburn (Jeb), Lynn Redgrave (Myrtle), Robert Hooks (Chicken).

The Glass Menagerie (1987, Cineplex Odeon). Director: Paul Newman; Producer: Burtt Harris; Screenplay: Tennessee Williams, based on his play; Cinematography: Michael Ballhaus; Production Design: Tony Walton; Editing: David Ray; Costume Design: Tony Walton; Original Score: Henry Mancini. 134 minutes. CAST: Joanne Woodward (Amanda Wingfield), John Malkovich (Tom Wingfield), Karen Allen (Laura Wingfield), James Naughton (Jim O'Connor).

The Loss of a Teardrop Diamond (2009, Paladin). Director: Jodie Markell; Producer: Brad Michael Gilbert; Screenplay: Tennessee Williams; Cinematography: Giles Nuttgens; Production Design: Richard Hoover and David Stein; Editing: Susan E. Morse and Jeremy Workman; Costume Design: Chrisi Karvonides; Original Score: Mark Orton. 102 minutes. CAST: Bryce Dallas Howard (Fisher Willow), Chris Evans (Jimmy Dobyne), Ellen Burstyn (Miss Addie), Ann-Margret (Aunt Cornelia), Will Patton (Mr. Dobyne), Jessica Collins (Vinnie).

Academy Award nominations for Tennessee Williams:

- **Best Screenplay** of 1951 for *A Streetcar Named Desire*
- **Best Screenplay** (Adapted) of 1956 for *Baby Doll*

(Williams received his two Oscar nominations for his two films directed by Elia Kazan.)

About the Author

JOHN DILEO'S first book was *And You Thought You Knew Classic Movies* (St. Martin's, 1999), hailed by Pauline Kael as "the smartest movie quiz book I've ever seen." His second book was *100 Great Film Performances You Should Remember—But Probably Don't* (Limelight Editions, 2002), which Adolph Green called "a valuable and touching work." TCM host Robert Osborne said, in the *Hollywood Reporter,* that the book "delightfully throws the spotlight on some remarkable film work," and the *Washington Post's* reaction was, "Not only is this helpful criticism, but *100 Great Film Performances* can serve as balm for anyone who has ever been disgruntled by the Academy's choices on Oscar night." Turner Classic Movies devoted a night of prime-time programming to films featured in John's third book, *Screen Savers: 40 Remarkable Movies Awaiting Rediscovery* (Hansen Publishing Group, 2007). Essays by him appear in two anthologies, *City Secrets: Movies* (2009) and *City Secrets: Books* (2009). John has been a contributing book reviewer for the *Washington Post's* Book World and currently writes DVD reviews for multiple publications. He frequently hosts classic-film series, appears on radio programs, lectures on cruise ships, conducts film-history seminars, and has been an annual participant in the Connecticut Film Festival (Danbury) and the Black Bear Film Festival (Milford, PA), where he interviewed Farley Granger (2005) and Arlene Dahl (2006). His web site is johndileo.com and his blog is screensaversmovies.com. Born in 1961 in Brooklyn, John was raised on Long Island and graduated from Ithaca College in 1982 with a B.F.A.